CHICAGO PUBLIC LIBRARY
BUSINESS / SCIENCE / TECHNOLOGY
400 S. STATE ST.   60605

CHICAGO PUBLIC LIBRARY

R01122 53911

D0205416

THE CHICAGO PUBLIC LIBRARY

FORM 19

DIVERGENT PATHS

DIVERGENT PATHS

How Culture and Institutions Have Shaped North American Growth

Marc Egnal

New York   Oxford
OXFORD UNIVERSITY PRESS
1996

Oxford University Press

Oxford   New York
Athens   Auckland   Bangkok   Bombay
Calcutta   Cape Town   Dar es Salaam   Delhi
Florence   Hong Kong   Istanbul   Karachi
Kuala Lumpur   Madras   Madrid   Melbourne
Mexico City   Nairobi   Paris   Singapore
Taipei   Tokyo   Toronto

and associated companies in
Berlin   Ibadan

Copyright © 1996 by Marc Egnal

Published by Oxford University Press, Inc.,
198 Madison Avenue, New York, New York 10016

Oxford is a registered trademark of Oxford University Press

All rights reserved. No part of this publication may be reproduced,
stored in a retrieval system, or transmitted, in any form or by any means,
electronic, mechanical, photocopying, recording, or otherwise,
without the prior permission of Oxford University Press.

Library of Congress Cataloging-in-Publication Data
Egnal, Marc.
Divergent paths : how culture and institutions
have shaped North American growth / Marc Egnal.
p.   cm.   Includes bibliographical references and index.
ISBN 0-19-509866-8 (cloth).—ISBN 0-19-510906-6 (pbk.)
1. Northeastern States—Economic conditions.
2. Southern States—Economic conditions.
3. Québec (Province)—Economic conditions.
4. Northeastern States—Social conditions.
5. Southern States—Social conditions.
6. Québec (Province)—Social conditions.
I. Title.
HC107.A115E37   1996   330.974—dc20   95-31904

1 3 5 7 9 8 6 4 2

Printed in the United States of America
on acid-free paper

CHICAGO PUBLIC LIBRARY
BUSINESS / SCIENCE / TECHNOLOGY
400 S. STATE ST.   60605

R01122 53911

For Judith, Barton, and Benjamin

Preface

Why are some countries or regions economic success stories, while others languish in the doldrums of slow growth? The role of culture and institutions must be placed near the top of any list of reasons. Take Japan, whose rapid development serves as an example for many nations. Abundant natural resources do not explain Japanese prosperity. Japan has little arable land, only limited deposits of coal and iron, and few oil or gas fields. Government policies, it is true, deserve scrutiny. But most extended discussions of Japanese growth look at the structure of the society, and at long-standing traditions that foster co-operation, loyalty, and hard work.

This work takes a similar tack. It is an historical enquiry into the nature of economic growth in North America. It explores the impact of institutions (such as slavery and the seigneurial system) and culture (including religion, literacy, the entrepreneurial spirit, and intellectual activity) on development. The book looks back to European origins, and discusses the course of growth in North America from the eighteenth century to the 1990s. But the greatest emphasis is on the hundred years between the 1750s and 1850s. During this period distinct, regional societies emerged and were sharply defined.

For the most part, *Divergent Paths* concentrates on a limited geographical area: the states and provinces settled by 1750. The analysis compares three regions: French Canada, the eight colonies (later states) of the North, and the five colonies (later states) of the South.

Only occasionally does the account of the years before 1860 treat the territories to the west. In many ways the development of the West paralleled that of the older areas. But fresh land and, at least initially, fewer cities were new factors in the mix. In Canada the territory immediately to the west of French Canada was settled by English-speakers, and has its own distinct course of development. The final three chapters, which carry the story from 1860 to the present, deal with the entire North and South, as well as with Quebec. By this era distinctions between the Northeast and Northwest (or "Midwest"), and between the Southeast and Southwest had lessened.

The book seeks to answer a question: why three societies—early Canada, the North, and the South—whose standard of living was similar in 1750 became so dissimilar in their development. By the midnineteenth century the original northern states had surged ahead in their growth. The southern states and French Canada trailed far behind. And the gap continued to widen until well into the twentieth century. The explanation of this pattern lies not with natural resources, the availability of foreign capital, or even government policies. Rather—and this is the central argument—culture and institutions shaped the divergent paths followed by the North, on the one hand, and the South and French Canada, on the other.

The South and French Canada, for all their obvious differences, were alike in important ways. Studying one sheds light on the other. Both were societies that emphasized hierarchy and social order more than the relentless drive for wealth. In the South this outlook can be traced back to the values of a slave society that placed some whites high above others and kept African Americans in bondage. In French Canada this world view emerged from the importance of the seigneurial system and Catholicism. As the two societies fell behind the Northeast and the leading European countries, their ideologies evolved along parallel roads. Both decried the baneful effects of materialism and condemned the reform movements of the North and Western Europe.

Divergent Paths thus brings together the writings on two similar regions—the South and French Canada—that too often have been considered apart. Students of the southern states have looked for parallels in Latin America, Prussia, South Africa, and even Russia.[1] But they rarely have studied a region which shares the same continent, and which experienced the same lengthy evolution from a traditional economy to post-industrial society. Scholars have compared Quebec to France and to Ontario.[2] But such studies miss an important opportunity in not exploring the development of the U.S. South. The slow growth of the South and French Canada contrasts with the steep ascent of the northern states. And both hierarchical areas were markedly affected by the rapid rise of the North.

The crucial era for defining these separate worlds was the century from the 1750s to the 1850s. Certainly, each of the three regions had its own values and behavior in 1750. Eighteenth-century commentators contrasted the "lazy" southerners, "industrious" northerners, and "vain" Canadians. But in the eighteenth century leading thinkers throughout North America shared Enlightenment beliefs. And ordinary folk (at least among the white population) farmed in similar ways, and had similar communal values. By the 1850s the contrast between the bustling, entrepreneurial North and the traditional, slower-growing South and French Canada was unmistakable.

Culture and institutions continued to evolve after the 1850s. But certain fundamentals were in place, and helped shape the response of the sections to the era of industrialization. An observer from the 1850s would not have been surprised by the contrasting success or the nature of the three societies in 1940. Only after 1940 did southerners and French Canadians break with patterns of behavior that had long shaped their lives. And only then did the paths of growth traced by the South and Quebec begin to converge with the course traced by the North. Since 1975 new links between culture, institutions, and development have been forged. These are treated in the final chapter.

Finally, three cautionary notes about this book. First, culture and institutions, as broad as those concerns are, hardly explain all aspects of growth. Historians rightly emphasize the impact of geography. The rocky soils of New England, the slow moving rivers of the South, the importance of the St. Lawrence River—all shaped development. So did proximity to markets. The most northerly states of New England stood further from the centers of U.S. commerce than did the commonwealths of southern New England. Hence New Hampshire remained poorer than Connecticut, despite a common Yankee heritage. And for shorter periods shifting patterns of trade or a sudden influx of capital could be decisive. I have written a companion book, *New World Economies: The Growth of Early Canada and the Thirteen Colonies* (forthcoming), that looks more closely at such short-term factors.

Second, this book examines societies—the North, the South, and French Canada—that had internal diversity. Are we justified in generalizing about these areas? The answer is yes, if we proceed with care. Contemporary opinion supports this approach. Commentators regularly viewed these sections as distinct places, and felt that the people in them had their own particular characteristics. Also the text notes the exceptions. It points, for example, to a state such as Maryland that became richer and more fully developed than the rest of the South.

Third, this work is an interpretative essay, one that relies on a broad mix of primary and secondary sources. Census data, diaries, and travelers' accounts are important for the story told here. So are the writings of many scholars. In grappling with the broad questions treated in *Divergent Paths*, historians often disagree with one another.

The text and notes deal with those debates, which are important for any full understanding of the issues raised. Even where the present work comes down on one side of a dispute, the other position often suggests a modification or refinement. Frequently a synthesis of opposing viewpoints seems the most cogent response.

In sum, *Divergent Paths* presents an argument about the importance of culture and institutions in guiding long-term growth. It is a thesis with implications for many developing societies. But it is an approach that never can be applied in a mechanistic or rigid manner. Ultimately, cultural change is about people and the decisions made by many individuals. There is a dialogue between the activities of particular men and women and the behavior of groups. That dialogue also helps shape the text of this work.

Like eighteenth-century farmers, historians in the late twentieth century depend on an extended community for support. Many readers have helped improve this book. They have given their time generously, recognizing that the only payment is gratitude and a promise to reciprocate. Several individuals read all or most of this manuscript. Joseph Ernst, David Hackett Fischer, Yves Frenette, Allan Greer, James Henretta, Fernand Ouellet, George Rappaport, and Gavin Wright tackled various drafts of this book. Others read a chapter or groups of chapters, and provided me with lengthy, thoughtful critiques. These individuals include Lois Green Carr, Nancy Humphrey Case, Avi Cohen, Robert Cuff, Eugene Genovese, Steven Hahn, Adrienne Hood, Jim Lemon, Fred Matthews, Jeanette Neeson, Jacques Rouillard, Chris Seymour, Lucy Simler, Paul Stevens, Lorena Walsh, and George Weider. Some of these readers enthusiastically concurred with my conclusions. Others dissented. But each of these scholars forced me to sharpen my arguments.

I am grateful to other individuals who helped me bring this book together. My research assistants—Elaine Naylor, Paula Vendramini, Sarah Elvins, Richard Dionne, and Tina Antoniou—made contributions that went beyond mere fact checking. Mirka Ondrak helped analyze the polling data discussed in Chapter 11. Juliana Drexler checked my translations from the French. Carolyn King of the York Cartographic Drafting Office prepared the maps and graphs. The Social Sciences and Humanities Research Council and York University provided grants and released time that allowed me to broaden this study. And Andrew Albanese, editor at Oxford University Press, remained supportive and helpful during the long process of transforming my manuscript into a book.

Finally, my family made the writing of this work a pleasure by constantly interrupting the project. Benjamin, our eight-year-old, chose my study as the terrain for various projectiles and remote control cars. Barton, our teenager, accepted his dad as a jogging companion and worthy adversary in board games. And my wife, Judith Humphrey, continually involved me in her own growing business. Without these breaks this book might have been finished sooner. But it would not have been half as much fun.

Contents

Appendices

List of Figures, Tables, and Maps

Figures

Tables

Maps

I

THE SHAPING OF REGIONAL SOCIETIES, 1750s TO 1850s

1

Introduction: The Paths Diverge

For Peter Kalm, the Swedish traveler and scientist, New France seemed no less prosperous than the northern Thirteen Colonies. Kalm, a student and friend of the great Swedish naturalist, Carl Linnaeus, traveled in North America between 1748 and 1751. He married a woman of Swedish descent in Philadelphia, and published his journals in three volumes after his return. Kalm was unstinting in his praise of Canadian farmers. "The high meadows in Canada are excellent and by far preferable to the meadows round Philadelphia and in the other English colonies," he remarked. And he observed in August 1749 that "the country on both sides [of the St. Lawrence] was very delightful today, and the fine state of its cultivation added greatly to the beauty of the scene." More generally, he felt that French Canadians lived as well as their English neighbors to the south. Kalm noted that "the French here eat nearly as much meat as the English on those days when their religion allows it."[1]

Kalm's remarks provide a good starting point for our undertaking. In the mid-eighteenth century the northern colonies, French Canada, and the southern colonies seemed roughly equal in wealth.* A century

---

* The Thirteen Colonies included 8 northern colonies: New Hampshire, Massachusetts, Rhode Island, Connecticut, New York, New Jersey, Pennsylvania, and Delaware. The 5 southern colonies were Maryland, Virginia, North Carolina, South Carolina, and Georgia.

3

later the northern states had far outdistanced their rivals. By 1850 northerners were more involved in commercial activities, more urbanized, and far more affluent—on the average—than southerners or French Canadians. This book argues that culture and institutions explain the divergent paths followed by the North, on the one hand, and the South and French Canada, on the other. The patterns established by the 1850s would shape the course of development during the late nineteenth and twentieth centuries.

The period from the 1750s to the 1850s was the crucial one for the definition of these three societies. To be sure, the regions were different in 1750. Labor systems varied; so did approaches to religion and land tenure. Contemporaries often commented about the distinct character of French Canadians, northerners, and southerners. But in 1750 there was much the areas had in common. As this chapter suggests, levels of wealth were similar, as were the ways people farmed and lived. (And as later chapters indicate, the elites shared common beliefs.) By 1850 the course of development of the regions clearly had diverged. Northerners were more successful, and more concerned than ever about money making. Southerners and French Canadians were now firmly committed to the defense of hierarchical societies, where the pursuit of profit ranked far below a set of traditional values.

This Introduction lays the groundwork for Part I of the book. This opening chapter looks at the economy of the three areas in 1750 and 1850, and documents the different paths followed by the North, on the one hand, and by the South and French Canada, on the other. The next seven chapters discuss the role of culture and institutions in shaping these regions during the century from the 1750s to the 1850s. Part II analyzes the economic development of these societies since the 1850s—and examines how deep-rooted patterns of belief and behavior have continued to guide the course of growth.

Equal Development—1750

In 1750 the North, South, and French Canada had much in common. They had a similar standard of living. And they took the same approach—called the "household economy"—to economic activities.

Similar Levels of Wealth

In the mid-eighteenth century the regions had achieved comparable levels of wealth and similar paces of growth. One must not think of 1750 as a starting line. By the mid-eighteenth century all three areas were over a century old. And all three had grown vigorously, allowing their citizens to live fairly well. Whatever factors slowed the development of French Canada and the South during the ensuing century, they seem to have had little impact before 1750.

What evidence supports this picture of regional equality? First, figures for the average wealth in the Thirteen Colonies suggest the same level of growth marked the North and South. In *Wealth of a Nation to Be* Alice Hanson Jones measures the various sorts of property the colonists held. Her study relies on probate records—the estate inventories ordered by a court after a person's death—and examines these documents for ten colonies. Jones's findings indicate that if the wealth in the South were distributed equally among all the colonists, black and white, each person could claim about £36 sterling. In the North each person would be worth only slightly more: £38 sterling (Table 1.1).[2]

Jones's findings document the *average* wealth in the North and South. For the North, a world of middling farmers, the average bears some semblance to reality. But for the South, where 41 percent of the population was enslaved in 1770, the results are only an abstraction. Southern whites lived comfortably because their slaves lived miserably. There is a place for abstractions, however; in the nineteenth century the southern average, as we will see, would not keep pace with the northern average. Jones's figures tell us that during the colonial era the North and South were equally successful in producing goods. On a per person basis, southern society, relying on slavery, generated about the same amount of wealth as northern free society.[3] Jones's work does not explore New France. Comparable figures could be developed for Canada, although no one has done so. The Canadian *inventaires-après-décès* are similar to colonial American probate records.[4]

Second, data for imports per person suggest similar standards of living in the different sections. Between the 1740s and 1770s the northern

Table 1.1 **Per Capita Wealth in the Thirteen Colonies, 1774 (in pounds sterling)**

	New England	Middle Colonies	Total North	South
Land	26.1	25.9	26.0	25.1
Livestock	2.8	4.8	3.8	4.8
Other producer goods	3.1	5.5	4.3	3.3
Consumer goods	4.4	4.0	4.2	3.1
Total	36.4	40.2	38.3	36.4

Source: Alice Hanson Jones, *The Wealth of a Nation to Be: The American Colonies on the Eve of the Revolution* (New York, 1980), 310. A very different picture emerges if only free wealthholders are considered. Then most African Americans become "producer goods" and southern wealth is far greater than holdings in the North. See Jones's figures on p. 310. Numbers may not add up to total because of rounding.

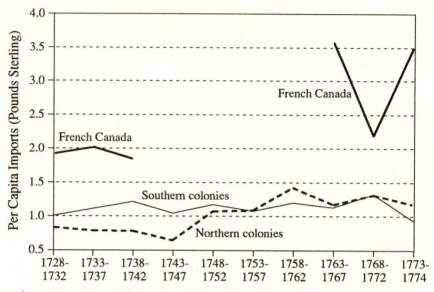

Figure 1.1   **Per Capita Imports into the Three Regions, 1728-74.** This
graph shows imports per person from the mother country. Shipments to
French Canada include goods directed to the aboriginal population. These
data suggest that in the eighteenth century the North was not wealthier than
the other two regions. (*Sources:* U. S. Bureau of the Census, *Historical Statistics
of the United States, Colonial Times to 1970,* 2 vols. (Washington, D.C., 1975),
II, 1168, 1176-78; A.J.E. Lunn, "Economic Development in New France,
1713-1760" (Ph.D. diss., McGill Univ., 1942), 443-44, 477; I. Craig, "Economic Conditions in Canada, 1763-1783" (M.A. thesis, McGill Univ., 1937),
14, 197; Robert Armstrong, *Structure and Change: An Economic History of Quebec* (Toronto, 1984), 16, 60. French livres were converted to pounds sterling
based on the ratio of 25 livres to 1 pound. John J. McCusker, *Money and Exchange in Europe and America, 1600-1775: A Handbook* (Chapel Hill, N.C.,
1978), 95-97; Denys Delage, "Les structures économiques de la Nouvelle
France et de la Nouvelle-York," *l'Actualité Economique,* XLVI (1970), 69.)

and southern Thirteen Colonies imported about the same quantity of
goods from Britain per person. (See Fig. 1.1.) These figures, based on official British trade statistics, are a reasonable guide to the consumption
of manufactures in the two sections. Smuggling was limited to a few
items, such as tea and luxury fabrics. The production of homespun only
slightly weakens the utility of these figures. Since northerners made
somewhat more cloth than southerners, import figures tend to underes-
timate northern consumption. However, in both sections the better
grades of fabric came from Britain. Trade data for Canada are less useful.
The incomplete series for Canadian imports at first glance suggests
higher levels of consumption. However, these numbers are inflated by
goods imported for the fur trade. In any case, the data for imports pro-

vides no evidence that the North had pulled away from its two rivals—as would be evident in the nineteenth century.[5]

Third, sundry observations suggest that levels of wealth and consumption were comparable in New France and the Thirteen Colonies. Peter Kalm's remarks open this chapter. The comments of the Jesuit historian Pierre-François-Xavier de Charlevoix, examined in Chapter 2, also indicate that Canada did not lag behind the Thirteen Colonies—at least in the appearance of prosperity. Allan Greer's study of three Canadian parishes compares the provisions made for retired or widowed parents in New France and in southeastern Pennsylvania. Greer concludes that rations in Canada were generous, and slightly better than the quantities allotted in Pennsylvania. Cole Harris's examination of grain production in New France indicates that output per acre was comparable to that in the northern colonies.[6]

Finally, such data as are available suggest that in the eighteenth century the rates of growth were similar in the three regions. Researchers estimate that the pace of development in the northern colonies, the southern colonies, and New France was around 0.5 percent a year. These statistics emerge from a variety of approaches and reflect long-term changes in the value of imports, exports, probated wealth, and agricultural production. There is a plausibility to the idea of similar paces of growth. The three sets of colonies began at the same place in the early seventeenth century, and had scaled similar heights by 1750.[7]

In sum, if our analysis turns on the question of standard of living or pace of growth, the three regions—Canada, the North, and the South—appear roughly equal in the mid-eighteenth century. The three were hardly equal in other ways. In 1750 the North had 660,000 people, the South 510,000, and New France only 50,000. New France had a tragic flaw—its weak growth in numbers—that cost it dearly in the imperial wars of the eighteenth century. But it was not backward in its standard of living or pace of development.[8]

The Household Economy

Not only were levels of wealth similar in 1750, but throughout the length of colonial North America most people adopted a similar approach to productive activities. They took part in a rural society that historians frequently refer to as a "household economy."* We can understand this world more fully by examining three farmers.

Samuel Swayne lived in Chester County, Pennsylvania, about

* A somewhat more cumbersome, but equivalent, way of talking about the rural world is one characterized by the "household mode of production." This concept is discussed more fully in Appendix A, which also examines the role of merchants in a society where most people were farmers.

thirty miles southwest of Philadelphia.[9] His prosperous Quaker parents had provided well for their children. When Swayne, age twenty-five, married Hannah in 1756 he received a 91-acre farm in East Marlborough Township. Gradually, he improved and expanded his holdings. At first he relied on hired workers, but later drew upon the labor of his many children (eight would outlive him). In 1772 Swayne purchased another 35 acres with a house that he would lease.[10]

Swayne planted a diversity of crops, and tended a variety of animals. Like most colonial farmers he thought first of the wide-ranging needs of his family. Making certain that these demands were addressed was more important than the possible profits that might come from expanding a single, cash staple. Wheat was Swayne's most valuable crop, but he also raised oats, barley, rye, hay, corn, potatoes, and flax. He kept cows, pigs, and chickens. His orchard was well known for its peaches and varieties of apples, which he pressed each fall to make cider.

The Swaynes frequently bought and sold goods and services. Most dealings were with individuals in the community. Although values were recorded in shillings and pence, only occasionally did cash change hands. Samuel made saddletrees (the leather frames that served as foundations for saddles) and sold these locally. Hannah's butter and cheese were also in demand. Some of the Swaynes' wheat was consumed within the township. When Samuel hired laborers he paid them partly in goods, such as potatoes, wheat, and bacon, and partly in cash. In 1767 Hannah's father moved in with them, and earned his keep by making and mending the family's shoes.

The Swaynes also purchased and sold commodities that involved them in the larger economy. Books and fabric came from England, sugar from the West Indies, and wine from southern Europe. Part of the produce of the farm was packed in oak barrels and sent to Wilmington, Delaware, or to Philadelphia. Wheat and flaxseed, and possibly other crops, entered international trade. While no precise breakdown is available for the Swayne farm, data for similar holdings in Pennsylvania suggest that about one-fifth (by value) of what the Swaynes raised was shipped outside the community. (See Appendix B.)[11]

If you had asked the Swaynes what their goals in life were, they would have likely said, first, being good parents and good Christians. (Among their possessions was a library of Quaker readings.) They would honestly have disclaimed any intention to get rich or "get ahead" in the world. In the language of the day they sought a "competency"—a comfortable living that was more than subsistence but less than luxury.[12]

More like the Swaynes than different in key values were the Allaires, who lived in the Canadian parish of St. Ours.[13] Like Samuel

Swayne, Théophile Allaire acquired land from his parents. But because he was one of eleven children, and the youngest of five sons, Théophile received only a small farm—some 60 arpents (51 acres). And he was forced to wait for this land, so he did not marry until he was thirty-one, in 1753. His first wife, Amable Ménard, died six years later, leaving Théophile with one daughter. Théophile then hired a housekeeper, Félicité Audet, who was a widow with a daughter. Within three months Théophile and Félicité were wed. In their marriage contract they promised to care for each other's child, and raise her as a Catholic. Together they would have three more children.

The Allaires' holding was the slender rectangular tract typical of New France. The narrow end bordering the Richelieu River was only 400 feet wide. But the farm stretched back over a full mile from the river. Again there was a diversity of crops. Wheat was most important, but Théophile also sowed fields in oats, peas, and hay. A garden near the house provided vegetables and tobacco. The 1765 census noted that the Allaires owned two horses, two cows, two sheep, and two pigs.

The Allaires were involved chiefly in local exchanges. Several of the items in the inventory taken when Théophile's first wife died undoubtedly were produced in the neighborhood. These include various tools, a pair of embroidered moccasins, a shawl, a cape, and a petticoat. The small size of the Allaire estate meant that there was little surplus left for export. Moreover, before any wheat could be offered to the local merchant, the claims of the Church (the tithe was one twenty-sixth of the grain reaped) and the seigneur of St. Ours had to be satisfied. Many of the Allaires' neighbors, however, had larger holdings, and regularly provided wheat to local traders. Few farms, however, sold more than a fourth of what they raised outside the community. (See Appendix B.) [14]

The Swaynes and Allaires farmed in similar, time-honored ways. The Swaynes could read, while it is unlikely the Allaires could (only about 10 percent of adults in rural Canada were literate at this time). But literacy made little difference in their approach to the land. Tradition was all important. We can sketch in the practices of these two households, using material from their records as well as more general information about farming in these regions. Both families broke the ground with plows drawn by a team of horses. The plows differed in construction (the Allaires' had wheels), but both were made of wood with a strip of iron on the moldboard. In both instances, the only other horse-drawn implement was the harrow that helped cover the seeds. Both farmers used a primitive two-field rotation. Fields were planted with grain one year, and left fallow the next. Carefully dug drainage ditches were the norm in both Chester County and St. Ours. Both farmers could point to neighbors who used scythes for cutting grain. But Samuel and Théophile were more typical in preferring sickles with their shorter handles and blades. During harvest all the Swaynes and Allaires worked from sunup to sundown to get the crop in. Once gathered in, the wheat was separated from the chaff on both farms by beating it with a wooden flail.[15]

The goals of the Allaires were strikingly similar to those of the Swaynes. They sought to be good Catholics and responsible parents. They wanted to live in comfort, but had no yearning to rise above their station in life. They hoped to provide well for their children. Théophile acquired an 80 arpent (68 acre) parcel on the other side of the Richelieu River. Presumably it was intended for his children, much as his parents had set aside land for him.

Before turning to our third farmer, we can step back to view the larger picture. The Swaynes and Allaires functioned within a common framework that we can call the household economy. What were its hallmarks? We can emphasize four. It was *agricultural*—with commerce and manufacturing incidental and subordinate. It was marked by *slow growth*. Children could expect a standard of living that was not much better than their parents. The outlook of individuals was conditioned by this reality. It was a *pre-literate* society. Knowledge was transmitted from parent to child, or from master to servant, by demonstration. For most persons, the ability to read was not an economic advantage. Finally, production was *locally oriented*. Most goods were produced and exchanged within the community. The mix of crops reflected the needs of the household and neighborhood—more than the demands of distant markets or considerations of profit.[16]

Historians, it should be noted, differ in their depiction of the early North American economy. This book and many other texts contend that a pre-capitalist household economy characterized colonial North America. Michael Merrill, for example, asserts that in the farming communities of the northern Thirteen Colonies "money did not mediate the exchange of products" and "individuals constantly cooperated in their work."[17] Various works on French Canada express a similar viewpoint. In his study of the Lower Richelieu valley Allan Greer notes that "the fundamental classes were self-sufficient peasants, on one side, and the priests and seigneurs they supported on the other." Only later was "this once commercially isolated area . . . brought into the world of buying, selling, and hiring."[18]

Other scholars disagree, and argue that farmers in the Thirteen Colonies were entrepreneurial and market-oriented. In his study of Kent, Connecticut, Charles Grant remarks: "One sees in certain of the Kent settlers not so much the contented yeoman, certainly not the 'slave' toiling for his master, but perhaps the embryo John D. Rockefeller." John F. Martin calls his book on seventeenth-century New England towns *Profits in the Wilderness*. Winifred Rothenberg emphasizes the "market imbeddedness" of early American farmers.[19] And some researchers paint a similar picture of early Canada. Maurice Séguin, for example, underscores the "trading and entrepreneurial spirit" of New France.[20]

The debate between the two groups of historians is a vigorous one. But when closely scrutinized, the two sides are not that far apart. To a surprising degree the dispute turns on matters of emphasis. Both the "social historians" and "market historians" (to use Allan Kulikoff's terms) agree that farmers were involved in commercial exchanges. The question is how to describe landowners who sold a fourth of their crops to outsiders, while keeping three-fourths for the community and their own needs. Similarly, both camps agree that some individuals (typically urban merchants) helped finance trade and, in the Thirteen Colonies, speculated in unimproved lands. At issue is whether such individuals set the tone for society. Appendix A, which explores these points further, suggests urban entrepreneurs coexisted with and indeed supported the household economy of the countryside. On balance, the household mode provides a useful framework for analysis—particularly when contrasted with the ascent of commercial capitalism in the nineteenth century.[21]

Finally, our third farmer suggests some modifications to the picture sketched in so far. William Deacon of St. Mary's County, Maryland, was far wealthier than Samuel Swayne or Théophile Allaire.[22] He had no children and no wife—at least in his later years. (Whether he had ever been married is not clear from the record.) Deacon lived well. At his death in 1759 he owned 350 acres of fertile land, but had for many years possessed a much larger estate. He also received an income from two positions he held: royal collector for the North Potomac District and justice of the peace. His house had four rooms on each floor, and candelabra on the walls and ceiling. In his cupboards were clothes worth 70 pounds, more than the worth of all movable possessions in most households. Deacon owned about 29 slaves—a group that included 10 children and 3 individuals too old to work.

Deacon took part in both local dealings and a broader set of exchanges. But in his case the proportion of farm produce sold outside the local community was much greater than it was for small farmers like Swayne and Allaire. Deacon's exact crop mix is not known. But he sold tobacco, and it is likely (following the pattern of wealthy individuals in his neighborhood) that this staple was valued at several times the worth of all his grain combined. Deacon also raised Indian corn for export and perhaps shipped some of his wheat abroad. Some of the thousands of shingles that his slaves made well might have entered intercolonial trade.

Local transactions were also important for Deacon. His plantation produced a great deal of wool. But perhaps because he had no wife or daughters, there was no spinning or weaving on his estate. Deacon's less wealthy neighbors undertook these tasks. One of Deacon's slaves, Toney, worked full-time as a blacksmith, and probably served the neighborhood as well as the plantation. In addition, Deacon's estate took part in the exchanges of foodstuffs so common to early America.[23]

The techniques of farming on the Deacon plantation were similar to those used on Swayne's farm and Allaire's *roture*. Again, literacy made little difference. William Deacon could read and write. But the implements and techniques he used differed not at all from those found on the farms of his less well-educated neighbors.[24] Deacon benefited from the shift, which had recently occurred in Virginia, from an agriculture based on the hoe to one based on the plow. By the 1750s wooden plows, tipped with iron, broke the soils in Virginia as they did in Pennsylvania or New France. And like farmers in the North and along the St. Lawrence, Deacon practiced only a primitive scheme of crop rotation.[25]

If we use William Deacon as an illustration, the South comfortably fits three of the four criteria of the household economy. It was agricultural, slow-growing, and pre-literate in the skills needed for production. But Deacon's estate was not locally oriented, at least not to the degree evident in small farms. In contrast to Swayne or Allaire, who sent less than a fourth of what they raised outside the community, Deacon likely sold almost half of his crop to distant markets. (See Appendix B.) The enforced poverty of Deacon's slaves accounts for much of the difference. Deacon had less need than the farmers to the north to raise a diversity of crops for home consumption. Two staples—corn and pork—made up the bulk of the slave diet.

But William Deacon, it must be emphasized, was not typical of the South. Most southern families held no slaves, and among slaveholders, the largest group had five or fewer bondspeople. The majority of farmers in the South resembled Swayne and Allaire. They produced chiefly for themselves and the local community. Deacon was an exception, if an important one, to the pattern of local self-reliance. He and other sizable slaveholders raised most of the southern staples shipped abroad. The example of Deacon modifies—but does not overturn—the picture of community-oriented farmers occupying the length of eastern North America in 1750.[26]

Northern States Lead the Way—1850

A century later the northeastern states had leaped far ahead of the other two regions. The activities of northerners now differed in striking ways from the pursuits of southerners and French Canadians. And the standard of living in the North was well above the levels in the South and French Canada.

The rise of the North must be viewed against the background of the changing economy of North America. Everywhere the bustle of commercial capitalism was displacing the close-knit exchanges of the household economy, even if this transformation was fully realized only in the Northeast. In 1750 the North American economy was agricultural, slow-growing, pre-literate, and (for the most part) locally oriented. By 1850 a contrasting set of four characteristics was reshaping economic life. Wealth came increasingly from non-agricultural activities, particularly commerce and manufacturing. The pace of development was far quicker. Literacy and, more broadly, education were becoming keys to growth. Transportation had improved, and individuals were now more dependent on distant markets. In short, the economy in 1850 was more *commercial, rapidly growing, literate,* and *externally oriented.*[27]

We can look more closely at the leading role played by the Northeast in each of these four areas. The states from New Hampshire to Delaware led the shift from agriculture to commerce and manufacturing. These states were home to the busiest ports and the largest industrial enterprises. Thousands of individuals worked in the shoe manufactories of Lynn, Massachusetts; in the cotton mill towns along the Merrimack River (which flowed through southern New Hampshire and northeastern Massachusetts); in the ironworks of Pittsburgh, Pennsylvania; and in the businesses making men's and women's clothing in New York City. By 1840 more than one out of four workers in the original northern states was in industry. That figure compares with one out of ten in the original southern states and fewer than one out of fourteen in French Canada. (See Table 1.2.)

And this shift from agriculture to commerce and industry was the high road to wealth. Each nonfarm worker produced goods or services worth almost twice the value of an agricultural worker's output. By

Table 1.2 **Industrial Workers as a Percentage of Total Labor Force in the Original States, 1840, and Lower Canada, 1851**

North	29.0	South	9.5	Lower Canada	7.2
New England	36.1	Upper South	15.8		
Middle Atlantic	26.6	Lower South	5.0		

Sources: Richard A. Easterlin, "Interregional Differences in Per Capita Income, Population, and Total Income, 1840–1850," in National Bureau for Economic Research, *Trends in the American Economy in the 19th Century,* Studies in Income and Wealth, vol. 24 (Princeton, 1960), 97–98; John McCallum, *Unequal Beginnings: Agriculture and Economic Development in Quebec and Ontario until 1870* (Toronto, 1980), 129. For the U.S. "industrial workers" are the non-agricultural workforce, excluding individuals in commerce.

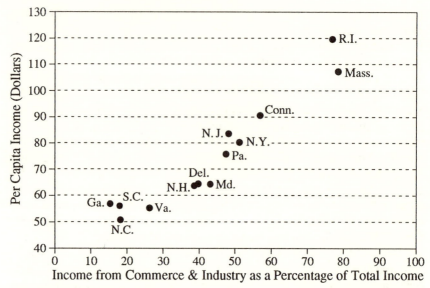

Figure 1.2 **Industry, Commerce, and Income Levels in the Original States, 1840.** Commerce and industry, rather than farming, formed the basis for a rising standard of living in the nineteenth century. The result? The commercial North was far wealthier than the agrarian South. Only Maryland, of the five original southern states, could be grouped with the poorer states of the North. (*Source:* Easterlin, "Interregional Differences," 97–104.)

1840 citizens of the original northern states received more income from non-agricultural activities than from farming. In the other two regions agriculture remained the chief source of wealth.[28] As Figure 1.2 suggests, there was a strong correlation between the income level of a state and the proportion of the population engaged in commercial activities. This graph makes clear the higher levels of earnings in the North, and particularly the relative affluence of states such as Massachusetts and Rhode Island.[29]

The rise of commercial activities in the Northeast was also reflected in the growth of towns and cities. By 1850 some 27 percent of the population of the eight northern states lived in urban places. By comparison, in the Southeast only 9 percent of the people were in towns, while in French Canada urbanization accounted for 15 percent of the population. (See Figure 9.3.)[30]

The pace of economic development accelerated, and here too the Northeast led the pack. During the eighteenth century the standard of living had climbed about 0.5 percent a year. By the mid-nineteenth century the rate of growth in both Canada and the United States was well over twice that pace. Small differences in the rate of growth translate into an enormous difference over time. Incomes rising at a rate of

1.5 percent a year more than double in half a century, while those climbing 0.5 percent a year increase less than a third in that span. A Rip Van Winkle who fell asleep in 1810 and awoke in 1860 would have marveled at the brave new world he saw. Trains, steamships, and canals transformed the way North Americans traveled and shipped their goods; the McCormick reaper made grain growers far more productive; the textile industry sharply reduced the production of homespun. More comforts were in the average home, more machinery in the barn. By contrast, a sleeper who drifted off in 1710 and arose in 1760 would have been less startled. A few more amenities, such as forks, knives, and coarse earthenware, could be found in the cupboards, and a few more yards of imported cloth in the drawers. But in the eighteenth century, unlike the nineteenth, there was no transformation of the material world.

And in the quickening economy of North America the lead of the Northeast was indisputable. Since the three regions had roughly the same standard of living in 1750, higher incomes in the North in the mid-nineteenth century (figures are presented below) testify to the faster rate of growth of that area. [31]

Northerners were also more likely to be literate, a skill that now made a difference in productivity and earnings. The Northeast benefited from the number and quality of its schools and from its relatively high expenditures for education. Most craft work demanded "book learning," and so did a surprising number of factory jobs. Horace Mann, who in the 1830s and 1840s helped make the Massachusetts school system one of the best in the country, found that local industrialists were enthusiastic about the value of well-trained operatives. Mann concluded: "There is scarcely any kind of labor, however simple or automatic, which can be so well performed without knowledge in the workman as with it." [32] Educated individuals had a similar advantage in agriculture. Proportionately, more northern farmers read agricultural journals, belonged to agricultural societies, and took part in efforts to improve farming techniques. An 1852 government report on farming in New York reported that "1,000,000 [acres] are so cultivated as to become richer from year to year—being in the hands of 40,000 farmers who read agricultural journals and nobly sustain the state and country societies of that commonwealth." No sizable group of educated, "improving" farmers existed in the South or French Canada. (Chapter 5 examines literacy and its impact on growth.) [33]

Finally, the North was more externally oriented: it led the other regions in abandoning the local exchanges of the household economy and embracing the long-distance commerce of capitalist society. The Northeast recorded the most striking gains in transportation, with far more highways, canals, and miles of track than the other regions. To be sure, products from Lower Canada,* such as lumber, and southern staples, such as cotton and tobacco, were lucrative exports. But revenues from these goods were overshadowed by the value of northern wares directed to domestic and foreign markets. Southerners and French Canadians were more inclined to raise needed foodstuffs and make clothing themselves, rely on neighborhood suppliers, or do without. By contrast, the residents of the Northeast, in part because of urbanization and in part because of the increased specialization of their farms, were more likely to buy manufactures and foodstuffs from distant producers.[34]

The decline of domestic manufactures is a good barometer of the shift from local producers to far-off suppliers. In the colonial era and early nineteenth century industrious northerners had made more textiles and other wares at home than had the inhabitants of the other areas. In 1810, for example, residents of the original northern states crafted, on the average, $5.97 worth of such goods, compared with $5.35 in the southeastern states. But the North was first to turn from the old ways. By 1850 per capita home manufactures were worth only $0.38 in the Northeast compared with $1.60 in the Southeast. Map 1.1 illustrates for 1850 the near disappearance of home manufactures in the North and their persistence in the South. In French Canada there was a resurgence of home production during the mid-nineteenth century.[35]

There was no escaping the furious commerce of the Northeast. Henry Thoreau, the homely-looking philosopher and pencil maker who went off into the woods near Concord, Massachusetts, to gain another perspective on his world, recognized the insistent exchanges that had come to define New England life. "The whistle of the locomotive," he observed in *Walden,* "penetrates my woods summer and winter, sounding like the scream of a hawk sailing over some farmer's yard, informing me that many restless city merchants are arriving within the circle of the town or adventurous country traders from the other side. . . . Here come your groceries, country; your rations countrymen! Nor is there any man so independent on his farm that he can say them nay."[36]

The eagerness the Northeast displayed in embracing commercial capitalism was reflected in the widening income gap that separated that section from French Canada and the Southeast. Various measures testify to the growing spread in levels of wealth. Relying on census returns as well as the results of earlier studies, Richard Easterlin has

---

* Modern-day Quebec experienced several name changes. This region was *Canada* (or part of *New France*) before 1763; *Quebec* from 1763 to 1791; *Lower Canada* from 1791 to 1841; *Canada East* from 1841 to 1867; and since 1867, *Quebec*. Popular usage, however, referred to the province as *Lower Canada* for several decades after 1841. This text, like many historical works, continues that custom.

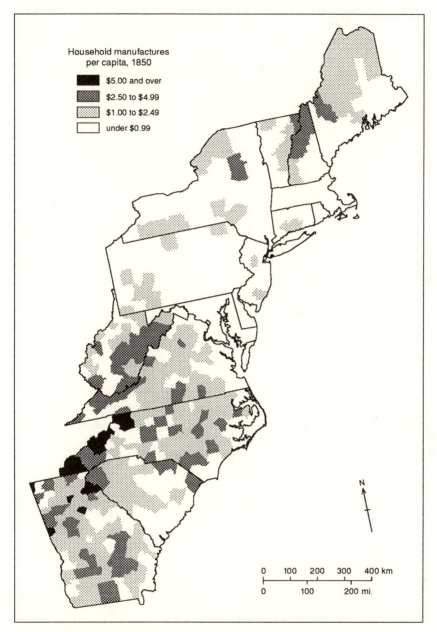

Map 1.1 **Home Manufactures in the Eastern U.S., 1850**. During the nineteenth century the North became more commercially oriented and the value of home manufactures dropped sharply. While domestic production also fell in the South, the decline was less pronounced. (*Source:* U.S. Bureau of the Census, *The Seventh Census of the United States: 1850* (Washington, D.C., 1853).)

developed estimates for income levels in the United States. These data, displayed in Table 1.3, underscore both the prosperity of the eight original northern states, where the average income was $82, and the lower standard of living in the five original southern states, where average earnings were only $56. Although there was a range of incomes in the North, all the original northern states were well above the southern average. And only Maryland, among the southern states, came close to the less wealthy northern states. A rough estimate for income levels in Lower Canada in 1840 can be derived from Canadian figures for 1850. The result is an average income of $52. This figure, which suggests French Canada was much poorer than the northern states (and indeed poorer than most southeastern states) is only a "guestimate." But other data reinforce this measure of income.[37]

The average annual income of farm workers, presented in Table 1.4, is another broad gauge of regional prosperity. This yardstick confirms the preeminence of the Northeast. In 1840 agricultural workers in the original northern states received $219, farmers in the five southern states earned $153, while farmers in Lower Canada—ten years later—$108. There was variation within the regions. For example, in Lower Canada those few counties where English speakers predominated provided higher wages than the French-speaking counties. But the northern states remained at the top of any list. And once again only Maryland among the southern states came close to the levels in the Northeast.[38]

Finally, contemporary observers in the mid-nineteenth century underscored these regional disparities. Hinton Rowan Helper was an acerbic critic of southern backwardness. He was a tall, athletic man, with blue

Table 1.3   **Income Per Person in the Three Regions, 1840 (in U.S. dollars)**

North	82	South	56	Lower Canada	
N.H.	64	Md.	63	Estimate	52
Mass.	107	Va.	54		
R.I.	118	N.C.	51		
Conn.	91	S.C.	56		
N.Y.	80	Ga.	57		
N.J.	83				
Pa.	75				
Del.	68				

Sources: Easterlin, "Interregional Differences," 97–98; O. J. Firestone, "Development of Canada's Economy, 1850–1900," ibid., 222–29; "[Francis] Hincks on Canadian Currency," in *Money and Banking in Canada,* ed. E. P. Neufeld (Toronto, 1964), 106–15. See note 37 for additional information. My figures for the North and South include only the states listed here, and so differ from Easterlin's aggregates.

Table 1.4 Agricultural Income Per Worker in the Original
States, 1840, and Lower Canada, 1851
(in current U.S. dollars)

North	219	South	153	Lower Canada	108
N.H.	182	Md.	207	French cos.	103
Mass.	199	Va.	154	English cos.	133
R.I.	170	N.C.	139		
Conn.	208	S.C.	139		
N.Y.	206	Ga.	155		
N.J.	276				
Pa.	255				
Del.	185				

Sources: Easterlin, "Interregional Differences," 97–98; Frank D. Lewis and
Marvin McInnis, "Agricultural Output and Efficiency in Lower Canada,
1851," *Research in Economic History,* IX (1984), 45–87, esp. 59–60. Population data from F. H. Leacy, ed., *Historical Statistics of Canada,* 2nd ed. (Ottawa, 1983), series A7. My figures for the sections and regions include
only the states listed here, and so differ from Easterlin's aggregates.

eyes and coal-black hair. Helper was born in North Carolina, schooled
in a small, local academy, and toughened by three years in the California
gold fields. He gradually developed a hatred of slavery—although his
later writings showed that his view of blacks was distorted by racism.
Helper's masterpiece, *The Impending Crisis of the South: How to
Meet It,* was published in 1857. Promoted in an abridged version by the
Republican party, the book received wide circulation. Helper crammed
his work with statistics drawn from the 1850 census—all designed to
contrast the slow pace of southern development with the gains registered in the North. He noted, for example, that even the "hay crop of the
free states is worth considerably more than all the cotton, tobacco, rice,
hay, and hemp produced in all the fifteen slave states."[39]

Focusing on pairs of states, Helper compared northern growth and
southern stagnation. For example, in 1790 New York had half the population of Virginia and exported fewer goods. By 1850 New York had
twice the population of Virginia and shipped wares valued at over thirty
times those of the Old Dominion. Helper repeatedly came back to the
same theme: the South had fallen far behind the North. "Less than
three-quarters of a century ago—say in 1789 . . . ," he observed, "the
South, with advantages in soil, climate, rivers, harbors, minerals, forests,
and, indeed, almost every other natural resource, began an even race
with the North in all the important pursuits of life; and now, in the brief
space of scarce three score years and ten, we find her completely distanced, enervated, dejected and dishonored." For Helper the culprit was
unmistakable: "Slave-drivers are the sole authors of her disgrace; as they
have sown so let them reap."[40]

John George Lambton, better known as Lord Durham, examined the problems afflicting French Canada. A strikingly handsome man, often charming but with a violent temper, Durham was both a wealthy aristocrat and a political reformer. Until his untimely death in 1841, he was viewed as a possible British prime minister. In 1838 Durham was sent to Canada, where short-lived armed rebellions had shown the need for far-reaching changes. Durham, who was appointed lieutenant-governor, was asked not only to administer this fractious possession but also to set its government on a sounder footing. He and his able assistants carefully studied Canadian society, and presented their findings in the lengthy *Report on the Affairs of British America.* Durham concluded that the French Canadians were a stumbling block for any program of political or economic reform. "They remain," he remarked, "an old and stationary society, in a new and progressive world." The French Canadians had prospered during the eighteenth century, but in the nineteenth century their cautious outlook slowed the pace of growth. Observed Durham: "They made little advance beyond the first progress in comfort, which the bounty of the soil absolutely forced upon them."

Durham compared the lackluster economy of Lower Canada (and indeed, the slow growth of British North America) with the prosperity of the northern part of the United States. There is, he remarked, a "striking contrast which is presented between the American and British sides of the frontier line in respect to every sign of productive industry, increasing wealth, and progressive civilization . . . . On the British side of the line, with the exception of a few favoured spots, where some approach to American prosperity is apparent, all seems waste and desolate." Lower Canada, Durham noted, has never "caught the spirit of American progress."[41]

Helper and Durham can be criticized as acerbic commentators, bereft of sympathy for the regions they studied. Durham certainly held many of the prejudices of the English upper class. But despite their shortcomings, both men offer thoughtful analyses of societies that failed to keep up with the North. Their evidence corroborates statistics that suggest the equality of development in the eighteenth century, and the supremacy of the northern states in 1850.

2

Eighteenth-Century Perceptions

For Thomas Jefferson northerners and southerners were without question different breeds of people. In 1785 he presented the Marquis de Chastellux with parallel lists of attributes:

In the North they are	*In the South they are*
cool	fiery
sober	Voluptuary
laborious	indolent
persevering	unsteady
jealous of their own liberties, and just of those of others	zealous for their own liberties, but trampling on those of others
interested	generous
chicaning	candid
superstitious and hypocritical in their religion	without attachment or pretensions to any religion but that of the heart[1]

Contemporary observers could well have provided a contrasting list for French Canada. In the nineteenth century the gulf separating an entrepreneurial North from the two regions less concerned with money making would widen precariously. But the three societies were hardly alike in 1750. Eighteenth-century perceptions allow us to examine differences in values and outlook that would have a far-reaching impact on growth in the nineteenth and even the twentieth century.

French Canadians: Cultured and Carefree

Commentators on the behavior of the settlers in New France emphasized three themes. The first was the contrast between the carefree
French and the industrious Yankees. The Canadians were the grass-
hoppers, fiddling the day away, while English colonists were the ants,
toiling for the future. No writer made this point more tellingly than
the Jesuit priest Pierre-François-Xavier de Charlevoix. Like Alexis de
Tocqueville a century later, Charlevoix was an observant traveler and
an astute historian. Voltaire, who studied with Charlevoix in Paris,
called his teacher "a most veracious man" and bought all his works.
Charlevoix visited New France twice: in 1705–8 and again in 1720–
22. He traveled widely, traversing the Great Lakes and canoeing with
his guides down the Mississippi to the rude settlement ("a hundred or
so shacks") at New Orleans. Everywhere he took notes on the plants
he saw, the terrain he covered, and the people he met. Back in France
he distilled his observations into a series of well-received works.[2]

For Charlevoix, the English and French in America exhibited strikingly different approaches to life. Superficially, the French seemed to be
more prosperous: "To judge of the two colonies by the way of life, behavior, and speech of the inhabitants, nobody would hesitate to say ours
were the most flourishing." But the shortcomings of the English were
largely in the area of "style"; they were the clear victors in the contest to
build a strong economy. Charlevoix commented: "In New England and
the other provinces of the continent of America subject to the British empire, there prevails an opulence which they are utterly at a loss how to
use; and in New France, a poverty hid by an air of being in easy circumstances." Charlevoix underscored the contrast between the carefree,
high-living French and the diligent, frugal English. "The English
planter," he explained, "amasses wealth and never makes any super-
fluous expense; the French inhabitant again enjoys what he . . . is not
possessed of. That [the English settler] labors for his posterity; this [the
French farmer] again leaves his offspring involved in the same necessi-
ties he was in himself at his first setting out." And finally: "You meet
with no rich men in this country [Canada], and it is really a great pity,
every one endeavouring to put as good a face on it as possible, and nobody scarce thinking of laying up wealth."[3]

Others echoed this contrast between cultured, improvident Canadians and the rough but diligent British colonists. Peter Kalm, the
Swedish naturalist, remarked: "I found that the people of distinction,
had here [in Canada] in general a much greater taste for natural history and other learning than in the English colonies, where it was
everybody's sole care and employment to scrape a fortune together."[4]
A French officer visiting the St. Lawrence colony noted that Canadians

"are not thrifty and take no care for the future, being too fond of their freedom and independence."[5]

Observers sounded a second theme: Canadians were excessively fond of luxuries. Good Lutheran that he was, Kalm was shocked by the display he witnessed. He reported from Quebec: "The English . . . do not idle their time away in dressing as the French do here. The ladies, especially, dress and powder their hair every day, and put their locks in papers every night. . . . People of rank are accustomed to wear lace-trimmed clothes and all the crown officers carry swords." Nor was the desire for finery limited to the towns. Observed Kalm: "The common people in the country . . . are content with meals of dry bread and water, bringing all other provisions . . . to town in order to get money for them, for which they buy clothes and brandy for themselves and finery for their women."[6]

French witnesses echoed Kalm's remarks. In the late seventeenth century Bishop Laval was scandalized by the behavior of the women attending church. They fussed over their hair and wore low-cut gowns, "contenting themselves by donning transparent veils which served only to add lustre to such scandalous nudities."[7] Jean Bochart de Champigny, who served as intendant—or chief civilian official of New France—complained in 1699 that the "women love display and are excessively lazy." A Sulpician priest arriving in the colony in 1737 noted that the people spent all their money on fineries. They were "as poor as artists and as vain as peacocks."[8]

The third theme touched by contemporaries was more delicately nuanced: a mixed evaluation of the willingness of Canadians to work hard. Champigny frankly regarded the inhabitants of New France as lazy. He observed that "the men are all strong and vigorous but have no liking for work of any duration."[9] Others set forth views that were ambivalent or contradictory. Charlevoix commented that New France was "supported by the industry of its inhabitants." But he also remarked that an "aversion to a regular and assiduous labor, and a spirit of independence, have ever carried a great many young people out of it [Canada], and prevented the colony from being peopled."[10] Kalm praised the industriousness of Canadian women. "In their domestic duties they greatly surpass the English women in the plantations . . . ," he observed. "The women in Canada on the contrary do not spare themselves, especially among the common people, where they are always in the fields, meadows, stables, etc. and do not dislike any work whatsoever."[11]

Another observer, Antoine-Denis Raudot, also provided a mixed view of Canadian work habits. Raudot served as intendant of New France between 1705 and 1710. He was only twenty-six when he arrived in Canada, but was astute, well connected, and determined to foster the growth of the struggling colony. In a passage fraught with ambivalence, he examined the willingness of Canadians to work hard. "The Canadian is lively, proud, haughty, strong, hardy and industrious, [and] capable of enduring extreme hardships," he remarked in 1709. But Raudot did not allow "industrious" to stand unmodified. He continued: "The soldiers have peopled this country with girls, who having led a riotous life in France, have instilled in their children idleness and arrogance instead of industry." But again Raudot modified his statement. He concluded: "Although the Canadian in general has a character such as I just described, he is steadily improving. He now works and makes his children work."[12]

Finally, portrait painting in New France reinforces the depiction of a society where entrepreneurial and even secular goals were subordinated to nonworldly concerns. Canadian painting in this era was largely religious, and was often designed to adorn a church. The portrait of Marguerite Bourgeoys, founder of the teaching order of the Congrégation de Notre-Dame, may be contrasted with paintings done in the Thirteen Colonies (Fig. 2.1). Typically, artists of New France, like Pierre Le Ber, who painted Bourgeoys, highlighted the devoutness of their subjects. In a few instances, painters depicted civilian administrators, emphasizing their aristocratic bearing. But absent from all these works were the middle-class virtues evident in the northern colonies.[13]

The commentary of many individuals and the vision captured by portrait painters suggest that the settlers in New France were less dedicated to frugality, hard work, and the accumulation of wealth than were northerners. This French-Canadian outlook, which is explored more fully in later chapters, would help shape the course of growth in the nineteenth century and beyond.

Industrious North versus Lazy South

Eighteenth-century commentators displayed remarkable unanimity in contrasting the northern and southern colonies. Northerners were hard-working, southerners lazy. Not surprisingly, such a comparison came easily to the pens of those living in the North. In the debate over the Constitution, James Winthrop of Massachusetts argued that no single set of laws could govern all Americans because the "idle and dissolute inhabitants of the South require a different regimen from the sober and active people of the North."[14]

Foreign visitors echoed this judgment. Andrew Burnaby was a well-to-do Anglican clergyman who visited the colonies in 1759 and 1760 and published an account of his travels after returning to England. Burnaby was impressed by the "laborious" northerners. "The Pennsylvanians," he noted, "as to character, are a frugal and industrious people. . . . They are by far the most enterprising people upon

Figure 2.1 **Pierre Le Ber,** *Marguerite Bourgeoys, 1700.* Most of the art of New France had a religious theme; few works displayed the concern for industry evident in portraits done in the northern Thirteen Colonies. Marguerite Bourgeoys founded the order of the Congrégation de Notre-Dame. Le Ber painted this work of great strength and somber tonality when Bourgeoys was on her deathbed. (*Source:* Marguerite Bourgeoys Centre, Montreal.)

the continent." New Yorkers stood not far behind. "The inhabitants of New York," Burnaby continued, "in their character, very much resemble the Pennsylvanians: more than half of them are Dutch, and almost all traders: they are, therefore, habitually frugal, industrious, and parsimonious." But a different approach to work marked the South. Southerners, Burnaby observed, were "indolent, inactive, and unenterprising: this is visible in every line of their character. I myself have been a spectator, and it is not an uncommon sight, of a man in the vigour of life, lying upon a couch, and a female slave standing over him, wafting off the flies, and fanning him, while he took his repose." [15]

Southerners concurred, and at times were harsher than northerners in condemning southern work habits. Robert Beverley was a wealthy Virginia planter. In his *History and Present State of Virginia* (1705) he denounced the "slothful indolence" of the region. Beverley presented his book to his countrymen to "rouse them out of their Lethargy and excite them to make the most of all those happy Advantages which Nature has given them." [16] Richard Henry Lee, another well-born Virginia slaveholder, also contrasted a lazy South with an industrious North. He remarked in the 1760s that "some of our neighboring colonies, though much later than ourselves in point of settlement, are now far before us in improvement." The reason? "With their whites they import arts and agriculture, whilst we with our blacks exclude both." [17]

The differences between the two regions were also evident in portraiture. Artists often portrayed northerners as hardworking, busy people. Painter Charles Willson Peale posed subjects such as Benjamin Franklin and Dr. Benjamin Rush with quill and paper at their side. John Singleton Copley, the greatest of the eighteenth-century American painters, took a similar approach. He depicted Paul Revere, a silversmith, not only with a teapot he had crafted, but also with the tools of his trade. He painted Boston merchant Isaac Smith at his writing desk. And as Figure 2.2 shows, Copley emphasized the industriousness of Thomas Mifflin and his wife. Thomas Mifflin, one of Philadelphia's wealthiest merchants, has paused in his reading—but only for a moment; his finger marks his place in the book. Mrs. Mifflin looks up from her weaving. [18]

By contrast, portraits of eighteenth-century southerners rarely highlighted the diligence of their subjects. More typically, painters portrayed the lavish clothes and leisure pursuits of a slaveholding upper class. Figures 2.3 and 2.4 present portraits of Colonel Barnard Elliott and his wife by Jeremiah Theus. The Swiss-born Theus, who painted the South Carolina elite over the course of more than three decades, was attuned to the outlook of the southern aristocracy. The elaborate outfits of the Elliotts form a sharp contrast to the plainer dress of the Mifflins, and suggest individuals who rarely worked with their hands. [19]

Figure 2.2 **John Singleton Copley,** *Mr. and Mrs. Thomas Mifflin,* *1773.*
Thomas Mifflin was a wealthy Philadelphia merchant and an outspoken patriot. Significantly, Copley chose to portray him and his wife as industrious individuals. This emphasis on diligence is echoed in other eighteenth-century
paintings of northerners. (*Source:* Historical Society of Pennsylvania, Philadelphia.)

Figure 2.3   **Jeremiah Theus, *Mrs. Barnard Elliott*, c. 1766.** Between the 1740s and 1770s Jeremiah Theus recorded the splendor of the South Carolina upper class. Contrast these portraits with Copley's portrayal of the Mifflins. Fine clothes and jewelry, not visible industry, characterize the Elliotts. (*Source:* Gibbes Museum of Art, Charleston, South Carolina.)

Figure 2.4 **Jeremiah Theus, *Colonel Barnard Elliott*, c. 1766.**

Portraits thus reinforce much other testimony that pronounced the North industrious and the South idle. Indeed, there were few crosscurrents of contradiction or eddies of uncertainty in the wide river of opinion depicting the two regions.

Because industriousness seemed the norm or at least the proper goal for all, contemporaries were concerned to explain the "inactive" nature of the South. Commentators offered three explanations. One was climate. In discussing the idleness of southerners, Reverend Burnaby noted: "The climate operates very powerfully upon them."[20] In *Notes on the State of Virginia*, first printed in 1785, Thomas Jefferson remarked: "In a warm climate no man will labour for himself who can make another labour for him."[21] David Ramsay was still another observer who pointed to the oppressive hot weather. Ramsay, who came from South Carolina, lived through the Revolution, but did not publish his account of that struggle until 1808. He noted that "warm, moist, unelastic air fosters habits of indolence." Ramsay added: a "propensity to indolence is common in Carolina as in other warm countries and seasons."[22]

A second reason was slavery. William Byrd was a writer of no mean ability, one of Virginia's wealthiest planters, and the owner of many African Americans. He told an English correspondent that the new colony of Georgia was wise to ban slavery. Slaves, Byrd remarked, "blow up the pride and ruin the industry of our white people, who seeing a rank of poor creatures below them detest work for fear it should make them look like slaves."[23] Jefferson too condemned bondage—despite the fact that his own leisure time depended on the labor of his blacks. "There must doubtless be an unhappy influence on the manners of our people produced by the existence of slavery among us," he observed in *Notes on the State of Virginia*. He continued: "With the morals of the people, their industry also is destroyed. . . . This is so true, that of the proprietors of slaves a very small proportion indeed are ever seen to labour."[24]

Finally, some writers link southern—and northern—behavior to national origins. In one version this is the story of the dashing "Cavaliers" and sober "Roundheads," two groups that clashed in seventeenth-century England. In his *History and Present State of Virginia*, Robert Beverley explained: "In the time of the Rebellion in *England*, several good Cavalier Families went thither [to Virginia] with their Effects. . . . The Roundheads went for the most part to *New-England*."[25] The Cavaliers were aristocrats, Anglicans, and royalists who supported the Crown in the English Civil War. The Roundheads were middling sorts, Puritans, and regicides who cheered Oliver Cromwell's New Model Army. From such origins, it was alleged, emerged the indolent, aristocratic South and the industrious, democratic North.

Robert Taylor's study, *Cavalier and Yankee*, shows that by the early nineteenth century this myth had a firm place in the popular imagination North and South.[26]

More recently, David Hackett Fischer, in *Albion's Seed: Four British Folkways in America*, has argued that there is substance to the myth. According to Fischer, four major regions in early America—New England, the Delaware Valley, Virginia, and the backcountry—drew their white settlers and dominant "folkways" from distinct parts of the British Isles. A majority of New Englanders, Fischer says, came from the Puritan towns of East Anglia, which had indeed supported Cromwell. By contrast, Virginians came from the west and south of England, where individuals were far more likely to back the royalist cause. The Delaware Valley, contends Fischer, was settled by Quakers and kindred spirits from the North Midlands. North Britain and Northern Ireland were the source of the colonists who settled the backcountry.

Critics have vehemently attacked Fischer's conclusions, and he has defended his work with equal gusto. On the empirical question—did colonists in the several New World regions come from distinct parts of the British Isles?—Fischer clearly has the better of his critics. The extraordinary amount of data he marshalls shows that at least during the initial waves of settlement the preponderance of individuals in the four regions came from different places in England, Scotland, Wales, and Northern Ireland. These differences in national origins affected speech patterns, as well as preferences in diet and dress. These migrations also helped shape the religions of the North and South—a topic explored more fully in Chapter 4.

A more difficult issue is the implications of these findings. Local accents are one question, an entrepreneurial spirit another. For example, did national origins make individuals more diligent? This text suggests that for the United States, Old World roots often were of secondary importance. Travelers in the colonial South noted the industriousness of foreign Protestants. Preacher George Whitefield visited a Swiss settlement in Georgia and remarked: "Surely they speak not the truth who say the Georgia people have been idle, for I never saw more laborious people than are in these villages." Unfortunately for southern development, such exemplary work habits were not preserved by subsequent generations. Slavery far more than national origins shaped the culture of all southerners.[27]

In sum, eighteenth-century observers agreed that the outlook of the settlers varied from region to region. Commentators concurred in their depiction of "laborious" northerners, "indolent" southerners, and "idle" French Canadians. Such comments hint at the future, and suggest a North that will grow richer, and a South and French Canada that will fall behind. But a survey of contemporary opinion is only a starting point. Subsequent chapters examine the roots of these different world views, and explore the impact and elaboration of these patterns of behavior. The qualities that distinguished northerners translated into more rapid growth only once commercial capitalism replaced the household economy. In the eighteenth century, southerners and French Canadians produced as much wealth as hard-working northerners. In 1750 the regions were marked by distinct values and institutions, but their paths of development had not yet diverged.

3

Peasants and Freeholders

Any exploration of New World culture and institutions necessarily begins with the Old World. Hence we examine Adam Winthrop. He was a London cloth merchant who responded eagerly when Henry VIII seized the monastery lands and offered them for sale. In 1544 Adam paid £409 for Groton Manor in Suffolk County. His son, also named Adam, and his grandson, John, devoted much of their energies to making Groton more profitable. They raised crops for the London market. By 1593 the second Adam was earning £62 from the sale of foodstuffs—more than the value of the rents he collected. The Winthrops acquired more land, and sold parcels when the opportunity seemed right. John, who was as keen a trader as his father and grandfather, observed: "Where I may have more money, I can depart with the more land." The Winthrops renegotiated leases with their tenants. Like other landowners they worked to get shorter terms, to raise rents, or simply to take over the land. When John finally sold his estate in 1631—to help finance his migration to Massachusetts—he received £4200 for it.[1]

The Winthrops, to be sure, were hardly freewheeling capitalists. The portraits of the second Adam and of John stare at us across the gulf of centuries. Adam with his gold earrings and John with his ruff and full Elizabethan beard look more like medieval courtiers than modern businessmen. Father and son presided at the manorial courts that governed the lives of their tenants. John was a justice of the peace and helped regulate prices and prevent economic "oppression" by merchants.[2]

But in their insistence on the commercial use of land, the Winthrops were the true forebears of the farmers that would spread across the United States. Their willingness to challenge customary relationships pointed to a day when the remnants of feudalism would disappear. The picture in Old France and New was very different. In France there were few families like the Winthrops. Few individuals attacked long-standing practices. And reflecting this heritage, farmers along the St. Lawrence had less of a commercial cast than those in the commonwealths to the south.

The approach people took to the land, which is examined in this chapter, played a crucial role in determining the pattern of growth. These customs, along with the role of religion and labor—which are discussed in the next chapter—form what might be called the *foundations* of the three North American societies. The topics treated in subsequent chapters—mobility, literacy, entrepreneurial spirit, and intellectual life—are in some ways outgrowths of these basic elements, and can be called *elaborations*. The distinction between foundations and elaborations is meant to suggest an order of priorities, rather than to be rigid or formulaic. Each of the chapters discusses institutions or aspects of culture that were important in shaping the pattern of growth.

The relationship between people and the land is a good place to start. In French Canada a hierarchical, static seigneurial system acted as a brake on development. By contrast, the emergence of freehold tenure accelerated the rise of the North. Such practices dovetailed with the entrepreneurial bent of the citizenry in the northern states. In the South the impact of this aggressive approach to land was more complex. Slavery was the dominant force shaping values. So the eagerness of southerners to take up land did not lead to a business mentality. But the rush to new lands boosted the standard of living, and helped introduce into southern society a note of belligerence lacking in French Canada.

The Hierarchical World of French Canada

French Background

The peasantry of France and its colony lived in a very different world than the freeholders of England and its North American possessions. Since the St. Lawrence colony mirrored the parent society, a study of property relations in New France must begin with an examination of Old France. We may particularly emphasize three aspects of life in France that shaped Canadian society: the seigneurial system, the strong sense of hierarchy, and the deep-rooted resistance to change.

The seigneurial system, which governed the use and ownership of the land, was a hardy transplant, brought from the soils of France to the St. Lawrence Valley. In France, however, seigneurialism was marked by more striking regional variations than would be the case in Canada. France was after all a sprawling kingdom that had been brought together during the course of many centuries. Newly acquired provinces often kept their privileges and local customs. In New France seigneurialism was imposed soon after settlement, and was administered in a more uniform manner.

Seigneurialism assumed multiple rights to the land. A lord might hold title to a seigneury, but when disposing of it, he had to respect the privileges of his wife and children as well as those of the peasants who lived on the soil. Within the seigneury peasants "owned" most of the land, but were restricted in their ability to buy or sell their estates. They had to provide their betters with labor services as well as with feudal rents, taxes and tithes. Peasants were caught up in a web of obligations to the Crown, nobility, and Church.

The highly stratified social structure of France also would be echoed in the New World. At the pinnacle of the social pyramid stood the nobility. Membership in this class was defined by birth, although entry was never entirely closed. The power of the nobility lay in its legal privileges—including exemption from taxation—and in the ownership of the land. Nobles comprised the most important group of seigneurs. The wealthiest members of the Church—the bishops, abbots, and others—had interests and an outlook similar to the nobles. At least 10 percent of the land in France lay within their seigneuries. The middle class was increasing in wealth, but had little political power until the French Revolution. Bourgeois seigneurs were important only near the cities. And at the base of the pyramid was the peasantry, the largest group in the realm.[3]

Finally, it is important to note the slow pace of social change in France between 1500 and 1750—a pattern of stasis that helped shape the cautious outlook of French men and women in the Old World and New. A brief comparison between England and France underscores the persistence of customary practices in France. Small holdings and strong feudal obligations were characteristic of England, as well as France, in 1500. But in England large, profit-oriented farms emerged in county after county between 1500 and 1750. Small estates disappeared. In France the peasantry successfully resisted the spread of commercial farming. True, on the wheat plains of northern France a few large estates were created in the seventeenth century. Some vineyards along the Atlantic coast expanded in response to the increased consumption of French wines. But throughout France tiny, poor peasant farms remained as characteristic of the countryside in 1750 as they had been in 1500. This lack of change in the size of holdings and in the use of land helped create a mindset that emphasized stability and community. Such values dovetailed with French Catholicism, and were at odds with an aggressive entrepreneurial approach to the economy.[4]

This society, shaped by the seigneurial system, a strong hierarchy, and a resolute resistance to change, would create a colony with similar values in the New World.

Feudalism in New France

The feudal system* in Canada perpetuated the hierarchical, anti-commercial values evident in seventeenth-century France and in French Catholicism. It elevated the nobility and clergy. It discouraged the speculative sale of farms, and restricted capital accumulation. It was as if someone had posted a sign at the mouth of the St. Lawrence: "Traditional society established here. Speculators and entrepreneurs not welcome."

Predictably, scholars have taken different viewpoints in discussing the system that governed land use in early Canada. Some historians highlight market forces and self-interested behavior. Cameron Nish asserts that the seigneurs were *bourgeois gentilshommes* (a "middle-class nobility") little removed in spirit from urban entrepreneurs. Nish argues the system "possessed several characteristics associated with bourgeois exploitation," and he underscores the "ambition of the seigneurs to engage in land speculation."[5] However, most writers contend that a strong sense of hierarchy and a non-entrepreneurial ethos characterized the seigneurial system. The analysis of economic activities presented below supports that point of view and suggests the weakness in the case for a bourgeois mind-set. Seigneurs, to be sure, wanted more wealth, but this desire for riches was hardly an indication of a modern outlook. More significant, lords and habitants (i.e., farmers) did not engage in the aggressive commercial activities that marked the new middle class.[6]

Feudalism in New France, as in Europe, placed power—and landed property—in the hands of the aristocracy. Decrees dating back to the first part of the seventeenth century had established for New France the principle of *nulle terre sans seigneur*—no land without a seigneur. And typically the lord was a titled individual, or a military officer with very similar values. True, a middle-class person could be a seigneur, and some were. But the royal officials who granted land did not encourage the bourgeoisie to become feudal lords. Rather, the intendants and governors who made the grants felt that nobles, with

---

* I follow Allan Greer in applying the adjective *feudal* to New France. Greer defines the "feudal mode of production" as one with a dominant aristocracy, an agrarian economy with peasants as the chief producers, a system that forces the peasantry to turn over some of its produce to the nobility, and multiple rights to the land. See Greer, *Peasant, Lord, and Merchant: Rural Society in Three Quebec Parishes, 1740–1840* (Toronto, 1985), xi–xiv.

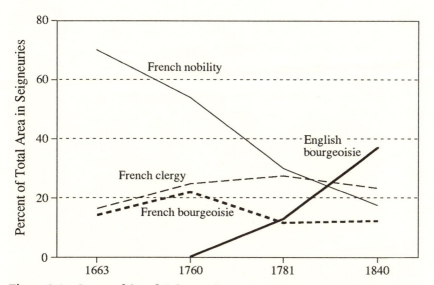

Figure 3.1 **Ownership of Seigneuries, 1663–1840**. During the French regime (that is, to 1760) the nobility were the dominant landholders. After the Conquest the English middle class came to the fore. During both periods the French-speaking bourgeoisie was a weak force. (*Source:* Fernand Ouellet, "Propriété seigneuriale et groupes sociaux dans la vallée du Saint-Laurent (1663–1840)," *Revue de l'Université d'Ottawa,* XLVII (1977), 183–214. In addition to the four groups presented on the graph, members of the English military owned 19 percent of seigneurial territory in 1781, and 11 percent in 1840.)

titles that stretched back for generations, should be the dominant class in Canada as they were in France. In 1660 the nobles and military men held 70 percent (by area) of the seigneuries granted in Canada. The clergy came next with 16 percent, and middle-class landowners third with 14 percent. The portion held by the aristocrats declined, but they continued to hold the lion's share of seigneurial land throughout the French regime. The bourgeoisie remained in third place among the owners of these fiefs (Fig. 3.1).[7]

Noble men and women in New France were acquisitive, but they sought riches within the framework of a traditional economy, not within the world of entrepreneurial activity. They demanded their feudal dues, and turned to the courts when they felt they were wronged. Despite regulations protecting the farmers, seigneurs raised rents. They changed the terms of payment from capons to cash, and from cash to wheat. They assiduously protected their monopoly of milling. As timber grew more valuable, they demanded control over trees cut on the habitants' land. But the lords did not introduce commercial farming on their own demesne—the area of the seigneury they cultivated themselves. They did not seek to enlarge that demesne for commercial purposes, as some of the most advanced members of the nobility did in France. Nor in most cases did they use their wealth to move into trade. General James Murray, who governed Canada in the 1760s, observed that the seigneurs "have an utter contempt for the trading part of the colony."[8]

Feudalism in New France also elevated the Church—which like the *noblesse* stood poles apart from trade. By 1750 the various religious orders controlled one-fourth of seigneurial land, and served as seigneur to one-third of the population. Church seigneuries were carefully administered and, as the colony grew, became highly profitable ventures. Moreover, all habitants, whether they lived in Church or lay seigneuries, had to pay tithes. This levy, which took one twenty-sixth of all grain harvested, helped support the local clergy. The Church was also responsible for key social institutions, including the hospitals, schools, and asylums. When critics of the seigneurial system emerged in the nineteenth century, Church leaders would be among the most outspoken defenders of this way of life.

Feudalism in New France also shaped the lives of farmers, and reinforced the traditional, noncommercial values evident in Catholicism. Various laws and customs discouraged land speculation. Some measures restricted individual habitants. *Lods et ventes* was a tax levied on the sale of land outside a family. One-twelfth of the purchase price in such transactions had to be turned over to the seigneur. The *retrait roturier* assured the seigneur that the habitant did not report an artificially low price for the sale to minimize the *lods et ventes*. It gave the seigneur forty days to acquire any farm sold by paying the buyer the purchase price. Other customs restrained the male head of the family—seigneur or habitant—from disposing of property as he chose. The *retrait lignager* allowed the wife and children to invalidate any deal. If they reimbursed the purchaser, they could take over the estate themselves. The *légitime* further protected the children. It said that any sale must recognize the rights of the children to the property. The eldest son was to receive (in the case of a seigneury) the manor and half the estate, while the other children were entitled to equal shares of the remainder. None of these restrictions was insurmountable. Taxes could be paid, and cash settlements could satisfy those waiting for an inheritance. But taken together these regulations obstructed the turnover of property. They limited the gains a landowner might receive from the sale of an estate.[9]

Feudal regulations also made it difficult for farmers to accumulate capital. It is true that seigneurs were obligated to grant undeveloped land at no charge. But once title was registered, the habitant had to pay several feudal dues. The annual payment made to the seigneur was called the *cens et rentes*. The *cens* was a token acknowledgment of the seigneur's rights. The annual rent, however, was more substantial.

It varied from seigneury to seigneury, and from farm to farm. But by the middle of the eighteenth century it typically could amount to twenty-seven livres on a ninety-arpent estate. Allan Greer's study of farms in the Richelieu Valley suggests the impact of this levy. Payment was made in grain. And for half the farms there was no surplus left after the family fed itself and paid the *cens et rentes*. Even most of the more prosperous farmers turned over at least 30 percent of their surplus to the seigneur. The seigneurial system required other payments. Habitants were prohibited from setting up their own mills, and had to pay the seigneur one-fourteenth of the grain ground. The amount was more than double the cost of providing this service. In some seigneuries farmers also had to provide *corvée* labor for the lord of the manor. The transfer of this wealth from habitant to seigneur checked economic growth. Farmers had less to invest in their holdings, and seigneurs did not put the funds they received to commercial use.[10]

In sum, the feudal system of New France affirmed the traditional relationships of a noncommercial society and discouraged the energies that might promote economic expansion. A few individuals, like the intendant Antoine-Denis Raudot, suggested easing the feudal burden on the habitants to promote economic expansion. But the force of religion, custom, and interest prevented any reforms before 1760.[11]

The Seigneurial System Under the British Regime, 1760–1854

The Conquest dealt a mortal blow to feudalism in New France, but seigneurialism—the regulations governing land use—lived on. Like slavery in the American South, the seigneurial system survived into the middle of the nineteenth century and was a brake on economic development. And like slavery, the seigneurial system had ardent defenders. In both cases the loudest critics were "outsiders." The end of the seigneurial system in 1854, like the abolition of slavery in 1865, altered society less than some of the most outspoken reformers might have wished.

It is hard to view Lower Canada as a "feudal" society after 1760. The old nobility was irremediably weakened. No new titled seigneurs received land; no new French-Canadian families were ennobled. British administrators governed Canada. However, the seigneurial system seemed to lose none of its vigor. If the French *noblesse* gradually lost its control of the land, English military officers and merchants increased their ownership of the seigneuries—and kept the old customs in force.

Historians differ in describing the nature of change in the countryside during this era. Some writers, such as Gilles Paquet and Jean-Pierre Wallot (who have co-authored several articles on this topic), contend that in the decades after 1800 the spread of market relations transformed the economy and outlook of rural French Canada.[12] Other scholars, such as Allan Greer and Fernand Ouellet, emphasize the slow pace of change outside the cities.[13] The two groups of historians also debate a related question: was it market forces (Paquet and Wallot) or the backward nature of agricultural practices (Ouellet) that explain the hard times that farmers in Lower Canada experienced in the first half of the nineteenth century?[14] The discussion below suggests that the case for far-reaching change in rural society is weak. Indeed, much of Paquet and Wallot's work is curiously abstract, and puts more emphasis on the conceptual framework than on the analysis of life in the countryside. Despite gradual alterations in the laws and regulations governing land use, most French Canadians continued to affirm a way of life and values whose roots went back to New France. This strong sense of tradition helped perpetuate seigneurialism and shaped the conflicts over its abolition.

We begin this account of the evolution and demise of seigneurialism with the changing institutional framework. British policy at first accepted French property law—if with some hesitation. The 1760 articles of capitulation guaranteed seigneurs and habitants the peaceful possession of their estates. The Proclamation of 1763 made no immediate changes in land ownership. But it muddied the waters by announcing that English law and English freehold tenure would be introduced into Canada. English law was now applied in some cases; French law in others. The Quebec Act of 1774 was designed to smooth the ruffled sensibilities of the French Canadians and keep them from joining the rebellious Yankees to the south. It reaffirmed the commitment of the English government to the seigneurial system and approved the collection of tithes by the Church. What else could the British do? In 1774 English speakers made up less than 4 percent of the Canadian population.[15]

Gradually, Britain limited the area dominated by the seigneurial system. The Constitutional Act of 1791 acknowledged the sway of French law in the St. Lawrence Valley. But it spun off the growing settlements to the west in a new province—Upper Canada—with freehold tenure. And in secret instructions accompanying the Act, the British government decided that the lands lying between the seigneuries and the American border would be granted with no feudal dues. This area, the Eastern Townships, would soon be filled with English-speaking settlers, including many Americans moving north from Vermont and New York. Bills approved by the British Parliament in 1822 and 1825 made possible the voluntary transformation of seigneurial property to freehold tenure. Few seigneurs volunteered. The Act of Union of 1840 marked another step toward the abolition of the seigneurial system. It created the United Provinces of Canada, consisting of Canada West (Upper Canada) and Canada East (Lower Canada). And it established a unified Assembly where the French-Canadian defenders of the seigneurial system could be outvoted and legislation ending seigneurial tenure might be adopted.[16]

The English in Lower Canada eventually became outspoken opponents of the seigneurial system—but at first they were happy enough to share the privileges of the French lords. Anglophones, initially military officers, and then, in increasing numbers, merchants, acquired seigneuries. By the 1840s members of the English middle class owned 41 percent of seigneurial land, significantly more than did the Church, the remnants of the French nobility, or the French middle class (Fig. 3.1). They invested more in their properties than did the French. They erected the biggest flour mills, and undertook the most extensive lumbering operations. They also exploited their feudal privileges even more aggressively than the French seigneurs. Like New Englander Simon Legree, the archetype of a hard-driving northern slaveholder in a leisurely South, many English seigneurs developed an unenviable reputation in French Canada. Even Lord Durham confessed: "The seigniorial tenure is one so little adapted to our notions of proprietary rights, that the new seignior, without any consciousness or intention of injustice, in many instances exercised his rights in a manner . . . which the Canadian settler reasonably regarded as oppressive."[17]

Increasingly, English Canadians turned against the seigneurial system. One grievance was the burden placed on cities, where property changed hands more often than in the countryside. Even before the turn of the century, loyalist traders had pointed to feudal exactions as their reason for abandoning the town of William Henry (later called Sorel). "If the *cens et rentes* and *lods et ventes*, etc. be enforced upon us," they announced, "it will prevent many valuable members of society from settling among us."[18] By the 1820s Edward Ellice, himself a seigneur and merchant, could remark that seigneurial tenure in the towns was the reason for the "objections of British-born subjects to the investment of the[ir] large profits" in Lower Canada. "No house can be sold in Montreal or Quebec, or no farm in the island of Montreal, without paying a heavy fine," he complained.[19] Feudal control of town land slowed the development of local government and retarded the emergence of essential services. The backwardness of rural seigneurs was also condemned. "How many of our seigneurs of fiefs have refused," a committee of the Canadian Assembly asked rhetorically, "and still refuse every day to encourage the establishment of profitable works and useful manufactures for the country, in order to retain exclusively, without profit to themselves or the public, the numerous water powers owned by them?"[20]

The outlook of the French-Canadian majority was another story. Before midcentury most French speakers supported the continuation of feudal tenure. But such views were not held uniformly. An examination of two leaders sheds light on the range of opinion in Lower Canada.[21]

Louis-Joseph Papineau was a supporter of the seigneurial system—

and the most prominent French-Canadian politician during the first half of the nineteenth century. Like John C. Calhoun, who carried the banner of southern nationalism (and who was but four years his senior), Papineau served as leader, tribune, and symbol for his people. We glimpse Papineau through a series of portraits done in oil, pastel, and finally daguerreotype. He changes from an intense young lawyer, with his dark locks brushed fashionably forward at the sides, to the imposing elder statesman with strong features and a shock of white hair. He was an inspired orator and held sway in the Assembly of Lower Canada where he served as Speaker most years between 1815 and 1837. Papineau was a French-Canadian nationalist, who wanted an assembly dominated by his countrymen to make decisions for the province—unchecked by British governors or an appointed upper house. His denunciations of British rule led to the rebellions of 1837 and 1838. But Papineau was also a seigneur and a defender of the seigneurial system. "I am a great reformer in the matter of necessary political changes," he remarked, "but I am a great conservative in the matter of preservation of the sacred right of property." After the failure of the 1837 rebellion, Papineau fled into exile, returning to Canada only in 1845. Now in his sixties, he was elected to the Assembly of United Canada, where he made clear his unrepentant nationalism.[22]

Cyrille-Hector-Octave Côté was also a French-Canadian nationalist but, unlike Papineau, was a critic of the seigneurial system. Côté came from a poor family, but was determined to get an education and eventually became a doctor. He practiced in the small towns of the Richelieu Valley and gained a reputation as a skilled, caring individual for his labors during the 1832 cholera epidemic. Côté, who admired Papineau, had been interested in politics since the mid-1820s. He grew ever more concerned about the problems faced by the farmers he served, and in 1834 was elected to the Lower Canadian House of Assembly. Côté denounced the lords for constantly raising feudal dues, and he began to question seigneurial tenure itself as well as Church efforts to dominate schooling. Many farmers in the Richelieu Valley, where economic conditions had been particularly hard, backed Côté's daring stand. They joined him in the large, outdoor meetings. And they mustered under his leadership in the spring of 1837 when the decision to take up arms was made. But in other parts of the province the habitants were cooler to rebellion—and even to Papineau's more moderate position.

When the 1837 uprising failed, Côté fled to the United States, as did Papineau. But now the *patriote* leadership split on the question of social change. With Papineau on the sidelines, Côté and an anglophone doctor, Robert Nelson, called for a revolt in 1838. They demanded a republic with religious freedom, the separation of Church and state, and freehold tenure. Few farmers, however, rallied to the banner of social change, and the rebels' small force was defeated near the American border. When that second rebellion collapsed, Côté left politics—and ended up a Baptist preacher.[23]

But the days of the seigneurial system were numbered. Pressed by the English and the increasing spread of commercial relations, many in the French-Canadian elite came to see by the 1850s the wisdom of ending this vestige of feudalism—on their own terms. Unlike the southern planters who defended slavery even to the point of war, prominent francophones now accepted the *compensated* abolition of feudal dues. Hippolyte Lafontaine, who emerged as leader of the French Canadians when Papineau went into exile, argued that a proposed plan of compensation was the best offer the seigneurs might expect. "Delay gives new occasions for the propagation of principles which tend to overturn society," Lafontaine warned. "There comes a time when the people say, 'It is too late.' In this case, as the seigneurs form the smallest number, they may expect to lose everything without compensation." In December 1854 the law abolishing seigneurialism received viceregal assent.[24]

The abolition of seigneurialism, as spelled out in the 1854 law, was not the thoroughgoing change that reformers like Côté had desired. Farmers were now free to buy and sell their land, without worrying that a sale outside the family might be treated differently than one to relatives. But payments to the former seigneur did not cease. With abolition, commissioners visited each seigneury and calculated the value of the various feudal dues. These charges were now replaced by the *rente constituée*. The habitants continued to pay this new tax well into the twentieth century. They continued to call their landlord "the seigneur," although that title no longer had any legal status. The former seigneur often retained other lucrative rights, such as control over a local waterfall. The reforms of 1854, significantly, were not dictated by an uprising from below. If there were rumblings of discontent, it was only the muffled, distant thunder that might precede a storm, not the storm itself. The habitant's outlook—deferential, locally oriented, and noncommercial—remained intact. Abolition of seigneurialism was a sensible, limited reform pushed through by anglophone pressure and by the urgings of enlightened French-Canadian leaders. It did not mark a radical change in the social structure or values of French Canada.[25]

The Changing World of the Thirteen Colonies and States

The English Background

Just as New France was the product of the static, organic world of Old France, so the northern and southern colonies reflected—in their approach to land—the commercial ethos of Tudor and Stuart England. Just how this dynamic combined with other aspects of northern and southern society is discussed in subsequent chapters. But in both sections the ties between people and the land helped shape the mind-set of the population.

More than any other European country (except perhaps Holland), England was rushing headlong from medieval to modern times. Between 1500 and 1700 Britain was a mix of old and new, medieval and modern, feudal and capitalistic. The triumph of the modern would not be complete, perhaps, until the middle of the nineteenth century. But the direction was clear. And nowhere were the changes in England more evident or more important than in the relationship between the people and the land. In 1500 inefficient, subsistence agriculture shaped the lives of most English farmers. In central and southeastern England the open field system predominated. In these areas farmers lived in nucleated villages, with their homes close together, often in the shadow of the church and manor house. Each individual worked several narrow scattered strips. Land had been distributed so that most persons had an acre or two of good soil, several patches of lesser quality, and a bit of meadowland for making hay. Some fields were used in common for grazing sheep and cattle. And once the crops were gathered in, the animals were turned loose on all the lands. The open field system was less common in northwestern and southwestern England. Before 1500 farmers in those regions less frequently came together in central villages; more often they worked poor, isolated plots.[26]

Gradually the open fields of the south and east and the small, individual holdings of the west and north were replaced by self-contained farmsteads. Strongly rising prices during the century after 1540 helped accelerate the enclosure movement. Increased returns from the sale of foodstuffs or wool made commercial farming all the more attractive. New lands also fueled the real estate market and stimulated change. The confiscation of the monasteries—a result of Henry VIII's break with Rome—was one source of new estates. In addition, the Crown sold much of its own lands to raise money. Other fields were reclaimed from forest and waste land. The result was a flood of transactions that, county by county, began to wash away the open field system of the southeast and the isolated farms of the north and west. Families like the Winthrops, whose account opens this chapter, were the agents of this transformation.[27]

John Aubrey, a Wiltshire writer, was but one of many individuals commenting on the changes. "This countrey was anciently a delicate campania," Aubrey remarked in the 1660s, "all [open] ploughed fields as about Sherston: much have been enclosed since my tyme, and more and more will every day."[28] The enclosure movement would not be complete until the nineteenth century. But no one leaving England in the seventeenth or eighteenth century could be unaware of the pace or direction of change.[29]

The Thirteen Colonies

England's New World children, the Thirteen Colonies, closely followed their parent's lead. During the colonial era there were remnants of older ways in North America. Some individuals hoped to continue the open field system; others wanted to erect manors and establish a feudal hierarchy. But the winds of commercial self-interest that were transforming England blew hard and steady in the colonies. Both the North and the South developed an aggressive, individualistic approach to the use of land. This dynamic alone did not shape either region. But it reinforced the entrepreneurial bent of the North. And it helped distinguish the South from that other hierarchical, traditional society, French Canada.[30]

We can examine the direction and pace of this change by surveying the colonies and some of the individuals who helped to form their institutions. We begin by looking at the decline of open-field agriculture and the triumph of enclosed farms in New England.

The adventures of Peter Noyes, a strong-willed Englishman, illustrate this evolution. Noyes arrived in Watertown, Massachusetts, in 1638, and was unhappy with what he found there. Most individuals owned self-contained farms. Noyes, however, had grown up amidst the scattered strips of open-field agriculture. He hailed from a part of southern England, Hampshire County, not yet swept by the enclosure movement. Noyes did not want to abandon habits that went back "till the memory of man runneth not to the contrary." He was accustomed to sharing equipment, relying on common land for grazing, and working several small plots that provided him with a variety of soils.[31]

At first it had seemed that Watertown would become an open-field village—the sort of town that would please Noyes. The founders declared their "reall intent to sit down there close togither" and had initially laid out a central village surrounded by carefully divided fields. But soon after its establishment in 1630, the leaders of Watertown had a change of heart. They were predominantly individuals from East Anglia, where commercial farming had made deep inroads. In an orgy of trading and in divisions of ungranted land—activities that involved fully 200 people and 16,000 acres—the town leaders altered their original vision. Within less than a decade, and certainly by the time of Noyes's arrival, Watertown had become a community of large, enclosed farms.[32]

Noyes would not live in Watertown. He and other like-minded men asked the General Court for a tract where they could farm in time-honored ways. In the fall of 1638 the General Court granted them the township of Sudbury, and pronounced that they could "go to their plantation and allot the lands." Sudbury thus joined the minority of New England townships that were laid out as open-field villages; Watertown with its individual homesteads fit squarely with the majority. The selectmen divided land in Sudbury into small plots, and adopted the myriad of regulations that governed open-field life.

But separate farms, not open fields, were the shape of the future. By the 1650s the younger generation in Sudbury was demanding the end of what they viewed as an outmoded way of farming. Noyes and the other older selectmen firmly resisted all such pleas. So the dissidents split off and established a new town—Marlborough. Change came to Sudbury as well. At the end of the seventeenth century Noyes's village (like other open-field towns) accepted the inevitability of enclosed, single-owner farms, and reapportioned its land.[33]

Outside of New England, open-field agriculture or even the planned settlement of a village was unusual. But other remnants of pre-modern property relations were evident. A visitor from New France would have found in the New York manors much that was familiar. These vast estates dominated the land along the east bank of the Hudson River, much as seigneuries did the landscape of the St. Lawrence River. Tenants paid their manor lord an annual rent, similar to the *cens et rentes*. Sale of a leasehold meant additional payments. Called the "quarter sale" in New York, this charge amounted to a year's rent and resembled the *lods et ventes*. Some of the manor lords demanded labor services (like the *corvée*) called the "riding." Landlords in both colonies retained control over streams and directed tenants where to mill (and in New York where to market) their wheat. [34]

But the contrasts are also instructive. Lease terms differed between New France and New York. Habitants held their land in perpetuity, reflecting the strong position achieved by French peasants. Leases on most New York patents were typically for "two lives"—meaning as long as the husband or wife was alive. The lease then had to be renewed and the "quarter sale" paid.

And unlike the French Canadians, the American colonists resented the manorial system. New York politician Cadwallader Colden remarked that "the hopes of having land of their own & becoming independent of Landlords is what chiefly induces people into America." Manor lords were forced to woo tenants with various inducements. Robert Livingston, for example, bought cows, horses, and hogs for the farmers who settled on his land. Other manor lords paid for passage to America, provided agricultural equipment, and offered favorable lease terms.[35]

Tenants in New York protested—often violently—against manorial tenure. Armed clashes were common in New York between the 1750s and the end of the manorial system in the 1840s. Land-hungry New Englanders helped foment uprisings in the early 1750s. During the Great Rebellion of 1766 hundreds of tenants joined together in armed bands, and were finally suppressed by British regulars. Such clashes continued after Independence. Reacting to such pressure, the legislature broke up and sold the estates of loyalist manor holders, and in 1787 ended many feudal obligations. But patriot manor owners, like the Livingstons and Van Renssalaers, held on to their lands, and important manorial dues, like "quarter sales," continued. Leaseholders remained less free than other tenants in the North. Only after more fighting—including riots in the 1790s and the "Anti-Rent War" of the 1840s—did the descendants of the manor lords agree to sell their lands to the tenants and allow freeholds to replace leaseholds. By contrast, few French Canadians ever denounced the seigneurial system; only briefly during the rebellions of 1837 and 1838 did a small group of farmers demonstrate against feudal tenure.[36]

There were few traces of pre-modern property relationships in Pennsylvania. William Penn, the founder and proprietor, wanted farmers to reside in villages "for the more convenient bringing up of youth . . . [and] so that neighbors may help one another." He called for the creation of communities with homes and a meetinghouse at the center, and holdings extending outward like the wedges of a pie. He also hoped that settlement would be continuous, so that one village would begin where the last one ended.[37] But such plans, as one observer remarked after Penn's death, carried "no more weight than the East Wind" in shaping settlement. Instead of planned villages, individual homesteads covered the Pennsylvania landscape. Only a handful of settlements conformed to Penn's desires. Pietistic church groups, such as the Moravians, who established Bethlehem and Nazareth, came together in nucleated villages—for a single generation. Instead of continuous settlement, Pennsylvanians preferred "indiscriminate location"— where the best sites, such as those along a river bank, were taken up first. The only feudal remnant that survived in Pennsylvania was the "quitrent."* This was a sum, set at one shilling for every hundred acres, that settlers were obligated to pay Penn each year.[38]

Property relations in the southern colonies followed a similar course. Attempts to bring feudal or communal practices to the New World were short-lived or were fiercely challenged by farmers who wanted full control over their own homesteads.

Cecil Calvert, the second Lord Baltimore, wanted to make Maryland a haven for Catholics—and a colony ruled by landed nobles. Calvert promised that anyone who brought over "five able men" would

---

* A *quitrent* was a feudal due, not a capitalist rent. It was paid to a feudal superior in place of services that might otherwise be rendered.

receive "a mannor of good Land, to the full quantity of 2000 Akers for them and their heyres." Ultimately some sixty manors were created between the time of the first settlement in 1634 and the 1670s. Patentees were allowed to conduct feudal courts, called "courts leet" and "courts baron." Such tribunals operated—in a few instances. Manor lords were also allotted permanent seats in the legislature, much as in the House of Lords. And in the early years of the colony, some of the manors were successful in attracting immigrants who lacked funds to farm on their own.[39]

What is remarkable, however, is how quickly and completely this experiment in manorialism disappeared. By the end of the seventeenth century the feudal estates had become plantations like any other in Maryland. Unlike New York, where a single manor might encompass over 100,000 acres, the patents in Maryland were small, averaging less than 3000 acres. The manor lords of Maryland never became a powerful political group. Beginning in the 1660s Calvert established proprietarial "manors" in each county. These estates would remain until near the end of the colonial period, when much of this land was sold off. But the proprietarial manors were not feudal patents. They were merely an attempt by the Calverts to take advantage of rising land values.

Maryland became, like much of the South, a land of large plantations and small freeholds. A "headright" system helped populate the colony during the seventeenth century by offering free land to those who paid for their passage or arranged for others to come to the colony. As in Pennsylvania the chief remnant of feudalism became the quitrent, which the Calverts collected throughout the colonial era.[40]

Some feudal practices persisted in the Northern Neck of Virginia. This was the area that lay between the Potomac and Rappahannock rivers. Based on a claim that went back to 1649, the Fairfaxes became the proprietors of the Neck. And while the colony disputed the patent, the Crown in 1746 ruled in favor of Lord Fairfax. The proprietorship gave Fairfax a large tract of western land and the right to collect quitrents throughout the Northern Neck. As more settlers moved into the area, these privileges proved valuable. By 1768 quitrent payments totaled £4000.[41]

But for the most part, Virginia, like the other southern colonies, was settled by individuals who viewed land as both a productive resource and a commodity for speculation. The wealthier planters acquired additional estates and purchased shares in frontier land companies. Planters and farmers came together in informal communities, centered around the activities of a church, courthouse, store, or tavern. Such gatherings were characterized by hierarchies of caste and class. But they remained looser and less formally structured than the feudal communities of New France or the corporate villages of New England.[42]

The Carolinas were, like Maryland, an example of a short-lived feudal experiment in the New World. Anthony Ashley Cooper, the guiding spirit in the founding of these colonies, worked with the philosopher John Locke to write the Fundamental Constitutions of Carolina. This document provided a blueprint for a highly stratified society. At the top were two orders of nobility. Then came the freeholders, and the tenants who would occupy the estates of the nobility. Beneath them was a class of serfs, who were bound to the soil. Finally, slaves were to provide a source of labor. Ashley did not expect to erect this complex edifice all at once. Rather he saw the Fundamental Constitutions as "the compasse [we] are to steere by." In fact, very little of the Fundamental Constitutions was implemented. Slavery flourished, but more because of the desires of the settlers than the directives of the owners. The proprietors received quitrents. But no feudal lords or manors emerged in the colonies that became, by the 1690s, North and South Carolina.[43]

Georgia was another example of a conflict of old and new, of the headlong collision between English plans for a traditional society and acquisitive American reality. James Oglethorpe, an English reformer, was preeminent in the group that founded Georgia. In 1730 the Board of Trade was considering establishing a colony south of South Carolina, to serve as a bulwark against the Spanish, French, and Indians. This plan dovetailed with the philanthropic interests of Oglethorpe and his friends. They hoped to send "poor unfortunate persons" to a new colony, where these debtors and others would find "vast tracts of fertile land lying uninhabited and uncultivated." The Crown awarded Oglethorpe and several associates a charter in 1732.[44]

Oglethorpe and the other Georgia Trustees laid down a set of strict rules for their New World utopia. Property was to pass only to males, so that every farm would support a citizen-soldier. There was to be no rum, no estates larger than 500 acres, and no slaves. Settlement would be focused around planned, fortified towns. This philanthropic plan, unlike the proposals of the Calverts or New York patroons, was not an effort to recreate a feudal order. But it did impose communal values on self-seeking American colonists.

Step by step the Trustees were forced to back away from their principles. By the early 1740s changes were evident. The Trustees allowed female inheritance. They instructed local officials to "wink at the importation of rum and discourage seizures thereof." They let planters acquire estates greater than 500 acres. Oglethorpe tried to draw the line on the introduction of slavery. He saw the spread of a black labor force as the end of his vision of a colony of industrious small farmers. The inhabitants, however, made clear that "we are all here generally of opinion that Georgia can never be a place of any great consequence without negroes." The flourishing South Carolina plantations, which relied on slave labor, were an example too strong to be ignored. In 1750 the Trustees yielded on the importation of blacks. Settlement in Georgia did center on planned, fortified villages; war with the Spanish in Florida during the 1740s testified to the wisdom of palisades and guardhouses. Only after hostilities ended would individual plantations spread in the low country. In 1752 the Trustees abandoned their charter, but by this date Georgia resembled the neighboring plantation province of South Carolina.[45]

Independence and Beyond

In the Thirteen Colonies, as in England, the modern, commercial approach to property relations triumphed over feudal, communal practices. Indeed, this victory was more complete in America than in Old England. The process of change was accelerated by the abundant resources of the New World. The colonies also had no landed aristocracy to slow the drive to an egalitarian, commercial society. Perhaps the transition to an individualistic society was somewhat slower in rural New England and in the manors along the east bank of the Hudson River. But too much should not be made of these differences. Everywhere American farmers were becoming self-seeking individuals.

In the eighteenth century, however, the outcome was not unbridled capitalism. Rather it was the household economy described in Chapter 1: agricultural, slow-growing, pre-literate (in its approaches to production), and locally oriented. Farmers in the Thirteen Colonies may have been more open to the possibilities of commercial farming than were individuals in New France. But the slow pace of change in the techniques of agriculture and manufacturing and in the nature of transportation offered few chances for commercially-minded individuals to leap ahead. The transformation of traditional society and the triumph of the enterprising farmers of the North would come only in the nineteenth century.

By 1776 the relations between people and the land were well defined in the United States. The break with England only confirmed the demise of communal practices. Quitrents were ended. The Penns, Calverts, and Fairfaxes lost control over ungranted lands. Feudal customs survived only in a few strife-filled New York manors. Independent farmers, with their eye on the main chance, became the dominant figures in the rich farmlands of the North and South.

The use that Americans made of the land in the nineteenth century is important for an understanding of growth. This topic, however, is closely linked to the movement westward and the clash between slave and free agriculture. These issues are examined under the heading of *mobility* (see Chapter 5).

Finally, we may reflect on how landholding practices shaped the mind-set of the three regions. For French Canada, the feudalism of the colonial era and the seigneurial system, which persisted until the mid-nineteenth century, helped create a strong sense of hierarchy. This approach to the land emphasized customary relations rather than the pursuit of profit. In the North the rapid dissolution of pre-modern practices fostered the entrepreneurial spirit of the region. In the South the impact of commercial landholding was less straightforward. The unceasing concern to carve out new farms imparted a remarkable sense of energy to the region. Slave society would be run by restless planters, used to moving west onto new soils. This abundant energy was not expressed as in the North, in the steady pursuits of entrepreneurs. Rather it came out in a strain of aggression and violence that characterized the South before the Civil War. Various books on the southern states—and several of the chapters that follow—explore this belligerent cast of mind.[46] But it is worth noting that for all the similarities between the South and French Canada (parallels that are emphasized in this work), the two were unlike in important ways—and the differences went back to dissimilar approaches to the land.

4

Religion and Labor

Preston Brooks of South Carolina sat in the Senate Chamber and listened to the speech of Massachusetts Senator Charles Sumner with mounting disgust. Sumner's vitriolic attack on the South offended Brooks. More personally, Sumner impugned the honor of Brooks's elderly cousin, Senator Andrew Butler of South Carolina. Senator Butler, said Sumner, "has chosen a mistress [slavery] to whom he made his vows, and who, though ugly to others, is always lovely to him; though polluted in the sight of the world, is chaste in his sight." Senator Butler spoke with a slight speech defect; Sumner mocked this too.

Brooks, who was a member of the House of Representatives and a veteran of the Mexican War, did not challenge Sumner to a duel. Brooks had fought one in his youth. But the code of the Old South dictated that a duel must be fought between social equals, and Brooks did not consider Sumner his equal. Besides, Brooks suspected that Sumner would refuse and might report the matter to the police. "To punish an insulting inferior," Brooks later explained, "one used not a pistol or sword but a cane or horsewhip." He debated: "I . . . speculated somewhat as to whether I should employ a horsewhip or a cowhide." But he decided to use his walking stick made of gutta-percha, a hard, rubbery substance.

He determined to cane Sumner at his seat in the Senate after the chamber had adjourned for the day. But when the opportunity presented itself, Brooks noted a woman sitting in the lobby nearby, and with chivalric concern refused to act until she left. Finally, he marched over to the Massachusetts senator. "I have read your Speech with care . . . ," he said, "I feel it is my duty to tell you that you have libeled my State and slandered a relative who is aged and absent and I am come to punish you for it." Then he delivered a series of blows to the defenseless Sumner. "I . . . gave him about 30 first rate stripes . . . ," Brooks recollected. "Towards the last he bellowed like a calf. I wore my cane out completely but saved the Head which is gold."[1]

The clash between Brooks and Sumner, which took place in May 1854, was not simply a conflict of two individuals. Nor was it even a fight between representatives of the slave and free states. Rather as was evident in the elaborate choreography that guided Brooks's actions, it was a bitter encounter between two cultures.

This chapter, which rounds out our discussion of the foundations of regional society, examines religion and slavery. Together they helped define French Canada and the South as civilizations that valued hierarchy and social order more than the drive for profit. Catholicism, as practiced along the St. Lawrence, turned minds toward the Church and away from the pursuit of wealth. The links between religion and the slow growth of the South are more debatable. Some observers contend that the southern strain of Protestantism encouraged easy living rather than hard work. But this argument is hardly conclusive. In the North religion reinforced entrepreneurial leanings.

The impact of slavery on the southern outlook was clearer. The "peculiar institution" created a hierarchical society and slowed economic development. Planters cherished their position in an ordered society that placed poor whites below wealthier ones, and African Americans at the bottom. For the southern elite, slaves were always more than a work force; they were also a measure of status. This commitment meant that the southern elite depended on laborers who were uneducated, unmotivated, and (compared with northern workers) unproductive.

Religion

The Catholics of Old and New France

Were Catholics different in their economic behavior from Protestants? In 1904 and 1905 Max Weber, a German scholar, wrote *The Protestant Ethic and the Spirit of Capitalism,* in which he emphatically answered, yes. He reworked and expanded the piece just before his death in 1920. The book now stands as an imposing arch through which any one investigating the links between religion and economic behavior must pass. Weber looks beyond the narrow bounds of theology and dogma. His analysis of Catholicism, for example, explores the clusters of beliefs held by Catholics—and not simply the pronouncements of theologians.

Guided by this broader approach to religion, Weber focuses on the sixteenth, seventeenth, and eighteenth centuries. He argues that the Protestant faiths created a capitalist mentality that regarded hard work and self-denial as the path to wealth. Those areas where Protestantism flourished—England, Holland, and the northern Thirteen Colonies are examples—developed societies with industrious middle classes. Catholic countries—for example, France—had many acquisitive people. But compared with the Protestant lands, the Catholic states had no class with a knack for business. They had no large group with a determination to get ahead in the world through industry and frugality.

Is Weber right? Were the Catholics of Old and New France less enterprising than the Protestants of that era? Weber has been criticized for some of his sweeping generalizations about Catholics. The citizenry of Renaissance Italy, for example, was devoted to business—and loyal to the Church. Weber also has been criticized for emphasizing the influence of ideas on behavior, while ignoring the role of material reality in shaping ideas. But his analysis of the links between religion and economic behavior in seventeenth- and eighteenth-century Europe seems on the mark. Indeed, by the middle of the seventeenth century the connection between business and creed was a commonplace. A pamphleteer observed in 1671: "There is a kind of natural inaptness in the Popish religion to business, whereas, on the contrary, among the Reformed, the greater their zeal, the greater their inclination to trade and industry, as holding idleness unlawful."[2]

Seventeenth-century Catholic France was a society that elevated the Church and the nobility—and looked down on those who pursued business. Early in the century the provincial nobility revived the custom of *derogation*. Simply put, this practice meant: engage in trade, and you risk losing your noble status. Exceptions were made for certain cities, and for some individuals involved in wholesaling and overseas exchanges. But the distinction between wealth gained in trade and an honorable life was not erased until the French Revolution. One result was that few Catholic families persisted in commerce over many generations. Typically, Catholic merchants who grew wealthy purchased an aristocratic title and abandoned trade.

The values of French Catholicism grew more restrictive and more hostile to commerce as the conflict with French Protestants—Huguenots—heightened during the seventeenth century. The century began with tolerance. Witty, dashing, and well-liked, Henry IV in 1598 promulgated the Edict of Nantes, granting the Huguenots civil and religious privileges. Henry himself had been born a Protestant but converted to Catholicism, supposedly remarking, "Paris is well worth a

Mass." His chief minister, Sully, was a Huguenot. But such liberality gave way to persecution after a madman assassinated Henry in 1610. A prolonged, sometimes bloody struggle commenced. It culminated in the revocation of the Edict of Nantes in 1685 and the expulsion of the Huguenots from France. The onslaught against the Protestants was not simply the clash of two religious groups. It was also a sign of the hardening of French Catholicism. The crusade against the Huguenots was an attack on a way of life. Huguenots stressed literacy and the need to read the Bible; French Catholics emphasized ritual and priestly guidance. Huguenots thrived in commerce; their strength lay in the port cities of southwestern France. French Catholics looked down on trade, and drew their sustenance from a static, landed regime.[3]

This seventeenth-century French Catholicism—with its anti-commercial, hierarchical orientation—helped shape the culture of New France. Decrees issued in 1627 and 1628 banned non-Catholics from settling in the St. Lawrence Colony. And Catholicism was to become the mainstay of French-Canadian culture. The English Conquest of Canada in 1760 dealt feudalism a mortal blow. Its most important vestige—the seigneurial land system—was abolished in 1854. But an anti-commercial, organic Catholic outlook continued to exercise a remarkable influence over economic behavior well into the twentieth century.

The Protestants of the Thirteen Colonies

Religion also shaped the culture of the English colonists. It helps explain the aggressive, entrepreneurial bent of the North. But only in small part does religion shed light on the similarities between the South and French Canada.

Weber is a useful guide to the links between Protestantism and economic behavior. Weber focuses particularly on the militant faiths of the seventeenth century, such as the Puritans, Quakers, and Mennonites. These sects—as Weber admits—did not endorse a capitalist credo. "We are dealing," says Weber, "predominantly [with] unforseen, and even unwished for results of the labours of the reformers."[4] Indeed, Puritan ministers regulated the activity of merchants, affirmed the doctrine of the fair price, and censured the drive for profits.[5]

According to Weber, the connection between the Protestant sects and a capitalist mentality does not come from their early economic doctrines, but emerges from other, core beliefs in those religions. It reflects the emphasis given by these faiths to the doctrine of the "calling"—the idea that we serve God by working hard at our profession. These denominations turned a harsh spotlight of introspection upon the individual. Calvinism and the faiths closely allied with it (such as Puritanism and Presbyterianism), as well as Quakerism, required all persons to look into themselves to see if they were worthy of salvation. The result, says Weber, was a society of driven men and women. Each person was determined to get ahead by hard work and self-sacrifice.

Stripped of doctrinal overtones, this mind-set—Weber argues— produced the philosophy of Benjamin Franklin. Sandy-haired, physically strong, and accomplished in so many areas, Franklin was one of the best-known individuals in the colonies. He was born a Presbyterian but adhered to no one church. Franklin is a central figure in Weber's book. The printer was one of the most outspoken advocates of the virtues of industry and frugality. Each year he served up generous helpings of these virtues in the adages printed in *Poor Richard's Almanac*. For example:

> [Industry]
> Keep thy Shop, and thy Shop will keep thee.
> He that hath a Trade, hath an Estate.
> Early to Bed and early to rise makes a Man healthy, wealthy, and wise.
> The sleeping Fox catches no Poultry.
> [Frugality]
> Beware of little Expences—a small Leak will sink a great Ship.
> Buy what thou hast no Need of, and ere long thou shalt sell thy
>   Necessaries.[6]

For Weber, Franklin's secular credo and the teachings of the Protestant sects together helped form a society of hard-working, frugal individuals.

We well may question Weber's idealistic explanation: his belief that ideas (Protestantism) were the key to social change (the rise of capitalism). And we might feel uneasy about Weber's application of the word "capitalist" to Franklin's teachings. Weber concedes that Franklin may not have spoken for the merchants, "the capitalist entrepreneurs of the commercial aristocracy."[7] But a larger point should not be lost amidst this criticism. There can be no doubt that the economic outlook of the Protestants of the Thirteen Colonies was very different from that of the Catholics of New France. French Catholics looked down on commerce and saw little need for literacy. They accepted a hierarchy that placed the nobility and clergy at the top and everyone else well below them. In contrast, the English Protestants exalted commerce and valued literacy. These dissenters moved—if ever so cautiously—toward a more egalitarian world view.[8]

Weber also suggests that religion explains the difference between North and South. Here the linkages are more questionable. "The early history of the North American Colonies," Weber remarks, "is dominated by the sharp contrast of the adventurers, who wanted to set up plantations with the labour of indentured servants, and live as feudal lords, and the specifically middle-class outlook of the Puritans." For

Weber the dichotomy is clear. Easy-going, Anglican representatives of "merrie old England" shaped the course of southern development. Hard-working Puritans and other like-minded religious sects, Quakers and Mennonites, guided northern society. Indeed, with only slight changes, Weber has presented the familiar tale of the Cavaliers and Roundheads, discussed in Chapter 2. Anglican Cavaliers, defenders of Charles I, settled the South. Puritan Roundheads, advocates of Cromwell's reforms, peopled the North.[9]

But the correlation between religion, sections, and economic activity is limited at best. Although distinct groups may have settled the several regions, the movement of people within the colonies and across the Atlantic in the eighteenth century blurred religious lines. A *tour d'horizon* in 1750 suggests the difficulties with Weber's categories. Most of New England was Congregational, but bustling, commercial Rhode Island had more Baptists than Puritans. The middle colonies were home to a potpourri of religions. Quakers, Presbyterians, Lutherans, Anglicans, as well as members of the Dutch Reformed and German Reformed Churches—all could point to large numbers of adherents in at least one of the middle colonies. Moreover, the mercantile centers of the North—Boston, New York, and Philadelphia—each had sizable groups of Anglican merchants. The trading activities of these Churchmen did not distinguish them from their Congregational, Quaker, or Presbyterian counterparts.

As for the "backward" South, Virginia, it is true, was overwhelmingly Anglican. But in Maryland the Church of England could claim only half the white population. And the Lower South was more akin to the middle colonies in its mix of sects. Baptists were probably the largest group in North Carolina. In South Carolina only a third of the population adhered to Anglicanism. Presbyterians, Lutherans, and Baptists had a noteworthy presence there. Lutherans were strong in Georgia.[10]

Weber's emphasis on the religious differences separating the North and South cannot be dismissed out of hand. Northern faiths such as Congregationalism and Quakerism fostered a more aggressive approach to individual initiative. Anglicanism may well have contributed to the non-entrepreneurial ethic of the South. Because it was the creed of the wealthy, Anglicanism had a far greater impact than any head count of its adherents might suggest.[11]

But the picture is hardly a tidy one. The religious distinctions between North and South are less useful in explaining sectional outlooks than the differences between a Protestant America and a Catholic New France are in showing national behavior. The mix of religions in both the North and South undercuts any firm divisions. Nor did political or economic behavior correlate closely with faith. The nineteenth century made clear the supremacy of section over religion. In the decades before the Civil War the major churches split, formally or informally, into southern and northern wings. Ultimately, the fault line within the United States was not shaped by religion. Rather it lay between a section that relied on slavery and one whose economy was based on free labor.[12]

Labor Systems: Slavery Shapes the South

The seigneurial system and Catholicism helped make French Canada a society that valued customary relations more than the relentless pursuit of money. Slavery had the same impact on the South. It was the cornerstone of a social system that kept productivity low, created a rigid social hierarchy, and fostered an unquestioning commitment to agriculture. The next three sections discuss how slavery shaped the South. The first looks at the low productivity of southern labor from the vantage of two observers: Virginia planter Landon Carter and the northern traveler Frederick Law Olmsted. The second section examines the hierarchical relations between white southerners. The final section engages recent scholarship. It argues that the South was unlike the hard-driving capitalist North and more nearly resembled the society of French Canada.

Two Observers on the Low Productivity of Slave Labor

To study Landon Carter is to see the Protestant Ethic reshaped by the realities of southern plantation life. In some respects, Carter, who came from a wealthy Virginia family, was an anomaly in the South: he was too diligent, too serious, and too tedious. "Let him relax," a critic wrote about Carter, "and we are all his own."[13] But Carter did not relax, and he cared little for the pastimes that amused other planters. He grumped that "gaming is one of the devil's divises to draw mankind from those social duties for which he was at first created."[14] Thomas Jefferson saw Carter simply as boring. His speeches, Jefferson observed, "like his writings, were dull, vapid, verbose [and] egotistical."[15]

Carter was determined to manage his vast plantations efficiently. His diary, which covers (with some gaps) the years from 1756 to 1778, records the endless experiments he undertook to improve his farming. The diary itself was an important part of the plan: "Every husbandman whether Planter or farmer would do well to keep a diary or Journal of all his observations on his own and the management that he sees of others: for as art can never be perfect, it is certain he himself might correct many of his own errors by such a journal Comparing one year with another."[16] His journal is filled with measurements and computations as he tried to figure out the right mix of seed and land, of manure and crop.

Landon Carter might sound like another "improving" farmer, comparable to the best husbandmen in the North or England. But there was a difference. Carter was a slaveholder, owning at his death perhaps 500 African Americans.[17] He depended on this labor force to translate his plans into reality. And the slaves constantly frustrated his best laid plans.

Look over Carter's shoulder as he tries to get his blacks to plant more corn on each acre. He reports: "I ordered every negro to put his hinder foot in working in the middle, behind the hill last made and his forefoot before, and so to hill up to that forefoot . . . but then the villains although not tasked, foreman and all, would straddle wide, and by often lifting up the hind foot stretch so far as to get the hills to 3 feet distance; so that although this way amended the evil something, yet instead of 3,111 hills in an acre, they got to but 2,074 in the acre. And how to remedy this I don't yet know."[18]

Here is Carter's effort to sow oats with care: "The piece measures only 31 or 2 acres and they have put in the ground 158 bushels which at 4 bushels to the acre should have been but 124. The negroe seeds men have no gage and therefore must have it proportioned at so many bushel to each land. There were 60 bushels sown on this side [of] the barn and I suppose with the same profuse hand."[19]

Carter's answer to the problem of recalcitrant or "lazy" slaves was discipline, which usually meant whipping. "Kindness to a Negroe by way of reward for having done well is the surest way to spoil him," Carter observed, and he rarely spoiled his slaves.[20] More typical was a firm response: "My threshers of oats made a shrift to thresh no more per day than they did when the days were 20 minutes shorter. . . . This was such evident lazyness that I ordered them Correction which they took three days running."[21] "Lazyness" and "Correction" are two themes which recur throughout Carter's journal, as they do in the writings of other slaveowners. But firmness was hardly an effective solution. "I find it is almost impossible to make a negro do his work well," Carter confessed. "No orders can engage it, no encouragement persuade it, nor no Punishment oblige it."[22]

Carter also displayed that southern aversion to entrusting his blacks with more equipment. Along with his neighbors Carter moved from agriculture based on the hoe to one based on the plow. But he introduced new implements with grave misgivings. "Carts and plows only serve to make Overseers and people [i.e., slaves] extremely lazy," he noted, "and it is certain truth that wherever they are in great abundance there is the least plantation work done." Carter felt work-saving devices promoted idleness; other slaveowners commented that African Americans mishandled any tools but the rudest.[23]

But Carter also showed no inclination to get rid of his refractory labor force. The slaves were not simply "capital goods," like so many plows or horses. They were a measure of his status in Virginia society. And in a paternalistic, condescending way, they were objects of his affection. Carter often called his slaves, "my people"; he tended them when they were ill, and spoke warmly of particular individuals. "I fear my very old Slave and fellow creature Jack Lubbar is now going to Pay the debt of nature . . . ," he remarked. "Farewell to as honest a human creature as could live; Who to his last proved a faithful and a Profitable servant to his Master as every remembered Conduct must testify." [24]

Landon Carter may have started off with the intentions of an "improving" farmer. But he resigned himself to the frustrations, the slow pace of life, and the low productivity associated with slave labor. The price of Carter's defeat (and the failure of others like him to bring northern values to the South) was not wholly apparent in the eighteenth century. There was as yet no yawning gap between the techniques of production used by free labor and those used by slaves. But by the mid-nineteenth century a reliance on unskilled, unmotivated labor and the lack of mechanization put the South at a grave disadvantage. [25]

Frederick Law Olmsted, a Connecticut Yankee who visited the South in the 1850s, also documents the low productivity of southern labor. In his lengthy account of his travels through the South, he describes a society characterized by poverty, a slow pace of life, and qualms about industrialization. Even if Olmsted's descriptions of the South had not been so well done and so widely read, he would have a secure place in American history as one of the country's first landscape architects. In a career that stretched from the 1850s to the 1890s he designed parks and estates, including Central Park in New York City and the grounds of the 1893 Chicago World's Fair. But before settling down in his chosen profession, Olmsted traveled. He wrote a book about farming in England, and was commissioned by the *New York Times* to report on conditions in the South. The articles he filed were later collected in several books. Although he disliked slavery, he was no abolitionist, and observers in both the North and South commented on the justice of his commentary. [26]

Olmsted's descriptions make clear the relative poverty of the South (reinforcing the figures on average income presented in Table 1.3). "For every mile of road-side upon which I saw any evidence of cotton production," he observed, "I am sure that I saw a hundred of forest or waste land, with only now and then an acre or two of poor corn half smothered in weeds; for every rich man's house, I am sure that I passed a dozen shabby and half-furnished cottages, and at least a hundred cabins—mere hovels, such as none but a poor farmer would house his cattle in at the North." [27]

He added his voice to those who remarked upon the slower pace of life and the absence of the work ethic in Dixie. The culprit was slavery. "To work industriously and steadily," noted Olmsted, "especially under directions from another man, is, in the Southern tongue, to 'work like a nigger'; and, from childhood, the one thing in their condition which has made life valuable to the mass of whites has been that the niggers are yet their inferiors."[28] But African Americans, Olmsted observed, were no more diligent laborers than were whites. And the need to supervise these recalcitrant workers helped shape the character of the region. "The calculating, indefatigable New Englander, the go-ahead Western man," stated Olmsted, would "lose patience with the frequent disobedience and constant indolence, forgetfulness and carelessness, and the blundering, awkward, brute-like manner of work of the plantation slave. The Southerner, if he sees anything of it, generally disregards it and neglects to punish it."[29]

These two observers, although writing a century apart, although hailing from different sections, provide similar descriptions of southern culture. They suggest a black labor force whose productivity was low. They portray a society that had serious reservations about mechanization. And they depict a white population that adopted or was forced to adopt a more leisurely approach to economic activities.

Upper-Class and Lower-Class Whites

Slavery shaped southern society in another fundamental way: it created a pervasive hierarchy that placed some whites far above others. The largest slaveholders and a few allies made up the ruling elite, while most nonslaveholders were consigned to the lower rungs of the socical ladder. Olmsted observed: "The government and society of the South is the most essentially aristocratic in the world."[30] This hierarchical social structure checked southern development. State governments, dominated by the large planters, voted only limited funds for education or internal improvements. Moreover, the South lacked the large group of sturdy middle-class consumers that helped drive northern growth. Instead, the market in the South was skewed toward the extremes: on the one hand, to the demands of the wealthy for luxuries, and on the other, to the rudimentary needs of the slaves and poor whites.[31]

Students of southern history, it should be noted, have long debated whether antebellum society was democratic (at least for adult white males) or dominated by the slaveholding elite—as this book argues. Those who make the case for democracy note that the suffrage broadened in the South as in the North, that some legislatures were reapportioned to reflect population, and that roughly the same percentage of the white population voted in the two regions. "By 1860," contends Fletcher Green, "the aristocratic planter class had been shorn of its special privileges and political power." Some writers underscore the independence, vigor, and numerical preponderance of the "plain folk" in a society where only one-fourth of free families held slaves. The common people of the South, George M. Frederickson observes, were "fiercely democratic in their political and social thinking." For Frederickson, the southern states were a *Herrenvolk* democracy—a democracy of the "master race."[32]

But other historians note that white manhood suffrage did not a democratic South make. In the years before the Civil War almost all governors of southern states were slaveholders; planters also formed a majority of the lawmakers in every state, except Missouri and Arkansas; and they dominated the county courts in the cotton south and Virginia. William L. Barney remarks: "When the yeoman farmer voted, and most did, there was little for him to decide. Both candidates were more likely than not to represent slaveholding interests." All southern states sent representatives to Washington based on the "federal apportionment"—that is, slaves counted as three-fifths of a person in determining the number of seats. Many southern states used the same basis in determining representation in the state legislature, thus assuring planters of influence beyond their proportion of the white population.[33] Historians have documented the tension that existed between a dominant slaveholding elite and the large number of free farmers. There was no Herrenvolk democracy. Rather there was a ruling group, and common folk who were sometimes compliant, sometimes restless.[34]

The social hierarchy in the South began with wealth, and was strongly reinforced by social codes and public displays. Unlike northern society, where a democratic ethos softened the distinctions between the rich and poor, southern society emphasized class lines. The planters not only dominated local politics, but stood out by their elegant dress and lavish homes. They shared the same pastimes, adhering to rules of conduct that made clear their lofty place in an ordered world. William Grayson, a South Carolina writer, observed: "A gambling debt is a debt of honour, but a debt due a tradesman is not." The distinction was clear: tradesmen came from the lower class, those one gambled with did not.[35]

Dueling provides a vantage point for an examination of class lines. Duels were public rituals, far more common south of the Mason-Dixon line than north of it. Thomas Hamilton, a Scottish novelist and traveler, noted: "To fight a duel in the New England States would, under almost any circumstances, be disgraceful. To refuse a challenge, to tolerate even an insinuation derogatory from personal honour, would be considered equally so in the South." Northerners preferred to settle their differences in court.[36]

The southern *code duello* reflected a strong awareness of social rank.

As seen in the Preston Brooks–Charles Sumner encounter, gentlemen refused to fight with their social inferiors. Such rejection could be far more painful than a wound of honor. When Andrew Jackson caned Thomas Swann, rather than duel with him, Swann desperately tried to prove he was a gentleman, and hence a worthy opponent. Jackson, Swann informed the local newspaper, "was told I had letters of introduction, and could procure certain certificates to prove I was entitled to that character." Similarly, James Wilkinson pleaded with Virginia congressman John Randolph for a duel. "I have no hesitation," stated Wilkinson, "to appeal to your justice, your magnaminity, and your gallantry, to prescribe the manner of redress." Randolph replied coldly: "I cannot descend to your level." On the field of honor the combatants often expressed their love and admiration for each other. After all, they belonged to the same elite club. As naval hero Stephen Decatur and James Barron lay mortally wounded, "Barron proposed that they should make friends before they met in Heaven . . . Decatur said he had never been his enemy, that he freely forgave him his death." After John Randolph and Henry Clay dueled, "the parties exchanged cards, and social relations were formally and courteously restored."[37]

Social hierarchy, with wealthy whites placed high above poorer ones, and both groups set over the African Americans, would be one of the most enduring legacies of the Old South. It would survive the Civil War and the demise of slavery, and continue to shape southern society well into the twentieth century.

A Dialogue about Capitalism and Slavery

The writings of Carter and Olmsted and the presence of a rigid social hierarchy suggest the South was a section with a different ethos than the North. It was a world like French Canada, where values other than the ceaseless pursuit of profit shaped people's actions. Eugene Genovese has written that "the planters, in truth, grew into the closest thing to feudal lords imaginable in a nineteenth-century bourgeois republic." Many scholars agree, and have built upon Genovese's insights.[38] But other historians argue that wealthy southerners were simply capitalists in slaveholders' clothing. Robert Fogel labels southern society "a flexible, highly developed form of capitalism."[39] Recent studies of the southern economy shed light on this debate. The dialogue that follows draws upon these works. It argues—with some reservations—that the South had more in common with the hierarchical, slow-paced world of French Canada than with the bustling, entrepreneurial society of the North.

QUESTION: *Didn't planters earn solid returns on their investment in land and slaves?*

ANSWER: Perhaps. In their landmark article Alfred Conrad and

John Meyer suggest 6 percent as a benchmark figure for judging the profitability of slave plantations. During the 1850s this rate of return reflected alternative, safe investments for those with large amounts of capital. Conrad and Meyer (and other researchers) argue that most planters matched or bettered this standard. Studies of the profitability of slavery typically present a range of returns that depend on the staple, soil, and size of the holding. For cotton, Conrad and Meyer conclude, earnings ranged from 4 percent for smaller operations on poorer soils to 12 percent for the largest plantations on the best soils.[40]

But the case for the profitability of slave-based agriculture is hardly as clear-cut as Conrad and Meyer would have it. Some economic historians review the data and suggest that typical earnings were well below 6 percent. And even those researchers who accept that returns were high point to the crucial importance of slave sales. Unlike northern farms, crop production alone did not make southern agriculture profitable. Finally, much of the debate over profitability turns on the date selected for analysis. Which census year is more typical: 1850 or 1860? Those making the case for an efficient, profitable slave society typically choose 1860, and regard the boom times of the 1850s as normal. Not fair, cry their critics. Cotton prices were high in 1859 and 1860, while the value of slaves reached an all-time peak. Pick another year, such as 1850, these historians suggest, and the extraordinary returns from slave agriculture disappear.[41]

QUESTION: *But let's say planter incomes were high. Doesn't that suggest that slaveowners were commercial capitalists, much like farmers or industrialists in the North?*

ANSWER: No. The presence of large profits is no assurance of capitalism. The seigneurs of French Canada eventually received substantial earnings from their estates, but were not capitalists. Capitalism cannot be equated with a desire to seek a profit or accumulate wealth. Such a desire has existed in many primitive and feudal societies. Rather capitalism reflects an approach to money making. In a capitalist society, the dynamic class takes a hard, unsentimental approach to tradition and customary relations. These entrepreneurs are governed by an ethic of hard work and relentless profit maximization. Individuals invest their money where they can make the best returns. Profitability, not considerations of prestige or tradition, shapes business activity.[42]

QUESTION: *But to put the question differently, weren't the planters simply profit maximizers? That is, wasn't it wiser for them to put their money into land and slaves than into any alternative investment?*

ANSWER: Perhaps such an argument can be made for the eighteenth century. But not for the nineteenth century. The flaw in the planters' economic behavior—and it was a grave shortcoming—lay in their disdain for industrialization. Despite much higher earnings in manufacturing, planters kept their money in agriculture. Using manuscript census returns, Fred Bateman and Thomas Weiss show that the average profitability of all southern industries in 1850 was 25 percent, and in 1860, 28 percent. In many enterprises—such as boot- and shoe-making; the fabrication of tin, sheet iron, and copper; or the production of wagons and carriages—returns topped 30 percent. Investments would have been fully repaid in three to four years. But the southern elite contributed only a trickle of funds to any industry. For the most part, slaveholders and southern industrialists remained mutually exclusive groups. Only 6 percent of wealthy slaveowners invested capital in manufacturing. Less than 15 percent of industrialists in the South belonged to the slaveholding elite. Bateman and Weiss conclude that it seems "plausible to accept the view espoused by Eugene Genovese and others: that the opportunities existed [in the South] and were known, but that investors chose to ignore them."[43]

The comparison of the investments made by northerners and southerners is instructive. The residents of the free states behaved as profit-maximizers should. Like southerners they recognized that there were much higher returns in manufacturing than in agriculture. But unlike southerners they eagerly pursued these opportunities. During the 1850s the North recorded greater investments in industry than in farming. The reverse was true in the South. We return to this issue in Chapter 6, which examines the cotton textile industry in the North and South.

A pattern of investing that was unprofitable for individual southerners was also harmful for the southern economy as a whole. Because each worker in industry produced nearly twice as much wealth as each agricultural worker, the lack of industrial development was tantamount to a sentence of economic backwardness. Figure 1.2 illustrates the strong links between non-agricultural activities and the standard of living in antebellum America.[44]

QUESTION: *What about the movement of slaveholders to the rich soils of the West? Doesn't that suggest a desire to maximize returns, that is, a capitalist mind-set?*

ANSWER: Yes and no. It's true that, unlike the French Canadians, many southerners moved west and the region benefited from this migration. Incomes were higher in new states like Mississippi, Louisiana, and Arkansas, than in the southeast. But this movement was hardly a long-term solution. Even before the Civil War the growth of western incomes had slowed. Also the southern ideology of expansion made the planters more bellicose and dogmatic in their defense of slavery and in their refusal to reform. The benefits and drawbacks of this migration are explored more fully in the next chapter.

QUESTION: *Was slavery truly such an obstacle to progress? Bound labor could have been used in manufacturing. What was to stop the South from keeping its slaves and industrializing?*

ANSWER: Southerners feared that any program of extensive manufacturing would disrupt the social fabric. A determination to preserve
an ordered society, in which slaves were a source of status as well as
income, overruled any calculations based merely on dollars and cents.

Planters saw grave dangers whether industrialization proceeded
with slaves or with white workers. The difficulties entailed in using
bondspeople were perhaps most serious. The most successful experiments with black workers—such as Joseph Anderson's Tredegar Iron
Works, or the tobacco houses of Richmond—involved monetary incentives. James Henry Hammond, who would serve as both South Carolina governor and senator, expressed the fears of many about the
spread of such practices. "Whenever a slave is made a mechanic,"
Hammond remarked, "he is more than half freed, and soon becomes,
as we too well know, and all history attests, with rare exceptions, the
most corrupt and turbulent of his class."[45] Urban slaves were notorious for their "uppity" ways. "The evil lies," a Charleston committee
asserted, "in the breaking down of the relation between master and
slave, . . . and the assumption of freedom and independence on the
part of the slave, the idleness, disorders, and crime which are conse-
quential."[46]

The broad trend—and there were exceptions to this pattern—was
away from the use of blacks in skilled occupations. Hammond's remarks above, delivered in 1849, reflected his own change of heart. In
the early 1840s he had been more open to the employment of blacks
in industry. The slave population of all southern cities declined in relative terms, and in most cases in absolute numbers as well. Between
1820 and 1860 bondspeople in southern towns fell from 22 percent to
10 percent of the population. During these same decades white laborers, either by legislation or simply by aggressive action, displaced slaves
from such crafts as carpentry and haircutting. The cotton mills erected
in the southern upcountry employed only whites.[47]

But planters also saw dangers in a growing white work force.
C. G. Memminger was an outspoken Charlestonian who would become Secretary of the Treasury in the Confederacy. "In this State and
City . . . ," he remarked in 1849, "I find an opinion gaining ground
that slaves ought to be excluded from mechanical pursuits, and everything but agriculture, so as to have their places filled with whites."
These white laborers, warned Memminger, are "the same men who
make the cry in the Northern Cities against the tyranny of Capital—
and there as here would drive before them all who interfere with
them—and would soon raise hue and cry against the Negro, and be
hot Abolitionists—and every one of those men would have a vote."[48]
Memminger's grim forebodings were borne out by the labor unrest
which surfaced in southern cities during the 1850s.[49]

Caught between two unpalatable choices—uppity blacks and re-bellious whites—the planters preferred not to encourage industrialization, even if that decision meant forgoing profitable investments.

QUESTION: *Well, perhaps planters shunned industrialization. But wasn't slavery an effective way of producing cotton and the other southern staples?*

ANSWER: Moral issues aside, a case could be made that in the eighteenth century slaves were an efficient labor force for the South. Although slaves were less skilled and less motivated than whites, they worked longer hours and their "labor force participation rate" was higher. That is, because black women worked in the fields (while white women did not) there were more laborers in a black population of a given size than in a comparable group of whites. In 1750 the South produced the same level of goods and services as the North or New France.

In the nineteenth century the argument for the utility of slave labor is much harder to make. Many northern farmers now expanded their output by implementing the latest advances in scientific farming. The bound labor of the South took no part in this progress. To be sure, some economic historians argue that slaves remained an efficient, highly productive work force. In their 1974 work, *Time on the Cross,* Robert Fogel and Stanley Engerman contend that slaves were "diligent workers, imbued like their masters with a Protestant ethic." But other researchers sharply challenge these findings, and present calculations showing that free labor was more productive than slave. These historians argue that bondspeople were ill-trained, unmotivated laborers who sabotaged efforts to work them harder. Even Fogel and Engerman have backed away from their more extreme claims about the motivation of the labor force.[50]

During the nineteenth century the increasing mechanization of northern farms heightened the advantages of free workers over slaves. Although bound labor gave masters extra hours and extra hands, such contributions could not match the additional output provided by the harvesters, cultivators, and grain drills found on free farms. The refusal of planters to educate blacks or improve their skills limited plantations to simple tools. As Table 4.1 indicates, the value of farm machinery per acre of improved land in the North was more than twice the value in the South. The average return to farm labor in the South, even with high cotton prices, was well below that in the North.[51]

In sum, slavery helped make the South into a society with a different ethos than the enterprising North. The individuals who dominated southern society valued hierarchy and accepted the low productivity of bound labor. The preservation of this ordered world was far more important than the relentless pursuit of profit.

Table 4.1   Farm Implements and Machinery in the Original States: Value
per Improved Acre, 1850
(in current dollars)

North	1.66	South	0.81
N.H.	1.03	Md.	0.88
Mass.	1.50	Va.	0.68
R.I.	1.39	N.C.	0.72
Conn.	1.07	S.C.	1.02
N.Y.	1.78	Ga.	0.92
N.J.	2.50		
Pa.	1.71		
Del.	0.88		

Source: Seventh Census of the United States: 1850 (Washington, D.C., 1853), lxxxii.

This examination of religion and labor completes our picture of
the institutions and culture that provided a foundation for the three
societies of eastern North America. Landholding, religion, and slavery—more than any other concerns—defined the path of rapid growth
that the North followed and the road of slower development taken by
the South and French Canada. The aspects of culture discussed in the
next chapters may be considered elaborations of these foundations.

5

Mobility and Education

Isaac Weld was an Irishman who came to North America in the 1790s to find an "agreeable place of abode." Weld never did find a place that suited him, and eventually returned home. But the result of his wanderings was a widely reprinted account of North American society. Weld was struck by the differences between French Canada and the United States, and especially by the rootedness of the French and the mobility of the Americans. "The French Canadians . . . ," he remarked, "are fond of living near each other. . . . In this respect a wonderful difference appears between their conduct and that of the young people of the United States, particularly those of New England, who, as soon as they are grown up, immediately emigrate, and bury themselves in the woods, where, perhaps, they are five or six hundred miles distant from every relation upon earth."[1]

Our examination of the cultural and institutional origins of growth now moves beyond those concerns—landholding, religion, and labor—that formed the foundations of these societies. This chapter examines two areas that were important if secondary: geographic mobility (both across the Atlantic and within the New World) and literacy. The refusal of French Canadians to move far from home reinforced the slow growth of that society. By contrast, a bustling, mobile population furthered the ascent of the North. The impact of high mobility on the South was more complex. It quickened growth in that section (which still remained far behind the North). But the southern approach to expansion firmly tied the section to the fate of slavery. It linked the South to a system that was less productive than free labor and lessened the possibility of reform.

Levels of literacy readily conform to the picture of a rising North and a more slowly growing South and French Canada. The Catholics of French Canada and the planters of the slave South placed less emphasis on schooling and the ability to read than did the citizenry of the northern states.

Migration to the New World

New France

The Catholic French were reluctant to move to the New World—a fact that had a profound impact on the development of French Canada. Few French came or wanted to come to Canada. Estimates vary. But researchers agree that no more than 500, and probably closer to 250, lay individuals paid their own passage and made their lives in New France. In all, between 1606 and 1760 just over 10,000 men and women settled in the St. Lawrence Valley. One plausible breakdown of these immigrants is 3300 soldiers, who were encouraged to remain by various inducements; 1200 indentured servants; 1500 women, sent over from poorhouses and orphanages; 200 petty criminals exiled to the New World; 500 male clergymen; 1800 Acadians who moved to the St. Lawrence Valley after the English attacked their villages in the 1750s; 900 slaves; 600 captured British subjects; and 250 voluntary immigrants.[2]

Many individuals who could return to France did. Despite generous offers of land, pay, and discharges, only one-fourth of the 13,000 soldiers stationed in New France remained. Fewer than one-third of the 3900 indentured servants sent to Canada stayed. And more men and women would have gone back to France had not official policy restricted departures for the mother country.

Why was voluntary migration so low and the desire to return to France so strong? Let us review some reasons that do *not* explain the low net migration.

1. *Conditions in New France were undesirable.* In fact, peasants lived much better in New than in Old France. Over 90 percent of farmers in the St. Lawrence Valley owned land, compared with less than half in France. Good quality, if uncleared, acreage was available throughout the French regime, and it was granted for the asking. Unlike French peasants, Canadian farmers had plows and draft animals, and reasonably comfortable homes. Where a French peasant owned two or three acres, a Canadian habitant might hold eighty acres. There were no direct taxes in Canada—a far cry from the oppressive conditions in

France. And life expectancy, after age one, was longer in the New World.[3]

2. *Prosperity and the lack of any "surplus" population in France kept emigration to a minimum.* Not so. The French population of twenty million was four times that of England. During the seventeenth and early eighteenth centuries French agriculture barely supported these teeming masses. Repeated famines brought misery to many peasants. The economy grew slowly, at least before 1713, and many individuals left their homes to seek their livelihoods elsewhere. The army absorbed some of the wanderers, growing from 20,000 in 1661 to 300,000 in 1710. Many individuals traveled about France or tried their luck in Spain. There was no shortage of potential emigrants.[4]

Other reasons better explain the trickle of transatlantic migrants.

1. *Canada had a poor image in France.* After the English Conquest, Voltaire observed: "We have lost in one day . . . fifteen hundred leagues of ground. These fifteen hundred leagues being frozen deserts, are perhaps not really a loss."[5] Some writers like Samuel de Champlain emphasized the rich resources of Canada. But many early accounts noted the bitter winters and Iroquois menace. Too much, however, should not be made of this explanation. Emigration did not quicken in the eighteenth century once the threat of Indian attacks lessened. And French settlers did not flock to the warm colonies in the West Indies. Saint-Domingue had a white population of only 20,000 in 1740.

2. *The prohibition of Protestants kept out many immigrants.* Decrees issued in 1627 and 1628 permitted only Catholics to settle in New France, effectively barring Huguenots and foreign Protestants. Between the 1680s and 1720 some 200,000 Huguenots left France, many emigrating to England, Holland, and other European countries. Perhaps 7000 came to the Thirteen Colonies—where some became prominent merchants and craftspeople. This group included, in Boston, Paul Revere, the Faneuils, and Bowdoins; in New York, the DeLanceys; and in South Carolina, the Guerards, Légarés, and Manigaults. New France closed the door to this pool of talent.[6]

3. *Communal values made the French reluctant to emigrate overseas.* Peter Moogk has studied the correspondence of individuals who went to New France. He concludes that many French people considered permanent resettlement in the New World as "unnatural, even as selfish and immoral." Every migration has voyagers who become homesick and who return soon after arriving. But to an extent that distinguished them from the English or other peoples, the French were reluctant to go to the New World and eager to return after arriving. A few Frenchmen and women were themselves puzzled by this behavior. Father Paul Le Jeune remarked that "there are so many strong and robust peasants in France who have no bread to put in their mouths; is it

possible that they are so afraid of losing sight of the village steeple . . . that they would rather languish in their misery and poverty, than to place themselves some day at their ease among the inhabitants of New France?"[7] The culture of France emphasized stasis, and contributed to a mind-set that encouraged individuals to remain in their native land.

Anyone who seeks to analyze transatlantic migration in narrow economic terms will have trouble explaining the paltry flow of individuals to New France. Both the "pull" of prosperity and the "push" of misery were strong. Deep-seated values kept most French in Europe where they would never be too far from their homes.

Thirteen Colonies

To move from Canadian to American immigration is to leap into another world. The outlook of the immigrants and the policies of the mother country are strikingly different. The number of arrivals is of a far greater magnitude. Between 1620 and 1760 only 10,000 individuals settled in the St. Lawrence Valley, while during roughly the same span (1630 to 1780) about 500,000 whites and over 250,000 blacks became residents of the Thirteen Colonies.[8] Most whites came as indentured servants. But perhaps a third or more of those sailing to America were voluntary immigrants, financing their own passage.[9] Taking the Thirteen Colonies as a whole, the gates were thrown wide open to men and women of many faiths and countries. Protestants formed the mainstay of this immigration. Maryland, however, started as a Catholic refuge, and several provinces had thriving Jewish communities. Most of the white settlers were English, but particular colonies had large groups of Germans, Scots, Scots-Irish, Irish, and Dutch. Some provinces like Pennsylvania advertised aggressively for settlers. Few immigrants displayed the reluctance to resettle in the New World that characterized the French.[10]

Some came to the Thirteen Colonies for religious reasons, to escape persecution or establish their Zion in the wilderness. But economic motives—the "pull" of New World prosperity and the "push" of Old World hardship—is explanation enough for most. Economic historians of the nineteenth century have shown that the waves of immigration mirrored fluctuations in the United States economy. The same relationship appears to hold in the colonial era. Two long swings—stretching from 1713 to 1745 and from 1745 to 1776—shaped colonial growth and net migration.[11]

During the eighteenth century the sharpest distinction in numbers of immigrants and the values they held lay between the Thirteen Colonies and New France. There was as yet no great divide separating the North and South. Pennsylvania was one magnet for new colonists, but most immigrants went to the South. Slaves were taken chiefly to the southern states, and whites arriving chose the South over the North by a ratio of two to one. This sectional imbalance reflected the incessant demands of planters for slaves and indentured servants. It also was a result of the relatively closed nature of New England and New York society. Few immigrants wanted to enter the tight-knit world of the New England Congregationalists. And most new arrivals avoided New York, where the large landlords refused to grant land outright to settlers.[12]

In the nineteenth century, slavery would change the pattern of immigration. Immigrants now shunned the South and made clear their preference for the North. The South had fewer cities, less industry, and a lower standard of living than the free states. In 1850 the foreign-born made up 15 percent of the eight northern original states, and only 2 percent of the five southern ones. Many southerners, regarding immigrants as potential abolitionists and labor organizers, rejoiced that few of the new arrivals settled in the South. Edmund Ruffin, a strong advocate of southern nationalism (he was given permission to fire the first shot on Fort Sumter in 1861), remarked: "One of the great benefits of the institution of African slavery to the southern states is its effect in keeping away from our territory, and directing to the north and northwest, the hordes of immigrants now flowing from Europe."[13]

Internal Migration

French Canada

According to classical theory, workers should move from a low-wage area to a high-wage one. (For economists such a movement illustrates "factor-price equalization.") Everyone benefits from this migration. New resources are brought into production. Wages rise in the older area as laborers move out. Society becomes more productive and achieves a new equilibrium.[14]

It didn't work that way in French Canada—at least not before the 1860s, when the pressure for out-migration became overwhelming. French Canadians were more hesitant than English settlers to move from place to place in the New World. Their behavior within North America thus echoes their reluctance to relocate across the Atlantic. This desire to stick close to home made little difference for the growth of French Canada in the eighteenth century. Habitants could find good land not far from their parents' farms. But it became one factor slowing development in the first half of the nineteenth century as the seigneuries along the St. Lawrence became overcrowded.[15]

Statistics underscore the French Canadians' lack of geographical mobility. Drawing upon the 1852 census, Frank Lewis and Marvin McInnis have studied the differences between farming in the English-

and French-speaking districts of Lower Canada. One of their findings was the higher ratio of people to land in the French districts. Where a French farm had four workers, an English one of the same size had three.[16] Another indicator of mobility is the comparison between the growth of population in Lower Canada and New England. Between 1790 and 1860 the population of Lower Canada increased almost seven times. New England only tripled its population. The contribution of immigration was comparable. Lower Canada appears to have had a slightly higher rate of natural increase. But New England was more urbanized. The key distinction was the willingness of New Englanders to move west, and the reluctance of French speakers to quit their native province.[17] Some French Canadians, to be sure, did leave Lower Canada. They went to New England and to midwestern states such as Michigan and Illinois. But before 1865 no more than a few thousand emigrated in any one year. And even this small exodus provoked cries of anguish from residents of Lower Canada who did not want to see French Canadians growing up on foreign soil. By contrast, several hundred thousand New Englanders moved to the western states during this era.[18]

Various observers (like Isaac Weld, whose statement opens this chapter) remarked on the reluctance of French Canadians to move long distances. The superior of the Montreal seminary commented in 1831 that the Canadian race "definitely does not have the adventurous spirit and the scorn for the bonds of birth and family that characterize the Americans. Only in the last extremity will the Canadien move away from his church steeple and parents."[19] A publicist promoting Montreal saw benefits in the attachment of French Canadians to the land. The writer observed in 1856 that "another advantage Montreal possesses is found in the density of the population of the surrounding districts. In many places the land has been subdivided until the holdings of each man are too small for profitable agriculture, and the people, deeply attached to the soil, are unwilling to leave the older settlements in the valleys of the St. Lawrence and Richelieu so long as they can obtain subsistence there." These crowded settlements, the writer pointed out, provided a large, docile work force.[20]

The French historian and statesman Alexis de Tocqueville also noted the immobility of French Canadians. A striking individual—short, with delicate features and dark hair that fell to his shoulders in the fashion of a Parisian gentleman—Tocqueville traveled widely in North America between May 1831 and February 1832. His trip included a visit of two weeks to Lower Canada. He was struck by the refusal of the Canadians to resettle far from their homes, and he explained it by referring to the behavior of the French. "In France," he remarked, "we regard simple tastes, quiet mores, family feeling, and love of one's birthplace as great guarantees for the tranquillity and happiness of the state. . . . The French of Canada, who loyally preserve the tradition of their ancient mores, are already finding it difficult to live on their land." He added: "I have met New Englanders ready to abandon their homeland, in which they could gain a comfortable living, to seek their fortunes in the wilderness. Nearby I saw the population of French Canada crowded into a space too narrow for them, although the same wilderness lay close at hand."[21]

The bonds of family and place may have helped preserve French culture in the New World. But during the first half of the nineteenth century, these ties slowed economic growth.

Restless Americans

Unlike French Canadians, Americans were only too eager to move from place to place. The pattern of migration in the southern states, however, differed sharply from that in the North. Closely viewed, the settlement of the Southwest reveals the fundamental weaknesses of the southern economy. By contrast, the movement of people into the Northwest (and the growth of these new states) shows the long-term strengths of the North. This discussion, which focuses on the period from 1800 to 1860, first provides an overview of migration in the South and North, and then examines the ideologies that defended and explained these movements.[22]

For the southern economy growth—and indeed survival—depended on the movement westward. Cotton culture was ravenous, drawing out nutrients from the land, and driving down returns in the older states. Hence the need to carve out new farms, and the initial, favorable earnings from plantations in the Southwest. In 1840 per capita income in Louisiana and Mississippi was exceptionally high—comparable with the levels in Rhode Island and Massachusetts. Northern traveler Frederick Law Olmsted was impressed by the prosperity of the westerners, if not by their breeding. "Herein is a radical difference between the social conditions of this [western] region," he remarked, "and that of the sea-board Slave States, where there are fewer wealthy families, but where among the few people of wealth, refinement and education are more general."[23]

Slaveowners were particularly mobile. They were more likely to migrate than northerners with comparable wealth. And when they moved they traveled further than nonslaveholders. These affluent southerners had relatively little of their holdings in land or buildings. Gavin Wright calculates that slaves accounted for almost two-thirds of the typical planter's wealth. Slaveholders and their bondspeople dominated the movement to new southern soils.[24]

In general, southerners were more likely to migrate than northerners. Consider these data. In 1850 out of every 100 white people born in New England or the mid-Atlantic states, 84 still lived in the section of their birth. By contrast, for every 100 white people born in the South Atlantic states, only 75 remained in that area in 1850. The Northeast had industry and growing cities to hold its people. The Southeast did not, and its residents were lured west by the high returns in the new states.[25]

But if the rich soils of the Southwest were a balm for southern ills, their potency was short-lived. Even before the Civil War soil depletion was evident throughout the West. In 1855 a Mississippi newspaper observed: "An improvident agriculture has already ruined millions of acres of our soil, and if persisted in, will ultimately turn the whole country into a wide, ruinous waste." The editor of the *Southern Cultivator* calculated in 1858 that 40 percent of southern land was worn out. This declining fertility was reflected in income levels. By 1860 growth had slowed markedly, and states such as Mississippi and Louisiana now dropped well behind the pace set by New England and the mid-Atlantic area. The fall in the relative income of the new states hinted at the post-Civil War era, when the Southwest was not much wealthier than the Southeast, and the two together formed the poorest region in the nation.[26]

Viewing western lands as a panacea, the Lower South shunned the path of reform blazed by Maryland. Residents of this border state gradually shifted away from a dependence on bound labor. Between 1830 and 1860 slaves declined from 35 percent of the population to 25 percent. Marylanders used the wealth from slave sales to fertilize their farmland. They also moved to towns: in 1860 urban places held 34 percent of Marylanders, well above the southern average of 10 percent of the population. They invested in manufactures, and Maryland despite its distance from the cotton fields led all southern states in building textile mills. But most members of the southern elite considered such a program anathema. They could not stomach reforms that questioned slavery or challenged the plantation system. They continued to see new lands as the cure-all for southern problems, even though many observers acknowledged that slave agriculture had reached its "natural limits" by midcentury.[27]

For the northern economy the movement west was important, but was not the mainspring of growth that it was for the South. Industry and commerce, rather than fresh soils, were the chief engines of development in the North. In 1840 Ohio, Illinois, and Indiana had average incomes less than half those of the leading New England states. But unlike the Southwest, the Northwest grew wealthier between 1840 and 1860 when measured against the national average. The new states of the North gradually became more industrial and urban—a trend that pointed to their rapid ascent after the Civil War. Cyrus McCormick's decision in 1847 to locate his reaper factory in Chicago suggested the strong tide of development that would lift both farmers and townfolk. The clashes before the Civil War make clear that northerners were determined to control the West. But they valued this expanse for the broad range of opportunities it offered, not just for the fertility of its soils.[28]

This overview provides a background for the expansionist ideologies that developed in the two regions. In the North the movement to the new territories reflected the outlook of a region of business-minded farmers and urbanites. In the South the slaveholding elite shaped the approach to the West.

The North and South Spell Out Opposing Ideologies of Expansion

During the middle decades of the nineteenth century politicians and editorialists in the North and South spelled out contrasting approaches to western expansion. These ideologies are important beyond the issue of settling the West. They illustrate the contrasting world views that guided the two sections.

Northerners enunciated a "free labor ideology." A prosperous, happy America, this credo argued, was one based on the labor of free, independent, hard-working people. Prominent among the individuals propounding these beliefs was William H. Seward of New York. He was a short, convivial man, with auburn hair that gradually turned "silvery and fine." An English visitor reported: "A good cigar, a good glass of wine, and a good story, even if it is *tant soit peu risqué* [a bit naughty], are pleasures which he obviously enjoys keenly." Seward served as governor of New York, senator, and later Secretary of State in Lincoln's cabinet.[29]

Seward argued that prosperity—as well as the reforms that were gradually perfecting northern society—depended on free labor. "Suppose that," he asked, "fifty years ago, New York, like Virginia and Maryland, had clung to slavery, where now would have been these three composite millions of freemen, the choice and flower of Europe and America?" He continued: "Where would, then, have been the Erie canal, the Genessee Valley canal, the Oswego canal . . . ? Where the imperial New York Central railroad, the Erie railroad, and the Ogsdensburgh railroad? . . . Where would have been the colleges, academies, and above all, the free common schools, yielding instructions to children of all sects and in all languages? Where the asylums and other public charities, and above all, that noble emigrant charity which crowns the state with such distinguished honor?"[30] The answer to these questions was obvious. Without free labor, the North would have none of the economic and social benefits of development.

As the sectional conflict heightened, Seward grew increasingly concerned about the West and the spread of slavery. Bound labor must not be allowed to triumph over free labor in the territories. "We have half a continent yet to be opened to the flow of one or the other," Seward observed. "Shall we diffuse slavery over it to react upon and destroy ourselves, or shall we extend freedom over it covering it with happiness throughout all its mountains and plains?"[31] And in a widely quoted speech, he observed: "It is an irrepressible conflict between opposing and enduring forces, and it means that the United States must and will, sooner or later, become either entirely a slaveholding nation, or entirely a free-labor nation."[32]

The beliefs Seward espoused must be set in a broader context. The ideology of free labor affirmed the destiny of a region of hardworking farmers and entrepreneurs. It helped provide the underpinnings for the optimism of this era. And it had important links with the doctrines that would emerge after the Civil War. To be sure, the Gospel of Wealth, which soon displaced free labor ideology, was less egalitarian and more fiercely individualistic. And corporate liberalism, which emerged after 1900, spoke to a mature industrial society, and seemed many removes from the earlier credo. But these northern ideologies shared strong roots in an entrepreneurial ethos. Free labor, and the doctrines that succeeded it, allowed northerners to link their passion for making money to a higher vision of the well-being of American society.[33]

A sharply contrasting body of beliefs guided southern expansion. The pole star for white southerners was an ideology that linked slavery and territorial growth—and argued that both were absolutely necessary. New territories were boosted as a source of political power. Many planters also believed that without new land the volatile southern mix of race and class would detonate. If northerners had their way, Thomas Clingman of North Carolina fretted, masters and slaves would be "pent up within a territory which after a time will be insufficient for their subsistence, and where they must perish from want, or from a collision that would occur between the races."[34] Prominent southerners agreed. "When you have forced into the cotton-growing States of this Union, eight millions of slaves, and have left them no outlet," remarked Mississippi Congressman Albert G. Brown, "you will have that sort of disaster which you would have if you dammed up the mouth of the Mississippi."[35]

No slaveowner enunciated these views more forcefully than John C. Calhoun. Over six feet tall, with strong features and piercing eyes, Calhoun impressed contemporaries with both his intensity and his intellect. During a political career that stretched from 1808 to 1850 he served as representative from South Carolina, senator, Secretary of War, Secretary of State, and Vice President. Always an expansionist, Calhoun before

1830 publicly supported the national government. The growth of the South seemed to dovetail with the rise of the United States.[36]

But after 1830 Calhoun abandoned his nationalism, and during the 1830s and 1840s spelled out a more narrowly sectional view of slavery and expansion. He defended slavery as a positive good and urged the annexation of Texas. This step, he declared, "ought to be unanimously and decidedly supported by the South."[37] Calhoun was delighted when Texas became part of the Union, but was troubled by the Mexican War (1846–48). He feared the conflict might strengthen federal power, and worried that the territory gained would be closed to bound labor. A bitter, confrontational tone marked his speeches on the West. "The North cannot have a deeper interest in asserting absolute power over the territories, than the South has in resisting it," he told the Senate in 1849. "If it be important to her, as the means of extending her power and ascendency over this Government, it is still more so to the South to resist it,— not only as indispensable to the preservation of her rights and equality, but her safety itself."[38] The threat of disunion lay not far beneath the surface. "The time is at hand, if the question should not be speedily settled," he pronounced, "when the South must rise up, and bravely defend herself, or sink down into base and acknowledged inferiority."[39]

Calhoun's views were repeated and amplified during the heated debates of the 1850s and during the secession crisis. Southerners looked not only to the West for new slave territory, but to the Caribbean and Central America as well. Many saw the formation of the Confederacy as a chance to extend the reach of the peculiar institution. A Vicksburg newspaper declared in October 1860, "We verily believe that the overthrow of the Union would not only perpetuate slavery where it now exists and establish it more firmly, but would necessarily lead to its widespread extension."[40] This belligerent ideology would not survive the defeat of the South. But many of the beliefs that contributed to this expansionist outlook—for example, the refusal to consider far-reaching reforms, the belief in caste and class, and the commitment to agriculture— would remain as important in the South after the Civil War as before.

Literacy and Education

Education also had a marked effect on economic growth. Differences in levels of literacy and schooling helped boost the prosperous North and slow the growth of French Canada and the South.

French Canada

Peter Kalm attended church in New France and disliked what he heard. "Most of the service was in Latin," the Swedish naturalist remarked. "It seemed as if the whole service was too much of an external *opus opera-*

tum. Most of it consisted in the reading of prayers with a rapidity which made it impossible to understand them. . . . The common man could certainly get nothing of it." Kalm looked at Canada through Lutheran eyes. But he saw clearly that Catholic New France did not exalt the spoken and written word as Protestant societies did. Unlike Puritan New Englanders or Lutheran Swedes, Canadians did not pore over the Holy Scriptures at home. "Although I paid particular attention to the matter," Kalm reported, "I never saw a Bible in any house, either in French or Latin, except at the residences of the clergy."[41] An upstanding citizen and parishioner in New France did not have to be educated. While education gradually improved, poor schools and high illiteracy continued to characterize French Canada and hindered economic growth in the nineteenth and twentieth centuries.

There were few schools in New France, and the result was a high level of illiteracy. Allan Greer's study of literacy in French Canada shows that in the middle of the eighteenth century roughly 10 percent of rural people could read. The overall rate was higher in the towns: in Trois Rivières half the population was literate. Literacy was judged more of a social grace than a vital skill. Although the percentages were low for both sexes, more women were able to read than men.[42]

The scarcity of books and the absence of newspapers compounded these problems. Catholic society in New France and Old regulated the circulation of all printed matter. In France government censors scrutinized works published in all fields. France had fewer newspapers than England, and the gazettes that were published had less news. And no works originated in Canada: New France had no printing presses. Kalm did not believe the explanation given him for the absence of printers— but he should have. "They pretend that the press is not yet introduced here," he reported in 1749, "because it might be the means of propagating libels against the government and religion." The real reasons, he asserted, were that "no printer could make a sufficient number of books for his subsistence" and that "France now has the profit arising from the exportation of books hither." Despite Kalm's concern about the size of the market, successful presses were opened soon after the Conquest.[43]

Education and literacy increased in French Canada in the nineteenth century, but remained well below the levels reached by whites in the United States or by anglophones in Lower Canada. By the 1840s about 31 percent of French speakers and 75 percent of English speakers in rural Lower Canada could read. Once again, rates were higher in the cities. And as earlier, more women could read than men. The 1861 census revealed that almost 18 percent of Quebeckers were illiterate, well above the rate of 3 percent in the original northern states. (See Table 5.1.)[44]

The links between religion and literacy were strong. While Protestants developed their own effective school system, the Catholic hierar-

Table 5.1 Rates of Illiteracy in the Original States, 1850, and Lower Canada, 1861
(All figures are percentages)

	Native Whites	Foreign Whites	Free Blacks	Total Population[a]
N.H.	0.3	14.5	10.0	0.9
Mass.	0.1	16.2	8.9	2.8
R.I.	0.8	9.9	7.3	2.4
Conn.	0.2	10.5	7.4	1.4
N.Y.	1.0	10.4	15.1	3.2
Pa.	2.2	8.2	17.4	3.3
N.J.	2.1	9.8	18.6	3.8
Del.	6.1	9.4	31.2	13.1
Average North	1.3	10.6	17.2	3.1
Md.	4.7	6.7	28.2	21.9
Va.	8.7	5.0	21.2	48.0
N.C.	13.3	13.3	25.0	40.8
S.C.	5.9	1.2	9.8	57.2
Ga.	7.9	6.3	15.9	44.7
Average South	8.7	5.9	24.2	43.6
Lower Canada counties				
8 English-majority counties	7.0			
52 French-majority counties	18.8			
Average Lower Canada	17.5			

[a] Total based on assumption that 95 percent of slaves are illiterate.
Sources: Seventh Census of the United States: 1850 (Washington, D.C., 1853); *Census of Canada, 1861* (Quebec, 1863–64). For the estimate of 95 percent illiteracy among slaves, W. E. B. DuBois, *Black Reconstruction: An Essay Toward a History of the Part Which Black Folk Played in the Attempt to Reconstruct Democracy in America, 1860–1880* (Philadelphia, 1935), 638; Eugene D. Genovese, *Roll, Jordan, Roll: The World the Slaves Made* (New York, 1974), 561–66.

chy was more concerned about the doctrines these institutions propounded than the number and quality of these centers of learning. Jean-Jacques Lartigue, the bishop of Montreal, led the crusade against the Assembly Schools Act of 1829. The bishop was angered that the measure allowed lay persons to control local schools. Remarked Lartigue: "It would be better for them [rural people] to have no literary education at all than to risk a bad moral education." The act was not renewed in 1836. Only in the late 1840s, after the assembly agreed that the clergy would direct the schools, did the Church support the spread of popular education. Even then school construction lagged. The census of 1850 showed that in the francophone counties of Lower Canada the number of schools was well below the levels in the United

States, North or South. And the rate of illiteracy remained markedly higher in 1861 in counties with a Catholic francophone majority than those where the Protestant English were dominant (Table 5.1). Religion and education were related even within the English-speaking community of Lower Canada. Literacy was markedly lower among anglophone Catholics (largely Irish immigrants) than among English-speaking Protestants.[45]

Widespread illiteracy had little impact on the growth of Canada in the French era. But it slowed development in the nineteenth century. With the spread of commercial capitalism, an increasing number of jobs demanded education. Artisans, merchants, and professionals had to be able to read and write. The pool of French speakers available for these occupations was small.[46]

Education North and South

A   In *Adam's* Fall
     We Sinned all.

B   Thy Life to Mend
     This *Book* Attend.

C   The *Cat* doth play
     And after slay.

D   A *Dog* will bite
     A Thief at night

E   An *Eagle's* flight
     Is out of sight

F   The Idle *Fool*
     Is whipt at school.

G   As runs the *Glass*
     Man's life doth pass.[47]

With these dour verses generations of New England school children learned their ABC's. Even in the colonial era levels of education were much higher in the North than in the South or French Canada, and this lead was maintained in the nineteenth century.

Nowhere in colonial North America could more people read and write than in New England. The Puritans were committed to education. In 1647 Massachusetts ordered every community with fifty families to support a teacher, while all towns with a hundred families or more were to "set up a grammar school." The reasons were frankly religious: God-fearing individuals had to be able to read the Bible. The preface to the school law declared that literacy was needed, "it being one chief project of that old deluder, Satan, to keep men from the knowledge of the Scriptures."[48] The full impact of the Puritan concern for learning became evident as society grew wealthier, and children could be spared from their chores and sent to the local schoolhouse. Literacy rose from the seventeenth to the eighteenth century, and by 1760 about 75 to 80 percent of New England men could read and write. Rates for women were lower. Patriarchal, Puritan society considered the education of women less crucial. In Boston 65 percent of women could read, but in the countryside only 33 percent were literate. By 1800 rural New England had achieved universal male literacy, although women continued to lag far behind.[49]

The exceptionally high rate of literacy in New England reflected the religious tenets of its founders, just as widespread illiteracy in New France can be traced back to French Catholicism. The Puritan colonies in America were following the same path as other militant Protestant states. In Calvinist Scotland compulsory schooling raised the literacy of men from 33 percent in 1675 to nearly 90 percent by 1800. In Peter Kalm's homeland—Sweden—the church demanded that all parishioners be able to read. Sweden achieved nearly universal literacy for both males and females by the middle of the eighteenth century.[50]

Literacy in the Middle Colonies was also relatively high. The work of Allan Tully suggests that in the 1720s about two-thirds of males in Pennsylvania could read. This was five points below the rate in New England. However, unlike the trend in Puritan New England, the rate in the Middle Colonies did not climb during the eighteenth century, but remained unchanged at about 66 percent. Evidence for female literacy in Pennsylvania is less abundant, but as in New England, the rate stood well below that of males.[51]

In the colonial South, white male literacy seems to have followed a pattern similar to that in Pennsylvania. Throughout the eighteenth century two-thirds of white men in Virginia could read. But the overall rate in the South was much lower because of the presence of the large slave population. Planters did not educate their bondspeople, and in all, fewer than 45 percent of southern males, black and white, were literate.[52]

During the first half of the nineteenth century the literacy rate and the quality of schools improved in both the North and South—but by all measures the North remained far ahead. A vigorous reform movement, demanding the creation of "common-school" systems, emerged in the northern states during the 1830s. While programs varied from state to state, these reformers typically campaigned for a system of tax-supported public schools, a state superintendent who would push local districts toward higher standards and greater uniformity, a longer school year, and improved training and qualifications for teachers. In New York, Governor William Seward led the crusade. Telling the legislature that the "improvability of our race is without limit," he success-fully urged a wide-ranging series of educational reforms.[53] In Massa-chusetts Horace Mann was the best known advocate of common schools. A tall, lean figure, with strong Lincolnesque features, Mann used his position as secretary of the Massachusetts Board of Education as a bully pulpit. He criticized the lack of uniformity and standards in Massachusetts education. "These schools, at the present time, are so many distinct, independent communities," he observed in 1837, and added: "If any improvement in principles or modes of teaching is dis-covered by talent or accident in one school, instead of being published to the world, it dies with the discoverer."[54]

Northern reformers built upon their successes. In the 1850s they encouraged many districts to extend the common-school system to include public high schools. Massachusetts took a further step and in-troduced a compulsory school attendance law in 1852. The common-school movement was also accompanied by a shift from poorly edu-cated male teachers to more professionally trained (but underpaid) women teachers.[55]

Universal literacy for males and females became the norm in the North for native-born whites, who formed the vast majority of the population. Northern school systems were less successful in educating the immigrants, largely Irish and Germans. Many of the new arrivals refused to send their children to the public schools, and preferred in-stead religious institutions. Blacks in the North received inferior educa-tion, typically in segregated schools. Table 5.1 provides data for the literacy of these groups, while Table 5.2 shows the comparatively high level of public spending on school children in the Northeast. Settlers from New York and New England also helped bring the common-school movement to the Northwest.[56]

Scholars disagree about the relationship between educational re-form in the North and the rise of commercial capitalism. Michael Katz and others argue that the new school systems were imposed on ordi-nary people by a capitalist class. The reformers, he asserts, "attempted to facilitate economic change through the transformation of social atti-tudes." Other scholars suggest a more complex reality and the impor-tance of benevolent motives.[57] But there can be no question that those crusading for better instruction recognized the economic value of edu-cation. "Let any one, who has resided or travelled in those States where there are no Common Schools," Horace Mann remarked, "com-pare the condition of the people at large, as to thrift, order, neatness, and all the external signs of comfort and competence, with the same characteristics of civilization in the farm-houses and villages of New England." Mann added: "These contrasts exist, notwithstanding the fertility of the soil and the abundance of mineral resources, in the for-mer States, as compared with the sterile surface and granite substratum

Table 5.2 Public Expenditure on Education for Each School-age Child in
the Original States, 1850
School-age population includes all children, 5–19 years old

	All School-Age	Free School-Age		All School-Age	Free School-Age
N.H.	$1.50		Md.	$0.77	$0.92
Mass.	3.19		Va.	0.35	0.84
R.I.	2.04		N.C.	0.41	0.67
Conn.	1.68		S.C.	0.31	0.77
N.Y.	1.31		Ga.	0.11	0.21
Pa.	1.62		Average South	0.35	0.68
N.J.	0.81				
Del.	1.21	1.30			
Average North	1.63	1.63			

Source: Seventh Census of the United States: 1850; Lawrence A. Cremin, *American Education: The National Experience, 1783–1876* (New York, 1980), 182–83. In the slave states the white school-age population was assumed to be 36 percent of total white population. Slight adjustments to this figure would not alter the regional contrast.

of the latter." In short, education, not natural resources, was the key to growth.[58]

The story of educational reform in the South is one of dashed hopes and angry denials of the need for change. No southern state developed the vigorous system of common schools that flourished throughout the North. North Carolina passed a common-school law in 1839 but never found the funds to breathe life into this legislation. Georgians briefly endorsed such a program, but soon repealed the measure. Instead southerners relied on tutors for the rich, privately funded "academies," and a haphazard, poorly supported set of public schools. Table 5.1 indicates the comparatively high levels of illiteracy among the native-born whites and free blacks, while Table 5.2 suggests the lack of public funds for schooling in the South. (The relatively high literacy of the foreign-born in the South reflects the presence of skilled craftspeople within this small segment of the population.)[59]

The weakness of educational reform in the South had roots that lay deep in the social structure and values of the region. The members of the elite, with their strong sense of social hierarchy, were unwilling to fund schools for the common folk. William Harper, a South Carolina lawyer, remarked: "The Creator did not intend that every individual human being should be highly cultivated. . . . It is better that a part should be fully and highly cultivated and the rest utterly ignorant." And the influential *DeBow's Review* suggested that the state should provide only a rudimentary education for most whites, adding, "beyond that it must educate the wealthy in order to maintain their position as members of the white, privileged class of our society." The upper classes in such states as Virginia and Georgia blocked proposals to establish public schools for the common folk. Instead, revenues in Virginia were directed to the state university, which served the children of the elite. Finally, deep-rooted social attitudes kept whites from educating the slaves. As southern society became more closed in the decades before the Civil War, the laws against teaching bondspeople became ever stricter.[60]

Education can be viewed both as a mirror of society and an engine of development. In each region the quality of schooling reflected religious beliefs, social hierarchy, and the demands of the economy. These factors came together to give the North the best system of schools and the most educated populace. French Canada and the South lagged far behind. But education was also a powerful force for growth. It fostered the development of the North by equipping the citizenry with the skills needed for success in commercial capitalism. High levels of education would continue to favor the North (and particularly the Northeast) during the long era of industrialization and in the post-industrial period.

6

Entrepreneurial Spirit in the North and South

The British officials were suspicious. Before letting Francis Cabot Lowell leave the country, they went through his baggage twice. After all, here was a wealthy Boston merchant who had spent an inordinate amount of time visiting British textile mills. The inspectors feared he was stealing industrial secrets. And they were right. But the plans for the power loom were in Lowell's head, not in his bags. When he returned to Boston in 1812, Lowell and a local mechanic, "planned and tried, altered and rearranged" the parts of the intricate machinery Lowell had remembered. Nor did Lowell's design skills stop there. He also imagined a complete factory, unlike any he had seen in Britain. It would take in raw cotton and produce cloth. And he envisioned an industrial center that would not resemble the crowded cities of England. ("We found the manufacturing towns very dirty," he remarked.) His new American mill town would be a clean, cheerful, healthy place to work.[1]

Francis Lowell, whose dreams would be realized, stands as a remarkable example of a northern entrepreneur. The industrial city that was named after him was a fitting tribute to his genius. He had drive, vision, and not incidentally, an unceasing determination to build his personal fortune. More broadly, Lowell illustrates the passion for business that characterized much of the North. This obsession was absent or much subdued in the South.

This chapter discusses the entrepreneurial spirit in the northern and southern states, while the next chapter focuses on French Canada. A knack for business is not a mystical, disembodied quality. It reflects the other concerns discussed in this book.[2] Patterns of landholding, Protestantism, a free labor force, extensive literacy, and high levels of mobility all contributed to the acquisitive outlook of northerners. Slavery, illiteracy, and sharply defined social classes shaped a different mind-set in the South. Southerners fretted about the spread of factories, and rarely displayed the love of enterprise that drove northerners.

The pages that follow examine the business spirit in the northern and southern states from two vantage points. The first section looks at the views of contemporary observers. The second section compares the development of the cotton textile industry in the two regions.

Yankee Sharpers and Indolent Southerners

What were Americans like during the middle decades of the nineteenth century? Visitors and longtime residents agreed that northerners were obsessed with making money, while southerners were addicted to their leisure. At first glance, the distinction between the two sections might seem similar to the one described by eighteenth-century commentators. And to a large degree it was. But in painting this canvas observers used new, intense colors—particularly in their description of the North.

The advent of commercial capitalism effected an unmistakable change in northern temperament. Eighteenth-century travelers called northerners hard-working and sober. Observers in the 1830s, 1840s, and 1850s introduced harsher notes. The widespread prosperity of the North was evident. But so were other qualities. For many commentators the northerner was now characterized by an "anxious spirit of gain."[3] He (the doctrine of two spheres set woman's place in the home, not in the world of business) was a "Mammon-seeking mortal." "He rises early," noted one British visitor, "eats his meals with the rapidity of a wolf, and is the whole day at his business."[4] Time and again observers emphasized the joyless, single-minded outlook of the citizenry. Religious fervor and a belief in the perfectibility of humanity kept Yankees and Yorkers from being totally immersed in the mundane. But for the most part, observers saw the inhabitants of the North in the 1830s, '40s, and '50s in much the same way that Americans view the Japanese in the late twentieth century: as a successful people who labor too much and play too little.

There was less change over time in the commentary about the South. In contrast to visitors during the colonial era, observers in the decades before the Civil War more often remarked upon signs of poverty and the readiness of southerners to join violent quarrels. But during both periods writers depicted a section given to leisure and display.[5]

Let us examine the remarks of four commentators on northerners—those prosperous, driven, joyless individuals. Other contemporary accounts might lengthen this discussion—but the message would not change.[6]

Americans did not always like what Frances Trollope had to say, but her picture of the North was insightful. She was a middle-aged Englishwoman who was used to living well, although her family had recently fallen on hard times. She came to America in 1827 in an effort to revive her family fortunes. But her store in Cincinnati went bust, and she decided to travel about the United States. Ironically, the business failure was the start of Trollope's success. The journal of her travels, *The Domestic Manners of the Americans*, which was published in 1832 after her return to England, sold extraordinarily well, and she went on to write 113 volumes of best-selling fiction and travel accounts.[7]

We join up with Trollope in Philadelphia, where she visited restful Washington Square, not far from the State House on Walnut Street. "The trees are numerous, and highly beautiful, and several commodious seats are placed beneath their shade. . . ," she remarked. "It was rarely, however, that I saw any of these seats occupied; the Americans have either no leisure, or no inclination for these moments of *delassement* [relaxation] that all other people, I believe, indulge in. Even their drams, so universally taken by rich and poor, are swallowed standing, and, excepting at church, they never have the air of leisure or repose." (Trollope and several of the writers discussed below spoke of *Americans* but meant *northerners*, who made up two-thirds of the population. The comments of these individuals—some quoted below—on the laziness of southerners makes this distinction clear.)[8]

The defects of the money-making North were, Trollope noted, taken to their extreme in New England. "I know not a more striking evidence of the low tone of morality which is generated by this universal pursuit of money," she stated, "than the manner in which the New England States are described by Americans. All agree in saying that they present a spectacle of industry and prosperity delightful to behold. . . . Yet I never met a single individual in any part of the Union who did not paint these New Englanders as sly, grinding, selfish, and tricking."[9]

Thomas Hamilton, a Scottish soldier, novelist, and traveler, reached a similar conclusion. "Wherever he [the New Englander] goes," remarked Hamilton, "the coils of business are around him. He is a sort of moral Laocoon, differing only in this, that he makes no true struggle to be free. Mammon has no more zealous worshipper than your True Yankee. . . . He views the world but as one vast exchange, on which he is impelled, both by principle and interest, to over-reach his neighbours if he can."[10]

James Buckingham echoed these sentiments. Buckingham was a Whig politician, journalist, and social reformer who visited the United States after his defeat in the 1837 parliamentary election. "The young men of America," he observed in discussing the North, "are all so busily engaged, from morning till night, in the affairs of commerce or professional occupations, and so engrossed with the one great aim of getting on in business, and acquiring wealth, that they have neither time nor inclination for . . . romantic dreams of love . . . ."[11]

Alexis de Tocqueville, the French writer and statesman, also pointed to the melancholia that afflicted many acquisitive northerners. "In America I have seen the freest and best educated of men in circumstances the happiest to be found in the world," Tocqueville observed. "Yet it seemed to me that a cloud habitually hung on their brow, and they seemed serious and almost sad even in their pleasures." He continues: "It is odd to watch with what feverish ardor the Americans pursue prosperity and how they are ever tormented by the shadowy suspicion that they may not have chosen the shortest route to get it." However, religion, Tocqueville noted, softened this preoccupation with gain, and turned the minds of these businesspeople to larger, non-worldly concerns.[12]

The South was another country. Most writers who noted the entrepreneurial spirit of the North remarked upon the lack of drive in the South. "The poles are not more diametrically opposed," Thomas Hamilton observed, "than a native of the States south of the Potomac, and a New-Englander. They differ in every thing of thought, feeling, and opinion. The latter is a man of regular and decorous habits . . . devoted to the pursuits of gain, and envious of those who are more successful than himself. The former [the southerner]—I speak of the opulent and educated—is distinguished by a high-mindedness, generosity, and hospitality. . . . He values money only for the enjoyments it can procure, is fond of gaiety, given to social pleasures, somewhat touchy and choleric, and as eager to avenge an insult as to show a kindness."[13]

After touring backcountry settlements in the South, James Buckingham reported: "In every farm-house you pass here, you see eight or ten lazy men and boys lounging idly in the veranda or piazza, in front of it, with their legs thrown up higher than their hips, their hats on, doing nothing, because the negro slaves can do the work; and what they do, though done badly, contents them. . . . The slave-system is, no doubt, one powerful cause of this general indolence and dirtiness of the whites, among the farmers and peasantry of the South."

Buckingham's comments about upper-class southerners were only slightly more favorable. After a visit to Virginia he noted that "all the males, except the very lowest, are brought up to the liberal professions, or to live upon the incomes of their plantations; and few enter into any kind of business by which their fortunes can be much improved. Habits of indolence, recklessness, and extravagance result from this."[14]

Tocqueville set forth a similar portrait: "In the southern states man's most pressing wants are always satisfied. Hence the southern American is not preoccupied with the material cares of life; someone else can look after that for him. Free on that score, his imagination turns to wider and less-defined objectives. The southerner loves greatness, luxury, renown, excitement, enjoyment, and, above all, idleness."[15]

Even in the eighteenth century, commentators had viewed northerners and southerners as different peoples. But by the middle of the nineteenth century, travelers sketched a landscape where the crevasse separating North and South had widened into a canyon. The North, in the language of the day, was filled with "go-ahead men." The South was populated with individuals who enjoyed their leisure and shunned the press of business.

These contemporary observations cannot stand on their own. Visitors to a region provide an impression, not a sustained analysis. We must examine the two societies more closely. A study of manufacturing confirms the comments of Trollope and others, and portrays a North committed to business and a South which lacked the spirit of enterprise.

Cotton Textiles: North and South

Measured by the value it added to the economy, the manufacture of cotton textiles was the leading industry in the United States before the Civil War. But while production skyrocketed in the North, it fizzled in the South. The cloth produced in a single Massachusetts county, Middlesex, was worth more than the output of all the mills in the southern states. Individual factories in the North were also larger and better capitalized. In 1860 the typical cotton mill in New Hampshire was worth over $280,000; the average factory in South Carolina, less than $50,000.[16]

A focus on the textile industry sheds light on the entrepreneurial spirit in the North and South. Our discussion begins with an examination of an alternative hypothesis: that economic self-interest, narrowly construed, explains these regional disparities. The next two sections look at the outlook and accomplishments of the industrialists, North and South. The final part shows that these regional differences were also evident in the views of employees. The underlying argument reinforces the larger themes of the book. This analysis contends that a passionate commitment to business accelerated factory building in the North, while a very different ethos braked development in the South.

The "Economic" Argument

All scholars agree that textile production in the North far outstripped the South. But historians disagree on the causes for this gap. Many studies—and this text—contend that markedly different ideologies explain the disparity.[17] But other works present an "economic" argument and suggest that rational, self-interested behavior accounts for the differences. The economic paradigm must be closely scrutinized. Its weaknesses suggest the need to explore the role played by deep-rooted values.

Historians affirming an "economic" paradigm assert that there was no fundamental difference between the outlook of northerners and southerners. Citizens in both regions were profit-maximizers with an eye on the main chance. The market simply gave entrepreneurs different signals in the North and South, and this led to distinct patterns of investment.

Scholars develop this line of reasoning in several ways. Stephen J. Goldfarb emphasizes the lack of adequate locations for southern cotton mills. "The South's early industrialization," Goldfarb remarks, "was impeded by its geography, which separated sites containing falling water, the most suitable motive power, by considerable distances from easy access to national markets."[18] Gavin Wright contends the labor market held back the South. Wright asserts: "In most times and places the South did not have 'cheap labor' much before 1875."[19] Other writers argue that slave agriculture was so profitable there was little encouragement to invest in industry. The "economic" historians affirm that this set of disincentives did not apply to the North. The northern states had abundant, well-situated mill sites; large numbers of potential workers; and few attractive alternatives for investment.[20]

However, these explanations have serious shortcomings. The contention that the North had better locations for mill sites is questionable. Virginia was closer to national markets than was Maine. But in 1860 that southern state had $1.4 million invested in textile factories; the northern state $6.0 million. Northern entrepreneurs and state governments sponsored internal improvements that tied otherwise remote centers into regional markets.[21] Nor did high labor costs slow the expansion of southern milling. Wright's own figures indicate that in 1850 the average annual wage paid in the cotton mills of six southern states was $99, while salaries in four New England states averaged $195. "Hidden" expenses, such as subsidized housing, were present in both regions. The price of slave labor soared in the 1850s, but by that

decade virtually all mills in the South had switched to white operatives. And southern entrepreneurs like William Gregg, who ran the
factory at Graniteville, South Carolina, found an ample supply of labor.
Gregg remarked in 1850: "From the day we commenced we have
never had the slightest difficulty in procuring hands who our overseers
(Eastern [i.e., New England] men) pronounce to be equal to any in
the Eastern States."[22]

The relative profitability of cotton planting also cannot explain the
slow growth of textile mills in the South. True, not all southern mills
provided solid returns. Some were small, poorly managed, inade-
quately capitalized, and short-lived. William Gregg criticized such enterprises in his *Essays on Domestic Manufacturing* but noted these problems were avoidable. Southern mills, Gregg and other writers
emphasized, had natural advantages over their northern competitors.
Raw cotton was cheaper in the South, because the mills were closer to
the fields. The cotton arrived at the factory cleaner. Labor costs were
lower. Southerners were able to buy the most up-to-date mill equipment from the North. "When we take all things into consideration,"
Gregg concluded, "it is really a matter of surprise, that we have not
long since made cotton manufacturing one of our leading occupations."[23]

Well-run mills reported higher rates of profit than were to be made
in cotton planting in the older states. Gregg's Graniteville factory, perhaps the largest cotton mill in the South, paid its first dividends soon
after operations began in 1848. By the mid-1850s the annual rate of
return was 10 percent. In these same years the Macon Factory in Georgia provided investors with earnings of over 30 percent on their capital. Fred Bateman and Thomas Weiss have studied southern industry
using manuscript censuses. Although their data for textile factories are
incomplete, the findings are suggestive. They conclude that the return
on cotton and woollen mills in the South was 8 percent in 1850 and
17 percent in 1860.[24]

Despite the high returns that could be gained in well-managed
mills, levels of investment in southern textiles remained low. The "economic" explanation will not stand; indeed, it should be set on its head.
We must ask why when rational calculation made investment in cotton milling attractive were so few factories built in the South? The
answer to this question demands a broad inquiry that looks at the
industrialists' ideology, achievements, and labor practices.

Ideology of Business in the North and South

Northerners lauded manufacturing and leaped at a chance to make
their fortunes from the new machines. Southerners had a different outlook. At most they accepted the presence of a few factories. But they

stood foursquare against a system of manufactures that might challenge the dominance of plantation society. And southerners rarely showed the keenness for money making so characteristic of northern entrepreneurs. These contrasting ideologies help explain the different paths traced by the textile industry in the North and South.

The northern states had few orators more skilled than Edward Everett. Tall, pale, handsome, Everett had a magic with words. His speeches helped propel his ascent from minister to Harvard professor, congressman, governor of Massachusetts, and Secretary of State. Everett would be chosen, along with Lincoln, to speak at Gettysburg. As congressman for Middlesex County, Everett was a natural choice to deliver the Fourth of July address at the great textile center of Lowell in 1830.[25]

Everett's remarks highlighted the patriotism, virtue, and harmony that (he was certain) characterized American manufacturing. Under British rule, Everett noted, the colonies had to "subserve the growth and wealth of the parent state." But the rise of manufacturing ended that subservience: "The establishment, therefore, of a prosperous manufacturing town like Lowell . . . may with propriety be considered as a peculiar triumph of our political independence." Moreover, New England industry had none of the "suffering, depravity, and brutalism" of European factories. "For physical comfort, moral conduct, general intelligence, and all the qualities of social character which make up an enlightened New England community," stated Everett, "Lowell might safely enter into a comparison with any town or city in the land." Everett closed his remarks with an apostrophe to the harmony between worker and employer. He told his listeners: "The alliance which you have thus established between labor and capital (which is nothing but labor saved) may truly be called a *holy alliance*."[26]

Everett's speech is representative of the hundreds of talks, tracts, and books celebrating northern industry.[27] To be sure, not everyone in the antebellum North agreed with these sentiments. Some urban workers denounced the "aggrandizement of an idle few," and trumpeted the conflict between labor and capital. However, these protesters were not like the English Luddites calling for a return to a preindustrial society. American workers accepted the factory system, if not the social relations it spawned.[28] A very few intellectuals, such as Henry David Thoreau, challenged the ascent of manufacturing. But, overwhelmingly, northerners welcomed the spread of industry.[29]

Entrepreneurs in the northern states also demonstrated a drive and acquisitiveness that had no counterpart in the South. Between 1817 (when Francis Cabot Lowell died) and the 1850s two families—the Appletons and Lawrences—led the New England textile industry. They were first among equals in the "Boston Associates," the tight-knit group of families that financed the mills at Waltham and Lowell. Nathaniel Appleton and Abbott and Amos Lawrence made their way to the top by dint of sheer energy and ability. These men left their middle-class farm families and came to Boston to seek their fortunes. Their rise was rapid. Nathaniel Appleton, who arrived in Boston in the 1790s with his worldly goods tied in a kerchief, was able by the 1820s to invest $180,000 in a Lowell company. The ascent of the Lawrences was equally breathtaking. By 1847 Abbott Lawrence was worth over two million dollars, and brother Amos was not far behind.[30]

What drove these men? Peer into their correspondence, read the commentaries of their families and friends, and you discover the obsessive, determined character that foreign observers so often remarked in the northern states. Accused of charging too much, Abbott Lawrence replied: "If you are troubled with the belief that I am growing *too rich*, there is one thing that you may as well understand; I know how to make money and *you* cannot prevent it." Nor did age slow Abbott. In 1842 Abbott's nephew described his uncle: "He still grasps at money tho' he has more than a million and is the richest man of his age here: he loves power too and office. He does not grow better nor happier as he grows older."[31]

The journals of Nathan Appleton's cousin, the successful merchant William Appleton, show the same drive—and lack of joy. "I am so much excited by business concerns that I have very little pleasure," he remarked in 1822. His outlook remained consistent. "I want no man's money," he noted in the 1830s, "but it gives me an unpleasant sensation to have others more successful than myself. These are feelings I am ashamed of and I endeavour to correct them." But there was no change in course. In the 1850s he remarked: "I attribute much of my anxiety the last few years to my business which has been profitable beyond the natural income." And even weeks before his death he was determined to succeed at one more venture, "to show the younger part of the Merchants that an old man of seventy-five has energy left."[32]

Southerners had a very different view of manufacturing and money making. Many showed an outright hostility to the establishment of factories. In the 1820s Thomas Cooper called industry "a dreadful curse," while two decades later another politician, Landon Cheves, observed that manufactures should be a "last resort." "They serve no interests," he remarked, "but those of the capitalists who set them in motion, and their immediate localities."[33] Editorialists thundered against factories during the debate over the tariff between 1828 and 1833. Reporting on a new cotton mill in Georgia, the Charleston *Mercury* remarked: "We depreciate the introduction of the manufacturing spirit in the South, as calculated to diminish our strength in relation to the tariff, if not to fix the odious system upon us."[34] Such criticism was reinvigorated in the 1850s as attacks against the North and northern manufacturing increased.[35]

Southern advocates of new enterprises went out of their way to reassure the planters that manufacturing would remain subordinate to agriculture. In 1849 James Hammond, a South Carolina leader, praised industrial development. But he quickly added that the landed class must retain the "preponderating" influence. "The thing is," noted Hammond, "to reconcile industry with free trade, slave labour, agricultural advancement & Southern tone."[36] William Gregg was a South Carolina mill owner and a tireless proselytizer for manufactures. But Gregg made clear his orthodoxy on the tariff ("we want no laws for the protection of those that embark in the manufacture of such cotton fabrics as we propose to make in South Carolina") and on agriculture: "Nor does it follow . . . that because we advance a system which will diversify the pursuits of our people . . . that we wish manufactures to predominate over other employments."[37] James Taylor, another southern manufacturer, emphasized that he and other like-minded individuals did not criticize the "established mode of thought or action."[38]

The drive and restless desire for gain that marked northern businesspeople was absent in the South. For many southerners, a trip north brought the contrast into sharp relief. John Linton, a Georgia manufacturer, visited Boston in the 1850s. "I am getting tired of this part of the World," he remarked, "and would rather be in Athens [Georgia] where everything is quiet, than to be in such a continued scene of noise and bustle as I have been in the last fifteen days. From all that I have seen of Massachusetts I have formed a more exalted opinion of the Puritan Blood, and the dogged determination and perserverance of its people than I have hitherto entertained."[39] William Gregg provided a similar commentary on the spirit of the two regions. He observed: "My recent visit to the Northern States has fully satisfied me that the true secret of our difficulties, lies in the want of energy on the part of our capitalists, and ignorance and laziness on the part of those who *ought* to labour."[40] His friend James Hammond agreed: "I am beginning to think our Southern people are, after all, a poor set of devils of narrow views and no spirit save such as may be exhibited in fisticuffs and duels. . . . If we cannot infuse more of the manufacturing and commercial spirit into them—more of *vim* in everything—they are gone."[41] The editor of the *Southern Cultivator* offered a similar explanation for the slow development of manufacturing. The problem, he remarked, "is a lack of energy in our Southerners."[42]

Finally, the distinction between the outlook of northerners and southerners is underscored by the forward role that individuals from the North played in bringing industry to the South. Like English-speakers in French Canada, northern men stood out in the South. The two leading industrialists in the Lower South—Daniel Pratt of Alabama and William Gregg of South Carolina—were not truly southerners. Pratt grew up in New Hampshire and moved south as a young man.[43] Gregg's mother was from Philadelphia, and his father from near Wilmington, Delaware. After the Revolutionary War his parents (both of them Quakers) settled with other Quakers on the Virginia frontier, where Gregg was born. Factories started by New Englanders dotted the southern backcountry. In 1816 and 1817 alone, Rhode Islanders opened up six small cotton mills in South Carolina. Batesville, South Carolina, which became a model for factory towns after the Civil War, was begun by New Englander William Bates. And some of the most outspoken advocates of southern industrialization, for example, General Charles T. James, who built several mills in the South, were northerners.[44]

In short, striking differences in ideology, more than short-term calculations, explain the paths followed by the textile industry in the North and South. But analysis cannot stop there. A full understanding of the industrialists (and their societies) must also include a close look at the achievements and frustrations of these textile lords.

The Worlds the Industrialists Created

In the North entrepreneurs erected not only mills, but an entire system that fostered industrial development. In the South planters, not manufacturers, dominated society. Industrialists had to make their peace with a society more inclined to erect barriers than smooth the path before them. The discussion below contrasts the world of manufacturers in Massachusetts and South Carolina.

Our account begins with the accomplishments of the Boston Associates, the leading group of factory owners in Massachusetts. The vision the Associates had of industrial society embraced textile mills, banks, railroads, and political office. The mills were the foundation of their empire. The success of Waltham and Lowell led to other million-dollar factories in towns such as Chicopee and Holyoke, Massachusetts; Manchester and Nashua, New Hampshire; and Biddeford and Saco, Maine. By 1850 the Associates controlled about one-fifth of the spindles in the country.[45] Their mills were technologically advanced, well managed, and highly profitable. The Associates carefully coordinated the activities of the various companies. Each mill or group of mills produced a different type of cloth, and managers cooperated in adjusting prices and wages. These same men controlled the agencies that bought the cotton and marketed the textiles. During their first twenty years the Waltham-Lowell mills were a remarkable success story, with annual dividends averaging over 11 percent. After the mid-1830s patents expired, competition increased, and profits dropped. Still, before the Civil War the factories run by the Boston Associates remained the most important group of textile factories in the country.[46]

The mill owners also created financial institutions to support the growth of their factories. The Suffolk Bank, chartered in 1818, was the linchpin of this system. Guided by Nathan Appleton, the Associates on the board of governors made it a central bank for New England. The Suffolk Bank agreed to accept the notes of country banks without discount—if those institutions deposited $5000 in its vaults. Two hundred banks, including all six major Boston repositories, accepted the offer. The result was sound currency for New England and, not incidentally, a million dollars in interest-free deposits for the Suffolk Bank.[47]

The Associates also founded a trust company, the Massachusetts Hospital Life Insurance Company. Despite its name, the new firm provided insurance only as a sideline. More significant, it allowed the Boston Associates to tap the wealth transferred from one generation to the next. John Lowell (Francis Cabot's brother) aptly described the enterprise: "It is *eminently* the *Savings bank of the wealthy.*" In the 1830s Massachusetts Hospital Life had more assets than the twenty-eight savings banks in the state combined. These funds were put at the disposal of the Waltham-Lowell mills. By the 1850s loans to the Associates totaled nearly four million dollars.[48]

The Associates helped construct railroads to link the factory towns with markets. During the 1830s mill owners and other capitalists financed four lines. These railroads originated in Boston and went to Lowell; Worcester; Providence, Rhode Island; and New Hampshire and Maine. Most of the funding came from private individuals, and the transportation provided was (for that era) splendid. The Boston and Lowell, for example, had iron rails on a granite roadbed and was double-tracked. In Boston the trains ran right to the docks.[49]

Finally, these entrepreneurs had a loud voice in state and national affairs. "This class is the controlling one in politics. . . ," grumbled reformer Theodore Parker. "It can manufacture governors, senators, judges to suit its purposes, as easily as it can manufacture cotton cloth."[50] Both Nathan Appleton and Abbott Lawrence served in Congress and were prominent in the Whig party. Indeed, John Quincy Adams called Lawrence "the most leading man of Whig politics in Boston."[51] President Zachary Taylor appointed Abbott Lawrence ambassador to Great Britain—a post that delighted the textile magnate. Edward Everett, Robert Winthrop, and Daniel Webster also spoke for the Boston Associates.[52]

In the South the picture was different. Industrialists stood at the periphery, not the center. The mills were smaller, and southerners rarely managed several companies as the Boston Associates did. Daniel Pratt's cluster of firms in Alabama—a group that included a cotton gin factory as well as cotton and woolen mills—stands out as an isolated example.[53]

The southern states had few financial institutions that measured up to those in the North. Charleston, South Carolina, had five commercial banks, but none championed a stable currency. "The banks," Gregg complained, "are interested . . . to drive out of circulation every hard dollar, and put in its place three of paper money." Gregg urged the state legislature to strengthen the banking system, but his suggestions were spurned. The commercial banks were reluctant to extend funds to industry. During a downturn in the 1850s Gregg had to use his own money to keep Graniteville running. "I could not get a dollar from any bank on the best mercantile paper," he noted.[54] Other facilities simply did not exist. South Carolina had no trust company to handle the fortunes of the wealthy. And while a savings bank was chartered in 1833, operations did not begin for a decade.[55]

South Carolina industrialists were also poorly served by the state railroads, which typically were built with public funds. In 1833 South Carolina completed a line from Charleston to Augusta, Georgia. But the roadbed was hastily laid, and relied on wooden rails with iron strips. The track, which held only the smallest locomotives, was constantly in need of repair. Lines built in subsequent decades were better, but were still below northern standards. And these railroads faced a grave burden: Charleston refused to allow trains in the city, so all exports had to be unloaded outside the town and carted to the docks.[56]

As for politics, the unwritten requirement for officeholding in the South was an acknowledgment of planter domination. Within that framework southern politicians accepted manufacturing and manufacturers. William Gregg and Daniel Pratt served in their state legislatures. No lawmaker offered a far-reaching critique of a society that placed so many obstacles—ideological, institutional, and economic—in the path to industrialization. During the war Pratt and Gregg backed the Confederacy, and expanded production.[57]

In short, manufacturers in the North and South adhered to contrasting views and fashioned very different worlds. Northern mill owners were determined to reshape institutions to serve industry better. By contrast, southern entrepreneurs accepted marginal status in a region given over to slavery and agriculture.[58]

The Labor Force

An examination of the work forces in northern and southern cotton mills also underscores the different outlooks of the regions. The operatives in the North breathed the same air of ambition and acquisitiveness as other citizens. By contrast, those who came to the southern mill towns held the older values of the household economy. We look at the labor force in the regions from two vantages: the motivation of the employees and the nature of their relations with the owners.

Why did individuals come to work in the Waltham-Lowell mills? Between the 1810s and late 1840s most employees in the factories were young, unmarried, native-born women from farm families. Thomas Dublin has studied their economic background and correspondence, and concludes that most of these women did *not* take jobs to support their families. They came to earn money for themselves. "I must of course have something of my own . . . ," a Lowell operative told her parents. "How can you blame me for wanting to stay here. I have but one life to live and I want to enjoy myself as well as I can while I live." "Others may find fault with me," another woman remarked, "and call me selfish, but I think I should spend my earnings as I please." On Saturdays the stores near the factories were crowded with mill workers who had taken up city fashions.[59]

These women reflected the Yankee ethic of acquisitiveness. Harriet Farley, editor of the *Lowell Offering*, a literary journal written by employees, explained to a critic the motivation of the mill "girls." A desire "to get money, as much of it and as fast as we can," she observed, has "drawn so many worthy, virtuous, intelligent, and well-educated girls to Lowell, and other factories." Farley added: "Strange would it be, if in money-loving New England, one of the most lucrative female employments should be rejected because it is toilsome, or because some people are prejudiced against it."[60]

Gradually, hours lengthened, the pace of work accelerated, and the mill workers began to protest against changes in the implicit contract between them and their employers. The first "turn out" or strike at Lowell came in 1834, and a more serious one occurred in 1836. During the 1840s thousands of workers supported the ten-hour movement, which demanded a shorter work day. Native-born women also expressed their dissatisfaction by leaving the mills. By 1850 half the operatives were Irish, who were willing to work longer hours for less. Only gradually would the new arrivals acquire the outlook and militancy of the Yankee women.[61]

Because the native-born operatives in the North were strongly motivated and relatively well educated, northern mill owners did not have to regulate their workers' lives to the same degree as entrepreneurs in the southern states. The Waltham-Lowell system, it is true, was paternalistic. The women had to live in boardinghouses, accept a curfew, and go to church on Sundays. But these rules gradually broke down, beginning in the 1840s, when mandatory church attendance ended, and accelerating in the 1850s, when most employees lived outside of company housing. And, significantly, northern factory owners exercised little control over the towns themselves. These centers had independent councils and often were home to union organizers and other critics. Moreover, the many northern plants not part of the Waltham-Lowell system did not build dormitories and exerted still less influence over their employees' lives. Jonathan Prude's analysis of factory life in central Massachusetts and Anthony Wallace's study of Rockdale, Pennsylvania, illustrate the ongoing tension between mill owners, on the one hand, and employees and communities, on the other.[62]

Southern mill workers had a different outlook and a different relationship with the factory owners. Initially, William Gregg hoped to employ young, single women at Graniteville. Copying the northern factories he had recently visited, Gregg built boardinghouses and hired matrons. "But this plan did not answer," noted James H. Taylor, another southern manufacturer. "Girls were unwilling to leave the home of their birth for strange places." The individualistic, acquisitive young women who supplied the labor for the factories of the Boston Associates had few counterparts in the South. Gregg, like most southern manufacturers, was forced to provide accommodations for whole families. Typically, the older children in each household worked in the mill.[63]

Gregg also created a mill town that was more tightly regulated than any in the North. His task was no less than transforming the preindustrial habits of the poor whites who arrived in Graniteville. James Montgomery, treasurer of the Graniteville Company, observed: "There are many who come to the factories who do not succeed—[who] do not like the work nor the regulations."[64] In Graniteville alcohol was prohibited and school attendance for children between six and twelve was compulsory. Gregg allowed no public dances and no "street sports or disorderly conduct" on Sundays. Gregg built his home near Graniteville and made sure his regulations were obeyed. Not every textile mill in the South, to be sure, operated in a company town. Some factories were in cities and some hired slaves or had a mix of slave and free operatives. But the trend was toward an all-white work force and a closely controlled environment. Mill towns like Graniteville and Batesville set the pattern that was copied and replicated after the Civil War.[65]

To summarize, while the North displayed the bright colors of the entrepreneurial spirit, the South was brushed by only the palest tones. Travelers noted the contrast; entrepreneurs spelled out different visions; and the work forces displayed distinct motives. These differences fostered the spread of commercial capitalism in the North and its slow growth in the southern states. French Canada, as the next chapter discusses, resembled the South and would lag in developing the industries that were the mark of the new era.

7

Entrepreneurial Spirit in French Canada

Petite-Nation was a poor seigneury located on the Ottawa River, mid-way between Ottawa and Montreal. Much of the land was given over to timber; only a third of the soil was suitable for farming. Louis-Joseph Papineau, the fiercely nationalist leader of the Patriote party, purchased the seigneury from his father in 1817. For Papineau, Petite-Nation was to be more than a source of revenue—it was to be an example of a French-Canadian path of rural development. Papineau wanted French Canadians, not English speakers, to oversee all activities in Petite-Nation. He disliked interference from the office of sheriff, which he condemned as a *"maudite invention anglais comme tant d'autres"* ("another damned innovation of the English"). He favored his younger brother, Denis-Benjamin, or at least another French Canadian as the principal merchant for the farmers. And Papineau did not want Americans or the British taking up his land. "Foreign squatters," he commented, are "infinitely less satisfactory than our Canadians."

But Petite-Nation followed a course of development far different from the one Papineau envisioned. The sheriff stayed, pocketing commissions Louis-Joseph felt were rightfully his. Easygoing Denis-Benjamin was displaced as chief merchant by a hard-driving New Englander, Stephen Tucker. Tucker was a Baptist and (noted Denis-Benjamin) "so filled with the missionary spirit that he has promised up to $40.00 to any of our poor Canadians who will agree to join his sect." Tucker became, next to Louis-Joseph, the chief creditor in Petite-

Nation. The local lumber industry and the few large, commercial farms all fell into the hands of English speakers—who comprised less than a fifth of the population of Petite-Nation. In short, virtually all the entrepreneurs in this corner of Lower Canada were English-speaking.[1]

Like southerners, French Canadians lacked a passion for business. Earlier chapters have discussed how Catholicism, the seigneurial system, and low levels of mobility and literacy helped form this mind-set. This chapter looks at business activity in French Canada before 1860 and adds to the discussion another crucial dimension: the role of the English. Some historians argue that the Conquest of 1760 and the high-handed behavior of the British are the key to understanding why nineteenth-century French Canadians stood on the margins of commercial life in their own province. "After 1760, and not before," observes Maurice Séguin, "it was more accurate to say of the *Canadien:* first and foremost, a farming man." Other scholars disagree.[2] The sections that follow point to longstanding traditions and not the Conquest as the cause of the subordinate role played by French Canadians. The story begins with the French era.

The Weakness of the Merchants of Early Canada

The flame of entrepreneurial spirit burned like a bonfire in the North. But in early Canada this light only flickered. Although the St. Lawrence colony could claim a group of local merchants, these individuals played a decidedly secondary role in the economy and provincial society. The nobility and the officials of the Church were clearly superior in wealth and prestige, and they looked down on those who derived their income from the exchange of goods. The merchants of Canada bore still another burden: French firms and their representatives in Quebec controlled much of the commerce of the colony.

Only a few well-to-do traders resided in Canada, and these individuals had not risen through their initiative in private business ventures. The few success stories were those persons who served a group of French merchants, gained a monopoly from the crown, or enjoyed grants from the royal treasury. Charles Aubert de la Chesnaye, who was probably the wealthiest trader in seventeenth-century Canada, pursued all of these roads to wealth. We can see him—from the inventory made of his belongings—modestly dressed in red flannel trousers, a lace-trimmed shirt, a jacket made of serge, and an old beaver hat. He came to the St. Lawrence colony in 1655 as the representative of a group of Rouen exporters. With this backing he secured the fur monopoly in the Tadoussac region north of Quebec. When the West India Company took over the commerce of New France in 1664 La Chesnaye became its agent. He purchased several seigneuries and was involved in lumbering, fishing, and agriculture, as well as the fur trade.

In 1693 Louis XIV granted him letters of nobility. Significantly, La Chesnaye's greatest failure was his attempt to bring together the Canadian business community in the Company of the Colony. His object was nothing less than control of the fur trade. But local resources were far too weak for this undertaking, and La Chesnaye lost his fortune. His last request was for a simple funeral and burial in a pauper's grave.[3]

Similarly, Pierre Trottier Desauniers, one of the most successful merchants in eighteenth-century New France, made his fortune through patronage and privilege. He was born at the turn of the century in Montreal to a well-connected family. His uncle was a seigneur and trader. By the 1730s Desauniers was a successful importer, holding his own in an area dominated by French houses and their representatives. But it was a partnership with his cousin, François Martel de Brouàgue, that dramatically expanded Desauniers's activities. Martel de Brouague was appointed commandant of the Labrador coast and given a monopoly of local trade. The two men eagerly exploited this privilege, and developed the Labrador fishery, with Desauniers building the vessels to serve this trade. In 1745 Desauniers received another rich plum—the contract to fortify Quebec—and was given an advance of 60,000 livres for this work. Two years later, his fortune made, Desauniers left Canada for France, and became a merchant in Bordeaux.[4]

La Chesnaye and Desauniers were unusual traders. But their stories illustrate the way to mercantile wealth in New France. It lay through preference, royal favors, and monopolies, not through private trading and a careful reading of markets as was true in the ports of the northern Thirteen Colonies.[5] Most Canadian businesspeople were many removes from La Chesnaye and Desauniers. The majority were the small traders of Montreal, who outfitted a few canoes and voyageurs for the trip west. Or they were the storekeepers of Quebec, resentful that the merchants of France not only dominated the importation of goods but also pushed into the retail trade. Only those few who stood within the favored circle of monopolists and rich families could hope to live well. And even these individuals were viewed as lesser creatures when compared with the nobility.[6]

The activities of local traders were disrupted by the phenomenal growth in government spending for war during the 1740s and 1750s. Private initiative, which had always been weak in New France, was overwhelmed by government activity. In the 1730s a group of merchants established the St. Maurice Forges, which produced bar iron, stoves, and implements for the local market and for export. Private funds and extensive government loans kept the enterprise afloat. But in 1741 the merchant group declared bankruptcy, and the government took over the ironworks. A similar fate overtook private shipbuilding.

Several dozen ships had come off the stocks in the 1730s. But after 1743 all construction was in the royal yards.[7]

The administration of François Bigot dealt another punishing blow to local entrepreneurs. These years were at once a further distortion of the Canadian economy and the culmination of a century of development in which the Crown was the prime mover. Bigot, who served as intendant from 1748 to 1760, was a vigorous, red-haired little man with a bad complexion. He loved his parties and was an avid gambler. He was also determined to enrich himself and his friends, and cared little for local traders. Bigot helped form a company, called the Grande Société, to provision the army. He took over the fur trade, ending the auctions that sold pelts to the highest bidders. He appointed his friends to the posts in the West, and told them to make the most of their opportunities. "Profit, my dear Vergor," he told a crony, "by your place; trim; lop off; all power is in your hands; do it quickly so that you may be able to come and join me in France and buy an estate near mine." After the fall of New France, Bigot was prosecuted and ordered to repay a million and a half livres.[8] But the big losers, as the wartime economy expanded, were the local merchants. Never a strong force, they were pushed to the periphery as government spending increased.[9]

A Military and Economic Conquest, 1760–1810

The French-Canadian merchant class—weak before 1760—was reduced to inconsequence by the English regime. Just why and how this happened demands close scrutiny. One argument is that the chill winds of the English Conquest killed the buds of the French-Canadian entrepreneurial spirit. But an examination of the half-century after 1760 tells a different tale.

The English Conquest *was* a serious setback for the Canadian merchant class. New competitors rushed into the province. In Montreal alone fifty new traders, most from England and Scotland, set up shop by 1765, and many others went to Quebec. French-Canadian traders also lost one of their most valuable privileges: the right to supply the western posts. The officers who now commanded these forts trusted English-speaking traders more than the Canadians. The British navigation acts severed connections between the New World French and their traditional suppliers in La Rochelle and Bordeaux. In addition, many French Canadians were hit hard by the decision of the French government to repudiate the paper money and bills of exchange issued to finance the war.

The tumultuous changes brought on by the Conquest certainly explain how a new English-speaking group of merchants quickly achieved prominence in French Canada. What they do not account for is the virtual disappearance—by 1790—of French traders in all but the most minor roles. To understand the reasons for the precipitous decline of this trading class, we must examine reasons that do and do not explain these events.

We begin with two explanations that do *not* account for the fall of the French-speaking business class.

1. *The British discriminated against the French Canadians socially, economically, and politically, and thus virtually excluded them from the business world.* Not so. In no area did the English firmly block the aspirations of the French. Socially, there was much mixing. "By all I can find," noted an English observer in 1766, "the English and French agree together tolerably well and speak well of each other: but there are great animosities between the English themselves one with another."[10] Many of the prominent English-speaking merchants—including James McGill, Joseph Frobisher, and Simon McTavish—married French-Canadian women. Wealthy traders from both groups mixed in the Beaver Club of Montreal.

Nor was there outright discrimination in the economic sphere. While the Conquest and imposition of the British navigation acts severed ties with France, credits were soon transferred to London. British merchants were eager to ship goods and extend funds, and particularly active among the London houses supplying the French Canadians were such Huguenot firms as Joseph & Henry Guinaud and Daniel Vialars. During the first decades after the Conquest, French-Canadian traders frequently entered into cooperative ventures with English-speaking merchants.[11]

The career of Jacques Baby, known as Dupéront, suggests that the Conquest hardly meant the end of opportunities for French-Canadian traders. Dupéront was an Indian trader in the Ohio Valley during the 1750s, and he fought with France's native allies against the British. His letters show him to be a straightforward individual, with considerable passion, and a readiness to denounce those who crossed him. After the Conquest he refused to swear loyalty to the English and considered returning to France to join his brother François. François had been taken to England as a prisoner-of-war, and then released. But Dupéront soon changed his mind about leaving Canada. François transferred the family business to London, while Dupéront found that the load of furs he had brought back with him from the West sold well in Montreal. Dupéront accepted the new regime, and during Pontiac's Rebellion in the early 1760s, he solidified his position by bringing supplies to the besieged British garrison at Detroit. Dupéront lost money because France repudiated the paper currency issued during the war. But still he prospered, and remained active in the fur trade until his death in 1789. When his estate was inventoried in 1800 it was worth about

£24,570, most of it invested with Alexander Ellice of London. His brother François (who lived on until 1820) became a seigneur and a member of the Legislative Council.[12]

Politically, French Canadians and their culture were given a privileged position in the new regime. The British could not afford to alienate the French population. In 1780 only a small percentage of Canadians were English-speaking. Trouble in the Thirteen Colonies made Britain all the more aware of the need to soothe French-Canadian sensibilities. Sir Guy Carlton, who served as governor of the province from 1768 to 1778, viewed the seigneurial class as the mainstay of his regime. The Quebec Act of 1774 affirmed the Catholic religion and the feudal land tenure of New France. And if most of the British posts were supplied by English-speaking merchants, the right to trade with the native peoples of the West was a more lucrative privilege—and was open to all.[13]

2. *The French-Canadian merchant class was overwhelmed by a group of wealthy traders arriving from Great Britain.* This too is a questionable generalization. Many of the English-speaking traders who rose to prominence in the Canadian economy arrived with little capital. The Frobishers—Joseph, Benjamin, and Thomas—disembarked in the 1760s with more ambition than funds. Simon McTavish came from a poor Highland family, and was penniless when he arrived in New York in 1763. After finding work with a merchant there he entered the fur trade, and by 1772 he was active at Detroit. Peter Pond—who hailed from Milford, Connecticut—was by turns a shoemaker, soldier, and sailor before he became a fur trader in the Canadian West. Charles Grant, a Quebec merchant who studied the fur trade, reported to the governor in 1780: "The Upper Country trade is chiefly carried on by men of low circumstances, destitute of every means to pay their debts when their trade fails."[14]

To be sure, some of the English and Scottish merchants who established themselves in the St. Lawrence Valley had ample funds or were agents of British houses. This was particularly true for those traders who focused on the import trade and rarely traveled into the continent's western reaches. William Grant and George Allsopp arrived in the 1760s as representatives of British firms. James Dunlop was a Scot who moved north from Virginia in 1774 when the patriots restricted the activities of merchants. But many English-speaking traders, like Robert Ellice, who came to enjoy wealth and valuable London connections, started with only modest capital.[15]

Other reasons better explain why the French traders—after their initial successes in the first decades after 1760—played only minor roles in the business community.

1. *The French traders were more reluctant than the English to join together in large-scale business ventures.* By the 1770s changes in the fur

trade pointed to the need for new forms of organization. Merchants had begun to deal with the native peoples in the Northwest, more than a thousand miles from the Great Lakes. The expenses and risks of such expeditions argued for a pooling of resources, as did the bitter competition that reduced the earnings of all the St. Lawrence outfitters. Moreover, as traders ranged further north and west, rivalry with the Hudson's Bay Company grew more intense. While the Montreal merchants had closer ties with many of the native peoples, the company had the advantage of unified direction and an all-water route to the interior.[16]

It was the English merchants, and not the French, who responded to these challenges and developed the new, larger enterprises. The decline of the French fur traders came not in the 1760s with the Conquest but in the 1780s with the emergence of the North West Company. The Frobishers and Simon McTavish were the organizational geniuses who created the new company. Consolidation had begun in the mid-1770s with the formation of loose compacts, or "pools," joining the leading merchants. In 1783 these arrangements were solidified by a formal agreement among eight firms—including the Frobishers and McTavish, but only one French Canadian, Nicholas Montour. Benjamin and Joseph Frobisher explained to the governor the reasons for the creation of the North West Company. "Taught . . . by experience that separate interests were the bane of the trade," they observed in 1784, "we lost no time to form with [various] gentlemen and some others, a company."

Through a series of reorganizations, the North West Company battled and then incorporated several groups of traders, and in each case, English-speaking individuals were the leaders. The stiffest challenge came in the 1790s, when a rival set of merchants formed the New North West Company (also called the XY Company). The two firms amalgamated in 1804 in an enlarged North West Company, with a hundred shares distributed among forty-eight different traders. Significantly, only two of the forty-eight individuals involved were French-Canadian. French speakers remained active in the trade. They were the *voyageurs* who trekked through the bitter cold and paddled the canoes. They served as clerks at individual posts. But no longer were they the owners or managers of this commerce.[17]

Simon McTavish, who directed the company from 1787 until his death in 1804, labored to build a dynamic and efficient organization. McTavish was a tall, slender, handsome man, who pronounced himself fond of "good Wine, good Oysters, & pretty Girls," and stated that he was "always like a fish out of water when not in Love."[18] McTavish had a vision of a company whose reach extended beyond British North America, and in the early 1790s he founded his own London house: McTavish, Fraser and Company. Under his guidance, the company also established an office in New York and built vessels for the China trade.

Ultimately, the North West Company would be defeated by geography and by the one organization it could neither buy nor outtrade: the Hudson's Bay Company. As the supply of beaver dwindled, lines of transportation helped decide a contest that had been waged for over a century between the St. Lawrence system and the Bay. In 1821 the Hudson's Bay Company took over the North West Company.[19] Although the battle between these two rival enterprises continued into the nineteenth century, the economic conflict between French and English traders had been decided many decades earlier.

2. *The English merchants were more innovative in the fur trade, and were more open to new, commercial activities than the French.* The differences in outlook between the two groups were evident in several areas. In the fur trade the great push into the North West was led by the English-speaking traders. French outfitters were active in the posts near the Great Lakes, but it was an Englishman, Thomas Frobisher, who in 1777 showed the value of exchanges on the edge of the great Athabasca watershed. It was a Connecticut Yankee, Peter Pond, who pushed still further north and west. Pond combined a passion for mapmaking and self-promotion with the skill of a consummate fur trader. He wintered on the Athabasca River and in 1779 emerged from the bush with 80,000 beaver pelts. And it was a Scot, Alexander Mackenzie, who explored the north as far as the Arctic Ocean. On these expeditions many of the strong backs belonged to the "pork eaters," the French-Canadian *voyageurs*. But the leadership was English-speaking.

French-Canadian merchants also were slower to shift from canoes to the larger, more efficient, flat-bottomed *bateaux*. According to a study by Fernand Ouellet, 75 percent of a group of English traders made the switch to *bateaux*, compared with 28 percent of a comparable set of French Canadians. Henry Hamilton, the governor at Detroit, remarked in 1776: "The industry and enterprising spirit of the [anglophone] traders of this post so far outgo the [French] Canadians, that I am persuaded the latter will in a very few years be dependent or bought out of their possessions by the former. The navigating the Lakes in large vessels is entirely in the hand of the new settlers."[20]

English-speaking traders were quicker to see the possibilities in the exportation of grain from French Canada. The era of Lower Canada as a noteworthy wheat shipper was short-lived, stretching from the 1780s to perhaps 1810. Anglophone merchants made the most of this export boom. Men such as Simon McTavish and William Grant invested in seigneuries and built large, commercial mills. In 1788 eight of the nine mill owners who ground 10,000 or more *minots* of wheat were English-speaking. More broadly, members of the anglophone bourgeoisie outpaced other groups in acquiring seigneuries during the first half-century after 1760. The portion held by the francophone middle class declined, reflecting that group's weakening economic position (Fig. 3.1).[21]

Similarly, anglophones dominated the lumber trade which climbed in importance in the 1790s. When the wars with France disrupted shipments from northern Europe, Britain turned to Canada for its supplies. By 1810 three-fourths of the exports by value from the port of Quebec were timber. English-speaking merchants controlled this commerce. For example, James McGill (who would leave part of his vast fortune to establish a college in Montreal) gradually moved out of dealings in peltries and redirected his energies toward the export of wood—and other activities. French Canadians undertook much of the hard work in the lumber trade, as they did in the fur trade, but were little involved in the direction of this commerce.[22]

What happened to French-Canadian merchants during these years? Like old soldiers, they quietly faded away. Individuals abandoned trade, or found that when they retired their children had no desire to continue the family business. Pierre-Joseph Gamelin, for example, came from a proud Montreal trading family: during the eighteenth century no fewer than ten Gamelins had been involved in commerce. But Pierre-Joseph, who remained an active, prosperous trader until his death in the 1790s, was the last of the line. His son had no interest in buying and selling wares. François Baby, mentioned above, was in 1769 the third largest investor in the fur trade. But by the 1790s he had given up commerce and had turned his energies to politics, his seigneury, and money lending. Pierre Guy, another prominent Quebec importer in the 1760s and 1770s, abandoned trading and pursued farming. One by one French Canadians withdrew from the commercial fray and left the field to English-speaking merchants.[23]

3. *None of the French-Canadian merchants had the sort of wealth that might have placed them at the top of the business community.* A class of rich French merchants might have continued to flourish into the nineteenth century, despite the organizational flare of the English and despite the willingness of the English to embark on new enterprises. But the French-Canadian traders could claim only the most meager capital base. The individuals who had profited most from wartime spending had returned to France—some to face prosecution. Those remaining in Canada frankly admitted their weakness. A petition sent by the citizens of Montreal to London in 1763 paraded a series of complaints: "The scourges of war and famine, long before the surrender of Canada, afflicted its unfortunate inhabitants. . . . Companies, as avaricious as they were powerful, were formed. . . . The merchants of Canada were helpless onlookers at business which should have been theirs."[24]

Many of the English-speaking merchants who entered the fur trade arrived with little capital and few connections. Even so, they soon matched and surpassed the investments of the French Canadians. In 1767 fifteen merchants outfitted canoes at Michilimackinac for the Northwest. Nine of these individuals were British, including such familiar names as Benjamin Frobisher and James McGill, while six out-fitters were French. The average value of the goods in the British canoes was £416, while the worth of goods in the Canadian canoes was only £278. Financial weakness compounded the other problems that the Canadians faced in the years after 1760.[25]

English Domination, 1810–60

English domination of entrepreneurial activities continued in the nineteenth century. Consider Horatio Gates—one of the richest and most successful merchants of Lower Canada. Born in western Massachusetts just after American Independence, Gates had moved to Montreal by 1807. During the War of 1812 he smuggled foodstuffs from Vermont and New York to the British forces. Desperate for provisions, the British commissariat arranged the sentries' schedule so Gates could bring his supplies through. After the war Gates moved through a series of partnerships, steadily expanding his activities. He imported goods from the United States and Britain, helped found the Bank of Montreal in 1817, and was active in shipping, railroad promotion, and real estate speculation. When Gates died in 1834 Montreal showed that it knew how to honor one of its leading citizens. The merchant community turned out en masse, ships in the harbor fired their cannons at one-minute intervals during the funeral service, and stores throughout the city closed. *Le Canadien* reported that "his death seemed to have cast a veil of mourning over the whole of the city which was losing him."[26]

Gates and the individuals he worked with, such as John Molson and Peter McGill, typified the group that directed the economic life of Lower Canada. They were English-speaking and were often involved in activities that reached beyond provincial boundaries. Successful French-Canadian entrepreneurs were few in number, and in most instances concerned only with the local scene. Only one of the commission merchants—those individuals who imported wares from Britain—listed in the 1845 and 1852 Montreal city directories was French-Canadian. Only one of the city's eight breweries was owned by a French firm. When industrialization began in the 1840s along the Lachine Canal near Montreal, only one of the more than 30 manufacturers was French-Canadian. English-speaking Canadians predominated in the list of those investing in the Bank of Montreal and railroads. The balance was different only in smaller-scale enterprises: 18 of 32 dry goods retailers in Montreal in the late 1840s were French-Canadian.[27]

English dominance of commercial activities was evident not only in the cities but also in the seigneuries. The Petite-Nation story, which opens this chapter, illustrates the remarkable strength of anglophone entrepreneurs—even on those estates where the lord was an outspoken French-Canadian nationalist.

The French-Canadian exceptions to these rules are worthy of scrutiny. Joseph Masson was the most successful French-Canadian merchant of his generation. He apprenticed in the shop of a Scottish retailer, Duncan McGillis of Saint Benoit, and then moved to Montreal where he met and impressed another Scot, the merchant Hugh Robertson. In May 1812 Robertson wrote his brother in Glasgow that he had just hired "a very canny lad who is going to work for me as a crier." By 1815 Masson, quite remarkably, had risen to partnership in the company. During the first half of the century, Masson was virtually the only French Canadian to ascend to such heights. But much of his business focused on local markets. Masson sold chiefly to French-Canadian traders in the Richelieu Valley and in the villages along the south shore of the St. Lawrence. He refused to support the Great Concern, a short-lived French-Canadian enterprise designed to wrest trade from the English-speaking merchants. It was founded by a group of French-Canadian traders in 1832 and, lacking adequate financing, collapsed in the Depression of 1837. Masson, however, thrived and in the 1830s purchased the seigneury of Terrebonne for £25,150.[28]

Etienne Parent also distanced himself from the cautious mind-set of many French Canadians. Parent was a respected journalist who urged his compatriots to enter business. A speech he gave in 1846 was entitled "Industry as a Means of Survival for the French-Canadian Nationality." But his remarks were a frank admission that most francophones shunned such activities. "Nowadays, in our country, thank heavens we no longer aspire to nobility," Parent observed. "But we yearn for membership in the professions: once again, a love of sedentary occupations. We may as well confess that we despise industry."[29]

More generally, during the first half of the century French-Canadian entrepreneurs were few in number, poorly funded, and more oriented to the local market than were English merchants. A shipping company, La Société des Navigations du Richelieu, competed vigorously for business within Lower Canada—but did not extend its sights beyond the province. French Canadians founded a bank, La Banque du Peuple, in 1835—but it was capitalized at far less than the Bank of Montreal. Not until the late twentieth century would French Canadians become preeminent in the business life of their own province.[30]

In sum, only in the northern states was the majority of the population imbued with a passion for making money during the first half of the nineteenth century. The spirit of enterprise was far less evident in the South and French Canada. These different outlooks help explain why the North was wealthier at midcentury, and why the gap would widen during the era of industrialization.

8

Intellectual Life

The day started off poorly. The small Wesleyan chapel in the upstate New York town of Seneca Falls was locked, and Elizabeth Cady Stanton had to send her nephew scampering through a window to open the doors from the inside. But the rest of the meeting went splendidly. Some of the individuals who had helped organize this first women's rights convention feared it would be poorly attended. But they needn't have worried. Even though announcements were issued only a few days before the July 1848 meeting, 300 people, mostly women, attended.

The gathering at Seneca Falls focused on improving the condition of women. But the convention was also representative of the broad waves of reform that rolled across the North in the 1830s, '40s, and '50s. Many of the delegates had taken part in other campaigns for perfecting humanity. Stanton and Lucretia Mott—the leaders at Seneca Falls—had first met as delegates to an antislavery gathering. Even the language of the Seneca Falls declaration, which affirmed a belief in the God-given potential of individuals, was familiar to northern reformers. "It is time," the meeting resolved, that "she ["woman"] should move in the enlarged sphere which her great Creator has assigned her. . . . Being invested by the Creator with the same capabilities, and the same consciousness of responsibility for their exercise, it is demonstrably the right and duty of woman, equally with man, to promote every righteous cause by every righteous means."[1] This expansive view of social change and belief in the divine nature of women and men fully suited the bustling, successful society of the North, with its rapidly rising standard of living. In the South and French Canada there was no counterpart to these reform movements or to the extraordinarily optimistic view of humanity held by many northerners.

This chapter looks at the life of the mind in the three regions. It also touches on some of the debates among historians over the course of intellectual development. At first glance, the role of ideas would seem to differ from the topics examined in the preceding chapters. Concerns such as landholding, religion, labor systems, and literacy clearly helped shape the behavior and values of people in the North, South, and French Canada. By contrast, the evolution of intellectual life appears to be more of a reflection of the different paths of growth than a cause. The dramatic changes in the outlook of leading thinkers in the three regions between 1750 and the 1850s might suggest that patterns of thought simply shifted with the times.

And yet the difference between intellectual life and the other concerns discussed here is more apparent than real. There were changes in labor systems and literacy. And while ideas evolved, they also coalesced in each region by the mid-nineteenth century. The outlooks that emerged during the formative period, 1750 to 1850, influenced behavior during the next hundred years. In Quebec a conservative, strongly Catholic world view guided the career decisions of generations of French Canadians. The brash, optimistic approach that emerged in the North and the hierarchical doctrines that appeared in the South had a similar importance for individuals in those areas. In short, these ideas were more than a mirror of the times. They shaped activities in each region and had an impact that continued well into the twentieth century.[2]

Northern Thought: The Perfectibility of Humans

Northern writers moved toward ever more stirring affirmations of human potential during the hundred years between the 1750s and 1850s, in sharp contrast to southern and French-Canadian thinkers, who increasingly emphasized obedience, ritual, and hierarchy. Rapid economic growth and a rising standard of living in the North helped create an optimism that by the middle of the nineteenth century seemed almost boundless.

Any understanding of the evolution of thought in the North must begin with an analysis of the strengths and shortcomings of northern writers and scientists during the Age of Enlightenment. Individuals such as Benjamin Franklin, John Bartram, and James Bowdoin epitomized the curiosity and faith in reason that were the hallmarks of the era. They displayed a remarkable confidence in the power of systematic inquiry to unlock the secrets of nature, and they undertook original investigations in fields such as botany, electricity, and astronomy. Like their counterparts in the southern states and Canada, they were part of a transatlantic "Republic of Letters."[3]

But the Age of Reason had limitations that provide a context for the evolution of ideology in the North. Franklin is a case in point. The virtues the printer espoused reflected the limited horizons of a slowly growing society. Industry and frugality are a way to wealth only for the very patient. And the other values he taught in his *Autobiography* suggest a world where self-discipline was more praised than exuberance. Franklin's moral catalogue elevated order ("Let all your things have their places"), moderation ("Avoid extremes"), tranquillity ("Be not disturbed at trifles"), and chastity ("Rarely use venery but for health or offspring"). The rapture of the senses, the delight in the natural world, the aura of boundless possibility that are found in nineteenth-century writers are missing from Franklin.[4]

John Adams's views are still less promising, if one measures progress toward a celebration of human worth. His great work, *Defense of the Constitutions of Government of the United States of America* (1787), has been called "the finest fruit of the American Enlightenment."[5] But one senses in his writings the dark, Calvinist view of humanity that shaped the thought of so many New Englanders. Adams was an intense, ambitious, introspective individual. After graduating from Harvard in 1755, he debated between becoming a Congregational minister and a lawyer. He chose law, but his outlook was unmistakably stamped by Puritanism. The Congregational (or Puritan) Church has its roots in Calvinism, with its emphasis on original sin and the depravity of human nature. Adams's early diary entries record the hellfire and brimstone preaching of the local minister ("You who are sinners, are in continual Danger of being swallowed up quick and born away by the mighty Torrent of God's wrath and Justice"). They also record Adams's cynical view of people: "No man is intirely free from weakness and imperfection in this life. . . . The greatest men have been the most envious, malicious, and revengeful."[6]

The same somber view of human nature is evident in Adams's political writings. In *Thoughts on Government* (1776) Adams argues for checks and balances in government to restrain the self-interest of people in any one branch. For the same reason, he insists that office holders be elected annually: "This will teach them the great political virtues of humility, patience, and moderation, without which every man in power becomes a ravenous beast of prey." Adams's lengthy tract, *Defense of the Constitutions,* is based on similar premises. "In the institution of government," he observes, "it must be remembered that, although reason ought always to govern individuals, it certainly never did since the Fall [of Man], and never will till the Millennium."[7] Just as the northern economy did not establish its superiority over the southern or French-Canadian economy before 1800, so northern intellectual life during these years was hardly more buoyant, progressive, or optimistic than its counterparts in the other two regions. Thomas Jefferson's view of humanity and his vision of American development outshone Adams's.

After 1800 the mounting wealth and bustle of the North helped introduce a more optimistic note into the intellectual life of the region. The writings of various individuals—including novelist Hugh Henry Brackenridge and dictionary-maker Noah Webster—reflect the economic quickening around the turn of the century.[8] But few figures epitomize the widening horizons of the early nineteenth century more than Washington Irving. Irving's tales, as various scholars have noted, accept the new, hard-driving money-making society, while dwelling sentimentally on an older, more peaceful society. In "Rip Van Winkle" the hero falls asleep before American Independence in a village marked by "drowsy tranquility." He awakens several decades later and finds a more dynamic world: "The very village was altered; it was larger and more populous. . . . The very character of the people seemed changed. There was a busy, bustling, disputatious tone about it." Rip Van Winkle (and Washington Irving) look at this new society and approve of what they see.[9]

Writers like Brackenridge, Webster, and Irving marked only the beginning of change. The great transformation of northern intellectual life came in the half-century after 1800. During these years a belief in human perfectibility replaced the more cautious doctrines of the Enlightenment, and a remarkable array of reform movements sought to remake society. Moreover, while Irving was a New Yorker and Brackenridge grew up in Pennsylvania, the strongest support for reform came from New England and from the areas of New England settlement. The raw materials for an artistic renaissance and for reform were present in the Puritan tradition. They were evident in the high value accorded learning, and in the traditional concern for each individual's salvation. However, before 1800 this sea of intellectual fervor was firmly contained by the dikes of Calvinism. Prominent divines and backwoods preachers had chipped away at these walls during the eighteenth century. But for much of the populace old-line Calvinism held sway in 1800.[10]

Historians have set forth several interpretations to explain the flowering of reform and intellectual activity in the North during the first half of the nineteenth century. Many writers emphasize the impact of the evangelical beliefs that dissolved the gloomy doctrines of Calvinism. Gilbert Barnes in *The Anti-slavery Impulse, 1830–1844* (1933) was among the first to make the link between religious change and the era of reform, and literally hundreds of scholars have followed suit. "The transformation of American theology in the first quarter of the nine-teenth century," John L. Thomas observes, "released the very forces of romantic perfectionism that conservatives feared." Bertram Wyatt-Brown notes that "the abolitionist movement was primarily religious in its origins, its leadership, its language, and its methods of reaching the people."[11]

There is no denying this argument, and indeed the weakening of Calvinism and the rise of new, perfectionist beliefs must be central to any discussion of northern thought in this era. Nonetheless, this explanation is hardly sufficient in itself. For it raises another difficult question: why did this new theology, with its increasingly optimistic view of humans, emerge in the North? There was no true parallel for this change in either the South or French Canada.

A second interpretation focuses on the importance of economic growth, and highlights the positive cast this expansion gave to the out-look of North Americans, and particularly those in the northern states. Russel Nye observes: "There were good reasons, American thinkers of the opening decades of the nineteenth century assumed, for believing that the rate of man's advancement could be spectacularly accelerated. They saw evidence, as they looked around them, that this was exactly what was happening. Conditions of life had improved visibly over the preceding century. . . ." This analysis is worth underscoring because it helps explain the differences between intellectual developments in the North and the other two regions. The northern states stood out because of their rapid pace of development. And they distinguished themselves by a pattern of growth—characterized by prosperous farms and small businesses—that provided the majority of the population with strong reasons for adopting a buoyant view of the future. The South and French Canada had social structures that undercut the links between regional development and individual prospects. Hence while a belief in progress was present in all three regions, only in the North did this credo become the dominant ideology.[12]

A third explanation of reform contends that the various campaigns were a response to a fear of social disorder. The founding of prisons and asylums during the Jacksonian era, David Rothman writes, was "an effort to insure the cohesion of the community in new and chang-ing circumstances." Other historians link "social control" to the evan-gelical movement. Paul Johnson in his discussion of revivals in Roch-ester, New York, asserts: "Evangelicalism was a middle-class solution to problems of class, legitimacy, and order generated in the early stages of manufacturing." Undoubtedly, religion and new institutions helped strengthen the bonds of society. But an emphasis on disorder and its consequences does not explain the new optimistic approach to society in the North. There was turmoil in both the southern states and Lower Canada; indeed, the two areas experienced armed rebellions in the

1830s. But neither followed in the perfectionist footsteps of the northern states.[13]

A fourth approach relates the crusades of this era to the upbringing and personal problems of the reformers. James Brewer asserts that antislavery leaders "commonly paid homage to strong-minded mothers or fathers whose intense religious fervor dominated their households." David Donald calls the abolitionists "an elite without function" and contends they attacked slavery to regain the status in the community denied to them by industrialists and others. This personal approach, often found in biographical studies and usually linked to the impact of the evangelical movement, can provide valuable insights. But any generalizations this method offers must surmount grave evidentiary problems. Donald's analysis of leading abolitionists has been subjected to withering criticism.[14]

Finally, a fifth interpretation ties the intellectual ferment of these years to efforts to strengthen commercial capitalism. The new institutions—common schools, mental asylums, penitentiaries—affirmed (in Michael Katz's words) ". . . [a] willingness to work, acquiesence in the legitimacy of the social order, and acceptance of one's place within it—all serviceable traits in early capitalist America." This argument, however, conflates causes and results. Typically these programs were undertaken to achieve moral or spiritual reformation, and only incidentally to promote capitalist goals. (Education may be an exception, but here too humanitarian aims were important.) Even Katz concedes that the reforms were initiated "by people swept simultaneously by optimistic theories of human nature and evangelical religion."[15]

Against this background of interpretation, we can scrutinize the transformation of northern intellectual life. A booming economy may have distinguished the North from the other regions. But it was a series of writers and preachers, influenced by the currents of religious reform, who helped recast the mind-set of the northern states. William Ellery Channing, the founder of Unitarianism, was a key figure in the rise of a more benevolent religion. On the base of the statue of Channing in the Public Garden of Boston is the inscription, "He breathed into theology a humane spirit." In sermon after sermon he denounced the gloomy faith of the Puritans. "This system indeed takes various shapes," he remarked in 1819, "but in all it casts dishonor on the Creator."[16] Channing's own elevated view of humanity was given full play in his talk, "Likeness to God." "I affirm, and would maintain," he wrote, "that true religion consists in proposing, as our great end, a growing likeness to the Supreme Being." What higher praise could Channing bestow on humanity than the message of this sermon? He affirmed that humans could be like God.[17]

Several preachers spread the new, buoyant faith in a wide-ranging revival that has been called the Second Great Awakening (the first was in the 1740s). Charles Grandison Finney, a Connecticut-born minister who preached to many thousands in upstate New York, was one of the most important of these itinerants. Finney was a tall, athletic man, with a remarkable singing voice and a forceful delivery honed during his years as a lawyer. (He told one client when he quit the law: "I have a retainer from the Lord Jesus Christ to plead his cause, and I cannot plead yours.") Finney threatened backsliders with eternal punishment—a harsher tack than Channing would have taken. But Finney also valued the potential of each human, and argued with Calvinists where he found them. He differed sharply with his teacher, George W. Gale. "He [Gale] held to the Presbyterian doctrine of original sin," Finney reported, "or that the human *constitution* was morally depraved. . . . These doctrines I could not receive."[18]

The new benevolent, anti-Calvinist creed, it should be noted, always remained a northern doctrine. There was no receptivity in the southern states to a message that trumpeted the full potential of human development. Southern ministers remained committed to slavery and its defense, and the schism between northern and southern churches gradually widened. In the 1840s the two largest denominations, the Methodists and Baptists, split along sectional lines.[19]

The optimism underlying the ferment of this era was brought to a pinnacle by various thinkers, and most notably by Ralph Waldo Emerson. Young Emerson was a disciple of Channing's, and would later eulogize his teacher: "Dr. Channing, whilst he lived, was the star of the American Church."[20] Emerson followed in Channing's footsteps, and became a preacher. But he found that even the Unitarian Church was too restrictive for his expansive views and he resigned his position. ("To be a good minister it was necessary to leave the ministry," he explained.) He soon embarked on his career as writer and lecturer. With his annual lecture tours, Emerson became a familiar figure in lyceums and public halls throughout the North.[21]

The message that Emerson brought his listeners and readers emphasized the divinity in each person. "Who can set bounds to the possibilities of man?" he asked in *Nature*, his first book, published in 1837. "Once inhale the upper air, being admitted to behold the absolute natures of justice and truth, and we learn that man has access to the entire mind of the Creator, is himself the creator in the finite."[22] Unlike Channing, who kept Christ and the Bible at the center of his beliefs, Emerson drew his philosophy from a remarkable range of sources. His lectures are peppered with references to Eastern mystics, Greek philosophers, and German and English romantics. The corollary to Emerson's belief in the god-like potential of each person (Emerson would say "man") was an emphasis on individualism. Emerson's admonitions on self-reliance have passed into the language as familiar sayings. "Whoso would be a man, must be a nonconformist." "A fool-

ish consistency is the hobgoblin of little minds, adored by little statesmen and philosophers and divines." "To be great is to be misunder-
stood." "An institution is the lengthened shadow of one man."[23]

The Age of Emerson was for the North an age of individualism,
optimism, enthusiasm, and reform. The belief in the perfectibility of
women and men underlay a series of movements to end slavery, extend women's rights, introduce temperance, improve diet and dress,
reform criminals, and bring world peace. Utopian communities demonstrated how property and marriage relations could be transformed.
New religious sects, such as the Mormons, emerged. A series of novelists, essayists, and poets—including such luminaries as Herman Mel-
ville, Nathaniel Hawthorne, Margaret Fuller, Henry David Thoreau,
and Walt Whitman—explored the expanses of the human soul. These
beliefs were also writ large in the ideology of "free labor." Northerners
exalted the opportunities that America offered and praised the entrepreneur whose honest efforts made the most of them.[24]

To be sure, the Age of Emerson in the North was also an era of
intolerance and of an obsession with work. Emerson was mocked, and
Thoreau ignored. Abolitionists were stoned; advocates of women's
rights were jeered; and sectarians, harassed. Thoreau commented
about his neighbors: "Most men, even in this comparatively free country, through mere ignorance and mistake, are so occupied with the
factitious cares and superfluously coarse labors of life that its finer
fruits cannot be plucked by them." Racism remained endemic in the
North. And it is also true that by the 1850s the rise of manufacturing
in the Northeast had begun to undercut the material basis of the free
labor ideology and the belief in all individuals realizing their potential.[25]

But the manufacturing nation lay in the future. And the work-
obsessed northerners retained a profoundly optimistic view of their future, in ways that Tocqueville and other observers noted. (It was an
optimism that had no counterpart in the South or French Canada.) At
least some of the intolerant northerners agreed to rewrite laws and
change local customs in the decades before the Civil War. States such
as Massachusetts expanded the rights of African Americans; others, for
example, New York, strengthened the legal position of women. And
millions marched to war singing about an abolitionist, John Brown,
and determined to eradicate slavery.

Closing of the Southern Mind

Like a train shunted from the main road to a rickety siding, intellectual
life in the South between the colonial era and the Civil War moved
from its Enlightenment origins to narrow, sectional concerns. Thus
southern intellectual activity, like the southern economy, traced an arc

that differed strikingly from the course of intellectual life in the North. The path of southern thought can be seen in the line that begins with the writings of Thomas Jefferson and James Madison and ends in the proslavery diatribes of Thomas Dew and George Fitzhugh.

Many, but not all historians of the South would concur with this overview. Some scholars argue that southern intellectuals were no less progressive than northerners in the middle decades of the nineteenth century. Hence these pages also confront the diversity of opinions on the path of southern thought.

We start with Jefferson and Madison. Most modern observers agree that these statesmen, in the years from 1770 to 1800, were among the leading thinkers of the day. Jefferson at age thirty-three was the author of the Declaration of Independence. He was a tall, sandy-haired individual, an excellent horseman, and an accomplished violinist. As a youth he mastered Greek and Latin, and while at the College of William and Mary his horizons were broadened by close contact with several remarkable individuals, including Dr. William Small, a Scottish professor of mathematics and philosophy. From Small, Jefferson later recollected, "I got my first views of the expansion of science, and of the system of things in which we are placed."[26]

What Small taught Jefferson was the essence of the Scottish Enlightenment—the most advanced thought of the times. The Scots moved beyond the formulations of John Locke, who had seen government as the defender of property. The Scots argued for a higher vision: the state should promote the well-being of its citizens. (The "greatest happiness for the greatest number" was Francis Hutcheson's phrase.) Hence Jefferson's ringing affirmation that all "men" have the "unalienable Rights" of "Life, Liberty, and the pursuit of Happiness." The Scots emphasized that people of all races, despite their different attainments, possessed a similar moral sense. Jefferson reflected these revolutionary ideas too. "We hold these truths to be self-evident," he pronounced, "that all men are created equal."[27]

Like Jefferson, James Madison in the years before 1800 was revolutionary in his thoughts as well as actions. A small, soft-spoken man, who usually dressed in black, Madison had a narrower range of interests than Jefferson. But he was more systematic and incisive in his study of political economy. He was first among equals in the writing of the Constitution in 1787 and was one of the three authors of the brilliant *Federalist Papers*. Madison's great contribution was his abiding faith in the republican experiment. Earlier writers, like Montesquieu, had felt republican government was suitable only for small nations, but Madison vigorously countered this traditional wisdom. "The people of America," he argued in Federalist #14, should not allow "a blind veneration for antiquity, for custom, or for names to overrule the suggestions of their own good sense." Madison was also a strong advocate of religious freedom. Along with Jefferson, he campaigned successfully for the disestablishment of the Anglican Church in Virginia.[28]

And slavery? Jefferson and Madison condemned it, as did most of the Revolutionary leaders in the South. Jefferson called slavery a "blot in our country" and a "great political and moral evil." Madison told the Constitutional Convention that "we have seen the mere distinction of colour made in the most enlightened period of time, a ground of the most oppressive dominion ever exercised by man over man." Both men called for gradual emancipation, and the colonization of blacks to another country. Colonization had more than a tinge of racism, but gradual emancipation was an "enlightened" stance, and somehow in the years before 1800 seemed possible. The staples cultivated by southern slaves—tobacco and rice—were not expanding. The success of the northern states in ending slavery suggested that the bondspeople of the South might be freed one day without a violent upheaval.[29]

In the decades after 1800 a gap between world opinion and the views of leading southerners emerged and gradually widened. The expansion of cotton cultivation reinvigorated the "peculiar institution," although it did not allow the South to match the pace of growth in the North. The resurgence of slavery undercut Jefferson's and Madison's optimistic faith in its demise. Both men continued to condemn the institution and favor colonization, but neither opposed its extension into new territories. Instead, they embraced the self-serving "diffusion" argument: the spread of slavery would lead to its eventual disappearance. Jefferson explained his views to the Marquis de Lafayette, who long had been a friend of the American republic. "All know," remarked Jefferson, "that permitting the slaves of the South to spread into the West will not add one being to that unfortunate condition, that it will increase the happiness of those existing, and by spreading over a larger surface, will dilute the evil every where, and facilitate the means of getting finally rid of it, an event more anxiously wished by those on whom it presses than by the noisy pretenders to exclusive humanity."

Lafayette, and other European observers, would have none of this contorted reasoning. "Are you Sure, My dear Friend," he replied to Jefferson, "that Extending the principle of Slavery to the New Raised States is a Method to facilitate the Means of Getting Rid of it? I would have thought that By Spreading the prejudices, Habits, and Calculations of planters over a larger Surface You Rather Encrease the difficulties of final liberation."[30]

After 1830 the terms of debate changed again, and the South (like French Canada) became even more of a bastion of conservative ideology in the Western World. Outside of the American South, slavery was in retreat. The revolutions that rocked Latin America in the first decades of the century struck hard at the institution. Britain emancipated its bondspeople in the West Indies in 1833, and beginning with the appearance of William Lloyd Garrison's *The Liberator* on January 1, 1831, a movement for the immediate abolition of slavery appeared and grew in the North. The leading thinkers in the South grew more defensive and ever more removed from the currents of progressive thought.[31]

Here we must pause to note the vigorous debate on the course of southern intellectual activity—and to support the contention that there was a "closing" of the southern mind. Many prominent intellectual historians agree with the argument presented in this text. They depict a society that moved from the openness of the eighteenth-century Enlightenment to the narrow, parochial concerns of a region defending slavery in a world swept by spiritual and material progress.[32]

But other scholars dissent. While hardly a unified "school," recent works on the South have affirmed three propositions. They argue that (1) the leading writers and thinkers in the southern states were sophisticated, well-read individuals. Notes Eugene Genovese: "On one subject after another the intellectuals of the Old South matched and in some cases overmatched the best the North had to offer."[33] (2) Southern thinkers were concerned about the issue of "progress." (3) Southern thought in the decades before the Civil War was modern and progressive. Notes Michael O'Brien:

> The desire to identify the modernization of nineteenth-century thought with New England and to deny the same title to the South has doubtless proceeded from honest and worthy motives. It has seemed hard to call a slave society progressive. But recent historiography has been moving to an appreciation of the Old South as far from premodern, precisely because our sense of the flexibility of industrial modernity has increased as the phenomenon has spread far beyond its original homes in Manchester or Lowell. . . . We must entertain the real possibility that . . . the Old South was a different and evolving version of what an American modernity might have come to look like.[34]

With the first two propositions there can be little argument, but they do not fundamentally challenge the traditional interpretation. The rich outpouring of recent works on southern thinkers has made clear these individuals were knowledgeable and sophisticated thinkers. But these erudite intellectuals could and did remain harsh critics of liberal trends.[35] As for the issue of "progress," Genovese and others have illustrated the importance of this question in the southern debate. Few in the South could ignore the rapid advances in well-being recorded in the northern states and Europe—and to a lesser extent in their own society. But for southern intellectuals the commitment to progress was always subordinate to the defense of slavery. There was a similar tension in French Canada. But while in French Canada the clash between the advocates of progress and the defense of hierarchy was fought out between different groups, in the South the debate over progress typically was evident within the thought of particular individuals. In both cases the defense of the traditional society was the dominant chord during the middle decades of the century, and the concern for liberal values a weak counterpoint.[36]

The third proposition—that southern thought became modern and progressive—simply does not hold up, unless one distorts the meaning of these words. Indeed, the case studies that Michael O'Brien presents contradict his generalizations. For example, his analysis of Hugh Swinton Legaré, a Charleston writer and politician, abundantly illustrates the "closing" of the southern mind. After the Nullification Crisis of 1832–33 Legaré became the loneliest of figures—a Unionist in a state that had turned with virtual unanimity to southern nationalism. He lost his friends and was ousted from local politics. "For my own part," Legaré wrote in 1833, "I do confess that the insolent & mad conduct of the [Nullification] convention has almost entirely alienated me from the state—which I do believe I loved more than any body in it." And a few years later he remarked: "The South Carolina in which & for which I was educated has some how or other disappeared, & left a *simulacrum* behind of a very different kind—which I don't understand, neither am understood by it." Southern intellectuals were erudite, yes. Concerned, even tortured by progress, yes. But modern and progressive, no.[37]

Several individuals played a prominent role in changing the intellectual climate in the South, even though recent writings have made clear that intellectual activity was broad-based. Thomas Roderick Dew was a college professor who in the 1830s helped shift the South toward a proslavery stance. Dew did not wholly break with the Founding Fathers on the justice of slavery. His 1832 pamphlet, "Review of the Debate in the Virginia Legislature of 1831 and 1832," condemned the slave trade, acknowledging it was "shocking to the feelings of mankind." And he conceded that the doctrine "all men are born equal" might have some validity in a certain abstract sense. This was a small concession, however. He commented acerbically: "No set of legislatures ever have, or ever can, legislate upon purely abstract principles, entirely independent of circumstances, without the ruin of the body politic, which should have the misfortune to be under the guidance of such quackery."[38]

With considerable vehemence Dew affirmed that slavery was a system with great benefits for all involved. It was sanctioned by the Bible. It kept the blacks happy: "A merrier being does not exist on the face of the globe, than the negro slave of the U. States." It eliminated social conflict among whites. ("The menial and low offices being all performed by the blacks, there is at once taken away the greatest cause of distinction and separation of the ranks of society.") It was a natural stage in the progress of civilization. And Dew harshly attacked the "monstrous absurdity" of colonization. The expense of purchasing slaves from their masters was too great, American blacks were ill adapted for a return to Africa, and these slaves were desperately needed as a labor force in the South.[39]

Dew defended slavery, but like other southern intellectuals during these decades, he was unable to ignore the material strides made by the North. Hence his essay contained an odd, unresolved, contradictory acknowledgment of the benefits of free labor. Dew lamented the "inferiority of Virginia to some of the Northern States, in energy and industry." He wanted to see bondage continued in the Deep South, but contemplated its removal from his own state. Internal improvements were key to the transformation of Virginia. "The first effect of the improvement," he remarked, "will be to raise up larger towns in the eastern portion of the state. . . . The rise of cities in the lower part of Virginia, and increased density of population, will render the division of labor more complete, break down the large farms into small ones, and substitute, in a great measure, the garden for the plantation cultivation; consequently, less slave, and more free labor will be requisite, and in due time the abolitionists will find this most lucrative system working to their heart's content, increasing the prosperity of Virginia, and diminishing the evils of slavery."[40]

Professor Dew did not bother to resolve the contradictions in his tract. Most southerners read it as a spirited defense of slavery. Individuals like John C. Calhoun rejoiced in the new intellectual climate that declared bonded labor beneficial for both races. Dew's piece was widely circulated, then reprinted in *The Pro-slavery Argument* (1852). But both sides of Dew's essay—the vehement defense of slavery and the acknowledgment that it slowed growth—illustrate how far the South had traveled since its equal partnership with the North in the eighteenth century.

It is also worth noting—in light of the parallels between the South and French Canada—that many southerners had kind words for feudalism and the seigneurial system. No southerner, in a society that had at least the trappings of democracy, could show unreserved enthusiasm for the polity of the Middle Ages. But many writers compared hierarchical, feudal practices favorably to the aggressive commercial capitalism of the North and England. For example, Daniel Hundley of Alabama observed: "It may be that the old order of things, the old relationship between landlord and villein, protected the latter from many hardships to which the nominal freemen of the nineteenth century are subjected by the blessed influences of free competition and the practical workings of the good old charitable and praiseworthy English maxim: 'Every man for himself, and the devil take the hindmost.' "[41]

The culmination of the odyssey of the South away from the main

currents of progressive thought came in the 1850s. George Fitzhugh, a
Virginia planter and lawyer, was the most influential of several writers
who insisted that slavery was a positive good. Gone was any vestige of
respect for the Declaration of Independence. After quoting from the
Declaration, Fitzhugh stated in *Sociology for the South* (1854): "Men are
not 'born entitled to equal rights'! It would be far nearer the truth to
say, 'that some were born with saddles on their backs, and other
booted and spurred to ride them,'—and the riding does them good.
. . . 'Life and liberty' are not 'inalienable'; they have been sold in all
countries, and in all ages, and must be sold so long as human nature
lasts."[42]

Much of *Sociology for the South* and Fitzhugh's other book, *Cannibals All!; or, Slaves Without Masters* (1857), is devoted to a critique of
the societies of the North and Western Europe. This pointed analysis,
which was echoed by other southern intellectuals, targeted the shortcomings of capitalist labor relations. Fitzhugh argues that slaves are far
better off than free workers. "The statistics of crime," Fitzhugh notes,
"demonstrate that the moral superiority of the slave over the free laborer is still greater than his superiority in animal well-being. There
never can be among slaves a class so degraded as is found about the
wharves and suburbs of cities." And further: "The capitalists, in free
society, live in ten times the luxury and show that Southern masters
do, because the slaves to capital work harder and cost less than negro
slaves." Some modern students of Fitzhugh argue his writings should
be taken as a call for enslaving southern whites.[43]

Fitzhugh was particularly enraged by northern reformers—individuals, he noted smugly, who could recruit few followers in the South.
Why do you find, he asked, "Bloomer's and Women's Right's men,
and strong-minded women, and Mormons, and anti-renters, and 'vote
myself a farm' men, Millerites, and Spiritual Rappers, and Shakers,
and Widow Wakemanites, and Agrarians, and Grahamites, and a
thousand other superstitious and infidel Isms at the North? Why is
there faith in nothing, speculation about everything?" The answer was
that a free labor economy was a poor foundation for a stable society.
Stated Fitzhugh: "Slavery, marriage, religion, are the pillars of the social fabric."[44]

But like Dew, Fitzhugh was not comfortable with the impact of
the peculiar institution on the southern economy. He admired the
progress made by the northern states and the most advanced countries
of Europe. "Holland and Massachusetts," he observed, "are two of the
richest, happiest, and most civilized States in the world, because they
farm very little, but are engaged in more profitable and enlightened
pursuits." Fitzhugh did not suggest, as Dew had, moving away from
slavery. But he did urge internal improvements, urbanization, more
schools, and more manufacturing. Here was a program—although

Fitzhugh did not draw the conclusion—that would have aided southern growth but also undermined slavery.[45] The most able of the southern nationalists could never be of one mind in their defense of slavery.
The evidence of the harm it had wreaked on their section was all too
apparent.

Such ambivalence about the slave economy was not the only
crosscurrent in the South in the decades before the Civil War. A very
small group of southerners remained outspoken in their condemnation
of slavery. However, most of these individuals, such as James Birney,
Sarah Grimké, and her younger sister Angelina, fled to the North.

Furthermore, southern evangelicals emphasized "benevolence"
and the moral reform of the individual. This outlook, which cut across
denominational lines, called upon all persons to improve themselves
and the world they lived in. There was in the South an emphasis on
the individual not found in French Canada. The southern states were,
after all, part of the bustling, Protestant, American democracy. But the
limitations of this evangelical world view must be emphasized. Southerners, preachers and parishioners alike, emphatically rejected the programs of social reform that swept the North. Their belief in the individual never reached the heights scaled by Channing and Emerson. They
rejected "moral perfectionism" and turned from the other "isms" of
the age, such as utopianism and Unitarianism.[46]

For all its contradictions and crosscurrents, the course of southern
intellectual life was clear. During the century from 1760 to 1860 it
moved from the open, Enlightenment world of Jefferson and Madison
to a beleaguered defense of slavery.

French Canada: The Triumph of the Church

Between 1750 and 1850 intellectual life in French Canada followed a
path that in its broadest outlines resembled the road traced by the leading writers of the South. The outlook of the most influential French
Canadians shifted from the broad mainstream of the Enlightenment to
a narrow Catholic vision that denounced liberal thought, women's
rights, and secular education. The evolution of the life of the mind thus
paralleled—and reinforced—the changes in the economy of a region
that fell ever further behind the North.

What was intellectual life like in Canada before the Conquest?
From one point of view, very limited. With no printing presses, and
with fewer than 20 percent of males and females literate, early Canada
lacked the breadth of cultural activity evident in both the northern and
southern colonies. But we can rephrase the question. What was the
outlook of the writers and thinkers of New France? Here the answer is
more positive. Literate Canadians, no less than the colonists to the
south of them, shared the outlook of the Age of Reason.

We begin with Peter Kalm's observations. In 1749 the Swedish scientist and traveler met the Marquis de la Galissonière, commandant general of the colony. La Galissonière was unimpressive physically. He was "of a low stature, and somewhat hump-backed," Kalm noted. But his mind was another matter. "He has a surprising knowledge in all branches of science," Kalm remarked, "and especially in natural history, in which he is so well versed, that when he began to speak with me about it, I imagined I saw our great *Linnaeus* under a new form." La Galissonière encouraged others to explore and report to him about the plants and animals of the New World. "Great efforts are made here for the advancement of *Natural History*," Kalm concluded, "and there are few places in the world where such good regulations are made for this useful purpose."[47]

Canada boasted other well-read individuals who shared the curiosity and faith in reason characteristic of the Enlightenment. Claude-Thomas Dupuy, a hot-tempered administrator who served as intendant during the 1720s, was an able scientist and inventor. He brought to Quebec his astronomical instruments, a fully equipped physics laboratory, and a library of over 1000 volumes. At his death the *Gazette of Holland* lamented: "The Republic of Letters has suffered a great loss." Another intendant, Antoine-Denis Raudot, wrote extensively about the native peoples. Many of the intendants owned libraries of several hundred books covering an impressive range of topics. Works on history, law, literature, and science were more common in these collections than those on theology. And among the religious books, treatises by dissenting Catholic writers frequently stood alongside more pious tomes.[48]

The Roman Catholic Church in Canada during the French regime was far weaker than it would be in the nineteenth century. On the local level, parishioners more than held their own in quarrels with the clergy. Tithes did not yet provide a steady income, so curés had to rely on the good will of the flock and on voluntary donations of money, labor, and materials. Churchwardens were elected and outspoken, and inclined to scrutinize closely any new building projects. On the provincial level, the bishops of Quebec recognized that their power in this frontier colony was less than that of the governor or intendant. This subordination of church to state also reflected the doctrines of the Gallican, or French, Church. The king, rather than the pope, appointed the bishops in France and Canada, and such subordination continued with the arrival of the English. "As the king of England is now through right of conquest sovereign of Quebec," pronounced Henri-Marie Dubreil de Pontbriand, bishop of Quebec, "we owe him all the sentiments of which the apostle Paul speaks."[49]

Finally, we may note that in eighteenth-century French Canada women had rights and status that would disappear in the closed society of the nineteenth century. Women were more literate than men, and they had property rights that were far more extensive than in the English colonies. The Constitutional Act of 1791 made no reference to gender, and so allowed women who met the property qualification to vote.[50]

In the nineteenth century the outlook of French Canadians grew more intensely Catholic and more critical of the freethinking that had marked the Enlightenment. The changes in Lower Canada were most pronounced after the defeat of the liberal-led uprisings of 1837 and 1838. But the movement toward a closed, Catholic society was evident even during the first decades of the century as priests gradually gained more control over parish affairs. A wealthier countryside made tithes a stable source of income. And the clergy, financially more secure, were able to end the practice of allowing parishioners to choose churchwardens.[51]

Historians are not of one mind in describing the course of intellectual life in Lower Canada during the first half of the nineteenth century. Many works (and this one) argue that in the middle decades of the century French Canada became increasingly closed and conservative. During these years the Catholic Church, "on the defensive before the 'modern world' " (as Jean-Paul Bernard puts it), triumphed over the advocates of liberal thought.[52] But not all studies agree. Some books contend that the Church played a positive role as standard-bearer of French-Canadian nationalism against the English. In large part the dispute between these two schools of thought is over not events but values. It is an aspect of the clash between those who uphold a secular approach and those who defend the role of religion.[53]

Up until the 1830s liberalism, not Catholicism, was the most important ideology in Lower Canada, and Louis-Joseph Papineau, not the bishop of Montreal, the most influential leader. Within French Canada, Papineau's philosophy was clearly progressive. But set in the North American context it more nearly resembled the republicanism of the American Revolution than the boisterous democracy of the Age of Jackson. Papineau (and his followers in the Patriote party) proclaimed their support for democratic institutions. The Patriote leader wanted more elected offices and the dissolution of the legislative council, which was appointed by Britain. "Spreading political instruction among the people," Papineau observed, "will place them in a condition to act with wisdom." But Papineau wanted the vote limited to property owners, and he often harkened back to eighteenth-century principles. He told the assembly: "I have found the good political doctrines of modern times explained . . . in a few lines of the Declaration of Independence of 1776 and the Declaration of the rights of men and citizens of 1789." Papineau advocated religious tolerance and limits on church involvement in schooling. But he was patriarchal in his view of women and little interested in the reforms sweeping the northern states.[54]

Even before the defeat of the uprisings in 1837 and 1838, Church leaders sharply challenged the liberal ideas of Papineau and his supporters. The bishop of Montreal, Jean-Jacques Lartigue, spearheaded the move toward a more conservative society. Lartigue, who came from a prominent Montreal family, trained to be a lawyer but chose the priesthood just before being called to the bar. He passionately admired those French writers, such as Hugues de Lamennais, who espoused ultramontanism. This was a doctrine that affirmed the absolute supremacy of the pope, and argued that the Church should be independent of any civil authority. Lartigue was heartbroken when Pope Gregory XVI condemned Lamennais in the 1830s, and for the moment the Montreal bishop was more Catholic than the pope. Lartigue did not disavow his beliefs, and by midcentury this viewpoint would triumph in both Canada and Rome.[55]

Lartigue, who served as bishop from 1820 to 1840, labored on several fronts for his vision of French Canada. He campaigned for Catholic-controlled schools, and was disappointed by a series of acts that created local boards and limited the role of the Church. Such measures, he felt, were tainted by democracy and the deistic liberalism of France. Lartigue also worked to limit the involvement of the English government in Church affairs. Without consulting the British authorities, he secured a papal bull creating a new diocese for Montreal. And he urged French-Canadian nationalists to abandon the freethinking Patriote party and follow the banner of the Church. The triumph of Lartigue and conservative Catholic ideology came with the suppression of the Rebellions of 1837 and 1838. Defeat discredited the Patriote party and forced its leaders, like Papineau, into exile. Lartigue moved quickly to consolidate the gains the Church had made.[56]

Lartigue's work was continued after his death by his hand-picked successor, the new bishop of Montreal, Ignace Bourget, who held office until the 1870s. With his purposeful stride, sparkling blue eyes, and quick mind, Bishop Bourget was a formidable opponent of those who questioned his cause. Under Bourget, Roman Catholics finally gained control of the school system from the primary grades through the classical colleges. Bourget also helped increase the number of priests, and expanded the religious orders in Lower Canada. He continued Lartigue's fight for independence from the state, and in 1849 secured recognition of the Church's right to govern itself. Bourget, who was no less an ultramontane than Lartigue, made five trips to Rome and brought back for adoption in Canada various rituals, dress, and architectural designs.[57]

Bourget also led the attack against the remnants of liberalism. The Rouge party, influenced by democratic ideas in the United States and

France, was the successor to the Patriote party. Les Rouges encouraged individuals to read widely and make up their own minds about the issues of the day. Bourget denounced such heresy. "No one is permitted to be *free in his religious and political opinions* . . . ," he thundered. "Any moral point comes within the domain of the church and essentially derives from its teaching. For its divine mission is to teach sovereigns to govern with wisdom and subjects to obey in gladness." A particular object of Bourget's wrath was the Institut Canadien, a center of liberalism and Rouge strength in Montreal. His attacks did not close the Institut, but led many members to resign.[58]

The rights of women also suffered in these years. One campaign targeted woman suffrage. Beginning in the 1830s some lawmakers sought to take the vote from women, and in 1849 these efforts were successful. One scholar has suggested that agitation in the United States, and particularly the gathering at Seneca Falls, heightened fears in Canada—and precipitated the 1849 decision. Another concerted effort was directed at limiting the right of women to control property. In the 1840s the Legislative Assembly adopted measures encouraging women to renounce their feudal rights (without compensation) and creating registry offices, so that purchasers of land could see which properties were encumbered and which could be sold freely. The Civil Code adopted in 1866 eliminated all such "dower rights" unless they were officially registered. And by the end of the century the old feudal privileges of women had all but disappeared.[59]

Finally, the changing intellectual climate of French Canada was reflected in the career of François-Xavier Garneau, the first great French-Canadian historian. One of ten children from a poor family, François-Xavier received an education thanks to the kindness of a wealthy patron, Joseph-François Perrault. Perrault, a former fur trader and an educational reformer, recognized the boy's gifts and encouraged him. Garneau became a notary—as well as an ardent nationalist. ("I shall write the history which you do not even know exists," he lectured an English boy who was a fellow clerk. "You will see that our ancestors yielded only when outnumbered.") As Garneau moved from being a notary to a brief involvement in politics to his true calling as historian, his nationalism remained a constant. The issue was only to which star this patriotism would be hitched: the liberalism of the Patriote party or the increasingly conservative outlook of the Church.[60]

At first it seemed that Garneau had cast his lot with liberalism. While visiting London in the early 1830s, he became secretary to Denis-Benjamin Viger, the agent of the Patriote-controlled assembly. Garneau applauded the 1837 Rebellion, and denounced the 1840 Act of Union—just as other liberals did. His freethinking, anticlerical outlook was unmistakable with the publication in 1845 of the first volume of his *History of Canada*. This work defended freedom of conscience, lamented the exclusion of Huguenots from New France, and condemned Bishop Laval's authoritarian rule. Ultramontane writers criticized the book as "anti-Catholic and anti-Canadian." Garneau admitted that the volume gave him a "terrible reputation with vestrymen and sextons."[61]

Garneau took the Church's criticism to heart, and his views, much like the climate of opinion in Lower Canada, gradually changed. The second volume, published in 1846, was more circumspect in discussing religion. And the third volume, which appeared in 1849 and covered the history of French Canada from 1775 to 1792, displayed a new outlook. He now proclaimed the unity of religion and nationalism. The clerical establishment welcomed the convert, and Joseph Signay, the archbishop of Quebec, opened his archives to Garneau. In 1856 Garneau issued an abridged version of his opus, eliminating all passages that might offend the Church.[62]

François-Xavier Garneau's intellectual odyssey sealed the triumph of Catholicism in Lower Canada. Conservative Catholic writers, not Voltaire and Rousseau, would set the terms of discourse for French Canadians. Dissenters remained, but they no longer threatened the dominant role of conservative leaders such as Bishop Bourget. Not until the middle of the twentieth century would many French Canadians question the commanding position of the Church. Until that time, Catholicism helped turn Quebeckers from the currents of reform as well as from the wiles of materialism that were changing the outlook of the industrializing world.

Thus in its broadest contours, the course traced by writers and opinion makers in French Canada resembled the road taken by southern intellectuals. During the nineteenth century thinkers in both regions defended societies that were falling behind economically, and unwilling to change their behavior. They exalted hierarchical, traditional ways of living.

But the differences must not be ignored. French Canada was the child of Catholicism and the seigneurial system. The South was the product of an individualistic, Protestant faith, and of a property system where feudal values had long since yielded to commercial ones. The South was also shaped by a militant ideology of expansion. William Gilmore Simms of South Carolina, the leading novelist in the Old South, caught the aggressive tone of his section in a letter to Governor James Hammond. "Take my word for it," Simms remarked, "conservatism, in name at least, will not do for a pressing, impetuous people like our own. It must be *ultraism, in profession at least,* if not altogether in practice."[63] The arc of southern thought led to secession and Civil War. The path of French-Canadian intellectual life turned inward and pointed to the growth of a clerical nationalism, not rebellion. Only after defeat in the Civil War would the resignation of the South match the quiescence of French Canada.

Despite such differences, the evolution of thought in the South and French Canada followed similar patterns. The curve of northern intellectual activity was far different, and mirrored the burgeoning economy of that area. And these ideologies, in turn, helped shape the activities and goals of the citizens of the three regions.

Finally, as we look ahead we can ask, What endured? Which institutions and aspects of culture remained important in the years after 1860? Here the story is different for the southerners and French Canadians, on the one hand, and for the northerners, on the other.

For southerners (white ones, at least) and for French Canadians what mattered most was respect for authority, hierarchy, and traditional ways. The pursuit of profit was secondary. Slavery and the seigneurial system, it is true, disappeared. But the structured world of thought and behavior established by the 1850s endured and was evident almost a century later. The closed southern society of Thomas Dew and George Fitzhugh and the devoutly Catholic province fashioned by Bishops Lartigue and Bourget were still recognizable in 1940. These were civilizations that disdained those individuals whose first goal in life was getting rich. Only after 1940 would the older patterns of behavior gradually break down.

The North was different. The rich, egalitarian, reformist culture of midcentury did not survive. Instead, the basic continuity was provided by an entrepreneurial outlook. The civilization of small farmers and commercial capitalism quickly gave way to an industrial society of wealthy robber barons and a hard-pressed working class. Still traces of the egalitarian North of Emerson and Channing, of Stanton and Mott, of Lincoln and Seward remained. Andrew Carnegie never tired of arguing that his own rise from poor boy to steel magnate showed the wonders of American democracy.[64] And the philosophy of the twentieth-century industrial North—corporate liberalism—rested on the linkage between the success of big business and the prosperity of all Americans. For all the extremes of wealth in the North, the region never donned the mantle of hierarchy that cloaked the South and French Canada.

II

FROM THE 1860s TO THE 1990s

9

The Gap Widens:
1860s to 1940

Elmire Boucher, who grew up on a poor farm in the province of Quebec, knew about the realities of comparative economic development. "In 1899 my parents decided to leave for the United States," she later recollected. "Life was difficult on the farm which was too small for us. We were 16 children, all lively. We already had aunts in the United States who told us wonderful things about that part of the world."

"We lived in Bic, near Rimouski. We were on the third row of farms. It was a rather rocky farm, even mountainous. . . . There was no modern machinery. Everything was done by hand. Papa went to fish six months each year and sold the fish. With 16 children, there were 18 persons to feed."

Boucher settled with her family in Fall River, Massachusetts, where (most years) there were jobs for all and the Bouchers were able to prosper. Elmire concluded her account: "I've lived the good life. I profited from the American system."[1] At the turn of the twentieth century, as in the 1850s, there was no question that the northern states were wealthier than French Canada.

The patterns of growth established by the culture and institutions of the three regions before 1860 persisted well into the twentieth century. Indeed, as Figure 9.1 suggests, the gap between the North, on the one hand, and the South and French Canada, on the other, widened during the era of industrialization. There was an excellent fit between

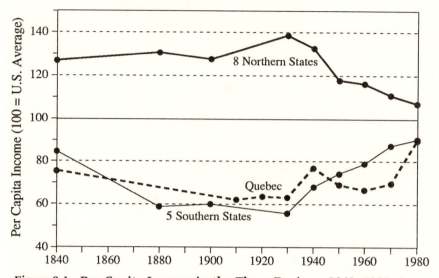

***Figure 9.1*   Per Capita Income in the Three Regions, 1840–1980, Compared with U.S. Average.** The gap between northern income levels and per capita earnings in the South and Quebec widened until about 1930. Then incomes gradually converged. This graph focuses on the original states to permit links with the 1840 data. (*Sources:* U.S. figures for 1840, 1880, and 1900 from Richard A. Easterlin, "Interregional Differences in Per Capita Income, Population and Total Income, 1840–1950," in National Bureau for Economic Research, *Trends in the American Economy in the 19th Century,* Studies in Income and Wealth, vol. XXIV (Princeton, 1960), 97–104; U.S. Bureau of the Census, *Historical Statistics of the United States, Colonial Times to 1970,* 2 vols. (Washington, D.C., 1975), I, 224, provides benchmark figures for U.S. per capita income; U.S. data for 1940 and 1980 from *U.S. Statistical Abstracts.* For Canadian data, consult F. H. Leacy, ed., *Historical Statistics of Canada,* 2d ed. (Ottawa, 1983), ser. A7, F95; Statistics Canada, *Canadian Statistical Review,* cat. No. 11-003; T. N. Brewis, *Regional Economic Policies in Canada* (Toronto, 1968), 92; R. M. McInnis, "The Trend of Regional Income Differentials in Canada," *Canadian Journal of Economics* I (1968), 447. Canadian figures for 1840 are an estimate based on data in O. J. Firestone, "Development of Canada's Economy, 1850–1900," in *Trends in the American Economy,* 222–29. *U.S. Statistical Abstracts* (various years) provide exchange rates.)

the busy, entrepreneurial ethic of the North and the new industrial economy. The belt of northern states stretching from Massachusetts to Illinois became the leading industrial area in the world. But there was much less harmony between the traditional values that shaped the growth of the South and French Canada and the demands of the new society. The Age of Industrialization belonged to the North.

The North Sets the Pace

The North* built upon its strengths in this era. The entrepreneurial spirit that had impressed visitors before the Civil War became the "Gospel of Wealth," which ennobled millionaires as long as they appeared socially responsible. ("Wealth passing through the hands of the few," steel magnate Andrew Carnegie explained, "can be made a much more potent force for the elevation of our race than if distributed in small sums to the people themselves.")[2] The bustling world of small businesses gave way to an economy of enormous firms. And after 1900 northern leaders developed a philosophy, "corporate liberalism," that showed how very much at home they were with the new industrial order.

The driving capitalist spirit that marked northerners after the Civil War was no accident. It emerged from the values evident at midcentury. And this northern gospel of wealth was every bit as influential as the Catholicism that shaped the outlook of Quebeckers or the planter-class mythology that guided southerners. In the decades after the Civil War few individuals in the North could escape the barrage of inspirational sermons, self-help books, and didactic novels that expounded on the virtues of industry and upward mobility. Children imbibed this credo as soon as they opened their McGuffey readers. "Persevering industry will enable one to accomplish almost anything," a New England schoolbook announced. "It makes the smallest man equal to the greatest labors. By it Lilliputians can bind a Gulliver, or a mouse can release a lion from captivity." The same message was set forth in the hundred novels Horatio Alger, Jr., wrote between the 1860s and 1890s.[3]

The capitalist ethos was not just for children. Lecturers who toured the North broadcast these doctrines to eager listeners. Russell Conwell delivered his sermon "Acres of Diamonds" more than 6000 times. (Conwell remarked, "There is a belt of civilization running across the country from a point about at Philadelphia on the south and extending north to the international boundary. In that belt, I find my most responsive audiences.")[4] Steel magnate Andrew Carnegie was a popular writer and speaker on themes such as "The Road to Business Success" and the "Gospel of Wealth." And authors who were northern by birth or outlook, such as Henry James and William Dean Howells, celebrated the self-made man.[5]

After 1900, however, this paean to entrepreneurial genius, with its rags to riches subtext, gradually changed. The age of the great ty-

---

* This chapter and the next two take a broader approach to the "North" and treat the states of the Northwest as well as the Northeast. Industrialization raised the relative standard of living in the Northwest and erased much of the distinction between it and the original states of the North.

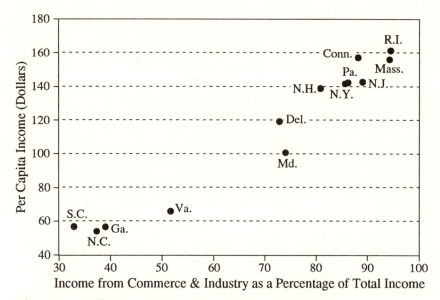

Figure 9.2 **Industry, Commerce, and Income Levels in the Original States, 1900**. Compare this graph to Figure 1.2, which presents data for 1840. In both 1840 and 1900 the northern states had more wealth and a larger proportion of people engaged in manufacturing and trade. During this sixty-year span the gap separating the North and South widened. The exception to the pattern is Maryland, which gradually became part of the northern economy. *Source:* Easterlin, "Interregional Differences," 97–104.

coons—the Carnegies, Rockefellers, and Swifts—was passing. Increasingly, large firms were directed by bureaucracies, not by entrepreneurial owners. A poor boy with pluck, it now seemed clear, was far less likely to rise than a middle-class individual with extensive education. Ambitious individuals now turned to articles like Bruce Barton's "What to Do If You Want to Sit at the Boss's Desk." Such tracts told readers how to move up the corporate ladder, not how to leap from poverty to affluence. The new hero was the organization man (rarely woman) rather than the rough-hewn business magnate. The new realities of mature industrial capitalism were reshaping the outlook of enterprising northerners.[6]

Inspired by the success ethos, several generations of entrepreneurs and skilled managers helped transform the North. These changes widened the gap between the well-off northern states, on the one hand, and the southern states and Quebec, on the other. Industrialization surged ahead in the northern states, and with it the standard of living (Fig. 9.2). Rapid urbanization accompanied the rise of manufacturing; by the 1880s most individuals in the Northeast lived in towns and cities (Fig. 9.3). Broadly viewed, the growth of big business went through

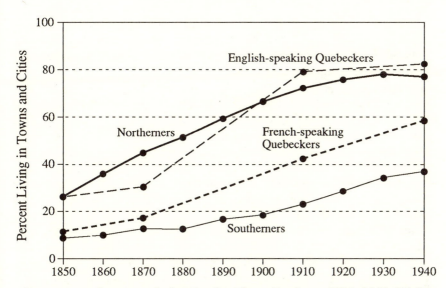

Figure 9.3 **Urban Population in the Three Regions, 1850–1940.** While towns and cities grew more important in all regions, the different populations showed strikingly different levels of urbanization. Southerners (and this graph includes the entire South) remained the most rural. The most urbanized groups were northerners (this graph shows the Northeast) and English-speaking Quebeckers. (*Sources:* U.S. data from *Historical Statistics of the U.S.*, I, 22; Quebec figures from Fernand Ouellet, *Colony, Class, & Nation in Quebec: Interpretative Essays* (Toronto, 1991), 242. The Quebec census was taken a year after the one in U.S., so the data are for 1851, 1871, 1911, and 1941.)

two phases: the triumph of the entrepreneur, 1870–1900, and the emergence of bureaucratic control, 1900–1940.

The development of a nationwide railroad network and a true national market provided the basis for the great age of corporate entrepreneurs. For historians the story is now a familiar one, thanks to the magisterial work of Alfred Chandler, Jr. Some northern businessmen combined existing firms into large units. John D. Rockefeller's consolidation of the oil refining business is a classic case study. Other individuals built corporations that produced new or newly standardized wares. Henry John Heinz, for example, mass-marketed pickles, sauces, and relishes; Henry P. Crowell developed Quaker Oats and taught Americans to enjoy breakfast cereal; Gustavus Swift transformed the distribution of meat. Many entrepreneurs directed their products largely to businesses. Andrew Carnegie headed the nation's largest steel firm; George Westinghouse and Thomas Edison sold electrical equipment. In most cases, the keys to success were transportation, economies of scale in manufacturing, and a large marketing budget. These firms were usually run and owned by the businessman who had established them.[7]

These individuals were (to borrow the terms of an old debate) both "robber barons" and "captains of industry." Rockefeller, for example, was ruthless in his campaign to buy out or close down his competitors. He made industrial espionage and predatory pricing standard practice. But Rockefeller was also innovative, cost-conscious, and relentless in his determination to strengthen the processes of production. Standard Oil chemists continually improved the refining process. Detailed cost accounting allowed individual refineries within the S.O. empire to compete against one another. When one refinery made advances, the others were told to match those gains.[8]

After 1900 the nature of American business changed, and the most successful northern businessmen were the ones who recognized and promoted these changes. For a broad range of industries oligopoly— where a small number of firms dominated production—became the norm. These corporations expected that they, and their competitors, would be in business for the long haul. Reluctant to cut prices, they were more inclined to compete through advertising and product differentiation. The entrepreneur-president gave way to a skilled administrator, who owned relatively little company stock. Corporations had grown so large that a new set of abilities, rarely displayed by the founders, was needed. Executives now had to be careful planners, able to supervise the activities of different divisions. They had to have a knowledge of finance and market trends. In keeping with the new demands of industrial society, northern business and engineering schools expanded. No comparable growth in professional training took place in Quebec or the South.[9]

Did the directors of these large firms continue the entrepreneurial ethos that had underlain northern success in the nineteenth century? In some cases, clearly not. Many of the companies put together in the merger wave around the turn of the century were overcapitalized, poorly organized, and soon failed. In other instances, such as the case of U.S. Steel (formed by J. P. Morgan based on Carnegie's holdings), the leader lost market share once competition and cost-cutting gave way to cooperation and fixed prices. In the world of oligopoly, there was always the danger that the managers of a large concern would yield to complacency. In the short run at least, profits and markets seemed assured. But for most top executives such smugness lay far in the future and would not emerge until the years after World War II. Between 1900 and 1940 most chief executive officers displayed an impressive mix of strengths—and an unmistakable entrepreneurial edge. Executives such as Alfred Sloan of General Motors or Gerard Swope of General Electric were able to organize efficiently various productive facilities and sources of supply. They took competition seriously. Their firms spent generously on research and development, and introduced a stream of new products and processes.[10]

The new industrial economy emerged in both the Northeast and Northwest—but there were significant differences between these regions. The area west of the Appalachians became the heartland of mass production. It was the home of the meatpacking, auto, tire, farm machinery, and steel industries. The economy east of the mountains remained mixed. Banks and insurance companies were more important. People were better educated. And while old industries, such as textiles, footwear, and clothing, employed large numbers of low-paid operatives, there were also metal-working and machine shops with highly trained workers and small production runs. Both the Northeast and Northwest would prosper for many decades. But when the industrial economy crumbled in the 1970s, the Northeast with its varied background and skilled labor force would prove more receptive to the rise of a post-industrial order.[11]

The policies of the federal government also boosted the northern economy. In the decade after the Civil War, for example, Congress allotted $103 million for public works with the lion's share going to the North. The eleven former Confederate states and Kentucky received only $9 million, while New York alone enjoyed $15 million. Tariffs, the National Banking Act, railroad subsidies, court decisions, the use of federal troops, and government contracts aided the North more than the South. Contemporaries and historians have debated the impact of these measures. While government actions did not create regional differences, they helped widen the gap.[12]

Northern agriculture also made rapid strides in this era, with productivity gains outpacing advances in the other two regions. Unlike the trend in the South, the average size of northern holdings steadily increased. And farms in the North remained better capitalized, more mechanized, and more involved in the labor market than those in the southern states or Quebec. For example, in 1930, for every 100 farms there were 25 tractors in the Northeast, 9 in the Southeast, and only 2 in Quebec.[13]

The fit between the North and the new world of mass production was underscored by the philosophy of "corporate liberalism" that emerged after 1900. This outlook, which shaped the views of the northern elite, was characterized by a vision of a harmonious, prosperous industrial society. By contrast, the leaders of French Canada and the South had mixed feelings about the new forces of production. In their eyes the benefits of industrialization were balanced by the dangers it posed to long-held traditions.[14]

The National Civic Federation, founded in 1900, was the organizational embodiment of corporate liberalism. One-third of the largest firms were represented in its membership. Business leaders in the federation included Andrew Carnegie, coal and shipping magnate Marcus

Hanna (who ran William McKinley's 1900 presidential campaign), and various partners from the House of Morgan. Some labor leaders endorsed the federation. Samuel Gompers, the cigar-chomping head of the American Federation of Labor, was the first vice president. John Mitchell of the United Mine Workers was also active in the group. Prominent politicians, including Grover Cleveland and William H. Taft, joined the discussions. These individuals hardly concurred on all issues. But they agreed that business, labor, and government could and should work together for the benefit of the country.[15]

A focus on two individuals suggests the dimensions of this philosophy. George Perkins was an executive who flourished in the age of bureaucratic control. He rose from insurance salesman to director of the New York Life Insurance Company. J. P. Morgan was determined to have Perkins as a partner and pursued him with a series of offers—until Perkins finally accepted. Perkins's work for Morgan shaped his view of a cooperative capitalism. He became a director of the newly formed United States Steel Corporation, where he lent decisive support to those who wanted to end predatory pricing and develop accords with other steel firms. He promoted a profit-sharing plan for workers and encouraged other welfare measures. Perkins's influence was even greater at International Harvester, a firm he helped create. He introduced health and accident insurance, profit sharing, and pensions. In 1909 he proudly reported his good works to the National Civic Federation: "If, as many of us have come to believe, co-operation in business is taking and should take the place of ruthless competition,—if this new order of things is better for capital and better for the consumer, then in order to succeed permanently it must demonstrate that it is better for the laborer."[16]

Gerard Swope was another standard bearer for corporate liberalism. When he retired in 1939 after serving as president of General Electric for seventeen years, *Fortune* praised him as an individual "whom many call the finest corporation executive officer that ever struck a balance sheet." Swope was also one of the more unusual corporate officers of this era. He came from a Jewish family and married a social worker, Mary Hill. Jane Addams, head of the settlement house where Hill worked, presided at the ceremony. World War I broadened Swope's view of the American economy. Secretary of War Newton Baker tapped the young executive to be co-director of the army agency responsible for procuring materials. Swope worked energetically to coordinate business activity on the national level. In the 1920s, as head of General Electric, Swope initiated a broad range of social welfare programs for employees. These included pensions, workmen's compensation, profit sharing, life insurance, and unemployment benefits. Swope also supported company unions, which gave workers some small voice in corporate policy.[17]

Swope's career highlights the links between corporate liberalism and the reforms of Franklin Roosevelt's New Deal. When the Depression struck Swope demanded forceful action. In a well-received 1931 speech, he urged that each industry be brought together in a trade association. These groups would meet to "outline trade practices, business ethics, methods of standard accounting . . . [and] to promote stabilization and give the best service to the public." Swope also insisted that "the psychology of fear must be removed." Hence workers should have "protection for their families in case of the breadwinner's death, protection for their old age, and protection against unemployment." He wanted all corporations to follow the GE model and establish welfare plans.[18]

President Herbert Hoover (who in other areas shared this corporate philosophy) rejected Swope's advice. But Roosevelt responded to the urgings of Swope and other business leaders. The National Industrial Recovery Act of 1933 bore a striking resemblance to Swope's plan for trade associations. And when Roosevelt tapped Hugh Johnson to run the National Recovery Administration, he called upon an administrator who had worked alongside Swope during the First World War. The reforms of the "second New Deal" of 1935 also echoed Swope's suggestions—but with the government rather than corporations as the provider of benefits.[19]

Most historians accept the importance of corporate liberalism. But scholars differ in describing the social harmony or conflicts that shaped these ideas. Some contend that business leaders guided a unified America. "The Progressive era," notes Gabriel Kolko, "was characterized by a paucity of alternatives to the status quo, a vacuum that permitted political capitalism [i.e., corporate liberalism] to direct the growth of industrialism in America, to shape its politics, to determine the ground rules for American civilization in the twentieth century, and to set the stage for what was to follow."[20] Other writers modify this picture in at least three ways.

First, many scholars emphasize that corporate liberalism was, to a remarkable degree, a response to pressure that came from socialists, labor, farmers, and women. Business leaders in the early decades of the century spoke openly about the threat from radical workers. George Perkins was hardly alone when he fretted in 1910 about the "very large increase in the Socialistic vote everywhere." There is, he noted, "a crisis in this country on the question of the relation between capital and labor." For Perkins and many others, reform was the answer.[21] Recent writers have also emphasized the importance of voluntary associations of women, who demanded and gained legislation to provide benefits for mothers.[22]

Second, some historians note that a desire for harmony with labor did not lessen the determination of employers to gain full control over the pace and nature of work. Business leaders enthusiastically backed the idea of "scientific management." In the late nineteenth century employees often had a great deal of knowledge—and hence power. An iron molder knew far better than his foreman when the molten mixture was ready to be poured. Scientific management helped deskill the worker and put knowledge and control into the hands of management. This new approach was pioneered by a Philadelphia patrician, Frederick W. Taylor. A mechanical engineer and superb athlete (he was part of the doubles team that won the first U.S. Lawn Tennis Association championship), Taylor made the efficient management of labor his life's work. The key was the analysis and redefinition of each job. "The shop, and indeed the whole works," he stated, "should be managed, not by the manager, superintendent and foreman, but by the planning department." Workers were to receive cards telling them what their tasks were and how to perform them. Taylor's disciples and others modified his practices, but the fundamentals remained in place. The new industrial order rested on employees who, while well paid, had little say in shaping their jobs.[23]

Third, other writers point out that a noteworthy minority of big businessmen rejected the more progressive aspects of corporate liberalism. The DuPonts, for example, adamantly defended the extraordinary profits they made in World War I. And the leader of the firm, Pierre DuPont, later reflected on corporate welfarism: "I have always been a believer in trying to make people conscious of their obligations to themselves and to society. Pension plans discourage such an idea." One of the DuPont executives, John J. Raskob, led the American Liberty League, which denounced the New Deal and "the demagogical theory that legislation provides a cure for all ills."[24]

Despite such reservations and modifications, it is clear that corporate liberalism had broad support within the North. The outlook of northern leaders was far more in harmony with the workings of an advanced industrialized society than were the views of the French-Canadian elite or wealthy southerners. In the era between 1860 and 1940 the gap between the North and the other two regions widened, and the North was riding high.

The New South Adheres to Old Values

If the North was buoyed by its strengths in the age of industrialization, the South* seemed burdened by its traditions. The agrarian values, racism, and concern for hierarchy that had defined relationships before

---

* In this chapter and the next two the discussion of the South includes all southern states, not simply the original five. As in the North, differences between east and west lessened during this era.

the Civil War slowed growth in an age where wealth came from large-scale manufacturing.

Historians studying the South in this era hotly debate the issue of change or continuity. They differ on whether entrepreneurial attitudes or older values were most important in shaping the "New South."[25] Some writers contend that a new middle class set the tone for society and that the typical southerner in this era was a "profit maximizer." These scholars emphasize the direction of change and note that the South grew steadily more urbanized and industrialized.[26]

Other works (and this text) disagree and underscore the persistence of traditional values. Most significant from this vantage is the slow pace of change and the widening gap between North and South. This school argues that the elite helped shape agriculture and industry more to protect caste and class lines than to produce the highest returns.[27] Those emphasizing a non-entrepreneurial ethos point to the continuities in the makeup of the southern upper class before and after the Civil War. Steven Hahn sums up much recent scholarship on this point:

> As a growing number of local studies are demonstrating—studies that have contributed to various "continuity" theses—the planters did maintain or reassert their dominance over much of the Southern countryside. Evidence from virtually every ex-Confederate state shows that the rate at which plantation owners persisted from 1860 to 1870 differed little from the previous decade and that the landed elite of the 1870s had firm roots in the antebellum era.[28]

For these historians signs of change in the outlook and behavior of southerners were unmistakable only during the last decades of the long era that stretched from the 1860s to 1940.

The ideology that shaped the views of white southerners in the seventy-five years after the Civil War resembled—in significant ways—the beliefs prevailing before 1860. It was an outlook that rested on the twin pillars of caste and class. African Americans were at the bottom, and wealthy white landowners were on top. Small white farmers stood somewhere in the middle. The aggressive pursuit of wealth was frowned upon. Industry was to remain subordinate to agriculture, and the defense of honor was exalted.[29]

These values were writ large in the pages of southern literary works penned by white authors. A familiar set of figures and settings characterized both highbrow and popular fiction. There were the faithful, happy African Americans; the high-minded patricians; and the sometimes good, sometimes conniving class of poor whites. The decades before the Civil War seemed to shimmer in a golden haze. Such themes were evident in the works of southern writers like Thomas Nelson Page, Joel Chandler Harris, William Faulkner, and Margaret

Mitchell. These authors and others reflected and helped shape the views of southerners.[30]

Let Thomas Nelson Page be your guide to this world. His popular stories and novels of the South were written between the 1870s and about 1910. The southern gentleman, Page observes,

> . . . was proud, but never haughty to dishonor. To that he was inexorable. He believed in God, he believed in his wife, he believed in his blood. He was chivalrous, he was generous, he was usually incapable of fear or meanness. . . . He believed in a democracy, but understood that the absence of a titled aristocracy had to be supplied by [the] class . . . to which he belonged.

The period before the Civil War for Page was a glorious time "when men treated women chivalrously and women relied on men implicitly, [and] when success bore no relation to wealth." The African Americans in Page's books share their masters' fondness for slavery. One faithful servant recollects: "Dem wuz good ole times, marster—de bes' Sam ever see. Dey wuz, in fac'! Niggers didn' hed nothin' 't all to do— jes' hed to 'ten' to de feedin' an' cleanin' de hosses, an' doin' what de marster tell 'em to do."[31]

Novelists were not the only individuals broadcasting these views. Church leaders and politicians sounded the same themes, as journalist Walter Hines Page (no direct relation to Thomas) made clear. Page observed in a 1902 article in the *Atlantic Monthly:* "Three influences have held the social structure stationary: first, slavery, which pickled all Southern life and left it just as it found it; then the politician, and the preacher. One has for a hundred years proclaimed the present social state as the ideal condition; and, if any has doubted this declaration, the other has told him that this life counts for little at best."[32]

Indeed, there were few dissenting white voices within this South.[33] Southerners for the most part were strangers to the northern obsession with success. The torrent of handbooks and novels that urged young men in the North to rise in the world was reduced to a trickle in the South. Even those few southerners who called for change displayed a remarkable respect for traditional ways. Henry Grady, editor of the Atlanta *Constitution*, was widely recognized as the leader of the New South Movement in the last part of the nineteenth century. He called for more industry and invited outside investment. But Grady fully shared the deep-rooted racism of the region. ("The supremacy of the white race must be maintained forever," he insisted.) And while he noted the discontent of some southern farmers, he would not attack the evils of sharecropping. Rather he blamed outsiders—greedy financiers and Republican politicians—for farm problems. An outlook that rested on such assumptions offered little possibility for far-reaching reform.[34]

Guided by this ideology the members of the old planter class, their descendants, and new additions to this ruling group worked hard to shape the region in their own image. These individuals, to be sure, did not have an entirely free hand in forming their "New South." Millions of African Americans, now free, refused some arrangements and only grudgingly accepted others. Poor white farmers sometimes supported the elite, but on occasion undertook their own protests. Northern politicians played a role in southern affairs, although after the end of Reconstruction usually a minor one. Northern capitalists were influential in certain economic activities. But by and large the planters were the creators of the New South. The emphasis they placed on hierarchy and social order rather than on productivity and long-term growth retarded southern development. While the North industrialized rapidly and found new ways of organizing workers and production, the South, like French Canada, grew more slowly.

In agriculture, tenant farming was the hallmark of the new order. Tenantry was a compromise, but a compromise that tilted heavily toward the desires of the southern elite. Initially, planters wanted African Americans to work the fields in gangs, much as in the days of slavery. These African Americans would be paid, but would have no choice about working. Blacks refused, countering with demands for land of their own. After three or four years of uncertainty in the late 1860s, tenant farming spread across the South. Ownership of the land remained in the hands of a class of affluent whites. But the great estates were divided into a series of small tracts and settled by farmers, black and white. These individuals were for the most part share-renters (who supplied equipment and animals) and sharecroppers (who provided only labor). The planter not only received a portion of the crop but also profited from the high markups charged by the general store, where the tenant had to shop.[35]

Tenant farming in the South was not only an economic relationship, it was also a means of social control. A survey in the 1920s indicated that planters oversaw work for 81 percent of sharecroppers and 61 percent of share-renters. Practices varied. In the Mississippi Delta close supervision meant that the day began with a wake-up bell. Bells were rung again to send people to the fields and to signal lunch, the resumption of work, and the end of the day. Throughout the South planters and overseers (or "riders") made sure the tenants behaved as they should.[36]

Such scrutiny was resented. "Any man under God's sun that's got anything industrious about him, you don't have to make him work—he goin' to work," remarked Nate Shaw, a black Alabama sharecropper. "But Tucker [the planter] didn't trust me to that. If a white man had anything booked against you, well, you could just expect him to ride up and hang around you to see that you worked, especially when the boll weevil come into this country."[37]

The patterns of southern agriculture contributed to the poverty of the region. Tenant farming fostered the growth of small, inefficient holdings. The average size of southern farms grew smaller between 1865 and 1930—unlike the trend in the rest of the United States and Quebec. Tenant farming also fixed cotton planting upon many areas that would have been wiser to move toward mixed farming. "We ought to plant less [cotton and tobacco] and more of grain and grasses," a North Carolina farmer observed in 1887, "but how are we to do it; the man who furnishes us rations at 50 per cent interest won't let us; he wants the money crop planted."[38]

The same values that shaped southern agriculture guided the course of industrial development. Southerners shunned industrial enterprises that might foster a riotous, urban proletariat and pose a challenge to the stable, agrarian social order. Lumber products and cotton goods illustrate this point. These were the only two southern enterprises to employ over 100,000 individuals during this era. What these two industries shared was the remarkable degree of control that owners had over workers.

Sawmills and logging operations typically were temporary, small, paternalistic enterprises. The mills moved when local timber supplies were exhausted, and so could hardly form the basis of a permanent labor force. Seasonal fluctuations in the number of employees also lessened militancy. Workers shifted from farming to lumbering and back again. Mills hired both blacks and whites. But all employees worked under the watchful eye of the local boss. The presence of African Americans helped keep wages low.[39]

Cotton mills were very different establishments—but they conformed to southern mores as fully as did the sawmills. Factories making cotton cloth might employ several hundred individuals. But the danger of a fractious labor force was undercut by the deliberate way that employers shaped the work force and the work environment. These businesses followed a pattern that had been worked out before the Civil War by entrepreneurs like William Gregg.[40] Operatives were exclusively white, and typically were recruited from the poor farms of the Piedmont or from hardscrabble mountain villages. These workers for many decades remained immune to the labor doctrines that spread in the North. Family labor was the mainstay of the cotton mills—at least until the 1910s. Children under 15 formed 15 percent of the work force in the factories in 1900, making the South the center of child labor in the nation. Females (including children) comprised over 40 percent of the operatives. And over 90 percent of workers lived in company towns, where employers exercised a remarkable degree of control.[41]

Only a very few southern entrepreneurs dared break this mold—and they seemed clearly out of place in a society that favored local, paternalistic businesses. James Buchanan ("Buck") Duke of Durham, North Carolina, was the driving force behind the American Tobacco Company. This trust, which commanded a 90 percent share of the cigarette market, was capitalized in 1889 at $25 million. Some who met Buck Duke considered him a quintessential southerner. He had "a Southern accent thick as butter," a New York merchant remarked, and frequently had a chaw of tobacco in his cheek. But Duke was hardly typical of the South. His father had voted for Lincoln and opposed secession. And while still in his teens Buck resolved to go to school in the North. "I am going to be a business man and make my pile," he told his father. "Now here's a place [the Eastman National School of Business in Poughkeepsie, New York] where a fellow can learn what I gotta know." On his return he introduced double-entry bookkeeping into his father's small tobacco firm. Once the family business acquired the Bonsack machine for mass-producing cigarettes, Duke went north again. He established his headquarters in New York City, and worked closely with northern financiers, advertising agencies, and businessmen.[42]

In all, few southerners joined the ranks of the business elite during this era. When Pitirim Sorokin compiled a list of American millionaires and multimillionaires in the 1920s he found that only 23 individuals of his total of 331 had been born in the South. By contrast, several northern states had more than the entire South, and New York alone claimed 104 of these wealthy individuals.[43]

Buck Duke's decision to go to school in the North was also a reflection of the poor state of southern education—another factor that slowed the growth of the southern economy. Lack of support for public schools reflected the priorities of a society where the "poorer sort" had little say in politics. Educated blacks were viewed as uppity. ("They're spoiling them [African Americans] now-a-days by educating them," grumped one employer.) African-American boys were expected to work in the fields, not sit behind a desk. For both races illiteracy was high. In 1880 some 80 percent of black farmers in the cotton South and 18 percent of white farmers could not read or write. The median level of spending per pupil in eleven southern states was less than a third of the national average in 1890. And while funding for white schools increased slowly during the ensuing decades, outlays for African Americans were cut. Between 1890 and 1910 southern blacks lost the right to vote as well as the vestiges of political power. Lily-white assemblies all too eagerly reduced the meager funds allotted for black schooling.[44]

While the most far-reaching changes would come after 1940, there were signs during the first decades of the twentieth century that the southern order was not immutable.[45] Between 1914 and 1930 one million African Americans left the South and went north. This "Great Migration" of blacks was paralleled by a comparable exodus of whites. The departure of nearly two million people suggests that the South was not entirely isolated from national developments. Nonetheless, this exodus had a surprisingly limited effect on southern society. Farm wages did not rise. Low cotton prices, not the departure of workers, shaped the rural economy during the 1920s.[46]

More far-reaching was the impact of the New Deal. Various federal programs affected the South. The Agricultural Adjustment Act of 1933 cut production and provided subsidies for reduced output. Landowners responded to these directives by driving off their tenants and keeping the government payments for themselves. The number of tenant farmers in the South dropped by almost 20 percent during the decade. Other New Deal programs, such as the National Recovery Administration and the Works Progress Administration, helped narrow the gap between northern and southern pay scales.[47]

Despite such gains, the South remained far behind the North in its standard of living. President Franklin Roosevelt hardly exaggerated when he pronounced in 1938: "The South presents right now the Nation's No. 1 economic problem." Only the changes that came after 1940 would bring the region closer to the mainstream of American development.[48]

Older Values Guide the Industrialization of Quebec

Between the 1860s and 1940 the province of Quebec, like the South, remained an underdeveloped area shaped by a philosophy that emphasized traditional, hierarchical values and questioned the pursuit of profit. Although Quebec gradually industrialized and urbanized, the province remained far behind the North.

In debates that broadly resemble discussions about the South, scholars provide several explanations for Quebec's path of development. Many essays, including this one, argue that long-held values slowed provincial growth.[49] But other works disagree. One school asserts that Quebec was hurt by its geographical position in North America. "Ontario has the advantage of location," observes Kenneth McRoberts. "The peninsula of Southwestern Ontario is directly adjacent to the US industrial centres of Michigan and Ohio. . . . Quebec's neighboring states of New England and New York were much weaker as industrial centres than were Ontario's neighbors."[50] Other writers dispute the premise of slow growth and argue that Quebec experienced a "normal" path of development. For example, in their history of Quebec, Paul-André Linteau, René Durocher, and Jean-Claude Robert remark: "The degree of urbanization in Quebec followed a similar pattern to that of Canada as a whole." These historians minimize the differences between francophones and anglophones.[51]

The balance of this chapter makes the case for the importance of values in shaping the growth of French Canada. Still the shortcomings of the alternative explanations should be noted. Writers who contend that location disadvantaged Quebec overlook the vitality of New York and New England. And those who argue that the province pursued a normal course of development have at best half a case. French Canada, it is true, urbanized and industrialized more rapidly than did the South. But it remained far behind the northern states. Moreover, the advances that Quebec made reflected, in large part, the wealth and direction of English speakers.[52]

We begin our examination of Quebec with a focus on the outlook of French Canadians. Let's listen to the remarks in the 1930s of a parish priest. The townsfolk of Drummondville, Quebec, have come together to celebrate St. Jean-Baptiste Day. Mass has just concluded. The crowd settles down again and the curé of the parish of Ste Anne addresses the gathering:

"The patriotic way for the true French Canadian to live is to save and become a small proprietor. English methods are not ours. The French become great by small savings and small business. Don't borrow the commercial ways of others. The prosperity of this community lies with us, not with the industries of England and United States, but in the number of small proprietors. Our country is not just any place where we make our living, as in the United States."

He continues: "Shun United States extravagances—radios, newspapers, and other expensive things and ways. Love your priests, go to Mass, and observe the feasts. It will be a great day when we have a real Catholic patriotism—a patriotism which not only makes every French Canadian ready to die for his country but ready to vote independently of parties."[53]

This ideology condemned the pursuit of riches, but it was not flatly anti-industrial. Local priests usually welcomed the establishment of a textile mill or a pulp and paper factory in their community. These businesses, which typically were directed by English-Canadian or American entrepreneurs, provided employment and kept people from emigrating to the United States. But French Canadians were not encouraged to build such grand enterprises. Their proper callings were more modest: farmer, worker, shopkeeper, or professional.[54]

The clergy were the most outspoken advocates of this traditional set of values. And gradually between the 1860s and 1940 their influence over the French-Canadian population increased. The number of clerics rose sharply during this era. During the middle decades of the nineteenth century Bishop Ignace Bourget of Montreal and other

Church leaders sowed many seeds that took root and flourished. The bishops fostered the growth of existing orders of nuns and brothers, and recruited foreign clerics. These leaders also established "classical colleges" to prepare young men for the priesthood. The number of Grey Nuns, Franciscans, Dominicans, Sulpicians, Jesuits, and other religious groups soared. In 1851 there was one member of a religious order for every 722 Catholics in Quebec; by 1931 there was one cleric for every 71 Catholics. As historian Fernand Ouellet notes, "the number of Catholics per cleric thus became the lowest in the Western world."[55]

Key to the growing power of the Church was its control over the education of French Canadians. (Protestants, who comprised 20 percent of the population, supported a separate school system.) During the 1840s the Church had won the battle to shape the curriculum. It now replaced lay teachers with nuns and brothers. Catholic schools gradually improved, but the quality of instruction remained poor, and illiteracy stayed relatively high. Students who went on in the Catholic system were steered away from business toward a limited group of professions: priest, notary, lawyer, and doctor. Catholic universities only confirmed the bent of the classical colleges. Early in the twentieth century more than a third of the students in the French-speaking universities in Quebec were studying religion; only 4 percent were taking the applied sciences. In the English-speaking higher institutions the balance was reversed: less than 1 percent took up theology, while 28 percent pursued applied sciences.[56]

In this era no single individual was more important in expounding and elaborating the ideology of French Canada than Canon Lionel Groulx. Born in the 1870s and living until the 1960s Groulx cast a long shadow across the Quebec landscape. His writings and campaigns influenced even those who disagreed with him. (Newspaper editor and politician Claude Ryan remarked: "He was the spiritual father of modern Quebec. Everything noteworthy, everything novel on the Quebec scene has carried the imprint of Groulx's thought.")[57] Groulx was a priest and a professor of history, but his activities went far beyond the pulpit and the classroom. He lectured widely, wrote two novels and many history books, and edited a nationalist journal.[58]

Groulx was determined to defend traditional society and values against outside influences. These dangers included "American paganism," "English agnosticism," and "French skepticism." During the 1920s Groulx led a small French-Canadian nationalist group, Action Française. It exalted the traditional role of women, promoted the use of French, defended Catholic unions, and praised rural life. "The settler and the farmer," he remarked, "have been the major artisans of our national destiny, the most faithful conservers of our religious and moral characteristics and of our dearest traditions." Groulx looked forward to the day when Quebec would become a sovereign nation. His many works of history revealed in the past the heroism and values he hoped to find in the present.[59]

The clergy were not the only ones propounding this set of beliefs. Editors, novelists, and union leaders affirmed the same values. Ronald Rudin's study of the *caisses populaires,* the small savings banks found throughout the province, shows that speeches at their annual meetings sounded similar themes. Officials exalted clerical leadership and denounced large-scale capitalism and class conflict.[60]

Recently, some historians have emphasized the voices of dissent that stood apart from this orthodoxy. But the presence of these critics only slightly modifies the picture of a closed, Church-directed society. Some women denounced a society where they had fewer rights than in any other North American jurisdiction. (Women could not vote in provincial elections until 1940, and married women had no rights over property or children.) But the protests were far weaker than elsewhere.[61] Catholic Quebec still had a few adherents of "liberalism"— that freethinking ideology with its strong roots in the Enlightenment. But these individuals kept their discussions within narrow bounds, and accepted the dominant role of the Church.[62] Many workers belonged to unions. But in this era these organizations typically were docile bodies loyal to the Church.[63] All in all, the outlook of most French Canadians was shaped by a durable, pervasive set of values whose origins can be traced back to New France.

This traditional outlook guided the development of the Quebec economy. It helps explain the slow pace of agricultural change and the patterns of out-migration that emerged as the growth of rural population outpaced the availability of new farmland. In 1891 the farm sector accounted for fully 45 percent of the Quebec work force, and this percentage only gradually decreased. Landowners took only halting steps to modernize their holdings and boost output. They changed their mix of crops and animals. But compared with their counterparts in the North, French-Canadian farmers remained far less productive, used much less machinery, rarely hired laborers, and were less likely to borrow money for improvements.[64]

Too many Quebec farms were poor tracts that barely supported one family. Quebecker Evelyne Provencher returned from the United States in 1923 for marriage and life on such a farm. "We were poor and had debts to pay," she recollected. "The second year of our marriage, hail destroyed all our crop. Oh, it was horrible. We had a lovely field of tobacco. We carted water because we did not have . . . a pump. We were too poor. From a well near the house, one went to get water to sprinkle the tobacco. . . . After the hail, in the fall the horse dies. It was the only one that we had. . . . That winter my husband had to go to a lumber camp. I remained all alone at my father-in-law's house. We decided to return to Manchester [New Hampshire]." These pockets of subsistence agriculture, strongly reminiscent of the household economy of the eighteenth century, slowed Quebec growth.[65]

The clear limits to the population the established farms could support created several streams of migration. These flowed to new areas in the province, to Quebec towns and cities, and to the United States. While farms were subdivided in some parishes, more typically, holdings were kept intact and passed from father to son. Such practices meant that most grown children had to seek work elsewhere. The Church hoped to find new soils within the province and launched an ambitious "colonization" movement in the nineteenth century. But many of the regions opened for settlement were rocky and inhospitable. Some French-speaking Quebeckers moved to the cities, particularly once industry developed in the early twentieth century. French Canadians became town-dwellers, but they did so at a slower pace than the anglophones. In 1910 when 78 percent of English speakers were urbanized, only 42 percent of francophones lived in towns and cities (Fig. 9.3).[66]

Many French Canadians also went to the United States. Between 1851 and 1931 about 700,000 people left Quebec, the majority going to New England. Emigration was greatest from 1865 to the late 1890s when industrialization in Quebec quickened, and jobs opened up in urban centers. This was the migration of a people who had long shown a reluctance to move (as discussed in Chapter 5). Thus, most French Canadians ignored the opportunities in the western reaches of Canada and the United States, where they might have continued farming. Instead, they chose the mill towns of New England, which lay much closer. They considered themselves migrants rather than immigrants. Like Evelyne Provencher, most returned to Quebec to try their fortune one more time before settling in the States. Once in New England, the French Canadians were slow to sell the property they held in Quebec and reluctant to take up U.S. citizenship. But the lack of opportunity in Quebec, and particularly in rural Quebec, meant that ultimately many settled in the States.[67]

The interplay between the traditional outlook of French Canadians and the initiatives of English-speaking entrepreneurs set the pattern for Quebec industrialization. Although they were four-fifths of the population, French Canadians made up only a small portion of the financiers and factory owners. There were a few notable exceptions to this rule, such as Louis-Joseph Forget, who was a securities broker and the force behind a series of important consolidations. Forget sat on the board of Canadian Pacific and other companies and became chairman of the

Montreal Exchange. Alfred Dubuc, a Chicoutimi bank manager, also stood out. Dubuc, who had little money of his own but a great deal of ability and determination, helped create one of the largest pulp mills in Quebec. Such individuals aside, anglophones dominated the upper reaches of Quebec industry. In the 1930s they made up almost 90 percent of the directors of large firms headquartered in Montreal. And in the smaller centers they typically ran the textile, paper, and other mills. English prejudice—a clear reluctance to hire francophones for managerial positions—reinforced the career decisions of French Canadians.[68]

For the most part, French Canadians contributed to the industrialization of Quebec by providing a large, low-paid, docile work force. A publication boosting the town of Shawinigan observed: "The contentment of the French-Canadian people is a factor of utmost importance to the employer in the district, and this great asset to human happiness is to be attributed directly to the wise and kindly guidance of their 'father confessor.' For centuries . . . it has been a cardinal principle of the habitant's religion to be contented with his lot."[69] The clergy, from bishops to parish priests, worked hard to preserve this mind-set. As in the South, the key question was how to guide the inevitable growth of industry so that hierarchical values remained intact. Curés urged workers to be obedient and fiercely attacked international unions, such as the American Federation of Labor. When unionization appeared imminent, the Church helped establish Catholic unions, which cooperated with the employers.[70]

Thanks to abundant hydroelectric power and the lure of a large pool of cooperative, low-paid workers, the pace of industrial growth in Quebec gradually accelerated. In 1910–11 fully 48 percent of the Quebec population lived in urban places, compared with 22 percent in the South and 57 percent in the North (72 percent in the Northeast) (see Fig. 9.3).[71] The per capita output of manufactures also was higher in Quebec than in the South, although here too the North retained its sizable lead. Manufacturing in Quebec typically meant large factories, poorly paid, low-skilled workers, and the processing of raw materials. Cheap electricity helped attract such industries as aluminum refining, chemicals, and pulp and paper to towns along the river valleys. But more than half the manufacturing in the province was located in Montreal and its environs. French-Canadian operatives working in Montreal factories crowded into the disease-ridden suburbs to the west and east of the rich downtown districts.[72]

Unlike the South, Quebec showed few signs before 1940 of abandoning its time-honored approach to development. Compared with levels in the United States, the average income in Quebec rose in the 1930s (see Fig. 9.1). But this advance was more a reflection of the disastrous fall in U.S. output during the Depression than French-

Canadian progress. These illusive gains were erased after 1940. The ideology which urged French Canadians to be farmers and small businesspeople prevailed in the 1930s, as earlier. Maurice Duplessis, premier of Quebec in the late 1930s, was a strong supporter of rural virtues, proclaiming, "Agriculture is an element of economic stability and social order." He worked closely with the clergy to check the influx of subversive ideas. Beginning with a huge rally in Quebec City in 1936, Duplessis led a spirited crusade against Communism. The first evidence of change would appear in the early 1940s. But the transformation of Quebec society did not come until the "Quiet Revolution" of the 1960s.[73]

In sum, a focus on the role of culture and institutions suggests that for all three regions the period from 1860 to 1940 was more one of affirmation than change. Tremendous growth accompanied industrialization. But the North remained far wealthier than the South or French Canada.

10

The Paths Converge: 1940 to 1975

In all three regions long-standing patterns of thought and behavior changed dramatically between 1940 and 1975. The traditional, non-entrepreneurial outlook of southerners and French Canadians gradually yielded to a more commercial mind-set. Powerful institutions—such as sharecropping in the South and the Catholic Church in Quebec—declined in importance. Such changes accelerated growth in these two sections, which for more than a century had lagged far behind the North. By contrast, the triumph of the corporate economy in the northern states dulled the business ethos that long had driven the growth of that area. The stage was set for economic decline. But (and the *but* here is important) these changes had only begun. Older patterns of thought and behavior persisted. In 1975 as in 1940 northerners remained more business-minded and more productive than southerners or French Canadians. The gap in the standard of living between the North, on the one hand, and the South and Quebec, on the other, had lessened but had not been erased.

The North: Successful and Complacent

Between 1940 and 1975 the northern states flourished. Success bred success. Or so it seemed. In fact this was an era when the outlook of northern businesspeople was marked by a dangerous complacency. The problems that would blight so much of northern industry after

1975 can be traced to this period. The fierce entrepreneurial approach of the nineteenth century was fading. The new watchwords were: don't stick your neck out, and be a team player. During these years foreign producers quietly made inroads into U.S. markets. Few in the North, however, noted such ominous developments. Most people were too busy enjoying their rising standard of living.

Our analysis of the North necessarily begins with a profile of its prosperity and the apparent triumph of its ideology—corporate liberalism. The northern states remained unquestionably the wealthiest part of the United States. If you colored in the richest ten states among the Lower Forty-eight—using per capita income as the yardstick—seven or eight of these states would be in the North. (The other two or three are California, Nevada, and Washington.) Among the leaders were Connecticut, New York, New Jersey, Delaware, Illinois, and Michigan. Other northern states fell not far behind. Northern factories sold cars, refrigerators, televisions, and other appliances to American consumers, who grew richer by the year. Northern plants supplied businesses with steel and chemicals and the government with computers and submarines. Most head offices (in 1967 over 80 percent of the Fortune 500 companies) were in the North. So were the chief banks and insurance companies.[1]

The few visible signs of northern weakness hardly seemed threatening. Not all areas in the industrial North shared the prosperity of the top states. In the Northeast many of the traditional industries, including textiles, shoes, and clothing were in decline. However, despite such problems, states like Massachusetts, Connecticut, and New York remained wealthier than the national average. The standard of living in the North, it was clear, was not rising as fast as levels in the South or French Canada (Figs. 9.1, 10.1–10.5). Nor after 1960 was the North creating jobs as fast as the southern states. The long-term movement of people from the South to the North was reversed. Northerners duly noted these trends, but few read them as evidence that the northern powerhouse might be in trouble.[2]

Not only was the economy of the North preeminent within the United States, it also shone on the international stage. In the 1950s America manufactured three-fourths of the motor vehicles made in the world and accounted for about half of global steel production. Even in the 1960s, with Japan and Germany back on their feet, 18 of the 20 largest firms in the world were American (and based in the northern states). For most U.S. businesses, foreign shipments posed no immediate threat. As late as 1970 imports amounted to less than 10 percent of the gross national product.[3]

Corporate liberalism remained the philosophy of the northern industrial states—although now this ideology was presented with bland self-assuredness that shaded into smugness. For corporate leaders the

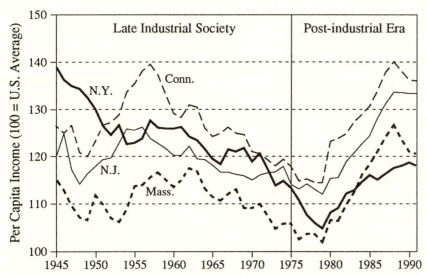

Figure 10.1 **Per Capita Income in Four Northeastern States, 1945–91, Compared with U.S. Average**. Although income levels remained above the national average, the economy of the Northeast weakened during the late industrial period. After 1975, however, this area displayed a remarkable resurgence.

Note that the graphs in this chapter show income levels *relative* to the U.S. national average. In most instances average earnings moved steadily higher, even when relative incomes declined. (*Source: Statistical Abstract of the U.S.*, various years. These are figures for "personal income.")

period from World War II to the mid-1970s appeared the heyday of a beneficent capitalist system. Profits were high, and real wages were rising. The labor movement was cooperative and no longer dominated by angry socialists. And the biggest firms accounted for an ever-increasing share of the national product. No wonder the business community felt an increased sense of self-importance. Charles Wilson, the head of General Motors, made clear his belief in the identity of corporate and national goals. Questioned during the hearings held to confirm his appointment as Eisenhower's Secretary of Defense, Wilson announced: "I have always believed that what's good for the country is good for General Motors, and vice versa."[4]

The same congratulatory note was evident in the remarks of other executives, as well as in the writings of journalists, historians, and economists. The overinflated rhetoric of Roger Blough, head of U.S. Steel, echoed Charles Wilson's sentiments. "To me the heart of the matter . . . ," Blough stated in a 1957 speech, "is not that corporate groups are the indispensable providers of the physical elements of our national well being; the heart of the matter is that through these freely

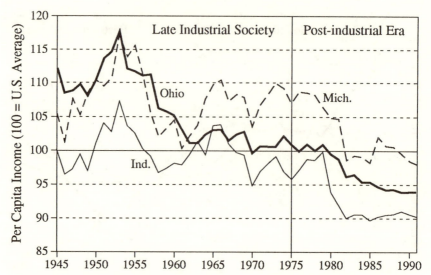

Figure 10.2 **Per Capita Income in Three Midwestern States, 1945–91, Compared with U.S. Average.** The 1950s were the heyday of the industrial Midwest. Although decline was evident well before 1975, the worst years came in the post-industrial era. (*Source:* See Fig. 10.1.)

formed and constantly evolving organisms of production, generative forces of great originality rise far above the individual imagination of any of its members, enhancing the role of *every* man and giving breadth and scope even to him who may be called the uncommon man." In short, corporations were wonderful.[5] New Dealer David Lilienthal in *Big Business: A New Era* and economist John Kenneth Galbraith in *The New Industrial State* were among the many individuals singing the praises of big business. These writers and others declared large units to be the most efficient way of organizing and planning production.[6]

With company and individual earnings so high, business leaders seemed to have every right to tell employees to follow corporate norms.The credo of conform and prosper pervaded the culture of the North. It was evident in movies such as *The Apartment* and in best-selling novels, for example, Sloan Wilson's *The Man in the Gray Flannel Suit*. This mind-set was expounded and analyzed in such treatises as David Riesman's *The Lonely Crowd* and William H. Whyte's *The Organization Man*. (The same ideology spelled out a subordinate role for women. They were to be homemakers or devoted secretaries.) Codes of behavior, even if unwritten, were operative everywhere. At General Motors John DeLorean, a group vice president, was hauled on the carpet for not conforming. "Goddammit, John," another executive yelled at him, "Can't you dress like a businessman? And get your hair cut,

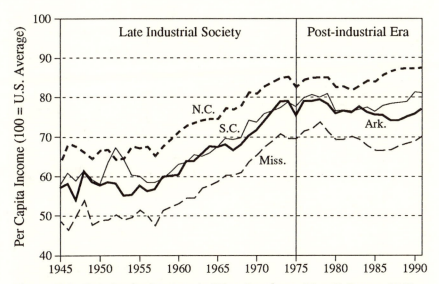

Figure 10.3 **Per Capita Income in Four Southern "Core" States, 1945–91, Compared with U.S. Average.** Like most of the South, the "core" states (discussed more fully in Chapter 11) grew wealthier during the late industrial period. But growth slowed in the post-industrial era. (*Source:* See Fig. 10.1.)

too." Other officials called his friends, and asked: "What's up with John? . . . Why doesn't he have dinner with the other executives? He's not acting like a team player." [7] DeLorean quit.

Those employees who played by the rules and rose in the ranks received marvelous benefits. Take Bethlehem Steel Corporation, the nation's second largest steel producer. In 1956 eleven of the eighteen best-paid executives in the U.S. worked for the company. Every vice president had his own dining room with linen tablecloths and full waiter service. Each Bethlehem plant had its own golf course, and the company employed three individuals whose only job was playing golf with clients.[8]

Big unions now came under the umbrella of corporate liberalism. Earlier in the century even the most liberal employers had resisted unionization. The auto and steel industries had been among the most notorious opponents of organized labor. But the Wagner Labor Relations Act of 1935 and the strikes that ensued changed the picture. By the 1950s generous industry-wide contracts were accepted as a way of keeping labor peace. There was no change in the Tayloristic formula by which managers made all production-related decisions and workers carried out those orders. But pay increases, especially to unionized workers, were regular and substantial. There were still strikes, but labor peace was the norm.[9]

The new ethos of conformity, it is true, did not wholly obliterate

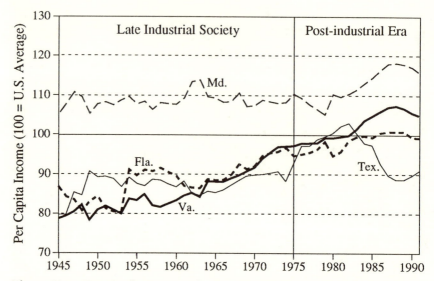

Figure 10.4 **Per Capita Income in Four Southern "Periphery" States, 1945–91, Compared with U.S. Average.** The states of the southern "periphery" (discussed more fully in Chapter 11) were wealthier and less characterized by traditional values than the states of the southern "core." By the 1980s per capita income in the "periphery" was around the national average—or higher. These states experienced stronger growth in the post-industrial era than did the "core." Texas, hard-hit by falling oil prices in the 1980s, was the exception to this rule. (*Source:* See Fig. 10.1.)

the northern respect for striving entrepreneurs. There were important start-ups during this era. Ken Olsen, for example, founded Digital Equipment Corporation in the 1950s, with a lean, aggressive approach to growth. ("We're a new company," he told his managers. "Nobody tells anybody else what to do. . . . You, you, you, and you are now entrepreneurs.") But a corporate outlook that emphasized conformity in thought and dress set the tone for these years.[10]

What was good for General Motors, IBM, General Electric, and the other leading firms certainly seemed to be good for America. Corporations made large profits. Managers lived well. Workers found more in their pay envelopes each year. And inequality in American society lessened. In the 1950s and 1960s the bottom fifth of society received a larger slice of the pie than it had in the 1920s. For many northerners who were reveling in an era of low inflation and high employment, it seemed paradise had arrived.[11]

But all was not right in paradise. The complacency and conformity that marked northern business culture obscured grave weaknesses. Too many business leaders had lost touch with the hard-driving entrepre-

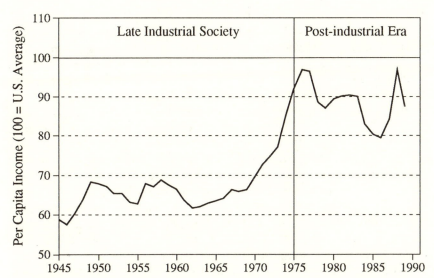

Figure 10.5 **Per Capita Income in Quebec, 1945–89, Compared with U.S. Average.** An era of strong growth began with the "Quiet Revolution" of the 1960s. However, the Quebec economy fared less well in the post-industrial era. (*Sources:* F. H. Leacy, ed., *Historical Statistics of Canada,* 2d ed. (Ottawa, 1983), ser. A7, F95, provides income figures 1926–76; for subsequent years, Statistics Canada, *System of National Accounts* (Ottawa, 1976), table 36 (catalogue 13-531); Statistics Canada, *Provincial Economic Accounts* (Ottawa, 1990), tables 1 and 2 (catalogue 13-213); for population, Statistics Canada, *Vital Statistics* (catalogue 91-210), vol. I; U.S. income figures and exchange rates, from *Statistical Abstract of the U.S.,* various years.)

neurial spirit that had helped enrich the North. Back in the 1880s and 1890s John D. Rockefeller was obsessive in his determination to wring an additional cent out of each barrel of crude oil he refined. Andrew Carnegie never hesitated to tear down a blast furnace he had just erected if he learned that a new one would lower costs and help him undercut the competition.

Compare that older approach with the fear of innovation voiced by leading executives in the decades after 1940. Let the other fellow make expensive mistakes was the accepted wisdom. Pete Estes (who was soon to be appointed president of General Motors) turned thumbs down on a proposal in the early 1970s to introduce front-wheel-drive cars. He confided to a colleague: "When I was at Oldsmobile, there was something I learned that I've never forgotten. There was an old guy there who was an engineer, and he had been at GM a long time, and he gave me some advice. He told me, whatever you do, *don't let GM do it first."* [12]

American businessmen (chiefly northerners) shunned advances

that had proven themselves in Europe or Japan. Tire makers were reluctant to introduce radials. Electronics firms were slow to use printed circuit boards. Steel companies too often relied on aging facilities and outmoded processes. Between 1950 and 1971 the Japanese built 11 steel plants with a total capacity of 115 thousand metric tons; the U.S. constructed only two with an output of 11 thousand metric tons. The Japanese shifted far more rapidly to the new steel technologies: basic oxygen furnaces and continuous slab casting. American steel executives saw no reason to invest in expensive new facilities. Foreign producers (they decided) posed no real challenge. The head of Bethlehem Steel remarked in 1971 that "the long-range threat of foreign steel competition seems to be diminishing." And four years later the president of Jones and Laughlin observed that "the steel import situation has changed dramatically and perhaps permanently during the past two years. . . . The era of cheap foreign steel has gone the way of cheap foreign oil, never to return." He was wrong.[13]

A portrait of Lee Iacocca during his years at the Ford Motor Company casts light on this corporate mind-set. In many respects Iacocca was a businessman to be admired. He was an executive with a sure feel for the market, and he became a dynamic president from 1970 until Henry Ford II fired him in 1978. (Iacocca subsequently would head the Chrysler Corporation.) He helped launch the sporty Mustang and redesigned the Lincoln, sharply boosting sales of that luxury car. He was articulate and outspoken in a Detroit where too many auto men were gray figures content to fade into the background.

But for all the flair that Iacocca brought to the job, he was as reluctant to innovate as any Detroit executive. He refused to push for safety features, arguing that "safety doesn't sell." He disliked the idea of building small cars, even though the success of the Volkswagen showed a strong market existed. (The popular wisdom in Detroit was, "small cars, small profits.") He pooh-poohed concerns about pollution. "We've got to pause and ask ourselves," he remarked, "how much clean air do we need?" Like his counterparts at GM, he rejected the idea of producing a front-wheel-drive car. It was a feature that consumers could not see. His response: "I say give 'em leather. They can smell it." And he was contemptuous of the challenge from Japan. In 1971 a friend, Carroll Shelby, was offered a large Toyota dealership in Houston. Iacocca told Shelby: "Let me give you the best advice you'll ever get. Don't take it." "Why not?" Shelby demanded. Iacocca replied: "Because we're going to kick their asses back into the Pacific Ocean." Shelby later estimated that following Iacocca's advice cost him $10 million.[14]

Not all northern industries can be tarred with the same brush. In some, research and development spending remained high. In others, such as data processing equipment, defense spending spurred growth.

But in too many areas—including autos, steel, and consumer electronics—it was an era of management by complacency. American plants gradually fell behind the competition abroad. Instead of putting money into product innovation, companies expanded by acquiring unrelated businesses. Total assets and earnings rose in these newly formed conglomerates, but productivity fell.[15]

But for a while the world of northern industry seemed an idyllic place. It was not until the 1970s that foreign producers finally overcame the enormous U.S. lead in product development. Plant closings and the devastating impact of foreign competition lay in the future. In 1975 as in 1940 the North was unmistakably the most prosperous section of the United States. Education levels remained high. Defense spending was a boon for some states, such as Connecticut and Massachusetts. The path ahead perhaps was uncertain. But for most people in the North, blue-collar and white-collar workers alike, these were years of welcome prosperity.[16]

The South: Farewell Sharecropping, Hello Industry

While the North was slipping from its lofty perch, the backward South was growing more prosperous. The section that Franklin Roosevelt had called the nation's number one economic problem became a mecca for job seekers and (in the view of its more enthusiastic publicists) the booming sunbelt. This dramatic ascent reflected profound changes in southern values and behavior. But any depiction of developments in the South during these years must be a balanced one. Progress was unquestionable. Old institutions, such as sharecropping, were swept away, and long-standing attitudes, such as the hostility to widespread industrialization, disappeared. African Americans gained rights they had not had since Reconstruction. Per capita income in the fifteen southern states climbed from just over 60 percent to more than 85 percent of the national average (Figs. 9.1, 10.3, and 10.4). Still, much of the old persisted in this "New South." Southerners remained poorer and less educated than other Americans. Blacks still were at the bottom of the economic hierarchy, and traditional values toward work and race continued to characterize much of southern society.[17]

The extensive literature that has emerged on the rise of the postwar South appears to be of one mind in arguing that momentous change took place during these years. Disagreements focus largely on the reasons for this transformation and on the benefits of southern economic growth. Various scholars have promoted, or questioned, the importance of agricultural reform, urbanization, migration, federal spending, state efforts to recruit new businesses, rising educational levels, civil rights reform, and the spread of air-conditioning.[18] Writers have also differed in evaluating the positive and baneful effects of the emergence of the Sunbelt South.[19] But to a remarkable degree, disputes seem to be over matters of emphasis. There is widespread agreement on the broad outlines of change.

We begin the story of this "new" New South with the transformation of agriculture. Why did farming change so remarkably after 1940, when for so long it had seemed fixed in its ways? The wartime shortage of labor served as a catalyst. But World War II only accelerated a process that was long overdue: the replacement of men and women by machines. This development had begun a century earlier in the North, and only deep-rooted social attitudes had kept southern farming so labor-intensive.[20]

New Deal programs reduced the number of sharecroppers, but the most striking changes came after 1940. Between 1940 and 1945 the farm population in the South fell by 20 percent. Bill Jenkins, an African American and resident of the South Carolina sea islands, remembered: "During World War II plants were looking for people to make fertilizer, and a lot of people out here who had been doing almost unskilled work were looking for other jobs because farming didn't pay that well. They started getting jobs in Charleston, and Daddy started using his truck to carry people to the fertilizer plant." Landowners now combined plots they once had tenanted, and brought in machinery. The number of tractors in fifteen southern states soared from 271,000 in 1940 to 496,000 in 1945, and to 918,000 in 1950.[21]

The labor shortage persisted after 1945, and spurred the mechanization of cotton picking. Racial attitudes had not changed. But white southerners glimpsed a new solution to the problem of working the land and keeping a restless underclass in check. They saw the possibility of expelling blacks from the rural South, and depending on machines rather than human labor. "I strongly advocate," announced Richard Hopson, a wealthy white landowner, "the farmers of the Mississippi Delta changing as rapidly as possible from the old tenant or sharecropping system of farming to complete mechanized farming. . . . Mechanized farming will require only a fraction of the amount of labor which is required by the share crop system thereby tending to equalize the white and negro population which would automatically make our racial problems easier to handle." The widespread adoption of mechanical cotton pickers began in the 1950s. In 1950 only 8 percent of cotton was mechanically harvested. By 1960 this figure had risen to 51 percent, and by 1968, fully 96 percent. Tobacco harvesting was also mechanized, although here dramatic progress came after 1970.[22]

The replacement of people and mules by machines had broad consequences. Much as white landowners had foreseen, African Americans left southern farms and moved in record numbers to the cities of the North and South. During the 1940s, 1950s, and 1960s, some 4.6

million blacks headed North. Those blacks remaining in the South moved from farms to towns. Where the black population in the U.S. in 1940 had been 77 percent southern, by 1970 it was only 53 percent southern. Where it had been 51 percent rural in 1940, by 1970 it was 81 percent urban.[23]

The end of sharecropping and the emergence of agribusinesses boosted productivity throughout the South. A region gains wealth as individuals abandon older, unproductive occupations. Hence the gradual disappearance of small, impoverished farms helped raise income levels in the South. The demise of sharecropping was also accompanied by a shift away from cotton toward more lucrative crops. In states like the Carolinas, Georgia, and Alabama, farmers sharply reduced the acreage devoted to cotton and expanded the production of such staples as peanuts and soybeans. President Jimmy Carter was a participant in these changes. After serving in the navy, Carter returned to Georgia in the mid-1950s to become a prosperous peanut farmer. He told a visitor to the White House: "In my little farming community, when I grew up, our agricultural methods and way of life were not greatly different from those of centuries earlier. I stepped from that world into the planning and outfitting of a nuclear submarine. When I returned to the land, I found that farming had been transformed in just a few years by new scientific knowledge and technology." Largely because of these changes in agriculture the rising tide of growth between 1940 and 1975 was one that buoyed virtually all southern states. [24]

Prominent southerners now regarded industry rather than farming as the engine of growth. Tax policy reflected these shifting priorities. Before 1950 corporate tax rates in the South were fully 85 percent above levels in the rest of the country. Beginning in the 1950s pro-business administrations in the southern states adopted new policies. Corporate taxes were reduced and eventually became the lowest in the nation. At the same time southern states aggressively sought new industry. Starting in the 1950s many states sent delegations to the North and Europe.[25]

The policies of the federal government also fostered the emergence of an industrial South. The interstate highway system, launched in 1956, was a blessing to a region that had fewer modern roads than the other, wealthier parts of the United States. Government outlays during World War II expanded the industrial capacity of the South by 40 percent. During the years after the war federal expenditures in the South rose steadily to the levels established elsewhere in the nation.[26]

Moreover, the spread of air-conditioning encouraged people and businesses to move south. Climate long had been touted as an explanation for the slow pace of southern development. But the widespread adoption of air-conditioning in the 1950s and 1960s seems as much the result as the cause of growth. Units for cooling buildings had been

available since the 1920s. Only when demand increased was this technology put to use. The advent of these machines changed the work
day and encouraged the influx of northerners. The *New York Times*
called the 1970 census (which documented the migration of whites to
the South) "The Air Conditioned Census" and commented: "The hum-
ble air conditioner has been a powerful influence in circulating people
as well as air in this country." [27]

While virtually all southern states participated in this economic
expansion, a more select group led in creating jobs and attracting
northern immigrants. Peninsular Florida with its warm climate, eager
land developers, and distinct racial history (marked by a small black
population) attracted many companies as well as northern retirees.
Texas with its oil boom was another magnet for affluent migrants,
while northern Virginia profited from its proximity to the rapidly expanding bureaucracy in Washington, D.C. There were also pockets of
northern settlement in Georgia, North Carolina, and Tennessee. This
influx would help remake Florida, Texas, and Virginia, although the
striking difference between these states and the rest of the South would
not be evident until after 1975 and the advent of the post-industrial
era.

Change occurred in the South in still another area: civil rights.
The federal government—pushed by civil rights leaders and by sit-ins,
marches, and boycotts—became a strong force for progress. The 1954
Supreme Court decision *Brown v. Topeka Board of Education* nudged the
South toward integrating its schools. The Civil Rights Act of 1964 at-
tacked discrimination in public accommodations, while the Voting
Rights Act of 1965 dramatically enlarged the black electorate in the
South. African-American voters provided a strong base for a new
group of influential black politicians, such as Andrew Young. Educated
at Howard University, Young rose to prominence in Martin Luther
King, Jr.'s, Southern Christian Leadership Conference. In 1972 Young
became (along with Barbara Jordan of Texas) one of the first African
Americans elected to Congress from the South since 1898. He would
later be ambassador to the United Nations and mayor of Atlanta. In
this "Second Reconstruction," as in the first, political rights were easier
to achieve than economic equality. But a cornerstone of modern
southern culture, racial discrimination in public facilities and at the
ballot box, had been dislodged. This change accelerated southern
growth. More opportunities were open to the black citizens of the
South. And northern firms now could move their head offices to Houston or Atlanta without offending a racially mixed staff.[28]

The progress recorded in the South is impressive. But the limits of this
transformation are equally significant. Despite years of steady growth
and much hype about a booming sunbelt only one southern state had

an average income in 1975 above the national average. And that one exception, Maryland, had long kept pace with the northern common-wealths. By any measure education lagged. Southerners were less liter-ate and completed fewer years of schooling than their counterparts in the North. Outlays on education were substantially lower in the South than elsewhere in the country. In 1971 almost all the states (11 of 13) that spent less than $680 per pupil were in the South. Only one south-ern state, Maryland, stood above the national average.

Industry came to the South, but typically in ways that reaffirmed the hierarchical social values of the region. Southern leaders wooed enterprises that relied on low-wage, non-union laborers. South Caro-lina, for example, advertised a work force that accepted "the primary position of capital" and respected "competent management." Unions were anathema. By 1954 all southern states (but relatively few states outside the South) had passed right-to-work laws, which prohibited closed union shops. And this was industrialization that did not chal-lenge the color line. Textile mills remained lily-white in the 1950s. In most other enterprises blacks were excluded, paid less for doing the same work as whites, or given jobs that were too poorly paid to attract white workers. Most of the new jobs were saved for whites. While 2.9 million blacks left the South during the 1950s and 1960s, net white immigration to the region was 2.1 million.[29]

Studying Luther Hodges casts light on the two sides—the progres-sive and the traditional—of the South during these years. Hodges was governor of North Carolina from 1954 to 1961 (and later Secretary of Commerce in John Kennedy's administration). Before entering poli-tics, Hodges managed the Marshall Field textile mills in North Caro-lina, and became a vice president of the company. As governor, he worked hard to recruit new industry, with trips to the northern states and Europe. "Since aggressive salesmen take their message directly to the prospects," Hodges recollected in his autobiography, *Business-man in the Statehouse*, "we decided that our administration would use this technique." He pushed for more money for the school system ("Education has been the basis of our economic progress") and for vocational training so that new firms could tap a pool of skilled work-ers. Hodges encouraged the development of Research Triangle Park, a high technology center located between Raleigh, Durham, and Chapel Hill.[30]

But Hodges also affirmed old-line southern values. He made clear his view of unions when a bitter strike closed the Harriet-Henderson Cotton Mills. The work stoppage dragged on from November 1958 to April 1959. When management decided to reopen the plant with non-union workers, Hodges supported the decision. He used the highway patrol and National Guard to make certain that strikers did not disrupt production. "I reaffirmed to the people," he remarked, "that the textile company had the right to operate and continue operating its mills as long as it did so within the law." Governor Hodges also orchestrated the North Carolina response to the 1954 Supreme Court decision that schools be integrated. While he counseled moderation and condemned lawless behavior, he also authored a resolution of protest. Hodges condemned the Court for "usurping the powers of the states and the people."[31]

The result of Hodges's policies was a mix of results characteristic of the South in this period. The state received new industrial investment of over $500 million during his administration. Per capita income rose, at least incrementally, from 66 percent of the national median in 1950 to 71 percent in 1960. North Carolina became the leading state in the U.S. in the proportion of workers employed in manufacturing. But racial segregation continued to characterize social and economic life. North Carolina led the nation in having the lowest rate (7 percent) of unionized workers. Outlays on education remained low, despite Hodges's stirring rhetoric. And Research Triangle Park remained an isolated outpost of high-tech development in a state of low-wage, low value-added industries.

This Janus-faced South, looking forward to the future and back to the past, was a region that grew steadily between the 1940s and early 1970s. However, and most ominously, the wave of growth which had lifted southern incomes during the years since World War II had subsided by the mid-1970s (Figs. 10.3 and 10.4). Agriculture was mechanized, and further substantial gains in farm productivity seemed unlikely. The low-wage industries also seemed weak reeds to support further expansion. They provided jobs but offered little impetus for raising the standard of living. This was, after all, an era in which advanced regions and countries all too willingly abandoned such manufacturing for higher value-added activities. After 1975 new patterns of development, which reflected the impact of post-industrial society on southern culture, would emerge.

Quebec Undergoes a "Quiet Revolution"

Like the South, Quebec experienced remarkable changes during this era. Venerated institutions, such as the Catholic Church, and long-standing assumptions, for example, about the proper livelihoods for French Canadians, were challenged. The appearance of new values and patterns of behavior accelerated economic growth. Entrepreneurial activity quickened and a new group of francophone businesspeople emerged. Still any discussion of French Canada during this period must, like an analysis of the South, emphasize both the extent of the transformation and the limits of change. Even in 1975 Quebec remained poorer and less business-oriented than the northern states.

We begin with the events that brought Quebec more fully into the modern era. Unlike the remaking of the southern states, the dramatic transformation of Quebec began only in the 1960s. A French-Canadian professor of sociology recently remarked: "In the early 1950s, my colleagues and I used to receive invitations from Canadian universities to explain why Quebec had not changed, why it hung on to its past and seemed to be rooted in the eighteenth century. However, since the late 1960s, we have been invited to talk about why Quebec has changed so rapidly." [32] There were challenges to the existing order in the 1940s and 1950s. But before 1960 the battlements of an older world stood intact. French Canada remained a fervently Catholic society with large families, Church-controlled education, and an ethos that disdained money-making.

Between 1940 and 1960, however, several developments helped prepare the ground for what Quebeckers would call the "Quiet Revolution." Some of these reforms came in the early 1940s when the Liberal party, headed by Adélard Godbout, held power in Quebec. The Liberals were not opponents of the Church. But their strength (in contrast to their opponents, the Union Nationale) lay more in the urban centers and less in the deeply conservative rural ridings. Hence they were more willing to press for long overdue changes. The Godbout government awarded the provincial vote to women, a step the Catholic hierarchy and many politicians had bitterly opposed. It introduced compulsory education for children under fourteen and adopted progressive labor legislation. It also nationalized some of the private power companies, laying the basis for Hydro-Québec, which would be an important engine of provincial growth. [33]

But there was no mandate for more sweeping changes, and in 1944 the Union Nationale, led by Maurice Duplessis, returned to power. Duplessis would continue to occupy the premier's office until his death in 1959. He was, in his later years, a paunchy man, given to Larenagas cigars (he smoked twenty a day) and the pomp of office. With his quick wit, he regularly assailed his opponents in the Legislative Assembly. Duplessis's long tenure was made possible, in part, by an apportionment that gave rural districts more representatives than their population warranted. The premier was an outspoken advocate of agrarian values, a staunch defender of the Church, and a determined opponent of "socialist" unions. In political affairs, he was a Quebec nationalist who stood up to Ottawa. But in economic matters, Duplessis was only too happy to continue the long-standing practice of allowing English-speaking entrepreneurs to dominate the provincial economy and pay French-speaking workers low wages. Critics denounced Duplessis for handing over the rights to such Quebec riches as the Ungava iron range, which was granted to Americans for minimal royalties. [34]

Dissent gradually mounted during the Duplessis years. The most important opposition came from the working class. Once-docile Catholic unions now displayed an unexpected militancy. The strike in 1949 against the Johns Mansville Asbestos firm revealed these changes. The stoppage was remarkable for its length and bitterness—and because it was led by Catholic unions. Duplessis used the judicial system and provincial police to break the strike, but the outlook of the workers had undergone a sea change. A small but influential group of intellectuals also criticized Duplessis and the world view he embodied. Labor lawyer and political scientist (and later Prime Minister) Pierre Elliot Trudeau was among those denouncing a French-Canadian outlook that was "hostile to all ideas for change, or even for possible improvement, that came from the outside."[35]

The turning point in the development of Quebec came in 1960 when the Liberal party ousted the Union Nationale and ignited the "Quiet Revolution." Like those who took part in the early days of Franklin Roosevelt's New Deal, the men (there were few women) who joined Premier Jean Lesage in remaking Quebec brimmed with excitement and pursued a variety of initiatives at once. Broadly viewed, the Quiet Revolution moved on two fronts. It helped secularize Quebec society, and it boosted the role of francophones in the economy, while limiting the power of English speakers. Both campaigns targeted long-established institutions and patterns of culture and helped remove obstacles that had slowed the pace of growth. The changes commenced in the early 1960s would not be reversed. Subsequent administrations, although drawn from different Quebec parties, consolidated and extended the work of Lesage.[36]

Most writers concur that the Quiet Revolution helped declericalize Quebec society and strengthened the position of French-speakers in the economy. The debates among historians turn on other questions (and are for the most part peripheral to the focus of this text). Scholars differ in their analysis of the years before the Quiet Revolution, and argue about how "modern" Quebec was in the 1950s.[37] Writers also disagree in assessing the role played by various groups—including intellectuals, the technocratic "new middle class," and the Quebec bourgeoisie—in initiating and sustaining these reforms.[38]

But there is agreement on the overall direction of the Quiet Revolution. With that in mind, we can examine the two major initiatives that characterized this period of reform. First, beginning in the early 1960s Quebec governments restricted the power of the Catholic Church. Church control over the education of francophones was dramatically reduced. The government established a system of nondenominational high schools and junior colleges and opened new universities with no religious affiliations. Church supervision in the lower grades was limited to religious instruction. Lay boards now set the curriculum. And this new educational system was better financed, helping to prepare Quebeckers for the challenges of industrial society. During the 1960s school attendance for sixteen-year-olds jumped from 51 percent to 84 percent. Education was not the only area declericalized. A new insurance plan established under Lesage gave the government effective control over hospitals. A provincial pension plan helped transfer social services from religious to public control.[39]

The efforts to secularize Quebec had a far-reaching impact. The number of clergy, which had reached a peak in 1960, now declined precipitously. While in 1961 there were 47,000 nuns, in 1979 there were only 27,000. Wholesale defections also depleted the ranks of priests. The values of the new society were reflected in the plummeting birth rate. In the late 1940s the rate of 30 births per 1000 population had been one of the highest in the industrial world. By 1972 the rate of 14 per 1000 population was one of the lowest.[40]

The Quiet Revolution moved on a second broad front: the government took steps to encourage French-Canadian businesses and loosen the grip of English speakers on the economy. The circle around Lesage was angered by the limited role that francophones played in their own economy and by the attitudes of anglophone employers. Here is the testimony of Jacques Parizeau, the rotund, wealthy politician and academic who was an adviser to Lesage and later leader of the nationalist Parti Québécois and provincial premier. "When I graduated from university," Parizeau recalled, "the American firms didn't even bother with francophones as part of their recruiting policy. They went to McGill, but most of them didn't even know where the Université de Montréal was." And further: "In 1960 . . . francophones were really at the margin of the business world in Quebec. Everything that was of any importance in the economy was controlled by people who were from outside. French Canadians were like cows in a field watching a train go by."[41]

Parizeau and other leaders of the Quiet Revolution wanted to see French speakers driving that train. One way of righting the balance was an activist state. In the 1960s the Quebec government established a series of institutions that made the state an important agent of development—and promoted francophone participation in the economy. Hydro-Québec, the provincial-run power company, was the flagship of the program. The Godbout administration in the early 1940s had laid the basis for this initiative. But before the 1960s Hydro-Québec controlled less than half the power generated in the province. The Lesage government, guided by its Minister of Hydraulic Resources, René Lévesque, compelled private firms to sell their assets to the province. When one English-speaking executive opposed Lévesque's arguments, the minister brought his fist down on his glass desk top, breaking the glass, and emphasizing that the government was determined to control provincial resources. French became the language of business in the new provincial power corporation—which also grew to be the largest employer in the province.[42]

Hydro-Québec was only one component of Quebec Inc., as the close relationship between government and business was called. Lesage established in 1962 a provincial investment agency, which bailed out faltering French-Canadian firms. A state-run pension plan (Caisse de dépôt et placement), created in 1965, soon controlled one of the largest capital pools in North America. The Caisse financed Hydro-Québec and bought government bonds when the anglophone investment houses were reluctant to do so.[43]

The provincial government took an active role in creating and strengthening francophone businesses. This statist approach to enterprise was reminiscent of New France, where the wealthiest merchants had depended heavily on government spending. Now, the provincial government intervened repeatedly to help the rising class of francophone entrepreneurs. The Caisse backed Antoine Turmel in the late 1960s when he merged three Quebec food wholesalers to form Provigo. The directors of the Caisse hoped Provigo would break the dominance of the supermarket chains run by English-speakers, and their expectations were amply fulfilled. Provigo became preeminent in Quebec and also one of the largest companies in Canada. Government outlays helped transform Bombardier from a maker of snowmobiles to an internationally respected manufacturer of transportation equipment. A contract to produce 423 cars for the Montreal Métro gave the company a much needed boost. And Lavalin, a construction and consulting firm, sharply expanded its revenues and horizons when it received (along with Bechtel) the contract to build the hydroelectric complex at James Bay. Lavalin earned $150 million for its work and gained experience that helped it undertake other projects around the world.[44]

These changes in the culture and institutions of Quebec strengthened the provincial economy. Before 1960 per capita income in Quebec usually was well below 70 percent of the U.S. average. By 1975 the standard of living in French Canada had reached over 90 percent of U.S. levels (Fig. 10.5). The growth of Quebec within the Canadian framework was also noteworthy. During the 1960s and 1970s Quebec narrowed the gap separating it from the wealthier province of Ontario.

Moreover, francophone entrepreneurs increased their ownership of the economy and for the first time made their mark in international trade. Thanks largely to the success of Bombardier, French-Canadian control of the production of transportation equipment in Quebec rose from 5 percent in 1961 to 34 percent in 1974. There were gains, if less striking ones, in other industries. Overall, francophone ownership of

Quebec manufacturing increased between 1961 and 1974 from 16 percent to 22 percent.[45]

But as was the case in the South, the limits on the progress made in Quebec also must be underscored. The industrial profile of the province remained more oriented toward the past than the future. Measured by number of employees, the largest manufacturing concerns were in the traditional areas: clothing, food and beverages, and pulp and paper. In the 1970s, as in the 1950s, extractive industries emphasized the export of raw materials. Fully 98 percent of iron ore left the province in unprocessed form in 1976. And despite the best intentions of Premier Lesage and others, francophones were hardly *maîtres chez nous*—masters in their own house. English speakers, often Americans, kept a tight grip on the largest manufacturing and mining enterprises.[46]

Moreover, literacy skills remained low. Even in 1975 after years of educational reform, more than a third of the adult population in Quebec had never attended high school. This was well below the levels in the North and in Canadian provinces such as Ontario and British Columbia.[47]

Equally worrisome, much of the progress made since 1960 reflected a fragile accord between the francophone majority and economically powerful anglophone minority. The government had aided French-speaking entrepreneurs, but had not challenged the privileges of the English-speaking elite. The reforms of the Quiet Revolution had frightened relatively few companies into leaving the province. Overwhelmingly, English remained the working language in the large corporate offices in Montreal. But for many Quebeckers the status quo seemed intolerable. The rise of the Parti Québécois and its victory in the provincial election of 1976 suggested this period of amity was about to end.[48]

In short, for the North, South, and Quebec a careful balance remains the key to understanding the changes of this era. Many northern business leaders seemed to lose the competitive edge that once had characterized this section. At the same time the South and French Canada became more entrepreneurial. Long-standing institutions—such as segregation and sharecropping in the South, or the Catholic Church in Quebec—now disappeared or were strikingly altered. The gap between the standard of living in the wealthier North and the poorer South and French Canada narrowed. But these changes were hardly complete. Even in 1975 the North remained richer and more oriented toward business than the other two areas.

11

The Post-Industrial Economy, 1975 to the 1990s

PictureTel, with headquarters in Danvers, Massachusetts, is the model of success in the post-industrial economy. It was started in 1984 by two twenty-two-year-old students, Jeffrey Bernstein and Brian Hinton, who attended the Massachusetts Institute of Technology. By the early 1990s PictureTel was the largest maker of videophones in the U.S., with sales of over $100 million and a market value of $170 million. The giant AT&T had been working for many years on sending pictures over phone lines, when Bernstein and Hinton figured out how to do it better. Norman Gaut, chief executive officer of PictureTel and another MIT graduate, explains: "No big company had the gumption to do what we did. Nobody had the guts but us." Bernstein stayed on as PictureTel expanded, becoming in his early thirties a blue-jean clad "corporate guru." Hinton went off to California to start still another high-tech company, Polycom.[1] The founders of PictureTel were the quintessential entrepreneurs of the Information Age: they were highly skilled, products of one of the great U.S. universities, and able to respond to market demand in a way that the large corporations could not. Not coincidentally, they were located in the Northeast, an area that flourished in this new economy.

The emergence of post-industrial society, much like the arrival of commercial capitalism 150 years earlier, helped redraw the map of economic development. Underlying these divisions was the interaction of the new productive forces with long-standing institutions and patterns of regional culture. Post-industrial society put a premium on superbly educated knowledge workers, who showed initiative and responsibility. Those qualities stand in sharp contrast to the obedience and subordination that industrial capitalism valued. The Information Age also rewarded entrepreneurial talent in a way that twentieth-century industrial society never had. Since 1975 the large corporations, long used to dominating the American economy, have steadily lost market share to smaller, aggressive firms.[2]

The Information Economy etched new lines of prosperity and stagnation in each region. The Northeast, which had stumbled during the 1960s and early 1970s, now surged ahead once more. High skill levels and an entrepreneurial outlook made this area a case study in how to respond to the demands of the new era. The Midwest, the heartland of mass production, displayed fewer of these attributes and suffered grave losses of jobs and income. For most of the South (the "core") the advent of post-industrial society was an unpleasant shock. However, some parts of the South (the "periphery"), including northern Virginia, southern Florida, and urban Texas, prospered as never before. Finally, the Quebec economy faltered with the advent of a society of knowledge workers. Figures 10.1 through 10.5 illustrate these trends in regional income.

The Entrepreneurial Spirit Reawakens in the North

For the northern states the period from 1975 to the early 1990s was the worst of times. It was also the best of times. The old industrial economy, whose origins went back to the 1870s and 1880s, collapsed. Hardest hit were midwestern states such as Michigan, Ohio, Indiana, and Wisconsin (Fig. 10.2). But during these same years a new post-industrial society emerged in the North. The new economy was centered in the Northeast, in such states as Connecticut, Massachusetts, New York, and New Jersey. In the 1990s, as in the 1840s, the Northeast reigned supreme. It had a higher standard of living and more wealth than the Midwest, the South, or the states of the Far West (Fig. 10.1).[3]

By the mid-1970s the mass-production industries of the North, despite a veneer of prosperity, displayed grave weaknesses. This corporate world was the lineal descendant of the dynamic economy of the late nineteenth century. But the entrepreneurial spirit, which had driven that earlier world of business, had gradually faded. High and seemingly assured profits had dulled the edge of innovation. Management had grown complacent and top-heavy with layer upon layer of executives. Unions too had grown fat. Organized labor was wedded to work rules that protected jobs—and hurt productivity. The contribution of many workers was limited by Tayloristic methods which in effect told blue-collar employees to leave their brains at the factory gate.

It was an industrial system ready to topple. But its precipitous decline in the years after 1975 was hastened by three developments. First
was the sharp rise in imports. Across a broad range of goods, Japanese
and European products were now better made and cheaper than
American manufactures. Consumers in the U.S. voted for these foreign
goods with their pocketbooks. In 1969 for every $100 Americans spent
on domestic manufactures they purchased only $14 of imported wares.
By 1979 they bought $38 worth of foreign goods, and by 1986 fully
$45 worth of imports. By that latter year two-thirds of all televisions
and radios and more than a fourth of all automobiles purchased by
Americans were made outside the United States.[4]

Second, the quickening pace of globalization encouraged U.S.
firms to rely more and more on labor in low-wage countries. Improvements in transportation and communications helped unify capital markets and speed the movement of goods across oceans and continents.
U.S. firms long had been involved with other countries. But now parts
of a car, home appliance, or computer could be made overseas and
brought back to the States for assembly. Direct investment abroad
soared, with American funds pouring into countries such as Mexico,
Brazil, Singapore, Korea, and the poorer European states. In 1966 U.S.
direct investment in manufacturing in Ireland was $66 million. By
1979 it was $1.6 billion. General Electric became the largest private
employer in Singapore. Whirlpool depended on Mexican workers to
produce its appliances. There were, to be sure, limits to this trend.
American firms did not dissolve into nebulous transnational corporations. Most of the productive facilities—over 80 percent—owned by
American firms were still in the United States. But the growing importance of foreign production hastened the decline of the old manufacturing economy of the North. It reduced the number of blue-collar jobs
and lowered the wages of those who remained employed.[5]

Third, the new shape of production helped deal a mortal blow to
the old factory system. State-of-the-art facilities now could produce
more goods with fewer workers. A greater use of robots and computer-
assisted manufacturing signaled the decline of those assembly lines that
Charlie Chaplin had labored on in *Modern Times*. Plants that wanted to
produce goods with the fewest defects turned Taylorism on its head
and insisted that each worker become a highly skilled decision maker.[6]

The response of old-line management to these forces of change
was simple: *cut, cut, cut.* Cut the number of U.S. workers, cut wages,
cut plants. Fundamentally rethinking the business or empowering
workers was not high on the agenda for these companies. At U.S. Steel
Tom Graham led the downsizing. Graham grew up in western Pennsylvania, became a metallurgical engineer, and rose to be president of
steelmaker Jones & Laughlin in the 1970s. In 1983 he was appointed
vice-chairman and chief of steel operations at USS. Graham entered an

overstaffed corporation, which lost $152 on every ton of steel shipped in 1982. He soon became known as the "people cutter." Non-union employees were dismissed—and not with two-week or two-day notices, but with pink slips handed them at the end of their shift. Employees were dropped, in some cases, weeks before they were eligible for pension benefits. Graham reduced his dependence on union labor by "contracting out" tasks to cheaper, non-union workers. Protests by various locals and major wage concessions in 1983 made little difference to Graham. He defended his approach to hiring non-union labor, telling organized workers not to "cling to a nostalgic past that is rapidly becoming irrelevant." And Wall Street loved Graham. Costs per ton fell. In 1987 USS (now renamed USX) with 18,000 to 19,000 workers produced as much steel as it had in 1983 with 48,600 employees. Ominously, though, costs still remained well above the "minimills" with their electric furnaces and flexible, non-union workers.[7]

The impact of these closings and layoffs was evident throughout the industrial North. Enormous factories were now boarded up, torn down, or made over in the hope of finding new tenants. Where Pittsburgh had once looked at the world through soot-laden skies, now the air was clear; the many steel works that dotted the river valleys had closed. The Allis-Chalmers plant in Milwaukee, which sprawled over 125 acres and had once produced thousands of tractors and combines, was shut. So were the great tire plants in Akron, and the General Motors facilities in Flint. The number of well-paying blue-collar jobs shrank drastically. Between 1979 and 1986 five midwestern states had a net loss of 990,000 manufacturing jobs, while the mid-Atlantic states of New York, Pennsylvania, and New Jersey shed 690,000 positions. The decline of unions, whose support had rested on just such workers, was indicative. Organized labor had represented 36 percent of workers in private industry in 1953, but it spoke for only 13 percent of these employees in 1987.[8]

The fall of industrial capitalism in the North was accompanied by a rise in inequality and a decline in those benefits that were the hallmark of corporate liberalism. Laid-off workers found other jobs, but usually at lower wages. Instead of making steel, they worked at the local K-Mart or learned how to repair refrigerators. Benefits also disappeared. In 1979, according to one estimate, 43 percent of new jobs provided pensions and 23 percent offered medical insurance. By 1988 only 38 percent had pensions and 15 percent supplied health benefits.The North was not poorer, but the slice of the pie given to less-educated workers was smaller.[9]

At the same time that the old industrial economy was crumbling in the midwestern states, a new post-industrial society was emerging in the Northeast. It was a society based on high value-added activities:

financial services, high technology, and the direction of large corporate and governmental organizations. These were activities that called for exceptional levels of education, knowledge workers rather than assembly-line workers, and individuals with keen entrepreneurial instincts. It was a set of specifications that fit the Northeast better than any other part of the nation. Robert Reich assigns most jobs in the U.S. to one of three categories: routine production (for example, data entry), in-person services (such as hairdressing and retail sales), and symbolic analytic services (for example, directing a large business). The Northeast had an unrivaled concentration of symbolic analysts.[10]

The rise of these new productive relations came just in time for the Northeast. During the 1960s and early 1970s the gradual economic decline of states like New York, Connecticut, and Massachusetts was unmistakable. These states boasted prominent educational institutions, banking and insurance centers, and a disproportionate number of head offices. So even in their worst years average incomes stood well above the national average. But part of their population labored in traditional industries, and these enterprises had been on even weaker footing than the factories of the Midwest. The northeastern industries were the miner's canary—the first to suffer from the noxious effects of increased foreign competition. Textiles, paper, and footwear in Massachusetts; metal working in Connecticut; clothing in New York—all were hard-hit by low-cost competitors. Between 1960 and 1975 per capita income in Connecticut fell from 129 percent of the national average to 117 percent. For New York the drop was from 126 to 114; for Massachusetts from 114 to 105 (Fig. 10.1).[11]

The decline in the Northeast was dramatically reversed after 1975 as the society of knowledge workers emerged. Massachusetts changed from "Taxachusetts" to the "Massachusetts Miracle." New Hampshire provided jobs for thousands of new arrivals. New York benefited from its role as the major port and chief financial center of a country where foreign trade and investment were becoming increasingly important. True, some of these advances were reversed in the years after 1986. New England was particularly hard-hit by the downturn of the early 1990s. But these setbacks moderated, and did not undo the gains of the preceding fifteen years (Fig. 10.1).[12]

Based on high value-added activities the post-industrial society of the Northeast expanded in wealth and geographical reach. It now extended north into New Hampshire, making this New England state, once relatively poor, one of the wealthiest in the country. To the south, Maryland and Washington, D.C., had for many years been part of the "Greater Northeast." During the 1980s northern Virginia became part of this area of high value-added enterprises. By 1991 eight of the ten wealthiest states—measured by per capita income—among the Lower Forty-eight were in this regional economy. They were New Hampshire,

Massachusetts, Connecticut, New York, New Jersey, Delaware, Maryland, and Virginia.[13]

There were, to be sure, rival "hot spots" in the United States. The most significant was in California, stretching south from San Francisco. Chicago was a vital regional center. (California and Illinois were the other two states in the top ten.) And there were important areas of post-industrial enterprise around Denver and in the South, particularly around Houston, Dallas, Atlanta, and southern Florida. But none of these areas had the size, wealth, or impact of the Northeast, which stood first in the new national economy. Map 11.1, which presents per capita income for 1981, displays these patterns for the eastern United States.[14]

Driving the new post-industrial economy were small innovative businesses, whose emergence signaled a reawakening of the entrepreneurial spirit in the North. A passion for money making and admiration for those who started companies had long been part of the northern outlook. But during the heyday of the corporate era small business seemed at best a sideshow in an economy dominated by large firms. Now with the advent of the post-industrial economy small and medium-sized enterprises became the main event. Significantly, women started many of these new businesses—although the size of most of these female-led firms remained small. Corporations had long excluded females from the highest ranks. The world of small business was more open, and during the 1980s the revenues generated by woman-owned companies rose at twice the rate recorded by all small firms.[15]

The decline of the large corporations and the rise of small business in the years after 1980 were unquestionable. In 1954, the first year *Fortune* listed the largest 500 industrial companies, their sales of $137 billion were equivalent to 37 percent of the GNP. That proportion steadily increased, until in 1979 the sales of the Fortune 500 companies were $1.4 trillion, accounting for 58 percent of the national product. Then the trend reversed. By 1989 the combined sales of the top companies were just under $2.2 trillion, or about 42 percent of the GNP. Employment figures tell the same story. The top companies employed an increasing proportion of American workers until the late 1970s. Then between 1979 and 1987 the Fortune 500 companies lost 3.7 million jobs, while the American economy added 19 million jobs. Three-fourths of new jobs were created by companies with fewer than 500 workers.[16]

The transformation of northern business was not limited to the rise of small companies. A few of the largest corporations, ones that had seemed so lumbering in the 1960s and 1970s, now learned to dance with sprightly new steps. General Electric, with its headquarters in Fairfield, Connecticut, is an example. When Jack Welch took over as

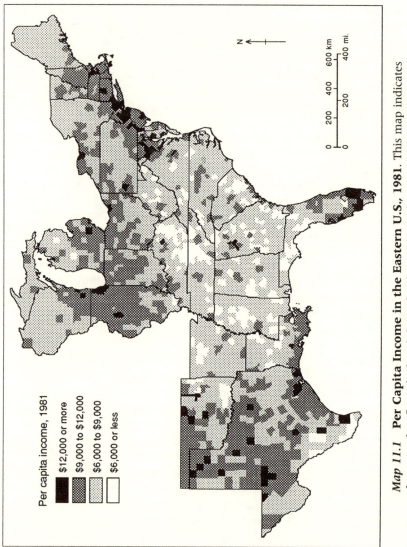

Per capita income, 1981

$12,000 or more

$9,000 to $12,000

$6,000 to $9,000

$6,000 or less

0   200   400   600 km

0   200   400 mi.

N

Map 11.1 **Per Capita Income in the Eastern U.S., 1981.** This map indicates the areas that flourished and those that lagged behind in the Information Age. (*Source:* National Geographic Society, *Historical Atlas of the United States* (Washington, D.C., 1988), 75.)

chief executive officer in 1981 he inherited a company with poor quality control and an administration that had more ranks than a modern
army. Like other CEOs Welch began with cuts, eliminating 100,000
jobs. He reassigned some work to overseas plants. But Welch was also
determined to change the corporate culture at GE. The firm must have,
he announced, the "speed, simplicity, and self-confidence" of a small
business. "We've got to take out the boss element," he declared.
Worker involvement became the rule. These reforms reshaped the way
GE made everything from diesel locomotives to jet engines to appliances. Productivity soared, climbing from 2 percent in the early 1980s
to over 5 percent in the early 1990s—a level well above the U.S. average. These changes benefited the workers in GE's many plants. But the
best-paid employees were those at the head office in Connecticut, and
particularly the person at the top. In 1991 Welch received over $10
million in the form of salary, bonuses, and stock options.[17]

But while the Northeast created high-paying jobs and spearheaded
the new economy, it did not create an abundance of these jobs. When
the industrial economy had expanded, rising wages and plentiful jobs
went hand in hand. The mass-production industries had over time provided millions of well-paying positions for workers drawn from Europe
and the South. But the successes of the post-industrial economy were
limited to a smaller group. A few of the high-tech companies dramatically expanded their work force. Digital Equipment of Maynard, Massachusetts, for example, hired 58,000 workers between 1981 and
1991. New Hampshire was one of the leading states for job creation
between 1979 and 1987. But most states in the prosperous Northeast
either lost people to out-migration during the 1980s (as New York did)
or attracted relatively few new residents.[18]

In this mix of depressed conditions and boom times in the North,
the resiliency of the Northeast is worth underscoring. Blessed with en-
viable human resources and an entrepreneurial outlook, the northeastern states have repeatedly shown the ability to adapt to new economic
conditions and flourish. These states led the nation economically in the
1990s much as they had during most decades since the mid-
nineteenth century.

The South: A Prosperous Periphery and a Stagnant Core

Post-industrial society also redrew the lines of development in the
southern states, creating two Souths. One was prosperous, urbanized,
and relatively well educated. This area of rapid growth lay largely on
the periphery of the fifteen-state region, and contained a minority of
the population and land area. It included Maryland and northern Virginia, southern Florida, urban Texas, and metropolises such as Atlanta.
This was the South that had moved furthest from the traditional cul-

ture and institutions of the region. This South engaged in high value-added activities, claimed a lengthy list of fast growing companies, and attracted the northerners who fled the snowbelt.

The other South fared less well in the new economy. This area formed the core of the region, and embraced most counties and a majority of the population. It included states such as Mississippi, Arkansas, Alabama, Kentucky, and South Carolina, as well as much of North Carolina, Tennessee, Georgia, and Louisiana. This area, with its older values, low levels of education and urbanization, and lack of skilled workers, was ill-prepared for the leading-edge industries of the 1980s and 1990s.[19] The post-industrial economy buffeted the core, and brought to an end an era of steady growth dating back to 1940.

We begin with the prosperous periphery. Why did this area flourish after 1975 when the rest of the South, despite strenuous efforts, grew far more slowly? We may emphasize four reasons for this surge of growth.

First, the many northern-born whites who settled in these states and cities helped give the periphery a more forward-looking, business-oriented outlook. The great flood of people rolling south during the 1960s, 1970s, and 1980s flowed in well-defined channels. In 1980 fully 41 percent of the Yankees in the South had settled in Florida, while 20 percent chose Texas and 10 percent lived in Virginia.[20] High concentrations of northerners characterized much of the periphery. In 1980 just over half the U.S.-born white population in Florida came from the North. The proportion of Yankees in the area from Tampa and Orlando to Miami was higher still. Maryland (which many texts now treat as a northern state) and the Norfolk area of Virginia, as well as the counties near Washington, D.C., also had a large number of northerners. So did Atlanta and eastern Texas.[21]

Where their numbers and wealth were sufficient, these modern-day carpetbaggers reshaped the economy and politics of their adopted states. Virginia is a case in point. By the 1980s newly arrived residents had helped expand the computer services and defense industries. General Dynamics, a leading defense contractor, moved its head office to Falls Church, just outside Washington. These northerners moderated the politics of the Old Dominion, a state that once had stood four-square against civil rights. L. Douglas Wilder benefited from these new realities. When Wilder, the grandson of a slave, entered state politics in 1970 one of his first demands was that the words "massa" and "darkie" be expunged from the state anthem, "Carry Me Back to Old Virginia." The electorate changed, and in 1986 Virginians made Wilder lieutenant governor and in 1989, governor. During his campaign for the statehouse Wilder noted the transformation of Virginia: "This is a far, far different state than it was when I got into politics 20 years ago.

After all, I'm now the Lieutenant Governor. A lot of people have moved into the State. There's been a lot of economic and social change, particularly up around Washington and down around Norfolk." [22]

Second, much of the success of the periphery reflected the rise of Texas, which now built upon its own entrepreneurial tradition. Texas long had had a diversified economy and a history of business activity that set it apart from other southern states. Along with cotton production, cattle raising was important in the nineteenth century and the oil industry in the twentieth. In his 1949 work, *Southern Politics in State and Nation,* V. O. Key, Jr., observed that "the changes of nine decades have weakened the heritage of southern traditionalism, revolutionized the economy, and made Texas more western than southern." He added: "White Texans, unlike white Mississippians, have little cause to be obsessed about the Negro. The Lone Star State is concerned about money and how to make it, about oil and sulphur and gas, about cattle and dust storms and irrigation, about cotton and banking and Mexicans." [23]

But until the advent of the post-industrial era Texas had not benefited from its entrepreneurial roots. The North had the industrial economy sewn up, and few factories or head offices were located in the Lone Star State. After 1975 the information economy replaced the world of smokestacks, and Texas boomed. Suddenly the virtues of a warm climate; modern, business-oriented cities; and an educated, non-union work force seemed irresistible. Between 1966 and 1991 the list of Fortune 500 companies with head offices in Dallas lengthened from 5 to 12 firms, while those located in Houston increased from 1 to 16. Equally significant was the broad mix of businesses that now flourished in Texas. Some were resource-based firms, like Exxon and Shell Oil. But many were on the cutting edge of American high-tech growth, including Texas Instruments, Compaq Computer, and Dell Computer. Small businesses, the dynamic element in the new economy, also thrived in the Lone Star State. [24]

Michael Dell, head of Austin-based Dell Computer, illustrates the entrepreneurial spirit that pushed Texas to the forefront of the information economy. Dell, who was born in Houston in 1965, had his own mail-order business at age thirteen. He listed, publicized, and auctioned the contents of his stamp collection. By age seventeen he was making thousands of dollars supervising a group of friends who sold the Houston *Post*. During his first year at college he bought computers from overstocked local dealers, upgraded them, and marketed them at a discount. Soon Dell had dropped out of school and was running his business full-time. By age twenty-six he headed a $679 million-a-year firm which sold computers direct to end users and supplied high levels of service. [25]

Despite such diversification, the Texas economy remains closely tied to the oil industry. The jump in the value of oil in the 1970s raised the standard of living, while falling prices in the 1980s threw the economy into a tailspin. Still Texas was less hard-hit by low oil prices than were neighboring Oklahoma and Louisiana, and since 1989 has benefited from a gradual recovery (Fig. 10.4).[26]

Third, large urban centers form a dynamic component of the periphery. Urbanization, to be sure, is a category that overlaps with northern settlement and the rise of Texas. In 1980 the three southern states with the highest proportion of city dwellers were Florida, Maryland, and Texas. These states also contained (or adjoined) the largest southern cities: Washington, Baltimore, Houston, Dallas, and Miami. But there were also important metropolitan areas in the core states. These include Atlanta, New Orleans, Memphis, Nashville, Birmingham, and Charlotte.[27]

These large cities are distinguished from the rest of the South by their values, their mix of occupations, and their strong growth. Thomas A. Lyson in *Two Sides to the Sunbelt: The Growing Divergence Between the Rural and Urban South* (1989) demonstrates the widening gulf that separates the major urban areas from the smaller cities and rural counties. The metropolitan areas had the best schools and universities in the region, the smallest proportion of illiterates, and the highest percentage of college graduates. They tended to be more moderate than the rest of the South on race issues. These major cities had proportionately more employees in finance, insurance, and real estate than the other areas of the South, and boasted the highest average incomes. The chief manufacturing industry in the big cities was electrical and electronic equipment, rather than the apparel and textile production found in the smaller centers and rural South.[28]

Atlanta is a good example of a southern city that has soared in the post-industrial economy. *Fortune* magazine put Atlanta on its cover (November 4, 1991) as the best city for business in the United States. Executives applaud its excellent transportation facilities, its proximity to regional markets, and its low costs for housing and office space. "Even the case-hardened New Yorkers, who sent out Bronx cheers at the thought of having to leave the sophisticated East . . . ," noted one corporate chairman who relocated his firm, "are singing the praises of warmer winters, and neighborhoods close to work that offer a lifestyle which was out of reach in New York." Atlanta jumped from ranking 18th among metropolitan areas in 1978 to 12th place in 1990. Calling itself "a city too busy to hate," Atlanta has consistently adopted a more moderate approach to the demands of the civil rights movement than has most of the South. The spoils of prosperity, however, are divided unequally in greater Atlanta. Whites who live and often work in the suburbs are the chief beneficiaries of the new affluence. Most African

Americans remained trapped in low-paying jobs and in the poverty of the central city.[29]

Fourth, government spending on defense and space has boosted the development of the periphery. In 1980 the Department of Defense spent in the South $50.1 billion, which amounted to almost 8 percent of the total regional income of $667.4 billion. Texas, Virginia, Florida, and Maryland were the chief recipients of these military outlays. Texas, which enjoyed weapons contracts and military pay totalling $12.1 billion, stood first in the region. The South also received $2.2 billion from NASA's budget of $5.4 billion. Again these funds were spent disproportionately in the states of the periphery, particularly Texas and Florida.[30]

The pace of development was slower in the core states of the South, where traditional values remained stronger (Fig. 10.3). Compared with the periphery, the core had fewer northerners, received less government funding, and was less urbanized. In 1990 big cities held less than 50 percent of the population of such "inner South" states as Arkansas, Mississippi, Kentucky, and West Virginia. By comparison, Maryland and Florida had over 90 percent of their inhabitants in metropolitan areas. All the states of the core stood well below the national average of 78 percent of the population in major cities. The core was also marked by lower levels of education. In much of the periphery and in the more prosperous areas of the North more than 65 percent of all adults were high-school graduates. But in the counties of the core typically less than half the adults had completed secondary school. (See Map 11.2.) Outlays per pupil and teachers' salaries were also lower in the core.[31]

The states of this inner South had large, impoverished African-American populations. In many of the core states (such as Mississippi, Alabama, Georgia, and South Carolina) over 25 percent of the population was black. In these states, which were poor to begin with, the income of African Americans was usually 55 percent or less of white income. By contrast black income was over 60 percent of white earnings in Texas and Florida, and over 70 percent in Maryland. For the core these statistics translated into abysmal pockets of poverty, where social services were lacking and infant mortality rates reached third-world levels. Rural African-American life in states such as Mississippi and Alabama reflected the long-standing priorities of a southern society that allotted few funds to the needs of the poor and less money still to the black poor.[32]

The polling data collected by the National Opinion Research Center between 1973 and 1991 further highlight the traditional values of the core. The findings are not broken down by core and periphery, but rather by the three census regions of the South: South Atlantic, East

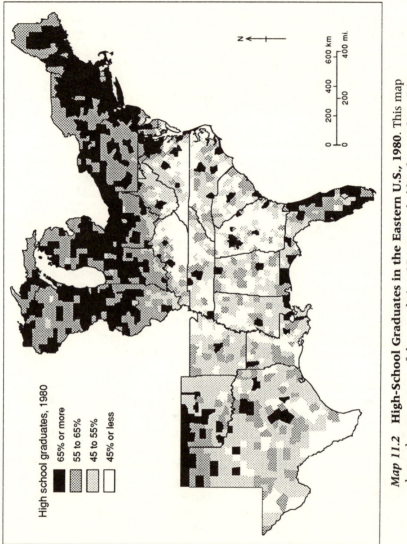

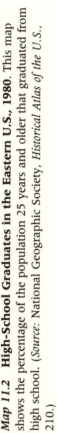

Map 11.2 **High-School Graduates in the Eastern U.S., 1980**. This map shows the percentage of the population 25 years and older that graduated from high school. (*Source:* National Geographic Society, *Historical Atlas of the U.S.*, 210.)

High school graduates, 1980

■ 65% or more

▨ 55 to 65%

░ 45 to 55%

□ 45% or less

South Central, West South Central. But since the core had more people than the periphery, results for the South document the majority
view and reveal a southern outlook that was distinct from the opinions
in the North. Several questions elicit the southern belief in hierarchy
and respect for authority. Southern respondents were more likely than
northerners to say that teaching children obedience is important. They
were more likely to affirm that people in high positions have special
abilities. They were more willing to silence a speaker who was critical
of religion. Similarly, attitudes toward work suggest a society more
inclined to look backward to the industrial era than forward to the
information age. Southerners, in contrast to their counterparts in the
North, preferred working for large companies rather than small ones.
And they were more likely to emphasize salary and less quick to point
to a sense of accomplishment as the most important criterion in select-
ing a job. Although the core states of the 1980s were hardly the South
of the 1880s, the past weighed heavily—and braked development.[33]

While the periphery attracted leading-edge industries, the core pursued a different course of development. Low skill levels and a lack of
home-grown entrepreneurs limited the range of possibilities. Communities worked hard to bring business in from the outside, with the emphasis on low-wage jobs. It was an approach that produced mixed results.

On the one hand, factories and mills from the North and from
overseas created many thousands of positions. During the 1980s half
of all the new foreign plants or expansions in the U.S. were in the
South. Some of these facilities, to be sure, were in the periphery. But
in relative terms the core was more dependent on outside firms and
claimed fewer locally owned enterprises. Japanese businesspeople refer
to Tennessee as *Tennessee-ken* ("the Prefecture of Tennessee") because
they built so many plants there. Locals called the stretch of I-85 near
Spartanburg, South Carolina, "the Autobahn" in recognition of the
presence of Swiss and German firms such as Hoechst Celanese.[34]

On the other hand, the benefits from these new jobs and factories
were surprisingly limited. Wooing northern and foreign firms often involved low-cost loans and major tax concessions. "If you don't step up
to the plate with a good financial package," a Greenville, Mississippi,
developer explained, "the thing [a Boeing plant] will pass you by."
Such generosity reduced or erased the revenues local governments
could expect from the new businesses. The emphasis on low-wage
non-union workers also was a two-edged sword. It attracted new employers, but did little to raise the standard of living. And competition
based on wages rather than skills remained a risky game. Even as new
plants opened in the South, others left for countries where costs were
still less. Complained an Alabama official: "Industrial jobs are going
out the back door faster than we can get them in the front door."
Finally, outside firms created employment but rarely the critical mass

for development produced by the interwoven activities of local entrepreneurs. Japanese companies, for example, often shunned local suppliers, preferring to get needed parts from other Japanese enterprises.[35]

What the core South must do to restart the engine of growth is no secret. Here's how Jesse White, Jr., a consultant and former director of the Southern Growth Policies Board, lays out the problem." Until the 1970s our economy really was based on a low-skill work force; then all of a sudden the earth plates of economic life in the world shifted," observes White. "All of a sudden, workers had to be skilled, they had to be flexible, and our work force was completely ill equipped because we hadn't really educated them. So our human capital base was our most impoverished. That's what we're trying to overcome, and we've still got a long way to go." However, building skills and changing mind-sets is not easy. In Mississippi a well-intentioned program of educational reform was abandoned because of a lack of funds in the state treasury. Perhaps federal money is the only answer. Steps must be taken before these southern states fall still further behind the national pace. Robert Mants, a civil rights worker and former county commissioner in Lowndes County, Alabama, understands: "This county was bypassed by the Industrial Revolution," he notes. "And if we, both black and white, don't move to meet the challenge at this time, we will find ourselves again being left out of this technological age."[36]

French Canada Faces an Uncertain Future

Like the southern "core," Quebec was more hurt than helped by the advent of post-industrial society. Broadly viewed, Quebec society lacked the skills and mind-set needed to stay on the cutting edge of change in the new economy. The expansion that began in the early 1960s ended in the mid-1970s as the pace of growth gradually slackened. While the standard of living in Quebec had climbed from about 62 percent of the U.S. average in 1961–63 to 95 percent by the mid-1970s, it fell back to perhaps 90 percent in the late 1980s (Fig. 10.5). Part of this drop reflected the weakened Canadian dollar. But the Quebec standard of living also declined relative to levels in Ontario. To be sure, any portrait of Quebec in the years after 1975 must sketch in the favorable trends as well as the broad setbacks the economy suffered. The expansion of high value-added businesses and the steady ascent of francophone entrepreneurs were hopeful signs. But the weakness of older industries, the exodus of many English speakers, and the persistence of traditional values slowed development and weighed more heavily in the balance scales.[37]

There were bright spots amid the clouds that darkened the Quebec economy in the post-industrial era. New high value-added businesses expanded during these years, reflecting growth in such sectors as aerospace, telecommunications, and pharmaceutical products. Typically, these firms were located in the Montreal area and were branch plants of American or English-Canadian concerns. Prominent in the list of leading-edge companies are Pratt & Whitney Canada, Bell Helicopter Textron, Merck Frosst Canada, and Northern Telecom. The production of transportation equipment (thanks to Bombardier) and financial services also expanded. These firms provided jobs for skilled francophones and maintained close ties with Montreal's research-oriented universities. While total employment in these enterprises remains comparatively small, their vigor is a favorable sign for the future of the Quebec economy.[38]

The French-speaking business class also grew stronger during these years. Like dynamite breaking up a logjam, the reforms of the 1960s had shattered old patterns of behavior and thought. The emergence of a large, successful group of French-Canadian entrepreneurs was one result. The change in the outlook of Quebeckers was hardly thoroughgoing, but business now became a desirable career for francophone youth. By 1987 Quebec had more Masters of Business Administration programs than any other province and turned out about half the Canadian business-school graduates. Some of the most successful French-speaking executives received the adulation often reserved for movie stars. Laurent Beaudoin has been widely praised for his achievements as head of Bombardier.[39]

Pierre Lortie is another executive who was an inspiration for many in Quebec. Tall, handsome, with prematurely silver hair, Lortie was extraordinarily successful—at least during the 1980s. He studied engineering at Laval University, was briefly involved in Quebec politics, and then went to the University of Chicago where he took his MBA. "For many French Canadians," Lortie observed, "going south of the border to the best schools was a way of solving the problem of self-confidence. They have been able to say, 'I've been with the best' and that brings confidence." And Lortie had ample self-assurance. Still in his twenties, he was appointed to the board of the Montreal Exchange. In 1980, at age thirty-three, he became the youngest president of the Montreal Chamber of Commerce. The next year he became president of the Montreal Exchange. He introduced a series of reforms that modernized the exchange and helped increase trading volume severalfold. Then in 1985 the directors of Provigo, the large food and retailing corporation (1985 sales, Can$4.7 billion), selected Lortie to succeed the founder, Antoine Turmel. In 1989 Lortie left Provigo, his luster only slightly dimmed by the poor performance of some of his acquisitions. Prime Minister Brian Mulroney promptly appointed him to head a commission on electoral reform and party funding.[40]

Francophone entrepreneurs also received a boost from the Quebec

Stock Savings Plan announced in 1979. This program, which provided tax benefits to Quebeckers investing in Quebec companies, proved an immediate success. More than $5 billion was poured into new shares, much of it in companies headed by French speakers. Francophones have now more control over the provincial economy than ever before. The list of French-owned firms includes such heavyweights as food distributor Provigo, Hydro-Québec, Socanav (which owns the supermarket chain Steinberg's), Bombardier, and the publishing giant Quebecor.[41]

The strength of the new, francophone business elite must not be exaggerated. The largest corporations with headquarters in Quebec—such as Canadian Pacific, Alcan, Bell Canada Enterprises, Seagram, Royal Bank, Air Canada, and Bank of Montreal—are controlled by English speakers. So are the most rapidly growing sectors of the Quebec economy, such as telecommunications and financial services.[42]

The continuing involvement of the provincial government in the economy also qualifies assertions about the power and independence of the French-speaking business community. Quebec Inc.—the union of government and business—is alive and well and flourishing in French Canada. Premier Robert Bourassa, who in the 1970s had viewed the James Bay hydroelectric project as an engine of growth, continued in the 1980s to push equally grandiose schemes for power development in the North. The Quebec Pension Plan (the Caisse de dépôt et placement) intervenes regularly and decisively in the provincial economy and the affairs of individual companies. Pierre Lortie became head of Provigo because the Caisse-appointed directors on the board preferred him to the individual handpicked by retiring CEO Antoine Turmel. The Caisse made sure that the supermarket chain Steinberg's ended up with a francophone owner. It helped block the efforts of anglophone Lorne Webster to control Trust général. And it brought together two great engineering firms: Lavalin and SNC Group.[43]

For all their limitations, francophone entrepreneurs are an exciting, positive force for growth. They show a new mind-set, many removes from the anti-business, agrarian, Catholic outlook of old. The traits Max Weber ascribed to the Huguenots are now in evidence. Or as Pierre Lortie recently observed, Quebeckers are experiencing an "underground Calvinistic revival."[44]

Set against those positive trends are other developments that have been less favorable for the expansion of the Quebec economy. There has been an uneasy fit between the institutions and culture of Quebec and the demands of post-industrial society. We can focus on three areas.

First, the new economic order accelerated the decline of many of the province's traditional industries. Long-established manufacturers closed their doors or shifted production to other countries and provinces. The textile and clothing industries, long a mainstay of employment in the Montreal area, lost market share and shed thousands of jobs. The Angus Shops, which repaired locomotives for the Canadian Pacific Railroad and was once the largest private employer in Montreal, providing work for more than 12,000 people, shut down early in 1992. Nor have the resource industries been spared. Concerns about the safety of asbestos fibers have hurt sales of that mineral. Migration of the pulp and paper industry to warmer climes, where trees grow faster, led to the closing of several large mills. The cumulative effects have been devastating. Since 1975 unemployment in Quebec has averaged more than 11 percent. And while metropolitan Montreal, much like greater Atlanta or Charlotte, is wealthier than the smaller towns and rural counties in the region, Montreal has not kept pace with its bustling southern counterparts. The heavy baggage of older industries has held Montreal back, while the southern metropolises rush ahead to meet the challenges of post-industrial society.[45]

Second, cultural nationalism has driven many English-speaking businesspeople from the province and slowed growth. Unlike the reforms of the Quiet Revolution, the cultural nationalism that has emerged since 1975 has hindered development. The Quiet Revolution helped bring francophones into the mainstream of business activity, and so added new energy to the economy. The restrictive language laws adopted in the 1970s and 1980s chased out many anglophones and hurt the economy.

Why have French-speaking Quebeckers given such fervent support to a program of cultural naturalism? Part of the explanation lies in the sharp decline in the birth rate, which has made francophones increasingly anxious about their future. French-speaking Quebeckers had long relied on *la revanche du berceau*—the revenge of the cradle—to assure their survival as a people. But now there are fewer children in each household and the disappearance of French-Canadian culture seems at least a remote possibility. A Toronto Star reporter heard familiar sentiments when he sat in a Montreal living room and listened to a discussion about constitutional change. "If I sign this, can you assure me that our language will be protected? Are there risks that tomorrow, our institutions will be anglicized?" asked school teacher Real Lamontagne, adding: "We're 6 million francophones surrounded by a North American sea of anglophones." During the 1970s such concerns were heightened by the obstinacy of some large anglophone companies. Sun Life, for example, employed in its Montreal office two thousand individuals—80 percent of them unilingual anglophones. Only two of its twenty-one directors were French Canadians. Stubborn anglophones and a declining birth rate among *pure laine* (old stock) Quebeckers pointed to the need for change.[46]

Language became the key to the defense of French-Canadian culture, particularly since the Quiet Revolution weakened the role played by religion in defining Québécois identity. René Lévesque, head of the Parti Québécois and premier from 1976 to 1985, underscored the importance of French: "Being ourselves is essentially a matter of keeping and developing a personality that has survived for three and a half centuries. . . . At the core of this personality is the fact that we speak French. Everything else depends on this one essential element and follows from it or leads us infallibly back to it."[47] Francophones demanded that immigrants coming to Quebec and businesses within the province use French. The result was Bill 101, adopted by the Parti Québécois in 1977. This act restricted access to English-language schools when both parents were not anglophones, specified that commercial signs be in French, and ordered all businesses with more than fifty employees to move toward the use of French in the workplace.[48]

The response of anglophones to Bill 101 (and more broadly to the changing cultural climate) was anger and flight. Early in 1978 Thomas Galt, head of Sun Life, announced the company was moving to Toronto because of the intolerable legislation. Other companies followed. Between 1978 and 1982 Montreal lost almost 30 percent of its head offices. Many headquarters remained in name only, with the real business done in Toronto. In the fifteen years after the PQ victory of 1976 perhaps 200,000 anglophones left the province, taking their money and expertise. Those leaving were often the highly skilled, better-educated members of the English-speaking community. Premier Lévesque, for one, appeared untroubled by the exodus. When businessman John Bulloch called Quebec an "economic sewer," Lévesque replied: "It's unfortunate that Mr. Bulloch doesn't choose his similes better. You know what a sewer evacuates, don't you?"[49]

Nor did language policy change in 1985 when the Liberals under Robert Bourassa succeeded the PQ. Soft-spoken, meticulously dressed, and extraordinarily cautious on cultural issues, Bourassa was determined not to offend the francophone majority. And the majority had grown ever more concerned about *survivance*—the survival of French-Canadian society. When the Supreme Court of Canada struck down the sign provisions of Bill 101, Bourassa introduced Bill 178. This measure reaffirmed that French must be used on commercial signs outside buildings. The only concession Bill 178 made was permitting English on signs inside stores—as long as the English lettering was less prominent than the French.[50]

The francization program was successful in achieving its stated goals. Quebec became more of a French-speaking province. More businesses, large and small, made French the language of the workplace. But the price for these gains was the loss of many head offices and jobs, the departure of talented anglophones, and slower growth.[51]

Third, the persistence of older cultural attitudes has slowed development in French Canada. Traditional ways are particularly evident in the smaller urban centers and rural areas. Compared with the Montreal region—which has about half the provincial population—the rest of Quebec is poorer, less educated, and less business-minded.[52] (See Map 11.3. Two secondary concentrations of wealth and business activity are around Quebec City and Ottawa/Hull.) The rate of functional illiteracy remains high in Quebec. A 1991 survey found that 19 percent of Quebeckers lacked the literacy and numeracy skills needed "to meet most everyday demands." Little more than half the population had the ability to understand written material of average difficulty.[53]

A variety of polls suggests that an older mind-set, which shuns business and independent, entrepreneurial activity, still characterizes many Quebeckers. For example, a 1991 poll conducted for *l'Actualité* asked, "Do you prefer people who do their duty or who seek happiness?" Francophones chose happiness over duty by a 51 to 42 margin. Outside of Quebec, Canadians favored duty by a 63 to 25 spread. When asked which groups they trusted, Quebeckers gave businesspeople a lower rating than did respondents in the rest of Canada.[54] Still another question points to the lack of an individualistic, entrepreneurial ethos in Quebec. When asked whether it was fair to pay a more productive employee a higher salary than a less productive colleague, fully 32 percent of francophones said such an arrangement was unjust. Only 17 percent of Americans felt that unequal pay was unfair.[55]

The future of the Quebec economy may well reflect the balance of these positive and negative trends. Buoyant growth depends on the expansion of high value-added activities and the continued ascent of French-speaking entrepreneurs. It also depends on the ability of Quebec society to move beyond the older declining industries, win the loyalty of entrepreneurs regardless of their language, and abandon values that question the worth of business activity.

Finally, this examination of the three societies raises broad questions about the costs and benefits of economic development. Should growth be the top priority? How does a country or region balance the need to preserve long-standing traditions against the possible financial gain that might come from a program of "modernization"? The determination of French Canadians to protect their culture is clear. This resolve is echoed, if more faintly, in the South. Economic development is not the only goal.

Unlike northerners, Quebeckers and southerners have been asked to abandon much of what defined their societies in order to facilitate growth. Most individuals are willing to bid farewell to certain aspects of the old. Many Quebeckers were pleased by the steps taken to end the dominant role of the Catholic Church. Many southerners, and par-

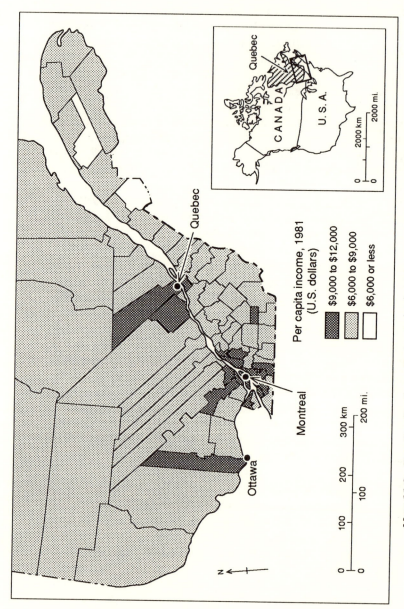

Map 11.3 **Per Capita Income in Quebec, 1981.** In Quebec the wealthiest counties were around Montreal and, to a lesser extent, Quebec City and the sister cities of Ottawa and Hull. Compare this map with Map 11.1, where the same wealth categories are used. (*Source:* Statistics Canada, Consumer Income and Expenditure Division, *Income Estimates for Subprovincial Areas* (Ottawa, 1982), 37–42. These statistics were multiplied by 1.17 to bring them into line with the data

ticularly black southerners, were only too happy to say "good riddance" to the Jim Crow laws that long characterized the region. But as the majority of francophones recognize and many southerners acknowledge, some of the changes proposed in the name of progress involve grave losses. The fierce battle by francophones to preserve the dominance of their language in Quebec testifies to the strength of this outlook. In the South similar concerns have been voiced. Marshall Frady, a Georgia writer, laments: "What one hears tolling over the South these days is a vast muted tinkling of—who would have ever supposed it?—dullness. Massively and uncomplainingly, the whole land is being trivialized. . . . The South may seem more sensible now; less outrageous and troublesome to the rest of the nation. But in the process, the old pipe-organ range of prodigal possibilities for life there—both gentle and barbarous, good and evil—has contracted to the comfortably monotone note of middle C." These losses and gains are also part of the turbulent process of growth as the regions contend with the demands of the post-industrial world.[56]

A Concluding Note

Mark Twain opens *The Adventures of Huckleberry Finn* by admonishing the reader: "Persons attempting to find a motive in this narrative will be prosecuted; persons attempting to find a moral in it will be banished . . . ."[1] Of course, Twain was being ironic. *Huckleberry Finn* is a profoundly moral book. Still, Twain's example is intriguing. The temptation to open or conclude a book with a disclaimer is strong. For this work the warning might be, "Persons attempting to predict the future based on the material in this book will proceed at their own risk."

Bookshelves are full of works that map the future based on present trends, and blunder badly. These include tomes written before 1940 that describe a never changing South or an eternal Quebec. They include more recent books that assumed these regions were on the verge of a total transformation. And one must add studies that in the 1950s and 1960s demonstrated the inevitable rise of corporate America and in the 1970s discussed the irreversible decline of the Northeast.

But any admonition against peering into the future must too be ironic. Works of history examine the past so we can better deal with the present and future. With that in mind, we can revisit the broader themes in this book.

Most striking in this study of the links between culture, institutions, and economic development are the continuities that mark each region. Even before Independence commentators picked the North as the section most likely to succeed. Eighteenth-century observers were struck by its "vigorous spirit of enterprise." Success in the nineteenth century only confirmed this analysis. Northern society drew its dynamic outlook from Protestantism, free labor, and a commercial approach to land. A democratic ethos as well as exceptional levels of education and mobility also fostered growth. The northern lead widened with industrialization and remained unchallenged for most of the twentieth century.[2]

Important continuities also characterize the development of the South. Writers in the 1700s emphasized the "indolence" of southerners, and the oft-repeated charge had substance. Slavery and the presence of a large African-American population shaped southern society. Planters deemed the status that came from holding bondspeople more important than economic efficiency. They accepted the slower rhythms of work set by an unmotivated, uneducated labor force. Slavery also created a strong hierarchy among whites, with respect for authority valued more than a determination to make money. The labor systems established after the Civil War reaffirmed these priorities. The result was a region that fell behind the North in the nineteenth century and remained less wealthy in the twentieth.

Fundamental patterns persisted in French Canada as well. The outlook of settlers along the St. Lawrence had deep roots that went back to the seventeenth-century colony. The seigneurial system and Roman Catholic Church created an ordered society, where the aggressive pursuit of wealth was frowned upon and ties of family and community were exalted. Levels of education were low and geographical mobility limited. The native merchant class was weak before 1760, and soon after the Conquest English-speakers gained control of commercial activities. In the nineteenth century Quebec, like the southern states, failed to keep up with the fast-growing North. During most of the twentieth century slow growth and English dominance characterized the province.

If continuity is the dominant theme, change is also evident. Regional cultures and institutions were ever more sharply defined during the century from the 1750s to the 1850s. Moreover, since 1940 the old order in the South and Quebec has gradually unraveled.

Several forces reshaped societies that can never be viewed as permanently set in their ways. The evolution of systems of production had a far-reaching impact and shifted the balance between regions and within regions. The decline of the household economy and the rise of commercial capitalism (which emerged by the 1830s) boosted the fortunes of the Northeast. The advent of industrial capitalism after the Civil War enriched both the Midwest and Northeast. Only at the end of the lengthy industrial era, that is, in the decades after 1940, did the South and Quebec begin to close the gap with the highly developed North. The arrival of a post-industrial or information-based society after 1975 again helped redraw the map of development. The New Economy reinforced the preeminence of a "Greater Northeast" but dealt a harsh blow to the industrial Midwest. Growth slowed in much of the South, although the southern "periphery" boomed. Quebec too was hurt by the new social order, even while greater Montreal remained the wealthiest and most dynamic area in the province.

Other factors helped transform the regions. The migration of people, businesses, and ideas acted as a corrosive acid, eating away at older structures. Since 1940 the trek of African Americans to the North and white northerners to the South has benefited both sections. The recent movement of firms to the sunbelt has been an important dynamic for southern growth. Legislation has also accelerated change. In Quebec measures adopted in the mid-nineteenth century strengthened the control of the Catholic Church over schools and other social institutions. Similarly, the reforms of the Quiet Revolution of the 1960s reduced the power of the Church and encouraged French-speaking businesspeople to play a more active role in the economy. In the South the pro-business legislation passed since 1950 signaled a new approach to industry. Civil rights acts strengthened the political rights of African Americans.

Finally, we might ask, what lessons can be drawn by legislators, businesspeople, and others who want to raise the standard of living in their state or region? If the themes of this work are valid, the keys to long-term growth do not lie with government mega-projects, a Keynesian infusion of dollars, or an industrial policy that picks winners and losers. Whatever the merits (or de-merits) of these measures, they provide band-aid solutions that disappear when the money runs out. Or they end up helping those regions best prepared to grow. Smokestack chasing also is not the answer. Policies that snare foreign plants with promises of low-wage non-union labor have at best had mixed success in Quebec and the South. Such firms might briefly buoy the local job market. But they perpetuate the psychology of dependence, and rarely boost the standard of living. Sustained growth must be home-grown and come from an educated, entrepreneurial local population.

But this work should not be read as a counsel of despair or an argument for a hands-off approach—just the opposite. The presence of deep-rooted cultures makes clear that our national economies are not self-regulating mechanisms. Unfettered capitalism will not lead to an equality of opportunity across regions. The marketplace left to itself is just as likely to reinforce the divergence of incomes from one area to another (as was true from the mid-eighteenth century to the 1930s) as convergence (evident from the 1940s to the 1970s). Since 1975 a new and growing disparity has characterized regional incomes in North America.

Rather, change is possible and concerted action by business, government, and educators is necessary—even if the results may come more slowly than many impatient souls might desire. Spending on infrastructure—roads, airports, and now the electronic networks that are the "highways" of the New Economy—can help boost poorer regions. But, most significantly, governments must support broad and inevitably expensive programs of quality education. Such initiatives are probably the best lever that a country or region can wield to effect long-term change. In the context of post-industrial society this does not mean training people for the next job, but for the challenges of a position that one might dream of creating. And the true payoff will not come next year, or in five years, but with the unfolding of the next generation. Because the poorest regions are unable to fund such programs fully, help must come from the central government.

There is a need to temper change with justice. The tradition of corporate liberalism—which tied increasing benefits for the worker to the expansion of capitalism—has come under fierce attack in the post-industrial era. But the fullest justice lies not in corporate largesse or in the increase of transfer payments. Rather it comes with a society that expands the skills and opportunities available to all individuals. It comes with a society that allows each of us to realize our potential and allows us to strengthen the communities that make up the rich tapestry of North America.

Appendix A

Some Thorny Concepts: Capitalism, the Capitalist Spirit, and the Household Economy

In writing *A Brief History of Time,* astrophysicist Stephen Hawking was warned that each equation he introduced into the text would halve his readership. I suspect that conceptual discussions have the same effect. Nonetheless, key terms must be examined. It is necessary to explore in more detail the meaning of *capitalism* and *capitalist spirit,* and their impact on the household economy.

This discussion expands upon ideas presented in Chapter 1, and addresses important issues. If life for the majority in the eighteenth century was characterized by the "household mode of production," what about the minority, the merchants in the towns? They were involved in far-flung exchanges. How do we assess the links between these capitalists and rural society? And how does the advice that Benjamin Franklin gave ("Industry" and "Frugality") tie in with the boisterous spirit of capitalism?

The Links Between Capitalists and the Household Economy

What was the relationship between the urban merchants—unmistakably capitalists—and the household economy? To begin with, it is important to note that capitalists did not require capitalism to flourish. The historian Fernand Braudel provides a useful definition of capitalism. He argues that it characterizes an economy or a sector of an economy run by capitalists. And what do capitalists do? Capitalists invest money to make more money. Shifting the definition from capitalism to capitalist allows us to use a much older word. "Capitalism" as a term dates from around 1850, but came into common use only around 1900. "Capitalist"—an individual who uses wealth to make more wealth—dates back to perhaps 1650 and was widely used by the late eighteenth century.[1] Braudel's definition allows us to talk about capitalism as a system that embraced only part of a society.

So capitalism and capitalists (typically urban merchants in the era before 1800) could coexist with the household mode of production. The two in fact relied on each other. Neighborhoods involved in the household economy were never self-contained. They required the services of merchants. Rural communities produced surpluses, if small ones, and bought imported wares. New settlements needed extensive funds during their first years. Often this money came from traders and others in the coastal cities. Capitalists worked alongside this rural economy but in the eighteenth century did not set the tone for society.[2]

Let's look more closely at the impact of capitalists on the three North American regions. In the eighteenth century small farms and production for local use characterized all three societies. But there were important differences within that framework. In the North regional institutions and culture gave rise to a free labor, freehold tenure society. In French Canada, to a feudal system. In the South, to a slave society.

Capitalists coexisted comfortably with the northern economy. Here more than anywhere else the movement of workers was free. The exchange of land was relatively unencumbered. Few aspects of society conflicted with the "rationality" of capitalism.

The story is different when we examine the impact capitalists had on feudal Canada and the slave South. The relationship between entrepreneurs and these hierarchical societies was two-sided. On the one hand, capitalism was antithetical in spirit and practice to feudalism and slavery. Those systems depended on customary relationships and limited the productive investments on which capitalism thrived. Money was not the measure of all things in a civilization based on seigneurialism or bondage. In the long run, which could mean several centuries, capitalism worked to destroy these societies. But on the other hand, capitalists could and did work closely with such systems. In the short run capitalism reinforced them. Slave and feudal labor produced goods that capitalists traded on the world market. The slave South and seigneurial French Canada could cooperate for a time with the capitalists of Europe and North America.[3]

Ben Franklin, the Capitalist Spirit, and the Rise of Capitalism

By 1850 the North had developed full-blown commercial capitalism, while the South and French Canada had not. Why? The text suggests a range of cultural and institutional factors. One area that must be further explored is the "mind-set" of the North. Was there a capitalist spirit? And how did it relate to the advice that Benjamin Franklin and other northerners espoused?

Here again Fernand Braudel is an excellent guide. Braudel rejects the contentions of individuals such as Werner Sombart and Max Weber that a mind-set caused capitalism. This is a sensible critique. Still, capitalists were marked by certain traits. Braudel acknowledges: "Capitalism could not exist without rationality, that is, without the continual adaptation of means to ends, without an intelligent calculation of probabilities."[4]

Was the "rationality" to which Braudel refers the same thing as Max Weber's emphasis on the importance of the virtues of industry and frugality? These are the qualities Benjamin Franklin advocated, and they are often referred to as the "Protestant Ethic." The relationship between such ideas and capitalism is hardly straightforward. Franklin's advice seems to be more fitting for the farmers and artisans laboring within the household economy, around 1750, than for the capitalists of the day, the overseas merchants in the colonial cities. The lives of those traders were hardly frugal. And they made their fortunes through speculation and risk-taking, not steady industry. After discussing these early capitalists, Braudel observes: "The reader will have noticed that reference is often made to the underlying notion of gambling, risk-taking, cheating; the rule of the game was to invent a counter-game, to oppose the regular mechanisms and instruments of the market, in order to make it work *differently*—if not in the opposite direction."[5] The merchant's philosophy was hardly "a penny saved is a penny earned."

Building on Braudel we might say that the capitalist—the individual who invested money to make money—was a relentless profit maximizer. And continually maximizing profits required an ethic or spirit that went far beyond the cautious virtues Franklin preached. The capitalist spirit included a willingness to take risks and a drive to control markets.

Still, the importance of industry and frugality for the development of capitalism cannot be laid to rest so easily. The Protestant Ethic may have been best attuned to the outlook of the artisan who served customers face to face or to the farmer who raised crops and tended livestock chiefly for local consumption. But industry and frugality suggested (as one of Franklin's tracts was titled) a Way to Wealth. And this outlook would evolve—as society changed—into the entrepreneurial, capitalist ethic of the nineteenth-century North. It should be no surprise that in the decades after the Civil War northern business leaders cherished the adages of Franklin.[6]

The North in 1750 may have been characterized by the household economy, just as the South and French Canada were, but its spirit—as discussed by the contemporary observers examined in Chapter 2—already differed from that of the other two regions. In important ways, northerners had begun to stand apart from the concern with custom, status, and prestige that defined relationships in feudal and slave society. This attitude contributed to the early development of commercial capitalism in the North.

Appendix B

Three Farms in 1750

The tables that follow provide snapshots of the household mode of production. In the eighteenth century the neighborhood, and not the larger world, dominated exchanges. Most goods produced on the farm remained in the community. Most items purchased came from nearby. Only the large slaveholding plantations violated this pattern, and sent half their produce to distant markets. The three farms profiled reflect data from many holdings. While set forth as plausible reconstructions, these estates are not intended to stand for the "average" in their regions.

Care was taken in constructing these tables—but some of the figures are conjectural. Commodities rarely shipped abroad, for example, hay and apples, are less well documented by price studies than are such familiar staples as wheat and corn. Similarly, any comparison of the total value produced on the three farms should be made cautiously. These figures represent 1750 prices (where available). The choice of a different year would create a different outcome.

Table B.1 Output of 140-Acre Farm in Pennsylvania, 1750
(Values are in pounds, Pennsylvania currency;
1 pound = 0.588 pound sterling)

Crop	Acres	Number of Animals	Quantity Produced	Value Produced	Value Sold Outside Community
Wheat	10		100 bushels	22.5	9.0
Rye	2		25 bushels	3.0	1.5
Oats	4		60 bushels	7.2	0.0
Barley	2		30 bushels	3.6	0.0
Buckwheat	2		30 bushels	3.6	0.0
Ind. corn	8		120 bushels	14.4	3.6
Hay	22		33 tons	23.1	0.0
Apples	2		800 bushels	12.0	0.0
Flax	2		300 pounds	7.5	4.5
Flaxseed			10 bushels	3.0	2.4
Cattle/beef		6	675 pounds	5.8	1.7
Milk			300 gallons	2.0	0.0
Pigs/pork		6	413 pounds	5.8	0.6
Sheep/wool		10	30 pounds	3.0	0.0
Total				113.5	23.4

Percentage of farm produce sold outside community: 20.6

Source: Data are drawn from Carole Shammas, "How Self-Sufficient Was Early America," *Journal of Interdisciplinary History,* XIII (1982–83), 250–53; James T. Lemon, *The Best Poor Man's Country: A Geographical Study of Early Southeastern Pennsylvania* (Baltimore, 1972), 150–83; Anne Bezanson et al., *Prices in Colonial Pennsylvania* (Philadelphia, 1935), passim.

This household contained six adults, including an indentured servant. I have assumed half the apples grown were made into cider. Also produced or raised on the farm were chickens, butter and cheese, root vegetables, honey, and yarn. All those items were consumed locally.

Table B.2 Output of 120-Arpent Farm in Saint Ours, 1750
(Values are in livres: 1 livre = 0.04 pound sterling)

Crop	Arpents[a] Planted	Number of Animals	Quantity Produced	Value Produced	Value Sold Outside Community
Wheat	15		120 minots[b]	360	178.2
Oats	4.5		50 minots	89	0.0
Barley	0.5		6 minots	10	0.0
Peas	1.5		12 minots	30	12.5
Tobacco	0.5		75 pounds	20	0.0
Hay	22		28 tons	75	0.0
Apples	1		200 minots	70	0.0
Flax	0.5		55 pounds	14	0.0
Cattle/beef		2	200 pounds	50	0.0
Pigs/pork		4	275 pounds	64	0.0
Milk			100 gallons	15	0.0
Sheep/wool		6	30 pounds	27	0.0
Total				824	190.7

Percentage of farm produce sold outside community: 23.1

[a] 1 arpent = 0.85 acre
[b] 1 minot = 1.107 bushels

Source: Data are drawn from Morris Altman, "Economic Growth in Canada, 1695–1739: Estimates and Analysis," *William and Mary Quarterly,* 3d Ser., XLV (1988), 705–8; Richard C. Harris, *The Seigneurial System in Early Canada: A Geographical Study* (Madison, Wis., 1966), 150–62; and Allan Greer, *Peasant, Lord, and Merchant: Rural Society in Three Quebec Parishes, 1740–1840* (Toronto, 1985), 20–47, 122–39.

This household contained four adults. In addition to the goods enumerated above, the farm grew root vegetables, produced maple syrup, and spun yarn. All those items were consumed locally.

Feudal exactions took a portion of the surplus, but some of these duties remained in the community. The farm produced 120 minots of wheat. The four adults consumed 56 minots. The tithe took 1/26 of the total harvested, or 4.6 minots. But this sum went to the local priest and so stayed in the neighborhood. The *cens et rentes* amounted to 9 minots, and was sold for export by the seigneur. This left 50.4 minots that the farmer exchanged for imported wares.

Table B.3 Output of 1000-Acre Plantation in Virginia, 1750
(Values are in pounds, Virginia currency: 1 pound = 0.794 pound sterling)

Crop	Acres	Number of Animals	Quantity Produced	Value Produced	Value Sold Outside Community
Tobacco	22		6600 pounds	54.0	53.0
Wheat	6		60 bushels	8.0	0.0
Ind. corn	32		480 bushels	43.0	10.0
Oats	4		60 bushels	5.5	0.0
Beans	1		10 bushels	1.5	0.0
Hemp	0.5		400 pounds	4.5	2.0
Apples	2		800 bushels	8.0	0.0
Cattle/beef		6	675 pounds	4.5	0.0
Milk			300 gallons	1.5	0.0
Pigs/pork		18	1240 pounds	12.0	0.0
Sheep/wool		4	12 pounds	1.0	0.0
Total				143.5	65.0

Percentage of farm produce sold outside community: 45.3

Source: Data are drawn from *U.S. Bureau of the Census, Historical Statistics of the United States, Colonial Times to 1970*, 2 vols. (Washington, D.C., 1975), II, 1197–98; Lewis C. Gray, *History of Agriculture in the Southern United States to 1860*, 2 vols. (1933; rpt., Gloucester, Mass., 1958), I, 161–277; Paul G. E. Clemens, "The Operation of an Eighteenth-Century Chesapeake Tobacco Plantation," *Agricultural History*, XLIX (1975), 517–31; Aubrey C. Land, "The Tobacco Staple and the Planter's Problems: Technology, Labor, and Crops," ibid., XLIII, 68–81; Lois Green Carr and Russell R. Menard, "Land, Labor, and Economies of Scale in Early Maryland: Some Limits to Growth in the Chesapeake System of Husbandry," *Journal of Economic History*, XLIX (1989), 407–18; Lorena S. Walsh, "Plantation Management in the Chesapeake, 1620–1820," ibid., 393–406; some prices extrapolated from Pennsylvania data in Anne Bezanson et al., *Prices in Colonial Pennsylvania* (Philadelphia, 1935).

This plantation contained four white adults and nine adult African Americans, all slaves. Seven of these slaves labored in the field. In addition to the goods enumerated the plantation raised chickens, root vegetables, and peas, and made tools, furniture, and yarn. All those items were consumed locally.

Notes

Abbreviations used in notes:

DAB   *Dictionary of American Biography.* 11 vols. 1928–37. Reprint. New York, 1946–58.

DCB   *Dictionary of Canadian Biography.* 13 vols. Toronto, 1966–94.

JEH   *Journal of Economic History*

WMQ   *The William and Mary Quarterly*

Preface

1. Examples of comparative works include Eugene Genovese, *The World the Slaveholders Made: Two Essays in Interpretation* (New York, 1969); Robert Brent Toplin, *Freedom and Prejudice: The Legacy of Slavery in the United States and Brazil* (Westport, Conn., 1981); Steven Hahn, "Class and State in Postemancipation Societies: Southern Planters in Comparative Perspective," *American Historical Review,* XCV (1990), 75–98; Shearer D. Bowman, "Antebellum Planters and Vormärz Junkers in Comparative Perspective," ibid., LXXXV (1980), 779–808; George Fredrickson, *White Supremacy: A Comparative Study in American and South African History* (New York, 1981); John W. Cell, *The Highest Stage of White Supremacy: The Origins of Segregation in South Africa and the American South* (New York, 1982); Peter Kolchin, *Unfree Labor: American Slavery and Russian Serfdom* (Cambridge, Mass., 1987). More generally, see Peter Kolchin, "Comparing American History," *Reviews in American History,* X (1982), 64–81. Canada rarely appears among the comparative works that Kolchin cites.

2. For example, François Lebrun and Normand Séguin, eds., *Sociétés vil-*

lageoises et rapports villes-campagnes au Québec et dans la France de l'Ouest (Trois-Rivières, Quebec, 1987); John McCallum, *Unequal Beginnings: Agriculture and Economic Development in Quebec and Ontario until 1870* (Toronto, 1980); J. P. Chateau, "Croissance et structure des industries manufacturières au Québec et en Ontario, 1949–63," *L'Actualité économique*, XLIV (1968), 492–527.

Chapter 1. Introduction: The Paths Diverge

1. Adolph B. Benson, ed., *Peter Kalm's Travels in North America: The English Version of 1770*, 2 vols. (1937; rpt., New York, 1966), II, 416, 458, 511. The anonymous author of *American Husbandry* (1775) also praises the meadows along the St. Lawrence. *American Husbandry*, ed. Harry J. Carman (1775; edited version, 1939; rpt., Port Washington, N.Y., 1964), 15–25.

2. Alice Hanson Jones, *The Wealth of a Nation to Be: The American Colonies on the Eve of the Revolution* (New York, 1980), 310.

3. These data also suggest that the inhabitants of the Thirteen Colonies did not lag far behind—at least in annual income—long settled European countries. Ibid., 303.

4. Various scholars have used these estate inventories as well as census data to discuss the distribution of wealth in New France. But to my knowledge no one has developed figures for New France comparable to Jones's for the Thirteen Colonies. See Allan Greer, *Peasant, Lord, and Merchant: Rural Society in Three Quebec Parishes, 1740–1840* (Toronto, 1985), 234–48; Lorraine Gadoury, "Les stocks des habitants dans les inventaires après décès," *Material History Bulletin*, XVII (1983), 139–47; Gilles Paquet and Jean-Pierre Wallot, "Structures sociales et niveaux de richesse dans les campagnes du Québec," ibid., 25–44; Christian Dessureault, "L'inventaire après décès et l'agriculture Bas-Canadienne," ibid., 127–37; Jacques Mathieu and Réal Brisson, "La Vallée du Saint-Laurent: un paysage à connaitre," *Cahiers de Géographie du Québec*, XXVIII (1984), 110–11; Richard Lalou and Mario Boléda, "Une source en friche: Les dénombrements sous la régime française," *Revue d'histoire de l'Amérique française*, XLII (1988), 47–72; Gilles Paquet and Jean-Pierre Wallot, "Les inventaires après décès à Montréal: préliminaires à une analyse," ibid., XXX (1976), 163–221.

5. Elizabeth B. Schumpeter, *English Overseas Trade Statistics, 1697–1808* (Oxford, Eng., 1960), 1–5, discusses the composition of the English data. On exchanges with New France, see Alice Jean Lunn, "Economic Development of New France, 1713–1760" (Ph.D. diss., McGill Univ., 1942), 443–44, 477; Denys Delage, "Les structures économiques de la Nouvelle-France et de la Nouvelle-York," *l'Actualité économique*, XLVI (1970), 69, 93–96; John J. McCusker, *Money and Exchange in Europe and America, 1600–1775* (Chapel Hill, N.C., 1978), 95–97. For several reasons comparisons between American and Canadian import data can only be approximate. First, the British series was based on prices that had been fixed at the beginning of the century. However, the divergence between the fixed prices and current ones was usually minor. Second, imports into New France must be "adjusted." Trade data include shipments from the West Indies and Louisbourg as well as France. Figures from 1739 suggest that imports from France were 87 percent of the total.

6. Greer, *Peasant, Lord, and Merchant*, 34–37. Greer's point of comparison

is the provision of grain, the chief component in the diet in both areas; Richard Colebrook Harris, *The Seigneurial System in Early Canada: A Geographical Study* (Madison, Wis., 1966), 150–55; Delage, "Les structures économiques," 104–5; James T. Lemon, *The Best Poor Man's Country: A Geographical Study of Early Southeastern Pennsylvania* (Baltimore, 1972), 152–54.

7. John J. McCusker and Russell R. Menard, *The Economy of British America, 1607–1789* (Chapel Hill, N.C., 1985), 55–60; Terry L. Anderson, "Economic Growth in Colonial New England: 'Statistical Renaissance,' " JEH, XXXIX (1979), 243–57; Duane Ball and Gary Walton, "Agricultural Productivity Change in Eighteenth-Century Pennsylvania," JEH, XXXVI (1976), 102–17; Morris Altman, "Economic Growth in Canada, 1695–1739: Estimates and Analysis," WMQ, 3d Ser., XLV (1988), 687–91, 703–4; Marc Egnal, "The Economic Development of the Thirteen Continental Colonies, 1720 to 1775," WMQ, 3d Ser., XXXII (1975), 200.

8. Immigration and population growth are examined in Chapter 5.

9. The depiction of Samuel Swayne is based on Samuel Swayne Account Book, Chester County Historical Society; Paul G. E. Clemens and Lucy Simler, "Rural Labor and the Farm Household in Chester County, Pennsylvania, 1750–1820," in *Work and Labor in Early America*, ed. Stephen Innes (Chapel Hill, N.C., 1988), 114–20. I am grateful to Lucy Simler and the Chester County Historical Society for providing a copy of the account book.

10. In addition to the material about the Swaynes, see Lemon, *Best Poor Man's Country*, 32–97.

11. Supplementing the Swayne material are Bettye Hobbs Pruitt, "Self-Sufficiency and the Agricultural Economy of Eighteenth-Century Massachusetts," WMQ, 3d Ser., XLI (1984), 333–64; Carole Shammas, "How Self-Sufficient Was Early America?" *Journal of Interdisciplinary History*, XIII (1982–83), 250–53; Lemon, *Best Poor Man's Country*, 150–83. See also the sources cited in note 17.

12. Daniel Vickers, "Competency and Competition: Economic Culture in Early America," WMQ, 3d Ser., XLVII (1990), 3–29; Sarah F. McMahon, "A Comfortable Subsistence: The Changing Composition of Diet in Rural New England, 1620–1840," ibid., 3d Ser., XLII (1985), 26–66; Allan Kulikoff, "The American Revolution, Capitalism, and the Formation of the Yeoman Class," in *Beyond the American Revolution: Explorations in the History of American Radicalism*, ed. Alfred F. Young (DeKalb, Ill., 1993), 80–119. Also see the discussion of capitalism and the household economy in Appendix A.

13. This account is drawn from the description of the Allaires in Greer, *Peasant, Lord, and Merchant*, 25–28, 37–47, 54–56, 75–76.

14. Some of the grain taken by the Church and seigneur found its way into markets outside the community. But in all the colony produced a limited surplus and exported only modest quantities; Lunn, "Economic Development," 443–44; Thomas Wien, "Peasant Accumulation in the Context of Colonization: Rivière-du-Sud, Canada, 1720–1775" (Ph.D. diss., McGill Univ., 1988); Morris Altman, "Seignorial Tenure in New France, 1688–1739: An Essay on Income Distribution and Retarded Economic Development," *Historical Reflections*, X (1983), 335–75; Altman, "Note on the Economic Burden of the Seignorial System in New France, 1688–1739," ibid., XIV (1987), 135–42. Louise Dechêne, *Le partage des subsistances au Canada sous le régime française*

(Montreal, 1994), 16, suggests that in the period 1725–44, 12 percent of the grain harvest went to feed Quebec and Montreal while 16 percent was exported (or provisioned the vessels trading with the colony). On local exchanges, see ibid., 24–36.

15. For farming practices in the Thirteen Colonies, see Percy W. Bidwell and John I. Falconer, *History of Agriculture in the Northern United States, 1620–1860* (Washington, D.C., 1925), 123–31; Lemon, *Best Poor Man's Country*, 174–78; McCusker and Menard, *Economy of British America*, 295–308; David O. Percy, "An Embarrassment of Richness: Colonial Soil Cultivation Practices," *Associates National Agricultural Library Today*, N.S., II (1977), 4–11; Richard L. Bushman, "Opening the American Countryside," in *The Transformation of Early American History: Society, Authority, and Ideology*, ed. James A. Henretta et al. (New York, 1991), 239–56. For French Canada, see Greer, *Peasant, Lord, and Merchant*, 28–32; Alan E. Skeoch, "Developments in Plowing Technology in Nineteenth-Century Canada," *Canadian Papers in Rural History*, III (1982), 156–77; Robert-Lionel Séguin, *L'équipement de la ferme canadienne aux XVIIe et XVIIIe siècles* (Montreal, 1959); Allan Greer, "The Pattern of Literacy in Quebec, 1745–1899," *Histoire sociale/Social History*, XI (1978), 298–301, 330–35. Louise Dechêne, "Observations sur l'agriculture du Bas-Canada au début du XIXe siècle," in *Evolution et éclatement du monde rural*, ed. Joseph Goy and Jean-Pierre Wallot (Paris, 1986), 189–202, takes a positive view of habitant farming practices. *American Husbandry*, 14–197, 236–359, provides valuable information about agriculture in all three regions.

16. These four points build on the studies of the "household economy" cited in this chapter, as well as on the large body of literature that discusses peasant society. See A. V. Chayanov, "Peasant Farm Organization," in *A. V. Chayanov on the Theory of Peasant Economy*, ed. Daniel Thorner, Basile Kerblay, and R. E. F. Smith (Homewood, Ill., 1966), 25–269; Diana Hunt, "Chayanov's Model of Peasant Resource Allocation," *Journal of Peasant Studies*, VI (1979), 247–56; Teodor Shanin, "Defining Peasants: Conceptualizations and De-Conceptualizations Old and New in a Marxist Debate," *Peasant Studies*, VIII, no. 4 (1979), 38–60; R. H. Hilton, "The Peasantry as a Class," in *The English Peasantry in the Later Middle Ages* (Oxford, Eng., 1975), 3–19; Eric Wolf, *Peasants* (Englewood Cliffs, N.J., 1966); Greer, *Peasant. Lord, and Merchant*, xi, 23.

17. Among those arguing for a locally oriented, noncapitalistic outlook are Michael Merrill, "Cash Is Good to Eat: Self-Sufficiency and Exchange in the Rural Economy of the United States," *Radical History Review*, No. 3 (1977), 42–71, quote on 54; Merrill, "So What's Wrong with the 'Household Mode of Production'?" *Radical History Review*, No. 22 (1979–80), 141–46; James A. Henretta, "Families and Farms: *Mentalité* in Pre-Industrial America," WMQ, 3d Ser., XXXV (1978), 3–32; Christopher Clark, "Household Economy, Market Exchange and the Rise of Capitalism in the Connecticut Valley, 1800–1860," *Journal of Social History*, XIII (1979), 169–189; Clark, *The Roots of Rural Capitalism: Western Massachusetts, 1780–1860* (Ithaca, N.Y., 1990); Pruitt, "Self-Sufficiency and the Agricultural Economy," 333–64; Michael A. Bernstein and Sean Wilentz, "Marketing, Commerce, and Capitalism in Rural Massachusetts," JEH, XLIV (1984), 171–73.

18. Historians of French Canada have long argued that habitants and others had a non-entrepreneurial mentality. Before the 1980s such views were

usually presented in the context of the debate over the impact of the Conquest. Beginning in the 1980s scholars have sketched in an interpretation closer to the work of such U.S. historians as Henretta, Clark, and Merrill. For the earlier debate see Fernand Ouellet, *Economic and Social History of Quebec, 1760–1850: Structures* and *Conjonctures* (Ottawa, 1980); Jean Hamelin, *Economie et société en Nouvelle-France* (Quebec, 1960); Marcel Trudel, *Introduction to New France* (Toronto, 1968); *Society and Conquest: The Debate on the Bourgeoisie and Social Change in French Canada, 1700–1850,* ed. Dale Miquelon (Toronto, 1977); Ramsay Cook, *The Maple Leaf Forever* (Toronto, 1971), 114–40. Recent writings on this topic include Greer, *Peasant, Lord, and Merchant,* quotes on xii; Bernard Bernier, "La pénétration du capitalisme dans l'agriculture," in *Agriculture et colonisation au Québec,* ed. Normand Séguin (Montreal, 1980), 73–91; Lise Pilon-Lè, "Le régime seigneurial au Québec: contribution à une analyse de la transition au capitalisme," *Cahiers du Socialisme,* VI (1980), 133–68; Gilles Paquet and Jean-Pierre Wallot, "Stratégie foncière de l'habitant: Québec (1790–1835)," *Revue d'histoire de l'Amérique française,* XXXIX (1986), 551–81; Christian Dessureault, "L'égalitarisme paysan dan l'ancienne société rurale de la vallée du Saint-Laurent: éléments pour une ré-interprétation," ibid., XL (1987), 373–407; Gérard Bouchard, "Paramètres sociaux de la reproduction familiale en milieu rural: systèmes ouverts et systèmes clos," *Recherches sociographiques,* XXVIII (1987), 229–51. Roberta Hamilton, "Feudal Society and Colonization: A Re-interpretation of the Historiography of New France," *Canadian Papers in Rural History,* VI (1988), 18–135, emphasizes the negative impact that France had on the colony; Gerald Bernier, "Sur quelques effets de la rupture structurelle engendrée par la Conquête au Québec," *Revue d'histoire de l'Amérique française,* XXXV (1981), 69–95, argues that the English Conquest gave a boost to economic development.

19. Lemon, *Best Poor Man's Country*; Lemon, "Comment on James A. Henretta's 'Family and Farms: *Mentalité* in Pre-Industrial America,' " WMQ, 3d Ser., XXXVII (1980), 688–96; Charles S. Grant, *Democracy in the Connecticut Frontier Town of Kent* (New York, 1961), quote on 53; Winifred B. Rothenberg, *From Market-Places to a Market Economy: The Transformation of Rural Massachusetts, 1750–1850* (Chicago, 1992); John F. Martin, *Profits in the Wilderness: Entrepreneurship and the Founding of New England Towns in the Seventeenth Century* (Chapel Hill, N.C., 1991). More broadly, see the discussion in Allan Kulikoff, *The Agrarian Origins of American Capitalism* (Charlottesville, Va., 1992), 13–33.

20. Several authors emphasize the entrepreneurial spirit of French Canadians before the English conquest in 1760. See Maurice Séguin, *La nation canadienne et l'agriculture (1760–1850): essai d'histoire économique* (Trois-Rivières,Que., 1970); Séguin, "La colonisation du Canada au XVIIIe siècle," *Cahiers de l'Académie canadienne-française,* II (1957), rpt. and trans. in *Society and Conquest,* 67–80, quote on 68; Michel Brunet, *La présence anglaise et les Canadiens* (Montreal, 1958); Guy Frégault, "La colonisation du Canada au XVIIIe siècle," *Cahiers de l'Académie canadienne-française,* II (1957), 53–81; Cameron Nish, *Les bourgeois-gentilhommes de la Nouvelle-France, 1729–1748* (Montreal, 1968). U.S. historians should be wary of seeking exact parallels in French-Canadian historiography because of the issues of national origins (French vs. English) and feudalism.

21. James T. Lemon, "Spatial Order: Households in Local Communities and Regions," in *Colonial British America: Essays in the New History of the Early*

Modern Era, ed. Jack P. Greene and J. R. Pole (Baltimore, 1984), 86–122, provides a balanced view of the two approaches to colonial society. For another synthesis, see Kulikoff, *Agrarian Origins,* 13–33.

22. This description draws upon the material in Lois Green Carr and Lorena S. Walsh, "Economic Diversification and Labor Organization in the Chesapeake, 1650–1820," in *Work and Labor,* 166–76.

23. On the importance of local transactions, see Lois Green Carr, "Diversification in the Colonial Chesapeake: Somerset County, Maryland, in Comparative Perspective," in *Colonial Chesapeake Society,* ed. Lois Green Carr, Philip D. Morgan, and Jean B. Russo (Chapel Hill, N.C., 1988), 342–88; Jean B. Russo, "Self-Sufficiency and Local Exchange: Free Craftsmen in the Rural Chesapeake Economy," in ibid., 389–432. On the extent of self-sufficiency in lowcountry South Carolina, see Philip D. Morgan, "The Development of Slave Culture in Eighteenth-Century Plantation America" (D.Phil. thesis, University College, London, 1977), 2–39.

24. Jack P. Greene, ed., *The Diary of Colonel Landon Carter of Sabine Hall, 1752–1778,* 2 vols. (Charlottesville, Va., 1965), provides an excellent example of the importance of pre-literate culture. Carter was well educated and read what books on farming were available. His reading, however, had little impact on his practice, which reflected trial and error and the close observation of his neighbors. See particularly, I, 156, 163, 229, 232, 256, 337, 576, II, 694, 697, 786. Carter is discussed further in Chapter 4.

25. Allan Kulikoff, *Tobacco and Slaves: The Development of Southern Cultures in the Chesapeake, 1680–1800* (Chapel Hill, N.C., 1986), 406–9; Lorena S. Walsh, "Plantation Management in the Chesapeake, 1620–1820," JEH, XLIX (1989), 393–406; Lois Green Carr and Russell R. Menard, "Land, Labor, and Economies of Scale in Early Maryland: Some Limits to Growth in the Chesapeake System of Husbandry," JEH, XLIX (1989), 407–18; Percy, "Embarrassment of Richness," 8; Carr and Walsh, "Economic Diversification," 176n. For a detailed portrait of a seventeenth-century planter who was in many respects similar to William Deacon, consult Lois Green Carr, Russell R. Menard, and Lorena S. Walsh, *Robert Cole's World: Agriculture and Society in Early Maryland* (Chapel Hill, N.C., 1991). For the change to plows in South Carolina, see Morgan, "Development of Slave Culture," 36–40.

26. Paul G. E. Clemens, "The Operation of an Eighteenth-Century Chesapeake Tobacco Plantation," *Agricultural History,* XLIX (1975), 517–31; Carr and Menard, "Land, Labor, and Economies of Scale," 413–16; see calculations in Appendix B. Agriculture in South Carolina paralleled that in Virginia, with the large rice plantations focusing on distant markets; Lewis C. Gray, *History of Agriculture in the Southern United States to 1860,* 2 vols. (Washington, D.C., 1933), I, 280–84, 295–97; Peter A. Coclanis, *The Shadow of a Dream: Economic Life and Death in the South Carolina Low Country, 1670–1920* (New York, 1989), 48–125. For estimates of the proportion of southern families holding slaves and the number of bondspeople owned by each household, see Kulikoff, *Tobacco and Slaves,* 6, 40–42, 134–54; Jones, *Wealth of a Nation to Be,* 54, 228–30; Peter H. Wood, *Black Majority: Negroes in Colonial South Carolina from 1670 through the Stono Rebellion* (New York, 1974), 155–66.

27. Historians reach various conclusions about the timing of the transition from the household economy to commercial capitalism — in part because

they focus on different regions and different activities. Gordon Wood, *The Radicalism of the American Revolution* (New York, 1992), esp. 313–47, argues that in the decades immediately following the Revolution the United States became "perhaps the most thoroughly commercialized nation in the world" (p. 313). See also Wood's essay, "Inventing American Capitalism," *New York Review of Books*, June 9, 1994, pp. 44–49, which emphasizes the 1780s as the turning point. Christopher Clark and John L. Brooke, who study western Massachusetts, suggest that commercial capitalism did not triumph in the countryside until after 1825, even if the first stirrings of change came earlier. See Clark, *Roots of Rural Capitalism*, 317–26; John L. Brooke, *The Heart of the Commonwealth: Society and Political Culture in Worcester County, Massachusetts, 1713–1861* (Cambridge, Mass., 1989), 269–309. James A. Henretta, "The War for Independence and American Economic Development," in *The Economy of Early America: The Revolutionary Period, 1763–1790*, ed. Ronald Hoffman et al. (Charlottesville, Va., 1988), 45–87, studies manufacturing and emerges with a more mixed evaluation. See also Henretta, "The Transition to Capitalism in America," in *Transformation of Early American History*, 218–38; Charles Sellers, *The Market Revolution: Jacksonian America, 1815–1846* (New York, 1991), 5–33; Allan Kulikoff, "American Revolution," 80–92; Kulikoff, *Agrarian Origins*, 13–126; Edward Countryman, " 'To Secure the Blessings of Liberty': Language, the Revolution, and American Capitalism," in *Beyond the American Revolution*, 123–48. Recent quantitative work by economic historians casts light on the issue of timing. These findings dispute the older notion of a marked acceleration around 1840 and suggest a gradual quickening beginning at the turn of the nineteenth century. Paul A. David, "The Growth of Real Product in the United States before 1840: New Evidence, Controlled Conjectures," *Journal of Economic History*, XXVII (1967), 168–171; Diane Lindstrom, "Macroeconomic Growth: The United States in the Nineteenth Century," *Journal of Interdisciplinary History*, XIII (1983), 679–705. For the impact of these changes on women, Nancy F. Cott, *The Bonds of Womanhood: "Woman's Sphere" in New England, 1780–1835* (New Haven, Conn., 1977).

28. David, "Growth of Real Product," 168–171; Serge Courville, "Un monde rural en mutation: le Bas-Canada dans la première moitié de XIXe siècle," *Histoire sociale/Social History*, XX (1987), 237–58; Paul G. Faler, *Mechanics and Manufacturers in the Early Industrial Revolution: Lynn, Massachusetts, 1780–1860* (Albany, N.Y., 1981), 1–76; Victor S. Clark, *History of Manufactures in the United States*, 3 vols. (1929; rpt., New York, 1949), I, 402–577; Thomas C. Cochran, *Frontiers of Change: Early Industrialism in America* (New York, 1981); Alfred D. Chandler, Jr., *The Visible Hand: The Managerial Revolution in American Business* (Cambridge, Mass., 1977), 15–78; Carl Siracusa, *A Mechanical People: Perceptions of the Industrial Order in Massachusetts, 1815–1880* (Middletown, Conn., 1979); Kenneth L. Sokoloff, "Was the Transition from Artisanal Shop to the Non-mechanized Factory Associated with Gains in Efficiency? Evidence from the U.S. Manufacturing Censuses of 1820 and 1850," *Explorations in Economic History*, XXI (1984), 351–82; Sokoloff, "Productivity Growth in Manufacturing during Early Industrialization: Evidence from the American Northeast, 1820–1860," in National Bureau for Economic Research, *Long-Term Factors in American Economic Growth*, Studies in Income and Wealth, vol. LI (Chicago, 1986), 679–736.

29. Robert W. Fogel, *Without Consent or Contract: The Rise and Fall of American Slavery* (New York, 1989), 103–4, argues that the South had more manufacturing than the census reported. His revisions, however, do not close the gap separating the levels of manufacturing in the South and North.

30. Lester Cappon, ed., *Atlas of Early American History: The Revolutionary Era, 1760–1790* (Princeton, N.J., 1976), 97–98, presents data on urban population in 1760; U.S. Bureau of the Census, *Historical Statistics of the United States, Colonial Times to 1970*, 2 vols. (Washington, D.C., 1975), I, 24–36, documents urban population in 1850. "Urban" is defined as places of 2500 or more people. Figures for Canada from Harris, *Seigneurial System*, 90–103. For Canada urban is defined as 1000 or more people. The difference between the 2500 and 1000 cut-off points suggests that Canadian figures should be lowered by roughly two percentage points to be comparable with those for the United States.

31. Simon Kuznets, "Notes on the Pattern of U.S. Economic Growth," in *The Reinterpretation of American Economic History*, ed. Robert W. Fogel and Stanley L. Engerman (New York, 1971), 18; Kuznets, *Modern Economic Growth* (New Haven, Conn., 1966), 64–65. See the "amenities index" constructed by Lois Green Carr and Lorena S. Walsh, and used by Gloria L. Main: Carr and Walsh, "The Standard of Living in the Colonial Chesapeake," WMQ, 3d Ser., XLV (1988), 135–59; Main, "The Standard of Living in Southern New England, 1640–1773," ibid., 124–34; Walsh, "Consumer Behavior, Diet, and the Standard of Living in Late Colonial and Early Antebellum America, 1770–1840," in *American Economic Growth and Standards of Living before the Civil War*, ed. Robert E. Gallman and John J. Wallis (Chicago, 1992), 217–61; Winifred B. Rothenberg, "The Productivity Consequences of Market Integration: Agriculture in Massachusetts, 1771–1801," ibid., 311–38; Lindstrom, "Macroeconomic Growth," 679–705.

32. Horace Mann, "Report for 1841," in *Life and Works of Horace Mann*, ed. Mary Mann, 3 vols. (Boston, 1865–68), III, 118–19; Maris A. Vinovskis, "Horace Mann on the Economic Productivity of Education," *New England Quarterly*, XLIII (1970), 550–571; more generally, see Richard D. Brown, *Knowledge Is Power: The Diffusion of Information in Early America, 1700–1865* (New York, 1989), David Jaffee, "The Village Enlightenment in New England, 1760–1820," WMQ, 3d Ser., XLVII (1990), 327–46; William J. Gilmore, *Reading Becomes a Necessity of Life: Material and Cultural Life in Rural New England, 1780–1835* (Knoxville, Tenn., 1989). Thomas Dublin, *Women at Work: The Transformation of Work and Community in Lowell, Massachusetts, 1826–1860* (New York, 1979), 149–51, disputes the connection between literacy and productivity. But his evidence shows that at Lowell educated workers received the best-paying jobs (such as weaving) while less-schooled individuals predominated in the more poorly paid positions, such as spinning.

33. U.S. Patent Office *Report*, 1852, quoted in Clarence H. Danhof, *Change in Agriculture: The Northern United States, 1820–1870* (Cambridge, Mass., 1969), 256; Simon Baatz, *"Venerate the Plough": A History of the Philadelphia Society for Promoting Agriculture, 1785–1985* (Philadelphia, 1985); Fred Bateman and Jeremy Atack, "The Profitability of Northern Agriculture in 1860," *Research in Economic History*, IV (1979), 87–125; Sue Headlee, *The Political Economy of the Family Farm: The Agrarian Roots of American Capitalism* (Westport, Conn., 1991), examines the mechanization of the family farm; Paul W. Gates, *The*

Farmer's Age: Agriculture, 1815–1860, vol. III in *The Economic History of the United States* (New York, 1960), 163, 183, 212–13, 239–47.

34. On change in the North, David Jaffee, "Peddlers of Progress and the Transformation of the Rural North, 1760–1860," *Journal of American History,* LXXVIII (1991), 511–35; Albert Fishlow, *American Railroads and the Transformation of the Ante-bellum Economy* (Cambridge, Mass., 1965), 262–301; Winifred B. Rothenberg, "The Market and Massachusetts Farmers, 1750–1855," *JEH,* XLI (1981), 283–314; Winifred B. Rothenberg, "A Price Index for Rural Massachusetts, 1750–1850," ibid., XXXIX (1979), 995–1001; Clark, *Roots of Rural Capitalism,* 228–90. On the South, consult Diane Lindstrom, "Southern Dependence upon Interregional Grain Supplies: A Review of Trade Flows, 1840–1860," in *The Structure of the Cotton Economy of the Antebellum South,* ed. William Parker (Washington, D.C., 1970), 101–15; Robert Gallman, "Self-sufficiency of the Cotton Economy of the Antebellum South," in ibid., 5–25; Steven Hahn, *The Roots of Southern Populism: Yeoman Farmers and the Transformation of the Georgia Upcountry, 1850–1890* (New York, 1983), 72–133, 240–83. For the advent of commercial capitalism in French Canada, see Courville, "Un monde rural," 237–58; Greer, *Peasant, Lord, and Merchant,* 194–231. Also see the sources cited in notes 27 and 28, and in Chapter 3, note 12.

35. Rolla Milton Tryon, *Household Manufactures in the United States, 1640–1860: A Study in Industrial History* (Chicago, 1917), 164–87, provides statistics for home manufactures; Adrienne D. Hood and David-Thierry Ruddel, "Artifacts and Documents in the History of Quebec Textiles," in *Living in a Material World: Canadian and American Approaches to Material Culture,* ed. Gerald L. Pocius (St. John's, Newfoundland, 1991), 63–71; John McCallum, *Unequal Beginnings: Agricultural and Economic Development in Quebec and Ontario* (Toronto, 1980), 88; Jonathan Prude, *The Coming of Industrial Order: Town and Factory Life in Rural Massachusetts, 1810–1860* (New York, 1983).

36. Henry David Thoreau, *Walden and Other Writings,* ed. Joseph W. Krutch (New York, 1962), 190–91; Walter Roy Harding, *Thoreau, Man of Concord* (New York, 1960); Leo Stoller, *After Walden: Thoreau's Changing Views on Economic Man* (Stanford, Calif., 1957); Jack Larkin, "Massachusetts Enters the Marketplace, 1790–1860: An Interpretation of Recent Work in Social History," in *A Guide to the History of Massachusetts,* ed. Martin Kaufman, John W. Ifkovic, and Joseph Cavalho III (New York, 1988), 69–82.

37. O. J. Firestone, "Development of Canada's Economy, 1850–1900," in National Bureau for Economic Research, *Trends in the American Economy in the 19th Century,* Studies in Income and Wealth, vol. XXIV (Princeton, N.J., 1960), 217–52, esp. 222–25. The extrapolation is made by assuming that income in Lower Canada was 85 percent of the national average, and that the Canadian economy grew at the rate of 0.9 percent a year during the 1840s. On the relationship of Quebec income to national income, Marvin McInnis, "The Trend of Regional Income Differentials in Canada," *Canadian Journal of Economics,* I (1968), 440–70. Gerald Gunderson, "Southern Ante-bellum Income Reconsidered," *Explorations in Economic History,* X (1973), 151–76, examines the strengths and shortcomings of the 1840 census data. See the "Reply" by Robert Gallman, ibid., XII (1975), 89–99, and a "Rejoinder" by Gunderson, ibid., XII, 101–2.

38. Richard A. Easterlin, "Interregional Differences in Per Capita Income,

Population, and Total Income, 1840–1950," in National Bureau for Economic Research, *Trends in the American Economy in the 19th Century*, Studies in Income and Wealth, vol. XXIV (Princeton, N.J., 1960), 97–98; Frank D. Lewis and Marvin McInnis, "Agricultural Output and Efficiency in Lower Canada, 1851," *Research in Economic History*, IX (1984), 45–87, esp. 59–60.

39. Hinton Rowan Helper, *The Impending Crisis of the South: How to Meet It* (1857; rpt., New York, 1963), quote on 54; Hugh C. Bailey, *Hinton Rowan Helper: Abolitionist-Racist* (Montgomery, Ala., 1965). Helper was not alone among contemporaries (and southerners) in arguing that slavery slowed southern growth. See Cassius Marcellus Clay, *Writings*, ed. Horace Greeley (New York, 1848), esp. 204–27, 346–47; [Daniel Reaves Goodloe], *Inquiry into the Causes Which Have Retarded the Accumulation of Wealth and Increase of Population in the Southern States* (Washington, 1846). J. B. D. DeBow, *The Interest in Slavery of the Southern Non-slaveholder* (Charleston, S.C., 1860), defended slavery despite an awareness that it weakened the economy. J. E. Cairnes, the British economist, presented a penetrating critique of the peculiar institution in *The Slave Power: Its Character, Career, and Probable Designs: Being an Attempt to Explain the Real Issues Involved in the American Contest*, 2d ed. (London, 1863).

40. Helper, *Impending Crisis*, 81. See the valuable essay on Helper in George M. Frederickson, *The Arrogance of Race: Historical Perspectives on Slavery, Racism and Social Inequality* (Middletown, Conn., 1988), 28–53. More broadly, on the role of the yeomanry in the South, see Paul Goodman, "White over White: Planters, Yeomen, and the Coming of the Civil War: A Review Essay," *Agricultural History* LIV (1980), 446–52; and see Chapter 4, notes 32, 33.

41. Sir C. P. Lucas, ed., *Lord Durham's Report on the Affairs of British North America*, 3 vols. (Oxford, 1912), quotes from II, 31, 28, 211–12, 99; Chester W. New, *Lord Durham: A Biography of John George Lambton, First Earl of Durham* (Oxford, 1929), ix-xiv, 41–61; Ged Martin, *The Durham Report and British Policy: A Critical Essay* (Cambridge, Eng., 1972), 49–92; Janet Ajzenstat, *The Political Thought of Lord Durham* (Montreal, 1988), 22–27, 78–80, 89–90.

Chapter 2. Eighteenth-Century Perceptions

1. Thomas Jefferson to the Marquis de Chastellux, Sept. 2, 1785, *The Papers of Thomas Jefferson*, ed. Julian P. Boyd, 25 vols. (Princeton, N.J., 1950–1992), VIII, 468. I have put the titles in italics.

2. "Pierre-François-Xavier de Charlevoix," DCB, III, 103–10.

3. Pierre-François-Xavier de Charlevoix, *Journal of a Voyage to North America*, 2 vols. (1761; rpt., Ann Arbour, Mich. 1966), II, 113, 114.

4. "Pehr [Peter] Kalm," DCB, IV, 406–8; Adolph B. Benson, ed., *Peter Kalm's Travels in North America: The English Version of 1770*, 2 vols. (1937; rpt., New York, 1966), I, 375–76 (July 2, 1749).

5. Quoted in W. J. Eccles, *The Canadian Frontier, 1534–1760* (New York, 1969), 91.

6. *Peter Kalm's Travels*, II, 446 (Aug. 8, 1749), 479 (Aug. 26, 1749).

7. Quoted in W. J. Eccles, *Canada under Louis XIV, 1663–1701* (Toronto, 1964), 228.

8. Quoted in Eccles, *Canadian Frontier*, 94, 96.

9. Quoted in ibid., 96.

10. Charlevoix, *Journal of a Voyage*, 264.

11. *Peter Kalm's Travels*, II, 403 (July 25, 1749).

12. Letter of 1709, [Antoine-Denis Raudot], *Letters from North America*, trans. Ivy Alice Dickson (Belleville, Ont., 1980), 11–19, quotes on 61. The introduction to these letters ascribes them to a Jesuit priest, Father Antoine Silvy. For the attribution to Raudot, see "Antoine-Denis Raudot," DCB, II, 549–54.

13. François-Marc Gagnon and Nicole Cloutier, *Premiers peintres de la Nouvelle France*, 2 vols. (Quebec, 1976); Gérard Morisset, *Coup d'oeil sur les arts en Nouvelle-France* (Quebec, 1941); Morisset, *La peinture au Canada français* (Ottawa, 1960); Guy Robert, *La peinture au Québec depuis ses origines* (Saint-Adèle, Quebec, 1978); J. Russell Harper, *Painting in Canada: A History*, 2d ed. (Toronto, 1977), 3–25; Patricia Godsell, *Enjoying Canadian Painting* (Don Mills, Ontario, 1976), 15–29.

14. Quoted in David Bertelson, *The Lazy South* (New York, 1967), 161; C. Vann Woodward, "The Southern Ethic in a Puritan World," WMQ, 3d Ser., XXV (1968), 343–70, contrasts the mind-set of the two sections.

15. Andrew Burnaby, *Travels through the Middle Settlements in North America in the Years 1759 and 1760. . .* (1798; rpt., New York, 1970), 96–97, 117, 150.

16. Robert Beverley, *The History and Present State of Virginia: A Selection*, ed. David F. Hawke (1705; Indianapolis, 1971), 319.

17. Bertelson, *Lazy South*, 155.

18. Jules D. Prown, *John Singleton Copley: In America, 1738–1774* (Cambridge, Mass, 1966), 59–93, appendices, plates; Wayne Craven, *Colonial American Portraiture: The Economic, Religious, Social, Cultural, Philosophical, Scientific, and Aesthetic Foundations* (Cambridge, Eng., 1986), 309–52, 374–405; James T. Flexner, *John Singleton Copley* (Boston, 1948); Richard H. Saunders and Ellen G. Miles, *American Colonial Portraits, 1700–1776* (Washington, D.C., 1987), 58–59, 230–46, 299–300, 316–17; Milton W. Brown, *American Art to 1900: Painting, Sculpture, and Architecture* (New York, 1977), 90–112.

19. On Theus and painting in South Carolina, see Craven, *Colonial American Portraiture*, 178–250, 353–73; Margaret S. Middleton, *Jeremiah Theus, Colonial Artist of Charles Town* (Columbia, S.C., 1953); Anna Wells Rutledge, *Artists in the Life of Charleston, Through Colony and State, from Restoration to Reconstruction* (American Philosophical Society *Transactions*, XXXIX (Nov. 1949), part 2, pp. 101–260); Frederick P. Bowes, *The Culture of Early Charleston* (Chapel Hill, N.C., 1942), 109–30; Francis W. Bilodeau, *Art in South Carolina, 1670–1970* (Columbia, S.C., 1970); Saunders and Miles, *American Colonial Portraits*, 183–86. More broadly on southern painting, Jesse Poesch, *The Art of the Old South: Painting, Sculpture, Architecture and the Products of Craftsmen, 1560–1860* (New York, 1983); Carolyn J. Weekley et al., *Painting in the South: 1564–1980* (Richmond, Va., 1983).

20. Burnaby, *Travels*, 150.

21. Thomas Jefferson, *Notes on the State of Virginia*, ed. William Peden (1785; Chapel Hill, N.C., 1954), 163.

22. Bertelson, *Lazy South*, 173. For more on climate and the impact of air-conditioning, see Chapter 10.

23. Quoted in Trevor R. Reese, *Colonial Georgia: A Study in British Imperial Policy in the Eighteenth Century* (Athens, Ga., 1963), 47.

24. Jefferson, *Notes on the State of Virginia,* 163.

25. Beverley, *History of Virginia,* 287.

26. William R. Taylor, *Cavalier and Yankee: The Old South and American National Character* (New York, 1957). This myth dovetailed with a belief that outsiders residing in the South—for example, foreign Protestants and northerners—were the only exceptions to regional indolence. On the industry of these unusual southerners, see Bertelson, *Lazy South,* 77, 91–92.

27. Bertelson, *Lazy South,* 77, quotes Whitefield; E. Merton Coulter, *Georgia: A Short History* (Chapel Hill, N.C., 1933, 1960), 139; David Hackett Fischer, *Albion's Seed: Four British Folkways in America* (New York, 1989); Harold E. Davis, *The Fledgling Province: Social and Cultural Life in Colonial Georgia, 1733–1776* (Chapel Hill, N.C., 1976), 15–18, 207–9, 233–39, discusses German-speaking settlers in Georgia. See the forum on Fischer's book in WMQ, 3d Ser., XLVIII (1991). Essays include Jack P. Greene, "Transplanting Moments: Inheritance in the Formation of Early American Culture," 224–30; Virginia DeJohn Anderson, "The Origins of New England Culture," 231–37; James Horn "Cavalier Culture? The Social Development of Colonial Virginia," 238–45; Barry Levy, "Quakers, the Delaware Valley, and North Midlands Emigration to America," 246–52; Ned C. Landsman, "Border Cultures, the Backcountry, and 'North British' Emigration to America," 253–59; and Fischer's reply, "*Albion* and the Critics: Further Evidence and Reflection," 260–308.

Chapter 3. Peasants and Freeholders

1. Robert C. Winthrop, *Life and Letters of John Winthrop,* 2 vols. (1864–67; rpt., New York, 1971), I, 212, quotes 1626 letter of John Winthrop; see also I, 13–26, 69–78, 151–55; Edmund S. Morgan, *The Puritan Dilemma: The Story of John Winthrop* (Boston, 1958), 3–15. Robert Brenner, "Agrarian Class Structure and Economic Development in Pre-Industrial Europe," *Past and Present,* LXX (1976), 30–75, discusses the emergence of capitalist agriculture.

2. Winthrop, *John Winthrop,* I, 215, 410–31; Morgan, *Puritan Dilemma,* 15–16, 22–25, 67.

3. Pierre Goubert, *The French Peasantry in the Seventeenth Century* (Cambridge, Eng, 1986), 6–34, 111–15, 166–75; Emanuel Le Roy Ladurie, *The French Peasantry, 1450–1660* (Oxford, Eng., 1987), 267–342, 409–19; Ralph Davis, *The Rise of the Atlantic Economies* (London, 1973), 108–22, 215–20, 290–93; Sydney Herbert, *The Fall of Feudalism in France* (1921; rpt., New York, 1969), 1–113, 188–98; George Lefebvre, *The Coming of the French Revolution,* trans. R. R. Palmer (Princeton, 1947), 1–20; Robert Forster, "Obstacles to Agricultural Growth in Eighteenth-Century France," *American Historical Review,* LXXV (1970), 1600–15. J. Jacquart, *La crise rurale en Ile de France, 1500–1670* (Paris, 1974), suggests the weakness of feudal tenure near Paris. More generally, these works depict both the norm, seigneurialism, and the exceptions, the areas marked by "allodial" or freehold tenure (which characterized less than 10 percent of the kingdom). Natalie Zemon Davis, *The Return of Martin Guerre* (Cambridge, Mass., 1983), 6–24, 51–58, portrays a community where seigneurialism had lost its hold.

4. Several important articles contrast the rapid growth of England and the slow course of development in France. See E. A. Wrigley, "Urban Growth and Agricultural Change: England and the Continent in the Early Modern Period,"

Journal of Interdisciplinary History, XV (1985), 683–728; Charles P. Kindle-berger, "Financial Institutions and Economic Development: A Comparison of Great Britain and France in the 18th and 19th Centuries," _Explorations in Economic History_, XXI (1984), 103–24; F. Crouzet, "England and France in the Eighteenth Century: A Comparative Analysis of Two Economic Growths," in _The Causes of the Industrial Revolution in England_, ed. R. M. Hartwell (London, 1967), 139–74; William Hagen, "Capitalism in the Countryside in Early Modern Europe: Interpretations, Models, Debates," _Agricultural History_, LXII (1988), 12–47.

5. Cameron Nish, _Les bourgeois-gentilhommes de la Nouvelle-France, 1728–1748_ (Montreal, 1968), 99–124, 173–84, quotes on 179–80; and see Léon Gérin, _Aux sources de notre histoire: les conditions économiques et sociales de la colonisation en Nouvelle-France_ (Montreal, 1946). Sigmund Diamond, "An Experiment in 'Feudalism': French Canada in the Seventeenth Century," WMQ, 3d Ser., XVIII (1961), 3–34, argues that New France rejected the values of French society. Richard Colebrook Harris, _The Seigneurial System in Early Canada: A Geographical Study_ (Madison, 1966), 163–64, 169–98, minimizes the influence that seigneurs and seigneuries had in shaping social structure and contends that the presence of the fur trade kept society in New France more open. Denis Monière, "L'utilité du concept de mode de production des petits producteurs pour l'historiographie de la Nouvelle-France," _Revue d'histoire de l'Amérique française_, XXIX (1976), 483–502, argues that the habitants were small producers rather than feudal peasants.

6. W. B. Munro, _The Seigniorial System in Canada: A Study in French Colonial Policy_ (New York, 1907), is the classic work on the seigneurial system and emphasizes the French feudal roots; Marcel Trudel, _La population du Canada en 1663_ (Montreal, 1973), underscores the power of the nobility; Fernand Ouellet, "Seigneurial Property and Social Structure, 1663–1840," in Ouellet, _Economy, Class, & Nation in Quebec: Interpretative Essays_, ed. and trans. Jacques A. Barbier (Toronto, 1991), 61–86, depicts a society dominated by an elite with a feudal mind-set; Allan Greer, _Peasant, Lord, and Merchant: Rural Society in Three Quebec Parishes 1740–1840_ (Toronto, 1985), ix–xiv, 3–19. See also Louise Dechêne, "L'évolution du régime seigneuriale au Canada: le cas de Montréal au xvii-e et xviii-e siècles," _Recherches sociographiques_, XII (1971), 143–83; and Dechêne, _Habitants et marchands de Montréal au XVIIe siècle_ (Montreal, 1974), 241–94, 353–402. Dechêne argues that the seigneurial system grew stricter in the eighteenth century and shaped social relationships. Also note two valuable discussions of recent literature on this question: Catherine Desbarats, "Agriculture within the Seigneurial Régime of Eighteenth-Century Canada: Some Thoughts on the Recent Literature," _Canadian Historical Review_, LXXIII (1992), 1–29; Roberta Hamilton, "Feudal Society and Colonization: A Reinterpretation of the Historiography of New France," _Canadian Papers in Rural History_, VI (1988), 18–135. See the works discussed in Chapter 1, note 18.

7. Ouellet, "Seigneurial Property," 61–86.

8. Murray quoted in Munro, _Seigniorial System_, 191; Greer, _Peasant, Lord, and Merchant_, 92–94; Harris, _Seigneurial System_, 63–87.

9. Greer, _Peasant, Lord, and Merchant_, 95–96, 124–25; Harris, _Seigneurial System_, 45–47, 75–76, 140–46; Munro, _Seigniorial System_, 95–100; Marcel Trudel, _Atlas de la Nouvelle-france: An Atlas of New France_ (Laval, Quebec, 1968,

1973), 161–81; Sylvie Dépatie, Mario Lalancette, Christian Dessureault, *Contributions à l'étude du régime seigneurial canadien* (Quebec, 1987), 37–55, 103–36, 283–85. More generally, women had rights and privileges in New France they did not have in the Thirteen Colonies. See "Marie-Madeleine Jarret de Verchères," DCB, III, 308–13; "Marie Guyart" [Marie de l'Incarnation], DCB, I, 351–59; Jan Noel, "New France: Les femmes favorisées," in *The Neglected Majority: Essays in Canadian Women's History*, ed. Alison Prentice and Susan Mann Trofimenkoff, 2 vols. (Toronto, 1985), II, 18–40; Lilianne Plamondon, "A Businesswoman in New France: Marie-Anne Barbel, The Widow Fornel," in *Rethinking Canada: The Promise of Women's History*, ed. Veronica Strong-Boag and Anita Clair Fellman (Toronto, 1986), 45–58.

10. Greer, *Peasant, Lord, and Merchant*, 122–39; Harris, *Seigneurial System*, 63–87; Thomas Wien, "Peasant accumulation in the Context of Colonization: Rivière-du-Sud, Canada, 1720–1775" (Ph.D. diss., McGill Univ. 1988), shows that the seigneurs expropriated much of the peasants' surplus.

11. "Antoine-Denis Raudot," DCB, II, 549–54; Dechêne, "L'évolution du régime seigneurial," 144–45.

12. Gilles Paquet and Jean-Pierre Wallot have authored several articles on this topic: "Le Bas-Canada au début du XIXe siècle: une hypothèse," *Revue d'histoire de l'Amérique française*, XXV (1971–72), 39–61; "Crise agricole et tensions socio-ethniques dans les Bas-Canada, 1802–1812: éléments pour une ré-interprétation," ibid., XXVI (1972–73), 185–237; "Sur quelques discontinuités dans l'experience socio-économique du Québec: une hypothèse," ibid., XXXV (1981–82), 483–521. Like Paquet and Wallot, Gérald Bernier places more emphasis on the conceptual framework than on the close study of changes in rural life. Bernier, "Sur quelques effets de la rupture structurelle engendrée par la conquête au Québec: 1760–1854," ibid., XXXV (1981–82), 69–95; and "La structure de classes québécoise au 19–e siècle et le problème de l'articulation des modes de production," *Revue canadienne de science politique*, XIV (1981), 487–518. Finally, Serge Courville does undertake a detailed study of aspects of rural life, but I would argue that his evidence does not support the case for far-reaching change. Serge Courville, "Villages and Agriculture in the Seigneuries of Lower Canada: Conditions of a Comprehensive Study of Rural Quebec in the First Half of the Nineteenth Century," *Canadian Papers in Rural History*, V (1986), 121–49; Courville, "Un monde rural en mutation: le Bas-Canada dans la première moitié du XIXe siècle," *Histoire sociale/Social History*, XX (1987), 237–58; Courville, *Entre ville et campagne: L'essor du village dans les seigneuries du Bas-Canada* (Quebec, 1990); Courville, "Le marché des 'subsistances': l'exemple de la plaine de Montréal au début des années 1830: une perspective géographique," *Revue d'histoire de l'Amérique française*, XLII (1988), 193–239. Courville suggests Lower Canada passed through a "proto-industrial" phase during these years.

13. Greer, *Peasant, Lord, and Merchant*, esp. 203–31; Fernand Ouellet, *Lower Canada, 1791–1840: Social Change and Nationalism* (Toronto, 1980); Ouellet, "Ruralization, Regional Development, and Industrial Growth before 1850," in *Economy, Class, & Nation*, 124–60; R. L. Jones, "Agriculture in Lower Canada, 1792–1815," *Canadian Historical Review*, XXVII (1946), 33–51. Claude Couture, "La conquête de 1760 et le probleme de la transition au capitalisme," *Revue d'histoire de l'Amérique française*, XXXIX (1985–86), 369–89,

provides a critique of Gérald Bernier's work. In *The Patriots and the People: The Rebellion of 1837 in Rural Lower Canada* (Toronto, 1993), 23–43, Allan Greer distinguishes his position from Ouellet's, but concludes about French-Canadian farming, "it remained basically peasant agriculture, and as such was bound to raise the ire of bourgeois commentators, especially those who came from the British Isles, then in the forefront of agricultural improvement" (34).

14. Paquet and Wallot, "Crise agricole," 185–237; T. J. A. LeGoff, "The Agricultural Crisis in Lower Canada, 1802–12: A Review of a Controversy," *Canadian Historical Review*, LV (1974), 1–31; Paquet and Wallot, "The Agricultural Crisis in Lower Canada, 1802–1812: *mise au point*. A Response to T. J. A. LeGoff," ibid., LVI (1975), 133–61; LeGoff, "A Reply," ibid., LVI (1975), 162–68; Fernand Ouellet, "Le mythe de 'l'habitant sensible au marché': commentaries sur la controverse LeGoff-Wallot et Paquet," *Recherches sociographiques*, XVII (1976), 115–32; R. M. McInnis, "A Reconsideration of the State of Agriculture in Lower Canada in the First Half of the Nineteenth Century," in *Canadian Papers in Rural History*, III (1982), 9–49; Greer, *Peasant, Lord, and Merchant*, 202–17. Robert Lavertue, "L'histoire de l'agriculture québécoise au XIXème siècle: une schématisation des faits et des interprétations," *Cahiers de géographie du Québec*, XXVIII (1984), 275–87, offers a summary of the debate.

15. Hilda Neatby, *The Quebec Act: Protest and Policy* (Toronto, 1972), 5–67; Neatby, *Quebec: The Revolutionary Age, 1760–1791* (Toronto, 1966), 6–17, 125–41, 253–63; Gustave Lanctôt, *Le Canada et la révolution américaine, 1774–1783* (Montreal, 1965), 29–39, 47–49; Alfred L. Burt, *The Old Province of Quebec* (Minneapolis, Minn., 1933), 74–101, 177–201.

16. Neatby, *Quebec: The Revolutionary Age*, 258–61; Fernand Ouellet, *Economic and Social History of Quebec: 1760–1850: Structures* and *Conjonctures* (Ottawa, 1980), 175–220, 317–31, 470–75, 538–46; Ouellet, *Lower Canada*, 201–10, 255–57, 328–41.

17. Sir C. P. Lucas, ed., *Lord Durham's Report on the Affairs of British America*, 3 vols. (Oxford, Eng., 1912), II, 36; Ouellet, "Seigneurial Property," 61–86; Greer, *Patriots and the People*, 270–74; Françoise Noël, *The Christie Seigneuries: Estate Management and Settlement in the Upper Richelieu Valley, 1760–1854* (Montreal and Kingston, 1992), provides an excellent case study of the clash between a hard-driving English seigneur and French-Canadian farmers. Simon Legree was the evil, New England-born slavemaster in Harriet Beecher Stowe's *Uncle Tom's Cabin*.

18. Petition to Lord Dorchester by James Sawyer and 23 others, 1796, quoted in Greer, *Peasant, Lord, and Merchant*, 200.

19. Ouellet, *Economic and Social History*, 361.

20. 1849, quoted in Ouellet, *Economic and Social History*, 471.

21. Greer, *Patriots and the People*, 258–93, provides a thoughtful analysis of French-Canadian views on the seigneurial system. Greer emphasizes that while there were few outright criticisms of seigeuerialism before the 1830s, habitants no more liked high feudal dues than modern citizens enjoy taxes.

22. *Papineau: His Life and Times* (catalogue of an exhibition held at the Public Archives of Canada) (Ottawa, 1986), presents a list of Papineau portraits and includes several reproductions; Mason Wade, *The French Canadians, 1760–1967*, rev. ed., 2 vols. (Toronto, 1968), I, passim, quote on 281; "Louis-Joseph Papineau," DCB, X, 564–78; Ouellet, *Lower Canada*, 275–326; and see

the documents in *Histoire des idées au Québec: des troubles de 1837 au référendum de 1980*, ed. Georges Vincenthier (Montreal, 1983), 16–30; Greer, *Patriots and the People*, 288–93, discusses the opposition of the seigneurs to the 1837 rebellion.

23. "Cyrille-Hector-Octave Côté," DCB, VII, 208–11; Nöel, *Christie Seigneuries*; Greer, *Patriots and the People*, 276–83, 344–50.

24. Lafontaine quoted in Wade, *French Canadians*, 280–81.

25. Munro, *Seigniorial System*, 240–51; Michael B. Percy and Rick Szostak, "The Political Economy of the Abolition of Seigneurial Tenure in Canada East," *Explorations in Economic History*, XXIX (1992), 51–68, asssesses the degree to which censitaires and seigneurs benefited from abolition; Jean-Pierre Wallot, "Le régime seigneurial et son abolition au Canada," in Wallot, *Un Québec qui bougeait: trame socio-politique au tournant du XIXe siècle* (Montreal, 1973), 225–51, emphasizes the role of English-speaking seigneurs in the events leading up to abolition.

26. Joan Thirsk, "The Farming Regions of England," in Joan Thirsk, ed., *The Agrarian History of England and Wales*, vol. IV: *1500–1640* (Cambridge, Eng., 1967), 1–112; C. S. Orwin and C. S. Orwin, *The Open Fields*, 3d ed. (Oxford, Eng., 1967), 1–2, 60–67, suggests that in a few counties, such as Essex and Kent, enclosure was widespread before 1500; Brenner, "Agrarian Class Structure," 30–37. Alan Macfarlane, *The Origins of English Individualism: The Family, Property and Social Transition* (Oxford, Eng., 1978), offers a different perspective. He argues that even in the late Middle Ages English people were "rampant individualists, highly mobile both geographically and socially, economically 'rational,' market-oriented and acquisitive" (163).

27. Mildred Campbell, *The English Yeoman: Under Elizabeth and the Early Stuarts* (New Haven, Conn., 1942), 72; R. H. Tawney, *Religion and the Rise of Capitalism: A Historical Study* (1926; rpt., Gloucester, Mass., 1962), 136–47, 172–88; Brian Manning, "The Peasantry and the English Revolution," *Journal of Peasant Studies*, II (1975), 133–58; John E. Martin, *Feudalism to Capitalism: Peasant and Landlord in English Agrarian Development* (Atlantic Highlands, N.J., 1983).

28. John Aubrey quoted in David Grayson Allen, *In English Ways: The Movement of Societies and the Transferral of English Local Law and Custom to Massachusetts Bay in the Seventeenth Century* (Chapel Hill, N.C., 1982), 85; Campbell, *English Yeoman*, 105–44; J. A. Yelling, *Common Field and Enclosure in England, 1450–1850* (London, 1977), 1–63; Thirsk, "Farming Regions," 65–92.

29. Roger Lockyer, *Tudor and Stuart Britain, 1471–1714* (New York, 1964), 323–27; J. M. Neeson, *Commoners: Common Right, Enclosures and Social Change in Common-Field England, 1700–1820* (Cambridge, Eng., 1992), emphasizes the "agency" of the common people involved in this process of change; Roger B. Manning, *Village Revolts: Social Protest and Popular Disturbances in England, 1509–1640* (Oxford, Eng., 1988); J. R. Wordie, "The Chronology of English Enclosure, 1500–1914," *Economic History Review*, XXXVI (1983), 483–505.

30. For a different point of view, see Rowland Berthoff and John M. Murrin, "Feudalism, Communalism, and the Yeoman Freeholder: The American Revolution Considered as a Social Accident," in *Essays on the American Revolution*, ed. Stephen G. Kurtz and James H. Hutson (Chapel Hill, N.C.,

1973), 256–88. Berthoff and Murrin suggest that in the eighteenth century there was a "feudal reaction" in the Thirteen Colonies.

31. Sumner Chilton Powell, *Puritan Village: The Formation of a New England Town* (Middletown, Conn., 1963), 3–79, quote on 75.

32. Allen, *In English Ways*, 31, 125–28, quote on 126; Powell, *Puritan Village*, 74–76.

33. Powell, *Puritan Village*, 79–138, quote on 79; David Cressy, *Coming Over: Migration and Communication between England and New England in the Seventeenth Century* (Cambridge, Eng., 1987); on the number of open field villages, see Joseph Wood, "Village and Community in Early Colonial New England," *Journal of Historical Geography*, VIII (1982), 333–46; Wood, "The Origin of the New England Village" (Ph.D. diss., Pennsylvania State Univ., 1978), esp. map on 149.

More broadly, historians set forth a "declensionist" model of New England development. This paradigm argues that the "Christian Utopian Closed Corporate Community" of the seventeenth century gave way in the eighteenth century to a fragmented society of self-interested Yankees. See Kenneth A. Lockridge, *A New England Town: The First Hundred Years, Dedham, Massachusetts, 1636–1736*, expanded ed. (New York, 1970, 1985), 3–22, 181–91, quote on 16. For other thoughtful syntheses of scholarship on the New England town, see James T. Lemon, "Spatial Order: Households in Local Communities and Regions," in *Colonial British America: Essays in the New History of the Early Modern Era*, ed. Jack P. Greene and J. R. Pole (Baltimore, 1984), 86–104; Darrett B. Rutman, "Assessing the Little Communities of Early America," WMQ, 3d Ser., XLIII (1986), 163–78; Jack P. Greene, *Pursuits of Happiness: The Social Development of Early Modern British Colonies and the Formation of American Culture* (Chapel Hill, N.C., 1988), 55–80.

34. Sung Bok Kim, *Landlord and Tenant in Colonial New York: Manorial Society, 1664–1775* (Chapel Hill, N.C., 1978), 162–234; Patricia U. Bonomi, *A Factious People: Politics and Society in Colonial New York* (New York, 1971), 188–94; Irving Mark, *Agrarian Conflicts in Colonial New York, 1711–1775* (New York, 1940), 50–74; Lawrence H. Leder, *Robert Livingston, 1654–1728, and the Politics of Colonial New York* (Chapel Hill, N.C., 1961), 3–40.

35. Kim, *Landlord and Tenant*, vii, 163–73, 238–40; Bonomi, *Factious People*, 195–200, with quote from Colden on 195; Dennis P. Ryan, "Landholding, Opportunity, and Mobility in Revolutionary New Jersey," WMQ, 3d Ser., XXXVI (1979), 571–92.

36. Mark, *Agrarian Conflicts*, 106–206; Bonomi, *Factious People*, 211–28; David M. Ellis, *Landlords and Farmers in the Hudson-Mohawk Region, 1790–1850* (Ithaca, N.Y., 1946), 1–50, 225–312; Alfred F. Young, *The Democratic Republicans of New York: The Origins, 1763–1797* (Chapel Hill, N.C., 1967), 6–32; Irving Mark and Oscar Handlin, "Land Cases in Colonial New York, 1765–1767: The King v. William Prendergast," *New York University Law Quarterly Review*, XIX (1942), 165–94.

37. James T. Lemon, *The Best Poor Man's Country: A Geographical Study of Early Southeastern Pennsylvania* (Baltimore, 1972), 49–61, 98–103, quote on 99; Gary B. Nash, *Quakers and Politics: Pennsylvania, 1681–1726* (Princeton, 1968), chaps. 1–2; Catherine Owens Peare, *William Penn: A Biography* (Lon-

don, 1956), 9–238; Mary Maples Dunn, *William Penn: Politics and Conscience* (Princeton, N.J., 1967), 3–43.

38. Lemon, *Best Poor Man's Country,* 49–57, 77, 81, 102–8, quote on 49.

39. Matthew Page Andrews, *The Founding of Maryland* (Baltimore, 1933), 1–35, 47–91, quotes on 51; Newton D. Mereness, *Maryland as a Proprietary Province* (1901; rpt., Cos Cob, Conn., 1968), 6–53. New York manor lords also were given the right to erect courts leet and baron, but seem not to have exercised this privilege; Kim, *Landlord and Tenant,* 17, 21, 69, 89–90, 103–6; Aubrey C. Land, *Colonial Maryland: A History* (Millwood, N.Y., 1981), 1–30.

40. Gregory A. Stiverson, *Poverty in a Land of Plenty: Tenancy in Eighteenth-Century Maryland* (Baltimore, 1977), 1–27, 104–42; Mereness, *Maryland,* 54–57; Charles A. Barker, *The Background of the Revolution in Maryland* (New Haven, Conn., 1940), 31–34, 123–24, 259–65; Lois Green Carr, Russell R. Menard, and Lorena S. Walsh, *Robert Cole's World: Agriculture and Society in Early Maryland* (Chapel Hill, N.C., 1991), 8–12.

41. Edmund S. Morgan, *American Slavery—American Freedom: The Ordeal of Colonial Virginia* (New York, 1975), 45–88, 93–116, 171–73, 213–23; Richard L. Morton, *Colonial Virginia,* 2 vols.: (Chapel Hill, N.C., 1960), II, 498–99, 546–48; James B. Gouger III, "Agricultural Change in the Northern Neck of Virginia, 1700–1760: An Historical Geography" (Ph.D. diss., Univ. of Florida, 1976), 54–81; Willard F. Bliss, "The Rise of Tenancy in Virginia," *Virginia Magazine of History and Biography,* CVIII (1950), 427–41; Stuart E. Brown, Jr., *Virginia Baron: The Story of Thomas 6th Lord Fairfax* (Perryville, Va., 1965); Virginius Dabney, *Virginia: The New Dominion* (New York, 1971), 93.

42. Allan Kulikoff, *Tobacco and Slaves: The Development of Southern Cultures in the Chesapeake, 1680–1800* (Chapel Hill, N.C., 1986), 205–60; Darrett B. Rutman and Anita H. Rutman, *A Place in Time: Middlesex County, Virginia, 1650–1750* (New York, 1984); T. H. Breen, "Horses and Gentlemen: The Cultural Significance of Gambling among the Gentry of Virginia," WMQ, 3d Ser., XXXIV (1977), 239–57; Richard R. Beeman, "Social Change and Cultural Conflict in Virginia: Lunenburg County, 1746 to 1774," ibid., 3d Ser., XXXV (1978), 455–76; Carville V. Earle, *The Evolution of a Tidewater Settlement: All Hallow's Parish, Maryland, 1650–1783* (Chicago, 1975); Rhys Isaac, *The Transformation of Virginia, 1740–1790* (Chapel Hill, N.C., 1982), 18–42, 115–38; Kevin P. Kelly, "Economic and Social Development of Seventeenth-Century Surry County, Virginia" (Ph.D. diss., Univ. of Washington, 1972).

43. Louise F. Brown, *The First Earl of Shaftesbury* (New York, 1933), 128–61; M. Eugene Sirmans, *Colonial South Carolina: A Political History, 1663–1763* (Chapel Hill, N.C., 1966), 5–16, quote on 9; the several drafts of the Fundamental Constitutions are reprinted in *North Carolina Charters and Constitutions, 1578–1698,* ed., Mattie E. E. Parker (Raleigh, N.C., 1963), 128–85.

44. Trevor Richard Reese, *Colonial Georgia: A Study in British Imperial Policy in the Eighteenth Century* (Athens, Ga., 1963), 1–39, quote on 10; Kenneth Coleman, *Colonial Georgia: A History* (New York, 1976), 13–49.

45. Reese, *Colonial Georgia,* 40–52, quotes on 48 and 51; Coleman, *Colonial Georgia,* 40–128.

46. The literature on this question is extensive. In particular, see Bertram Wyatt-Brown, *Southern Honor: Ethics and Behavior in the Old South* (New York,

1982), 62–87, 149–74, 402–61; John Hope Franklin, *The Militant South, 1800–1861* (Cambridge, Mass., 1956), 63–95, 227–49; Edward L. Ayers, *Vengeance and Justice: Crime and Punishment in the 19th-Century American South* (New York, 1984), 9–53; Richard M. Brown, *Strain of Violence: Historical Studies of American Violence and Vigilantism* (New York, 1975), 67–90, 185–235.

Chapter 4. Religion and Labor

1. Robert L. Meriwether, ed., "Preston S. Brooks on the Caning of Charles Sumner," *South Carolina Historical and Genealogical Magazine,* XII (1951), 1–4, quote on 2–3 ; *Alleged Assault upon Senator Sumner* (*House Report,* No. 182, 34 Cong., 1 Sess.); Appendix to the *Congressional Globe,* May 19, 1856, pp. 529–43, quote on 530; a full summary of this episode is presented in David Donald, *Charles Sumner and the Coming of the Civil War* (New York, 1960), 285–311, quote on 291.

2. Quoted in R. H. Tawney's forward to Max Weber, *The Protestant Ethic and the Spirit of Capitalism* (New York, 1958), 6. The writing relevant to Weber's thesis is voluminous. A good starting place (with particular emphasis on Weber's critics) is Robert W. Green, ed., *Protestantism, Capitalism, and Social Science: The Weber Thesis Controversy* (Lexington, Mass., 1959). Of particular value are the critiques offered by Fernand Braudel, *The Wheels of Commerce,* trans. Siân Reynolds (vol. II of *Civilization and Capitalism, 15th-18th Century*) (1979; trans., New York, 1982), 566–81; R. H. Tawney, *Religion and the Rise of Capitalism: A Historical Study* (1926; rpt., Gloucester, Mass., 1962); and Christopher Hill, *The English Revolution, 1640: Three Essays* (London, 1949); Hill, *Puritanism and Revolution: Studies in Interpretation of the English Revolution of the 17th Century* (London, 1958). Also see Henry Walter Brann, "Max Weber and the United States," *Southwestern Social Science Quarterly,* XXV (1944), 18–30; Herbert Luethy, "Once Again: Calvinism and Capitalism," *Encounter,* XXII (1964), 26–38; and Appendix A.

3. J. F. Bosher, *The Canada Merchants, 1713–1763* (Oxford, Eng., 1987), 60–69; R. B. Grassby, "Social Status and Commercial Enterprise under Louis XIV," *Economic History Review,* XIII (1960), 19–39.

4. Weber, *Protestant Ethic,* 90.

5. John Winthrop's Journal, Nov. 9, 1639, in *The Puritan Tradition in America, 1620–1730,* ed. Alden T. Vaughan (New York, 1972), 174; Bernard Bailyn, "The *Apologia* of Robert Keayne," WMQ, 3d Ser., VII (1950), 568–87; Emery Battis, *Saints and Sectaries: Anne Hutchinson and the Antinomian Controversy in the Massachusetts Bay Colony* (Chapel Hill, N.C., 1962), esp. chap. 17.

6. All quotations are from Benjamin Franklin, "The Way to Wealth," 1757, *The Papers of Benjamin Franklin,* ed. Leonard W. Labaree et al. (New Haven, Conn., 1959–), VII, 334, 341–45; these are sayings Franklin culled from his *Almanacs. The Autobiography of Benjamin Franklin,* ed. Leonard W. Labaree et al. (New Haven, Conn., 1964), also emphasizes the importance of industry and frugality. Carl Van Doren, *Benjamin Franklin* (London, 1939), 106–11, 265–66, suggests Franklin's views were more far-ranging. Marc Egnal, "The Politics of Ambition: A New Look at Benjamin Franklin's Career,"

Canadian Review of American Studies, VI (1975), 151–64, argues that Franklin consciously distorted the role hard work and frugality played in his rise; and see the essays in Charles L. Sanford, ed., *Benjamin Franklin and the American Character* (Boston, 1955).

7. Weber, *Protestant Ethic,* 65.

8. Appendix A continues this discussion of Weber, Franklin, and the rise of capitalism.

9. Weber, *Protestant Ethic,* 55–56, quote on 173–74; William R. Taylor, *Cavalier and Yankee: The Old South and American National Character* (New York, 1961); Robert M. Calhoon, "Religion and Individualism in Early America," in *American Chameleon: Individualism in Trans-National Context,* ed. Richard O. Curry and Lawrence B. Goodhart (Kent, Ohio, 1991), 44–65; also see Chapter 3 above.

10. Lester J. Cappon, ed., *Atlas of Early American History: The Revolutionary Era, 1760–1790* (Princeton, N.J., 1976), 28–39; Marc Egnal, *A Mighty Empire: The Origins of the American Revolution* (Ithaca, N.Y., 1988), passim, discusses religious divisions and their impact on factional politics; National Geographic Society, *Historical Atlas of the United States* (Washington, D.C., 1988), 37; Babette M. Levy, "Early Puritanism in the Southern and Island Colonies," American Antiquarian Society *Proceedings,* LXX (1960), Pt. I, 603–48, argues that many Puritans came to the South; E. Digby Baltzell, *Puritan Boston and Quaker Philadelphia: Two Protestant Ethics and the Spirit of Class Authority and Leadership* (New York, 1979), uses Weber to try to understand the differences between Boston and Philadelphia.

11. David Hackett Fischer, *Albion's Seed: Four British Folkways in America* (New York, 1989), emphasizes the importance of the original settlements in shaping the regions.

12. Anne C. Loveland, *Southern Evangelicals and the Social Order* (Baton Rouge, La., 1980), 161–62; Donald G. Mathews, *Religion in the Old South* (Chicago, 1977), 159–64.

13. Jack P. Greene, ed., *The Diary of Colonel Landon Carter of Sabine Hall, 1752–1778,* 2 vols. (Charlottesville, Va., 1965), I, 28.

14. Ibid., II, 638.

15. Ibid., I, 23.

16. Ibid., II, 697.

17. Ibid., I, 9.

18. Ibid., II, 679.

19. Ibid., I, 207.

20. Ibid., I, 429.

21. Ibid., I, 138.

22. Ibid., II, 755; on the frequency of whipping, Herbert Gutman and Richard Sutch, "Sambo Makes Good, or Were Slaves Imbued with the Protestant Work Ethic?" in *Reckoning with Slavery: A Critical Study in the Quantitative History of American Negro Slavery,* ed. Paul A. David et al. (New York, 1976), 57–77.

23. *Diary of Landon Carter,* I, 386; Eugene D. Genovese, *The Political Economy of Slavery: Studies in the Economy & Society of the Slave South* (New York, 1965), 48–61.

24. *Diary of Landon Carter,* II, 834; for other insights into this passage, Mechal Sobel, *The World They Made Together: Black and White Values in Eighteenth-Century Virginia* (Princeton, N.J., 1987), 41–43.

25. James Oakes, *The Ruling Race: A History of American Slaveholders* (New York, 1982), 153–91, also discusses the gap between slaveholders' intentions and the reality of low productivity; for another pointed example of a slaveholder's futile efforts to increase output, see Drew Gilpin Faust, *James Henry Hammond and the Old South: A Design for Mastery* (Baton Rouge, La., 1982), 69–134.

26. "Frederick Law Olmsted," DAB, VII, part 2, p. 24; Frederick Law Olmsted, *The Cotton Kingdom: A Traveller's Observations on Cotton and Slavery in the American Slave States,* ed. Arthur M. Schlesinger (1861; New York, 1966), ix–xxv.

27. Olmsted, *Cotton Kingdom,* 11.

28. Ibid., 19.

29. Ibid., 614–15.

30. Ibid., 620.

31. Genovese, *Political Economy,* 13–39, 159–73; Robert W. Fogel, *Without Consent or Contract: The Rise and Fall of Slavery* (New York, 1989), 84, notes that "nearly two out of every three males with estates of $100,000 or more lived in the South in 1860." The South had this lead despite its lower standard of living and smaller population.

32. Fletcher M. Green, *Constitutional Development in the South Atlantic States, 1776–1860: A Study in the Evolution of Democracy* (Chapel Hill, N.C., 1930); Green, "Democracy in the Old South," *Journal of Southern History,* XII (1946), 3–23, quote on 23; Frank L. Owsley, *Plain Folk of the Old South* (Baton Rouge, La., 1949); J. Mills Thornton, *Politics and Power in a Slave Society: Alabama, 1800–1860* (Baton Rouge, La., 1977); George M. Frederickson, *The Black Image in the White Mind: The Debate on Afro-American Character and Destiny, 1817–1914* (New York, 1971), 58–70, quote on 67; Lacy K. Ford, Jr., *Origins of Southern Radicalism: The South Carolina Upcountry, 1800–1860* (New York, 1988), 174–75, 281–307; Randolph B. Campbell, "Planters and Plain Folks: The Social Structure of the Antebellum South," in *Interpreting Southern History: Historiographical Essays in Honor of Sanford W. Higginbotham,* ed. John B. Boles and Evelyn T. Nolen (Baton Rouge, La., 1978), 48–77, provides an insightful survey of this issue. The quotes from Frederickson and Barney also appear in Campbell's text (pp. 72, 77).

33. The argument for slaveholder domination of the South goes back to the antebellum era and the contentions of the abolitionists. Many modern historians have made the same case. See Ulrich B. Phillips, "The Origin and Growth of the Southern Black Belts," *American Historical Review,* XI (1906), 798–816; Lewis C. Gray, *History of Agriculture in the Southern United States to 1860,* 2 vols. (Washington, D.C., 1933), I, 444–74, 532–37; Genovese, *Political Economy,* 3–36; Genovese, *The World the Slaveholders Made: Two Essays in Interpretation* (New York, 1969), 13–23; Raimondo Luraghi, *The Rise and Fall of the Plantation South* (New York, 1978); Fred Siegel, "The Paternalist Thesis: Virginia as a Test Case," *Civil War History,* XXV (1979), 246–61; Emory M. Thomas, *The Confederate Nation, 1861–1865* (New York, 1979), 6–10; William L. Barney, *The Secessionist Impulse: Alabama and Mississippi in 1860* (Princeton,

N.J., 1974), quote on 91. The evidence in Michael Wayne, "An Old South Morality Play: Reconsidering the Social Underpinnings of the Proslavery Ideology," *Journal of American History*, LXXVII (1990), 838–63, fully illustrates the power of the planters, although Wayne's conclusions are more ambivalent. On planter domination of officeholding, see Ralph A. Wooster, *The People in Power: Courthouse and Statehouse in the Lower South, 1850–1860* (Knoxville, Tenn., 1969); Wooster, *Politicians, Planters and Plain Folk: Courthouse and Statehouse in the Upper South, 1850–1860* (Knoxville, Tenn., 1975); Wooster, "Wealthy Southerners on the Eve of the Civil War," in *Essays on Southern History Written in Honor of Barnes F. Lathrop*, ed. Gary W. Gallagher (Austin, Tex., 1980), 131–59. Still other scholars have documented the unequal distribution of wealth in the South: Robert E. Gallman, "Trends in the Size Distribution of Wealth in the Nineteenth Century: Some Speculations," in *Six Papers on the Size Distribution of Wealth and Income*, ed. Lee Soltow (New York, 1969), 1–30; Lee Soltow, *Men and Wealth in the United States, 1850–1870* (New Haven, Conn., 1975).

34. William W. Freehling, "The Editorial Revolution, Virginia, and the Coming of the Civil War: A Review Essay," *Civil War History*, XVI (1970), 64–72; Steven A. Channing, *Crisis of Fear: Secession in South Carolina* (New York, 1970); Steven Hahn, "The Yeomanry of the Nonplantation South: Upper Piedmont Georgia, 1850–1860," in *Class, Conflict, and Consensus: Antebellum Southern Community Studies*, ed. Orville V. Burton and Robert C. McMath, Jr. (Westport, Conn., 1982), 29–56; William L. Barney, "Towards the Civil War: The Dynamics of Change in a Black Belt County," ibid., 146–72; Bertram Wyatt-Brown, "Community, Class, and Snopesian Crime: Local Justice in the Old South," in ibid., 173–206; Barney, *Secessionist Impulse*; Michael P. Johnson, *Toward a Patriarchal Republic: The Secession of Georgia* (Baton Rouge, La., 1977). Hinton Rowan Helper remarked: "Notwithstanding the fact that the white non-slaveholders of the South, are in the majority, as five to one, they have never yet had any part or lot in framing the laws under which they live. There is no legislation except for the benefit of slavery and slaveholders." Hinton Rowan Helper, *The Impending Crisis of the South: How to Meet It* (1857; rpt., New York, 1963), 48, 49, 107.

35. Bertram Wyatt-Brown, *Southern Honor: Ethics and Behavior in the Old South* (New York, 1982), 327–61, quote on 345.

36. Thomas Hamilton, *Men and Manners in America*, 2 vols. (1833; rpt., New York, 1968), II, 284. Harriet Martineau commented: "It is in Washington that varieties of manners are conspicuous. . . . One fancies one can tell a New-England member in the open air by his depractory walk. He seems to bear in mind perpetually that he cannot fight a duel, while other people can." *Retrospect of Western Travel*, 2 vols. (London, 1838), I, 145.

37. These examples are from Kenneth S. Greenberg, *Masters and Statesmen: The Political Culture of American Slavery* (Baltimore, 1985), 23–41, quotes on 36–38. Also see Steven M. Stowe, *Intimacy and Power in the Old South: Ritual in the Lives of the Planters* (Baltimore, 1987), 5–49, 122–59; Edward L. Ayers, *Vengeance and Justice: Crime and Punishment in the 19th-Century American South* (New York, 1984), 9–33, 267–72; Wyatt-Brown, *Southern Honor*, 350–61.

38. Genovese, *Political Economy*, quote from p. 31; Eugene Genovese and Elizabeth Fox-Genovese, *Fruits of Merchant Capital: Slavery and Bourgeois Prop-*

erty in the Rise and Expansion of Capitalism (New York, 1983), 3–60; Elizabeth Fox-Genovese, *Within the Plantation Household: Black and White Women of the Old South* (Chapel Hill, N.C., 1988), 53–71. See also Barbara Jeanne Fields, *Slavery and Freedom on the Middle Ground: Maryland during the Nineteenth Century* (New Haven, Conn., 1985); Luraghi, *Rise and Fall*; Jonathan M. Wiener, "Planter Persistence and Social Change: Alabama, 1850–1870," *Journal of Interdisciplinary History*, VII (1976), 235–60; Steven Hahn, *The Roots of Southern Populism: Yeoman Farmers and the Transformation of the Georgia Upcountry, 1850–1890* (New York, 1983).

39. The most outspoken case for capitalist slaveholders (and hardworking slaves) is presented by Robert W. Fogel and Stanley L. Engerman in *Time on the Cross: The Economics of American Negro Slavery* (Boston 1974) and *Time on the Cross: Evidence and Methods—A Supplement* (Boston, 1974); with only slight modification, this argument is restated in Fogel, *Without Consent or Contract*, quote from 64. Taking a similarly positive view of the efficiency of plantation labor is Claudia Goldin, *Urban Slavery in the South, 1820–1860* (Chicago, 1976). Frederick F. Siegel, *The Roots of Southern Distinctiveness: Tobacco and Society in Danville, Virginia, 1780–1865* (Chapel Hill, N.C., 1987), also affirms the importance of capitalist activities and rhetoric in the South. So does Edward Pessen, "How Different from Each Other Were the Antebellum North and South?" *American Historical Review*, LXXXV (1980), 1119–49; James Oakes, in *The Ruling Race* and *Slavery and Freedom: An Interpretation of the Old South* (New York, 1990), makes a case for the central role of "liberal capitalism" in the South. See the review of Oakes's work by Edward L. Ayers, *Reviews in American History*, XIX (1991), 194–99.

40. A good place to begin any investigation of the economics of slavery is with the essays in Alfred H. Conrad and John R. Meyer, eds., *The Economics of Slavery and Other Econometric Studies* (Chicago, 1964), and Hugh G. J. Aitken, ed., *Did Slavery Pay? Readings in the Economics of Black Slavery in the United States* (Boston, 1971). Harold D. Woodman, "The Profitability of Slavery: A Historical Perennial," *Journal of Southern History*, XXIX (1963), 303–25, underscores the distinction between the profitability of slavery for individuals and the benefits of the system of slavery for the South. Among those arguing that slavery was profitable are Gray, *History of Agriculture*, I, 301–41, 462–80, 545–67; Thomas P. Govan, "Was Plantation Slavery Profitable?" *Journal of Southern History*, VIII (1942), 515–35; Alfred H. Conrad and John R. Meyer, "The Economics of Slavery in the Ante-bellum South," *Journal of Political Economy*, LXVI (1958), 95–130; Yasukichi Yasuba, "The Profitability and Viability of Plantation Slavery in the United States," *Economic Studies Quarterly*, XII (1961), 60–67; Robert Evans, Jr., "The Economics of American Negro Slavery, 1830–1860," in National Bureau of Economic Research, *Aspects of Labor Economics* (Princeton, N.J., 1962), 185–256; James D. Foust and Dale E. Swan, "Productivity and Profitability of Antebellum Slave Labor: A Micro-Approach," in *The Structure of the Cotton Economy of the Antebellum South*, ed. William N. Parker (Washington, D.C., 1970), 39–62; Dale Swan, *The Structure and Profitability of the Antebellum Rice Industry* (New York, 1975); Richard Sutch, "The Profitability of Ante-Bellum Slavery Revisited," *Southern Economic Journal*, XXXI (1965), 365–77; Stanley L. Engerman, "The Effects of Slavery upon the Southern Economy: A Review of the Recent Debate," *Explorations in Entrepreneurial His-*

tory, 2d ser., IV (1967), 71–97. Richard K. Vedder, David C. Klingaman, and Lowell E. Gallaway, "The Profitability of Ante-bellum Agriculture in the Cotton Belt: Some New Evidence," *Atlantic Economic Journal,* II (1974), 30–47, argues that slave agriculture was even more profitable than Conrad and Meyer suggest.

41. Various historians have argued that slavery was an inefficient system and not profitable for individual planters. For the writings of contemporary critics, such as Helper, Goodloe, and Cairnes, see Chapter 1, note 39. Many of their arguments would later be repeated. U. B. Phillips was the first modern scholar to argue that slavery held the South back and provided low returns to the planters. See Phillips, "The Economic Cost of Slaveholding in the Cotton Belt," *Political Science Quarterly,* XX (1905), 257–75. Others have pursued this line of reasoning. Among the most trenchant critics of Conrad and Meyer's conclusions is Edward Saraydar. See his "The Economics of Slavery in the Ante Bellum South," *Journal of Political Economy* (1958), 85–130; "The Profitability of Ante Bellum Slavery—A Reply," *Southern Economic Journal,* XXXI (1965), 377–83. Also note Marvin Fischbaum and Julius Rubin, "Slavery and the Economic Development of the American South," ibid., 2d Ser., VI (1968), 116–27; and Genovese, *Political Economy,* 275–87. Gavin Wright, "The Efficiency of Slavery: Another Interpretation," *American Economic Review,* LXIX (1979), 219–26, argues cogently that the 1860 census depicts an exceptionally prosperous year.

42. See several discussions of the "rationality" of planter behavior: Eugene Genovese, "Commentary: A Historian's View," *Agricultural History,* XLIV (1970), 143–47; William K. Scarborough, *The Overseer: Plantation Management in the Old South* (Baton Rouge, La., 1966); Jacob Metzer, "Rational Management, Modern Business Practices, and Economies of Scale in the Ante-bellum Southern Plantations," *Explorations in Economic History,* XII (1975), 123–50.

43. Fred Bateman and Thomas Weiss, *A Deplorable Scarcity: The Failure of Industrialization in the Slave Economy* (Chapel Hill, N.C., 1981), 99–127, quote on 113. See also the critique of Bateman and Weiss in Gavin Wright, *The Political Economy of the Cotton South: Households, Markets, and Wealth in the Nineteenth Century* (New York, 1978), 115–16. Robert C. McMath, Jr., "Variations on a Theme by Henry Grady: Technology, Modernization, and Social Change," in *The Future South: A Historical Perspective for the Twenty-first Century,* ed. Joe P. Dunn and Howard L. Preston (Urbana, Ill., 1991), 84–85, observes that many of the textile manufacturers in the South were northern-born. William H. Pease and Jane H. Pease, *The Web of Progress: Private Values and Public Styles in Boston and Charleston, 1828–1843* (New York, 1985), 18–20, 40–53, 222–24, contends that slavery slowed industrial development in Charleston; Peter Wallenstein, "From Slave South to New South: Taxes and Spending in Georgia from 1850 Through Reconstruction," JEH, XXXVI (1976), 287–90, notes that commercial activities were hurt by taxes that fell more heavily on merchants than planters; Thomas F. Huerta, "Damnifying Growth in the Antebellum South," ibid., XXXIX (1979), 87–100.

44. Bateman and Weiss, *Deplorable Scarcity,* 3–6, 115–20.

45. Quoted in Genovese, *Political Economy,* 225; Richard C. Wade, *Slavery in the Cities: The South, 1820–1860* (New York, 1964), 33–64; Robert S. Starobin, *Industrial Slavery in the Old South* (New York, 1970), 14–28, 120–78; Ron-

ald L. Lewis, *Coal, Iron, and Slaves: Industrial Slavery in Maryland and Virginia, 1715–1865* (Westport, Conn., 1979); Charles B. Dew, "Disciplining Slave Iron-workers in the Antebellum South: Coercion, Conciliation, and Accommodation," *American Historical Review,* LXXIX (1974), 393–418; Dew, "David Ross and the Oxford Iron Works: A Study of Industrial Slavery in the Early Nineteenth-Century South," WMQ, 3d Ser., XXXI (1974), 189–224; Dew, "Black Ironworkers and the Slave Insurrection Panic of 1856," *Journal of Southern History,* XLI (1975), 321–38; Dew, *Bond of Iron: Master and Slave at Buffalo Forge* (New York, 1994), 172–219.

46. Wade, *Slavery in the Cities,* 256–79, quote on 245.

47. Ibid., 3–26, 243–79; Goldin, *Urban Slavery in the South,* provides an alternative explanation of the decline of slavery in the cities. Goldin argues that rural demand for workers drew slaves from the cities. But see the critique of Goldin in Wright, *Political Economy,* 121–23. See also Starobin, *Industrial Slavery,* 212–16; Broadus Mitchell, *The Rise of Cotton Mills in the South* (1921; rpt., Gloucester, Mass., 1966), 9–49; Ernest M. Lander, Jr., *The Textile Industry in Antebellum South Carolina* (Baton Rouge, La., 1969); Diffee W. Standard and Richard W. Griffen, "The Cotton Textile Industry in Antebellum North Carolina," *North Carolina Historical Review,* XXXIV (1957), 131–60; Tom E. Terrill, "Eager Hands: Labor for Southern Textiles, 1850–1860," JEH, XXXVI (1976), 84–99; Heywood Fleisig, "Slavery, the Supply of Agricultural Labor, and the Industrialization of the South," JEH, XXXVI (1976), 572–97.

48. Quoted in Starobin, *Industrial Slavery,* 209–10.

49. Genovese, *Political Economy,* 232–35; Starobin, *Industrial Slavery,* 118–19; Ira Berlin and Herbert G. Gutman, "Natives and Immigrants, Free Men and Slaves: Urban Workingmen in the Antebellum American South," *American Historical Review,* LXXXVIII (1983), 1175–1200.

50. Fogel and Engerman, *Time on the Cross,* I, 191–257, quote from 231. Fogel and Engerman back away from their depiction of slaves imbued with a Protestant ethic, although not from their assertion that bondspeople were more productive than free workers. See Fogel and Engerman, "Explaining the Relative Efficiency of Slave Agriculture in the Antebellum South," *American Economic Review,* LXVII (1977), 275–96; Fogel, *Without Consent or Contract,* 72–80, 155–62. For criticism of these views, see Paul A. David and Peter Temin, "Explaining the Relative Efficiency of Slave Agriculture in the Antebellum South: Comment," *American Economic Review,* LXIX (1979), 213–18; Wright, "Efficiency of Slavery," ibid., LXIX, 219–26; Donald F. Schaeffer and Mark D. Schmitz, "The Relative Efficiency of Slave Agriculture: A Comment," ibid., LXIX, 208–12; Thomas L. Haskell, "Explaining the Relative Efficiency of Slave Agriculture in the Antebellum South: A Reply to Fogel-Engerman," ibid., LXIX, 206–7; Gavin Wright, "Prosperity, Progress, and American Slavery," in *Reckoning with Slavery,* 302–36. Also see William L. Van Deburg, *The Slave Drivers: Black Agricultural Labor Supervisors in the Ante Bellum South* (Westport, Conn., 1979), 5–8, 31–44. Fred Bateman and Jeremy Atack, "The Profitability of Northern Agriculture in 1860," *Research in Economic History,* IV (1979), 87–125, suggest that farming in the North and South had comparable rates of return. But note: (1) They use Fogel and Engerman's data which focus on 1860, an exceptionally good year for the South. (2) Even in that year returns

in the Northeast were well above those in the cotton South: 13.2 percent vs. 10 percent. If figures for the Southeast were available this gap would be still wider.

51. Paul W. Gates, *The Farmer's Age: Agriculture, 1815–1860* (vol. III, *The Economic History of the United States*) (New York, 1960), 279–94; Clarence Danhof, *Change in Agriculture: The Northern United States, 1820–1870* (Cambridge, Mass., 1969), discusses the mechanization of northern farms; Wright, *Political Economy*, 52, provides figures for the value of implements per farm worker— $66 in the free states, $33 in the slaves states. On the earnings of farm labor in the North and South, see Chapter 1 above, and particularly Table 1.4.

Chapter 5. Mobility and Literacy

1. Isaac Weld, Jr., *Travels Through the States of North America, and the Provinces of Upper and Lower Canada . . .* , in *Early Travellers in the Canadas, 1791–1867*, ed. Gerald M. Craig (Toronto, 1955), 14–27.

2. I follow Peter N. Moogk, "Reluctant Exiles: Emigrants from France in Canada before 1760," WMQ, 3d Ser., XLVI (1989), 502–3, which uses and modifies the figures in Mario Boleda, "Les migrations au Canada sous le régime français" (Ph.D. diss., Univ. of Montreal, 1983), 41–55, 105–12, 339. See also Boleda, "Les migrations au Canada sous le régime français (1607–1760)," *Cahiers québécois de demographie*, XIII (1984), 23–28; J. N. Biraben, "Le peuplement du Canada français," in *Annales de démographie historique* (Paris, 1966), 105–38. For a different set of emigration statistics, consult Leslie Choquette, "French Emigration to Canada, 1660–1760" (paper presented to American Historical Association, December 1989).

3. Allan Greer, *Peasant, Lord, and Merchant: Rural Society in Three Quebec Parishes, 1740–1840* (Toronto, 1985), 20–21, 45, 61; Pierre Goubert, *The French Peasantry in the Seventeenth Century*, trans. Ian Patterson (Cambridge, Eng., 1986), 23–115.

4. Michael W. Flinn, *The European Demographic System, 1500–1820* (Baltimore, 1981), chap. 5; Moogk, "Reluctant Exiles," 503–4; André Corvisier, *Armies and Societies in Europe, 1494–1789*, trans. Abigail T. Siddall (Bloomington, Ind., 1979), 45, 131–33; J. F. Bosher, "French Colonial Society in Canada," *Transactions of the Royal Society of Canada*, Ser. IV, XIX (1981), 152–53; J.-P. Poussou, "Les mouvements migratoires en France et à partir de la France . . . ," *Annales de démographie historique* (1970), 11–78, and esp. 72–73.

5. Quoted in F. G. Stanley, *New France: The Last Phase, 1744–1760* (Toronto, 1968), 269; in *Candide* Voltaire referred to the struggle over Canada as one for a "few acres of snow" ("quelques arpents de neige").

6. Jon Butler, *The Huguenots in America: A Refugee People in New World Society* (Cambridge, Mass., 1983), 23–25, 49, provides figures for the number of Huguenots leaving France and the number coming to America; working back from the U.S. population with French roots in 1790, Morris Altman, "Economic Growth in Canada, 1695–1739: Estimates and Analysis," WMQ, 3d Ser., XLV (1988), 695, estimates 7000 Huguenots arrived in the Thirteen Colonies; also see Warren C. Scoville, *The Persecution of Huguenots and French Economic Development, 1680–1720* (Berkeley, Calif., 1960), 118–21, for other

figures on Huguenot refugees; Wayland F. Dunaway, "The French Racial Strain in Colonial Pennsylvania," *Pennsylvania Magazine of History and Biography,* LIII (1929), 322–42, discusses one group arriving from France.

7. Moogk, "Reluctant Exiles," passim, quote on 473; there was also debate in France over the wisdom of allowing people to leave. While the general policy was to encourage such settlements, some officials disagreed. See Guy Frégault, "The Colonization of Canada in the Eighteenth Century," in *Society and Conquest: The Debate on the Bourgeoisie and Social Change in French Canada, 1700–1850,* ed. Dale Miquelon (Toronto, 1977), 94–95; John D. Brite, *The Attitude of European States Toward Emigration to the American Colonies . . . 1607–1820* (Chicago, 1939).

8. For white immigration I have generally followed the figures in David W. Galenson, *White Servitude in Colonial America: An Economic Analysis* (Cambridge, Mass., 1981), 216–17; these have been supplemented by the data in Henry A. Gemery, "Emigration from the British Isles to the New World, 1630–1700: Inferences from Colonial Populations," *Research in Economic History,* V (1980), 215. For black immigration, see Philip D. Curtin, *The Atlantic Slave Trade: A Census* (Madison, Wis., 1969), 119, 140; and the modifications made in Richard S. Dunn, "Servants and Slaves: The Recruitment and Employment of Labor," in *Colonial British America: Essays in the New History of the Early Modern Era,* ed. Jack P. Greene and J. R. Pole (Baltimore, 1984), 165. See also Henry A. Gemery, "European Emigration to North America, 1700–1820: Numbers and Quasi-Numbers," *Perspectives in American History,* new ser., I (1984), 283–342.

9. Dunn, "Servants and Slaves," 159, estimates 300,000 servants and 50,000 convicts arrived between 1580 and 1775. Abbot Emerson Smith, *Colonists in Bondage* (Chapel Hill, N.C., 1947), 336, argues that between one-half and two-thirds of all white immigrants to the British colonies, 1630–1775, were servants. This contention has been repeated by other investigators. See Galenson, *White Servitude,* 17; Dunn, "Servants and Slaves," 159; James Horn, "Servant Emigration to the Chesapeake in the Seventeenth Century," in *The Chesapeake in the Seventeenth Century,* ed. Thad W. Tate and David L. Ammerman (Chapel Hill, N.C., 1979), 51–95.

10. On the distribution of religious and national groups, see Lester J. Cappon, ed., *Atlas of Early American History: The Revolutionary Era, 1760–1790* (Princeton, N.J., 1976), 24, 36–39; for a closer look at the reasons people came, Bernard Bailyn, *Voyagers to the West: A Passage in the Peopling of America on the Eve of the Revolution* (New York, 1986). Also consult important studies of national groups, including R. J. Dickson, *Ulster Emigration to Colonial America, 1718–1775* (London, 1966); Ian C. C. Graham, *Colonists from Scotland: Emigrants to North America, 1707–1783* (Ithaca, N.Y., 1956).

11. Brinley Thomas, *Migration and Economic Growth: A Study of Great Britain and the Atlantic Economy* (Cambridge, Eng., 1954), 83–132; Moses Abramovitz, "Long Swings in American Economic Growth," in *New Views on American Economic Development: A Selective Anthology of Recent Work,* ed. Ralph L. Andreano (Cambridge, Mass., 1965), 377–434, esp. graph on 416; Marc Egnal, "The Economic Development of the Thirteen Continental Colonies, 1720–1775," WMQ, 3d Ser., XXXII (1975), 191–222.

12. Galenson, *White Servitude,* 216–17. On the movement of slaves to the

New World, U.S. Bureau of the Census, *Historical Statistics of the United States, Colonial Times to 1970*, 2 vols. (Washington, D.C., 1975), II, 1172–74; Curtin, *Atlantic Slave Trade*; John J. McCusker, "The Rum Trade and the Balance of Payments of the Thirteen Continental Colonies, 1650–1775" (Ph.D. diss., Univ. of Pittsburgh, 1970), 548–767; James A. Rawley, *The Transatlantic Slave Trade: A History* (New York, 1981); W. E. Minchinton, "The Slave Trade of Bristol with the British Mainland Colonies in North America, 1699–1770," in *Liverpool, the African Slave Trade, and Abolition: Essays to Illustrate Current Knowledge and Research*, ed. Roger Anstey and P. E. H. Hair (Liverpool, 1976), 39–59.

13. J. Potter, "The Growth of Population in America, 1700–1860," in *Population in History: Essays in Historical Demography*, ed. D. V. Glass and D. E. C. Eversley (Chicago, 1965), 680–81; Ruffin quoted in Eugene D. Genovese, *The Political Economy of Slavery: Studies in the Economy & Society of the Slave South* (New York, 1965), 231.

14. For theoretical discussions, see Paul A. David, "Fortune, Risk and the Microeconomics of Migration" in *Nations and Households in Economic Growth*, ed. Paul A. David and Melvin W. Reder (New York, 1974), 21–88; Charles F. Mueller, *The Economics of Labor Migration: A Behavioral Analysis* (New York, 1982).

15. For insights into the reluctance of French Canadians to leave Quebec, see the essay by Lysiane Gagnon, "For relocated Quebeckers, there's a vast difference between losing a city and losing a culture," *Globe and Mail*, Dec. 24, 1993, p. D3.

16. Frank Lewis and Marvin McInnis, "The Efficiency of the French-Canadian Farmer in the Nineteenth Century," JEH, XL (1980), 512–13.

17. *U.S. Historical Statistics*, I, 24–37, 90–91, presents figures for population and migration—data that allow an approximation of the rate of natural increase; Potter, "Growth of Population," 680–81, gives figures for foreign born. G. Langlois, *Histoire de la population canadienne-française* (Montreal, 1934), 157–84; Province of Quebec, *Statistical Yearbook* (Quebec, 1914), 69, indicates that foreign-born made up 11 percent of the provincial population in 1851. This is the same level as in New England in 1850. Immigration was more significant for the Middle Atlantic states than for New England, but was less important in the South.

18. Fernand Ouellet, *Economic and Social History of Quebec, 1760–1850: Structures* and *Conjonctures* (Ottawa, 1980), 297–98, 355–56, 465, 481–82; Yolande Lavoie, *L'émigration des Québécois aux Etats-Unis de 1840 à 1930* (Quebec, 1979), 3–17; Yolande Lavoie, *L'émigration des Canadiens aux Etats-Unis avant 1930: mesure du phénomène* (Montreal, 1972), 9–14, 27–52. Between 1871 and 1911 Ontarians were far more likely than Quebeckers to move to other provinces. William L. Marr and Donald G. Paterson, *Canada: An Economic History* (Toronto, 1980), 183, presents decennial figures for migration by province; *U.S. Historical Statistics*, I, 107–8. On migration before the 1860s, see D. Aidan McQuillan, "French-Canadian Communities in the Upper Midwest During the Nineteenth Century," in *French America: Mobility, Identity, and Minority Experience across the Continent*, ed. Dean R. Louder and Eric Waddell (Baton Rouge, La., 1993), 117–42; Danielle Juteau, "Ontario and Quebec as Distinct Collectivities," ibid., 54–60; Gilles Paquet and W. R. Smith, "L'émigration des Cana-

diens français vers les Etats-Unis, 1790–1940: problématique et coups de sonde," *L'Actualité économique*, LIX (1983), 423–53.

19. Quoted in Greer, *Peasant, Lord, and Merchant*, 85. Greer also maps the characteristically short moves of families in three parishes he studies. See pp. 85–88. For a similar argument about New France in the period, 1642–1731, Louis Dechêne, *Habitants et marchands de Montréal au xvii-e siècle* (Montreal, 1974), 43–48, 287–94, 414–87; Marcel Trudel, *Les débuts du régime seigneurial au Canada* (Montreal, 1974), 1–10, 255–73, sees more mobility, but his focus is the period 1627–1663; also valuable is the comparison of an English- and French-speaking community in J. I. Little, "The Social and Economic Development of Settlers in Two Quebec Townships, 1851–1870," *Canadian Papers in Rural History*, I (1978), 89–113. Little concludes: "The cultural identity of the French Canadians seems to have been a handicap primarily because it discouraged them from leaving Quebec, except as a last resort. Scots and English Canadians, on the other hand, did not hesitate to emigrate to greener pastures south and west" (p. 98).

20. John McCallum, *Unequal Beginnings: Agriculture and Economic Development in Quebec and Ontario until 1870* (Toronto, 1980), 96–97; for similar comments see Ouellet, *Economic and Social History*, 489–90.

21. Alexis de Tocqueville, *Democracy in America*, 2 vols. (1835, 1840; rpt. and trans., New York, 1966), vol. I, part II, chap. 9; André Jardin, *Tocqueville: A Biography*, trans. Lydia Davis (New York, 1988), 119–47; Jean-Michel Leclercq, "Alexis de Tocqueville au Canada," *Revue d'histoire de l'Amérique française*, XXII (1968), 353–64; George W. Pierson, *Tocqueville in America* (New York, 1938), 347–430; J. Vallée, *Tocqueville au Bas-Canada* (Montreal, 1973).

22. Alexis de Tocqueville, who commented pointedly on the rootedness of the French in North America, noted: "An American will build a house in which to pass his old age, and sell it before the roof is on. He will plant a garden and rent it just as the trees are coming into bearing; he will clear a field and leave others to reap the harvest." See Tocqueville, *Democracy in America*, vol. 2, part II, chap. 13; Michael J. Greenwood, "Research in Internal Migration in the United States: A Survey," *Journal of Economic Literature*, XIII (1975), 397–433; Morton Owen Schapiro, *Filling Up America: An Economic-Demographic Model of Population Growth and Distribution in Nineteenth-Century United States* (Greenwich, Conn., 1986), examines several theories of migration.

23. Frederick L. Olmsted, *The Cotton Kingdom: A Traveller's Observations on Cotton and Slavery in the American Slave States*, ed. Arthur M. Schlesinger (1861; New York, 1970), 417; Robert W. Fogel, *Without Consent or Contract: The Rise and Fall of American Slavery* (New York, 1989), 89–92, notes the economic benefits of the westward movement of slave agriculture; Richard A. Easterlin, "Interregional Differences in Per Capita Income, Population, and Total Income, 1840–1950," in National Bureau for Economic Research, *Trends in the American Economy in the 19th Century*, Studies in Income and Wealth, vol. XXIV (Princeton, N.J., 1960), 97–98.

24. Gavin Wright, *Old South, New South: Revolutions in the Southern Economy since the Civil War* (New York, 1986), 19–20; Donald F. Schaefer, "A Statistical Profile of Frontier and New South Migration: 1850–1860," *Agricultural History*, LIX (1985), 563–78; James Oakes, *The Ruling Race, a History of Ameri-*

can Slaveholders (New York, 1982), 77–78; Jonathan M. Wiener, "Planter Persistence and Social Change: Alabama, 1850–1870," *Journal of Interdisciplinary History,* VII (1976), 235–60; Wiener, *Social Origins of the New South: Alabama, 1860–1885* (Baton Rouge, La., 1978), 3–33; Frank Owsley, "The Pattern of Migration and Settlement on the Southern Frontier," *Journal of Southern History,* XI (1945), 147–76; Fogel, *Without Consent or Contract,* 91–92.

25. Population density was much greater in the North than the South. Consult *U.S. Historical Statistics,* I, 24–36; for mobility figures, ibid., I, 89–92; Potter, "Growth of Population," 680–681, also indicates that southerners left their home states more often than did individuals in the North. See also Richard Easterlin, "Population Change and Farm Settlement in the Northern United States," JEH, XXXVI (1976), 45–83. For a map showing patterns of westward migration, John F. Rooney, Jr., Wilbur Zelinsky, and Dean R. Louder, eds., *This Remarkable Continent: An Atlas of United States and Canadian Society and Cultures* (College Station, Tex., 1982), 10; Wilbur Zelinsky, *The Cultural Geography of the United States* (Englewood Cliffs, N.J., 1973), discusses the theories explaining these patterns of American migration; Robert P. Swierenga, "The Settlement of the Old Northwest: Ethnic Pluralism in a Featureless Plain," *Journal of the Early Republic,* IX (1989), 73–105, reviews current scholarship; also see Lois Kimball Mathews, *The Expansion of New England: The Spread of New England Settlement and Institutions to the Mississippi River, 1620–1865* (Boston, 1909).

26. William L. Barney, *The Secessionist Impulse: Alabama and Mississippi in 1860* (Princeton, N.J., 1974), 8–16, quote on 11; Richard A. Easterlin, "Regional Income Trends, 1840–1950," in *The Reinterpretation of American Economic History,* ed. Robert W. Fogel and Stanley L. Engerman (New York, 1971), 38–49; Genovese, *Political Economy of Slavery,* 85–105.

27. Barbara Jeanne Fields, *Slavery and Freedom on the Middle Ground: Maryland during the Nineteenth Century* (New Haven, Conn., 1985), 1–22; Avery Craven, *Soil Exhaustion as a Factor in the Agricultural History of Virginia and Maryland, 1606–1860* (Urbana, Ill., 1926), 120–61; Charles W. Ramsdell, "The Natural Limits of Slavery Expansion," *Mississippi Valley Historical Review* [later *Journal of American History*], XVI (1929), 151–71; Charles W. Turner, "Virginia Agricultural Reform, 1815–1860," *Agricultural History,* XXVI (1952), 80–89; James C. Bonner, "Advancing Trends in Southern Agriculture," ibid., XXII (1948), 248–59; Genovese, *Political Economy,* 114–53; Genovese, "Recent Contributions to the Economic Historiography of the Slave South," *Science & Society,* XXIV (1960), 53–66; *Historical Statistics of the U.S.,* I, 22, 29. Data on cotton textiles are presented in U.S. Bureau of the Census, *Compendium of the . . . Sixth Census* (Washington, D.C., 1841), *The Seventh Census of the United States* (Washington, D.C., 1853), *Manufactures of the United States in 1860* (Washington, D.C., 1865). Maryland led southern states in investments in textile manufacturing in all three years, and in production in 1840 and 1860. Also see the discussion of textile production in the next chapter.

28. Robert Sobel, *The Entrepreneurs: Explorations within the American Business Tradition* (New York, 1974), 60–64; Douglas Lamar Jones, *Village and Seaport: Migration and Society in Eighteenth-Century Massachusetts* (Hanover, Mass., 1981), 104–113; Hal S. Barron, *Those Who Stayed Behind: Rural Society in Nineteenth-Century New England* (Cambridge, Mass., 1984); Susan L. Norton,

"Marital Migration in Essex County, Massachusetts . . . ," *Journal of Marriage and the Family,* XXXV (1973), 406–18, finds New Englanders moved further than their contemporaries in England and Italy; Easterlin, "Interregional Differences," 97–98; Easterlin, "Regional Income Trends," 38–49. The East North Central states (Ohio, Indiana, Illinois, Michigan, and Wisconsin) grew wealthier, 1840–60, relative to the national average, but the West North Central states (Minnesota, Iowa, and Missouri) did not.

29. Frederick Bancroft, *The Life of William H. Seward,* 2 vols. (1900; rpt., Gloucester, Mass., 1967), I, 4–5, 500–520, quote on 513.

30. Speech, Oct. 19, 1855, ibid., IV, 251–52.

31. Speech, Oct. 21, 1856, ibid., IV, 282.

32. Speech, Oct. 25, 1858, ibid., IV, 292.

33. Eric Foner, *Free Soil, Free Labor, Free Men: The Ideology of the Republican Party before the Civil War* (New York, 1970), provides the fullest depiction of this ideology; G. S. Boritt, *Lincoln and the Economics of the American Dream* (Memphis, Tenn., 1978).

34. Genovese, *Political Economy of Slavery,* 250. Many southerners saw possibilities for expansion not only in the West but also in the Caribbean (particularly Cuba) and Central America, for example, Nicaragua. See J. Preston Moore, "Pierre Soulé: Southern Expansionist and Promoter," *Journal of Southern History,* XXI (1955) 203–33; Basil Rauch, *American Interest in Cuba, 1848–1855* (New York, 1948); Ray F. Broussard, "Governor John A. Quitman and the Lopez Expeditions of 1851–1852," *Journal of Mississippi History,* XXVIII (1966), 103–20; William O Scroggs, *Filibusters and Financiers: The Story of William Walker and His Associates* (New York, 1916); John McCardell, *The Idea of a Southern Nation: Southern Nationalists and Southern Nationalism, 1830–1860* (New York, 1979), 236–73.

35. McCardell, *Idea of a Southern Nation,* 227–76, quote on 262–63.

36. Gerald M. Capers, *John C. Calhoun—Opportunist: A Reappraisal* (Gainesville, Fla., 1960); Lacy Ford, "Republican Ideology in a Slave Society: The Political Ideology of John C. Calhoun," *Journal of Southern History,* XLV (1988), 405–24; prior to 1810 Calhoun had served as representative to the South Carolina legislature. Senate speech, Jan. 27, 1838, *The Works of John C. Calhoun,* ed. Richard K. Crallé, 6 vols. (New York, 1851–56), III, 137, reveals that his expansionist outlook dates back to his childhood in the war-torn South Carolina backcountry.

37. John C. Calhoun to George McDuffie, Dec. 4, 1843, *The Papers of John C. Calhoun,* ed. Clyde N. Wilson, 22 vols. (Columbia, S.C., 1959–95), XVII, 588. Once Texas had been annexed in 1845, Calhoun opposed a war of conquest against Mexico. He feared the growth of federal power, and he worried that some of the new territory might not be hospitable to slavery. Ernest McPherson Lander, Jr., *Reluctant Imperialists: Calhoun, the South Carolinians, and the Mexican War* (Baton Rouge, La., 1980). For the broader context, Charles S. Sydnor, *The Development of Southern Sectionalism, 1819–1848* (Baton Rouge, La., 1948); David M. Potter, *The Impending Crisis, 1848–1861* (New York, 1976), emphasizes the divisions within a South that only gradually united against the North.

38. Speech, Aug. 12, 1849, *Works of Calhoun,* IV, 514.

39. Speech, June 27, 1848, ibid., IV, 504.

40. Quoted in McCardell, *Idea of a Southern Nation*, 276; also see Edmund Ruffin, *Anticipations of the Future* (Richmond, Va., 1860).

41. Adolph B. Benson, ed., *Peter Kalm's Travels in North America: The English Version of 1770*, 2 vols. (1937; rpt., New York, 1966), II, 541–42 (Oct. 5, 1749).

42. Allan Greer, "The Pattern of Literacy in Quebec, 1745–1899," *Histoire sociale/Social History*, XI (1978), 295–335; Michel Verrette, "L'Alphabétisation de la population de la ville de Québec de 1750 à 1849," *Revue d'histoire de l'Amérique française*, XXXIX (1985–86), 51–76; Roger Magnuson, *Education in New France* (Montreal and Kingston, 1992); L.-P. Audet, *Le système scolaire de la province de Québec*, 6 vols. (Quebec, 1950–56), I, 46–75.

43. *Peter Kalm's Travels*, II, 473 (Aug. 21, 1749); John Bosher, *The Canada Merchants* (New York, 1987), 156–58.

44. More women could read than men in New France, but by the 1830s more men had mastered the two skills of reading and writing than had women; Greer, "Pattern of Literacy," 295–335; Verrette, "L'Alphabétisation de la population," 51–76.

45. Fernand Ouellet, "L'enseignement primaire: responsabilité des Eglises ou de l'Etat? 1801–1836," *Recherches sociographiques*, II, no. 1 (1961), 171–87; Ouellet, *Lower Canada, 1791–1840: Social Change and Nationalism*, trans. Patricia Claxton (Toronto, 1980), 167–71; Jean-Jacques Jolois, *Jean-François Perreault (1753–1844) et les origines de l'enseignement laïque au Bas-Canada* (Montreal, 1969); A. Labarrère-Paulé, *Les instituteurs laïques au Canada français, 1836–1900* (Quebec, 1965), 49–83, 117–49; L.-P. Audet, *Histoire de l'enseignement au Québec, 1608–1971*, 2 vols. (Montreal, 1971), I, 356–84, II, 3–99; Jacques Monet, "French-Canadian Nationalism and the Challenge of Ultramontism," *Canadian Historical Association Historical Papers* (1966), 41–55; Greer, "Pattern of Literacy," 317–18.

46. W. G. Bowen, "Assessing the Economic Contribution of Education," in *Economics of Education*, ed. M. Blaug, 2 vols. (Baltimore, 1968), I, 67–100; Mary Jean Bowman and C. Arnold Anderson, "Concerning the Role of Education in Development," in *Old Societies and New States: The Quest for Modernity in Asia and Africa*, ed. Clifford Geertz (New York, 1963), 247–79; T. W. Schultz, "Investment in Human Capital," *American Economic Review*, LI (1961), 1–17.

47. From *The New England Primer* in *The Puritan Tradition in America, 1620–1730*, ed. Alden T. Vaughan (New York, 1972), 242.

48. James Axtell, *The School upon a Hill: Education and Society in Colonial New England* (New York, 1974), quotes on 13, 169; Kenneth A. Lockridge, *Literacy in Colonial New England: An Enquiry into the Social Context of Literacy in the Early Modern West* (New York, 1974), 49–51; Lawrence A. Cremin, *American Education: The Colonial Experience, 1607–1783* (New York, 1980), 19–74.

49. Lockridge, *Literacy in Colonial New England*, 13–71; other scholars have suggested levels of female literacy were somewhat higher. Consult Joel Perlmann and Dennis Shirley, "When Did New England Women Acquire Literacy?" *WMQ*, 3d Ser., XLVIII (1991), 50–67; Mary Beth Norton, "Communication," and Joel Perlmann, "Response," ibid., 3d Ser., XLVIII (1991), 639–48; E. Jennifer Monaghan, "Literacy Instruction and Gender in Colonial New England," in *Reading in America: Literature and Social History*, ed. Cathy N. Davidson (Baltimore, 1989), 53–80.

50. Lockridge, *Literacy in Colonial New England*, 99–101; Carl F. Kaestle et al., *Literacy in the United States: Readers and Reading since 1880* (New Haven, Conn., 1991), 12–18.

51. Alan Tully, "Literacy Levels and Educational Development in Rural Pennsylvania, 1729–1775," *Pennsylvania History*, XXXIX (1972), 301–12.

52. Lockridge, *Literacy in Colonial New England*, 72–97.

53. Among the works discussing the common-school movement are Carl F. Kaestle, *The Evolution of an Urban School System: New York City, 1750–1850* (Cambridge, Mass., 1973), 4–5, 112, 159–91; Kaestle, *Pillars of the Republic: Common Schools and American Society, 1780–1860* (New York, 1983), 104–17, quote on 104; Stanley K. Schultz, *The Culture Factory: Boston Public Schools, 1789–1860* (New York, 1973), 69–85, 261–94; David B. Tyack, *The One Best System* (Cambridge, Mass., 1974), 33–56, 78–88.

54. Lawrence A. Cremin, *American Education: The National Experience, 1783–1876* (New York, 1980), 148–85, quote on 155; Jonathan Messerli, *Horace Mann: A Biography* (New York, 1972); Alexander Field, "Educational Reform and Manufacturing Development in Mid-Nineteenth Century Massachusetts" (Ph.D. diss., Univ. of California, Berkeley, 1974).

55. William M. Landes and L. Solomon, "Compulsory Schooling Legislation: An Economic Analysis of Law and Social Change in the Nineteenth Century," JEH, XXXII (1972), 54–91; Michael B. Katz, *Class, Bureaucracy, & Schools: The Illusion of Educational Change in America*, expanded ed. (New York, 1971, 1975), 56–73; Kaestle, *Pillars of the Republic*, 120–22; Kaestle, *Evolution of an Urban School System*, 107–8; Schultz, *Culture Factory*, 138–45, 209–77.

56. Leon F. Litwack, *North of Slavery: The Negro in the Free States, 1790–1860* (Chicago, 1961), 114–15, 132–38, 144–52; Carter G. Woodson, *The Education of the Negro Prior to 1861: A History of the Education of the Colored People of the United States from the Beginning of Slavery to the Civil War* (Washington, D.C., 1919); Kaestle, *Evolution of an Urban School System*, 141–52; Kaestle, *Pillars of the Republic*, 161–81.

57. Katz, *Class, Bureaucracy, & Schools*, 3–55, quote on 37; Katz, *The Irony of Early School Reform: Educational Innovation in Mid-Nineteenth Century Massachusetts* (Cambridge, Mass., 1968), 1–50, 163–202; Katz, "The Origins of Public Education: A Reassessment," *History of Education Quarterly*, XVI (1976), 381–407. And see Samuel Bowles and Herbert Gintis, *Schooling in Capitalist America: Educational Reform and the Contradictions of Economic Life* (New York, 1976). Among those disputing Katz's conclusions are Diane Ravitch, *The Revisionists Revised: A Critique of the Radical Attack on the Schools* (New York, 1978); Carl F. Kaestle and Maris A. Vinovskis, *Education and Social Change in Nineteenth-Century Massachusetts* (Cambridge, 1980); but see Katz's replies to his critics in "An Apology for American Educational History," *Harvard Educational Review*, XLIX (1979), 225–66, and in the "Epilogue" to *Class, Bureaucracy & Schools*, 147–94.

58. Horace Mann, "Report for 1842," in *Life and Works of Horace Mann*, ed. Mary Mann, 3 vols. (Boston, 1865–68), III, 117–18; Maris A. Vinovskis, "Horace Mann on the Economic Productivity of Education," *New England Quarterly*, XLIII (1970), 550–71.

59. Kaestle, *Pillars of the Republic*, 192–217; Edgar W. Knight, *The Academy Movement in the South* (Chapel Hill, N.C., 1919); Elizabeth B. Pryor, "An

Anomalous Person: The Northern Tutor in Plantation Society, 1773–1860," *Journal of Southern History*, XLVII (1981), 363–92; Jane G. Weyant, "The Debate over Higher Education in the South, 1850–1860," *Mississippi Quarterly*, XXIX (1976), 539–57.

60. Thomas Webber, *Deep like the Rivers: Education in the Slave Quarter Community, 1831–1865* (New York, 1978); Eugene D. Genovese, *Roll, Jordan, Roll: The World the Slaves Made* (New York, 1974), 561–66; Kaestle, *Pillars of the Republic*, 195–207, quotes on 206, 207. Several works discuss the state of southern education before the Civil War. See, in particular, Fletcher M. Green, "Democracy in the Old South," *Journal of Southern History*, XII (1946), 2–23; Roger W. Shugg, *Origins of Class Struggle in Louisiana* (Baton Rouge, La., 1939), 69–75; Gavin Wright, *The Political Economy of the Cotton South: Households, Markets, and Wealth in the Nineteenth Century* (New York, 1978), 40–41; William R. Taylor, "Towards a Definition of Orthodoxy: The Patrician South and the Common Schools," *Harvard Educational Review*, XXXVI (1966), 412–26; Laylon W. Jordan, "Education for the Community: C. G. Memminger and the Origins of Common Schools in Antebellum Charleston," *South Carolina Historical Magazine*, LXXXIII (1982), 99–115.

Chapter 6. Entrepreneurial Spirit in the North and South

1. Robert F. Dalzell, Jr., *Enterprising Elite: The Boston Associates and the World They Made* (Cambridge, Mass., 1987), 5–25, quote on 12; Hannah Josephson, *The Golden Threads: New England's Mill Girls and Magnates* (New York, 1949), 11–32, quote on 20; Nathan Appleton, *Introduction of the Power Loom and Origin of Lowell* (Lowell, Mass., 1858), 7–9, 14–15; Robert Sobel, *Entrepreneurs: Explorations Within the American Business Tradition* (New York, 1974), 17–21, 25–26; Ferris Greenslet, *The Lowells and Their Seven Worlds* (Boston, 1946).

2. For a fuller, theoretical examination of the "entrepreneurial spirit," see the discussion in Appendix A.

3. Henry W. Bellows, "The Influence of the Trading Spirit upon the Social and Moral Life of America," *American Review*, I (1845), reprinted in *Antebellum American Culture: An Interpretative Anthology*, ed. David Brion Davis (Lexington, Mass., 1979), 112, refers to an "anxious spirit of gain." Bellows is an example of a native-born American whose comments echo those of foreign travelers.

4. Quotes from Captain Frederick Marryat, *Diary in America* (1839; rpt., London, 1960), 43, 73.

5. Nineteenth-century commentary is amplified by a rich body of modern writing that emphasizes the difference between northerners and southerners. In particular, consult W. J. Cash, *The Mind of the South* (New York, 1941); Eugene D. Genovese, *The World the Slaveholders Made: Two Essays in Interpretation* (New York, 1969); Bertram Wyatt-Brown, *Southern Honor: Ethics and Behavior in the Old South* (New York, 1982); Wyatt-Brown, *Yankee Saints and Southern Sinners* (Baton Rouge, La., 1985); William H. Pease and Jane H. Pease, *The Web of Progress: Private Values and Public Styles in Boston and Charleston, 1828–1843* (New York, 1985); Lewis P. Simpson, *Mind and the American Civil War: A Meditation on Lost Causes* (Baton Rouge, La., 1989). Some writers, however, minimize the differences between the two regions. See Edward Pes-

sen, "How Different from Each Other Were the Antebellum North and South?" *American Historical Review*, LXXXV (1980), 1119–49.

6. For examples of testimony similar to that presented below, see Isabella L. Bird, *Englishwoman in America* (1856; rpt., Toronto, 1966), 321–75; Fanny Kemble Wister, ed., *Fanny the American Kemble: Her Journals and Unpublished Letters* (Tallahassee, Fla., 1972), 101–59; Marryat, *Diary in America*, 42–43, 73–77, 284; Charles Dickens, *American Notes* (London, 1859), 429–35; Harriet Martineau, *Retrospect of Western Travel*, 2 vols. (London, 1838), I, 142–45, 214–41; Thomas C. Grattan, *Civilized America*, 2 vols. (1859; rpt., New York, 1969), I, 70–85, 114–36, 190–203, II, 92–95, 318–27; Anthony Trollope, *North America* (New York, 1862), 100–101, 184–87, 250–51, 322–23, 392–95. More broadly, on visitors to North America, see Henry T. Tuckerman, *America and Her Commentators* (1864; rpt., New York, 1961); Jane L. Mesick, *The English Traveller in America, 1785–1835* (1922; rpt., New York, 1970); Max Berger, *The British Traveller in America, 1836–1860* (1943; rpt., Gloucester, Mass., 1964); Marvin Fisher, *Workshops in the Wilderness: The European Response to American Industrialization, 1830–1860* (New York, 1967). Edward Pessen, *Jacksonian America: Society, Personality, and Politics* (Homewood, Ill., 1969), 5–38, 353–58, discusses contemporary observers and provides a full list of sources.

7. Frances Trollope, *Domestic Manners of the Americans*, ed. Donald Smalley (New York, 1949), vii–lxxvi.

8. Ibid., 266.

9. Ibid., 301–2.

10. Thomas Hamilton, *Men and Manners in America*, 2 vols. (1833; rpt., New York, 1968), I, 212–13. The Laocoön Group is a famous statue that dates from the second century B.C. It shows three individuals in the grip of a serpent that coils around their limbs.

11. James S. Buckingham, *Slave States of America*, 2 vols. (1842; rpt., New York, 1968), II, 15.

12. Alexis de Tocqueville, *Democracy in America*, ed. J. P. Mayer and Max Lerner, 2 vols. (1835, 1840; rpt. and trans., New York, 1966), vol. II, part II, chap. 13. On religion, see vol. II, part II, chap. 15; David J. Rothman, *The Discovery of the Asylum: Social Order and Disorder in the New Republic*, rev. ed. (Boston, 1971, 1990), 110–15, notes that contemporaries viewed this northern obsession with success as a cause of insanity.

13. Hamilton, *Men and Manners*, II, 283–84.

14. Buckingham, *Slave States*, II, 198–99, 562. Buckingham makes an important distinction between *industry* (not found in the South) and *speculation* (which some southerners were fond of): "Industry, in the sense in which we understand that term, as implying a love of active bodily exertion, is rarely seen among the white inhabitants of the South. They are always ready for a talk, a bargain, or a speculation, by which, without much bodily effort, they may make money; but hard work is certainly much more distasteful to them than to the same class of persons in England." Ibid., II, 198.

15. Tocqueville, *Democracy in America*, vol. I, part II, chap. 10; George W. Pierson, *Tocqueville in America* (New York, 1938), 347–430.

16. U.S. Bureau of the Census, *Census of the United States*, volumes for 1840, 1850, and 1860.

17. Eugene D. Genovese, *The Political Economy of Slavery: Studies in the Economy & Society of the Slave South* (New York, 1965), 180–220.

18. Stephen J. Goldfarb, "A Note on Limits to the Growth of the Cotton-Textile Industry in the Old South," *Journal of Southern History*, XLVIII (1982), 545–58, quote on 549.

19. Gavin Wright, "Cheap Labor and Southern Textiles before 1880," JEH, XXXIX (1979), 655–80, quote on 657.

20. Lacy K. Ford, Jr., *Origins of Southern Radicalism: The South Carolina Upcountry, 1800–1860* (New York, 1988), 244–80; Heywood Fleisig, "Slavery, the Supply of Agricultural Labor, and the Industrialization of the South," JEH, XXXVI (1976), 572–92; Robert S. Starobin, *Industrial Slavery in the Old South* (New York, 1970), 186; Robert W. Fogel and Stanley L. Engerman, *Time on the Cross: The Economics of American Negro Slavery* (Boston, 1974), 254–57.

21. *Census of the United States, 1860*; Goldfarb, "Note on Limits," 554; Genovese, *Political Economy of Slavery*, 184, 196.

22. William Gregg to Amos A. Lawrence, Sept. 2, 1850, in Thomas P. Martin, ed., "The Advent of William Gregg and the Graniteville Company," *Journal of Southern History*, XI (1945), 421; Wright, "Cheap Labor," 672; Tom E. Terrill, "Eager Hands: Labor for Southern Textiles, 1850–1860," JEH, XXXVI (1976), 84–99. Terrill's study shows that there was an abundance of poor whites available for work at the textile mills.

23. William Gregg to James H. Hammond, May 30, June 20, 1849, in "Advent of William Gregg," 415, 417; Richard W. Griffin and Diffee W. Standard, "The Cotton Textile Industry in Ante-bellum North Carolina. Part II: An Era of Boom and Consolidation, 1830–1860," *North Carolina Historical Review*, XXXIV (1957), 132–42; Broadus Mitchell, *William Gregg: Factory Master of the Old South* (1928; rpt., New York, 1966), 66; William Gregg, *Essays on Domestic Industry* (1845; Graniteville, S.C., 1941), quote on 76, and see 43–44. This well-made book is covered with cloth woven in Graniteville and dyed Confederate gray.

24. Richard W. Griffin, "The Origins of the Industrial Revolution in Georgia: Cotton Textiles, 1810–1865," *Georgia Historical Quarterly*, XLII (1958), 368–73; Ernest McPherson Lander, Jr., *The Textile Industry in Antebellum South Carolina* (Baton Rouge, La., 1969), 107; Fabian Linden, "Repercussions of Manufacturing in the Ante-bellum South," *North Carolina Historical Review*, XVII (1940), 313–14; "The Manufacture of Cotton Goods in the South," Freeman Hunt's *The Merchants' Magazine and Commercial Review*, XXII (1850), 107.

25. Arthur M. Schlesinger, Jr., *The Age of Jackson* (New York, 1945), 145; Garry Wills, *Lincoln at Gettysburg: The Words That Remade America* (New York, 1992), 32–36, 41–55.

26. Edward Everett, "Fourth of July at Lowell," 1830, in *The Philosophy of Manufactures: Early Debates over Industrialization in the United States*, ed. Michael B. Folsom and Steven D. Lubar (Cambridge, Mass., 1982), 281–94, quotes on 282–83, 292–93.

27. Thomas Bender, *Toward an Urban Vision: Ideas and Institutions in Nineteenth-Century America* (Lexington, Ky., 1975), 47–50; and more broadly, Leo Marx, *The Machine in the Garden: Technology and the Pastoral Ideal in America* (New York, 1964); Carl Siracusa, *A Mechanical People: Perceptions of the*

Industrial Order in Massachusetts, 1850–1880 (Middletown, Conn., 1979), 58, 69–75, 116; see also the documents and notes in *Philosophy of Manufactures.*

28. The literature on the antebellum American working class is now a rich one. In particular, see Sean Wilentz, *Chants Democratic: New York City & the Rise of the American Working Class, 1788–1850* (New York, 1984), 237–54, 326–59, quote on 332; Bruce Laurie, *Working People of Philadelphia, 1800–1850* (Philadelphia, 1980), 75–83; Alan Dawley, *Class and Community: The Industrial Revolution in Lynn* (Cambridge, Mass., 1976), 173–93; Paul G. Faler, *Mechanics and Manufacturers in the Early Industrial Revolution* (Albany, N.Y., 1981), 167–88.

29. Henry David Thoreau, *Walden and Other Writings,* ed. Joseph W. Krutch (New York, 1962), 124–25; Thoreau, "Paradise (to be) Regained," 1843, in *Philosophy of Manufacturers,* 411–19; Ralph Waldo Emerson, "Wealth," 1856, 1860, in ibid., 447–62.

30. Frances W. Gregory, *Nathan Appleton, Merchant and Entrepreneur, 1779–1861* (Charlottesville, Va., 1975), 10, 269–96; Frederic C. Jaher, "Businessman and Gentleman: Nathan and Thomas Gold Appleton—An Exploration in Inter-generational History," *Explorations in Entrepreneurial History,* IV (1966), 17–39; Sobel, *Entrepreneurs,* 19–28; Dalzell, *Enterprising Elite,* 57–59, 77–78, 115–20; Louise Hall Tharp, *The Appletons of Beacon Hill* (Boston, 1973), 94–111; Caroline Ware, *Early New England Cotton Manufacture: A Study in Industrial Origins* (Boston, 1931), 61, 91–105; Josephson, *Golden Threads,* 115–77. See also the valuable contemporary account, Appleton, *Power Loom.*

31. Josephson, *Golden Threads,* quotes on 149, 173; Paul Goodman, "Ethics and Enterprise: The Values of a Boston Elite, 1800–1860," *American Quarterly,* XVIII (1966), 437–51; Frederick C. Jaher, "The Boston Brahmins in the Age of Industrial Capitalism," in *Age of Industrialism in America: Essays in Social Structure and Cultural Values,* ed. Frederick C. Jaher (New York, 1968), 188–262; also see *Extracts from the Diary and Correspondence of the Late Amos Lawrence,* ed. William R. Lawrence (Boston, 1855).

32. Dalzell, *Enterprising Elite,* quotes on 64–65; Dalzell draws these quotes from *Selections from the Diaries of William Appleton, 1786–1862,* ed. Susan M. Loring (Boston, 1922).

33. Thomas Cooper, "The Disadvantage of Machinery," 1823, in *Philosophy of Manufactures,* 256; Cheves quoted in Broadus Mitchell, *The Rise of Cotton Mills in the South* (1921; rpt., Gloucester, Mass., 1966), 58n. On the ambivalence in John C. Calhoun's approach to manufacturing, consult Theodore R. Marmor, "Anti-industrialism and the Old South: The Agrarian Perspective of John C. Calhoun," *Comparative Studies in Society and History,* IX (1966–67), 377–406; Charles A. Wiltse, *John Calhoun: Nationalist, 1787–1828* (1944; rpt., New York, 1968), 119–21; Richard N. Current, *John C. Calhoun: An American Portrait* (New York, 1966), 87–105.

34. Quoted in Griffin, "Industrial Revolution in Georgia," 360; Chauncey S. Boucher, "The Ante-bellum Attitude of South Carolina Towards Manufacturing and Agriculture," *Washington University Studies,* III (1915), part 2, 243–70.

35. George Fitzhugh, for example, railed against "the filthy, crowded, licentious factories . . . of the North." Quoted in Linden, "Repercussions of Manufacturing," 321. See also Wilfred Carsel, "The Slaveholder's Indictment of Northern Wage Slavery," *Journal of Southern History,* VI (1940), 504–20.

36. Drew Gilpin Faust, *James Henry Hammond and the Old South: A Design for Mastery* (Baton Rouge, La., 1982), 275–76, quotes Hammond; Vicki V. Johnson, *The Men and the Vision of the Southern Commercial Conventions, 1845–1871* (Columbia, Mo., 1992), 90–124.

37. Gregg, *Essays*, 39; William Gregg to William B. Seabrook, May 10, 1850, "Advent of William Gregg," 419. Daniel Pratt, the leading industrialist in Alabama, took a similar stance. He advocated industry while accepting the values of southern society; Randall M. Miller, *The Cotton Mill Movement in Antebellum Alabama* (New York, 1978), 43–51.

38. Quoted in Herbert Collins, "The Southern Industrial Gospel before 1860," *Journal of Southern History*, XII (1946), 387.

39. John S. Linton to Annie [Linton?], July 19, 1853, *Cotton History Review*, I (1960), 76.

40. Gregg, *Essays*, 12–13; also see William Gregg to James H. Hammond, Feb. 18, 1849, "Advent of William Gregg," 411–12.

41. Boucher, "Ante-bellum Attitude," 258.

42. Richard W. Griffin, "Poor White Laborers in Southern Cotton Factories, 1789–1865," *South Carolina Historical Magazine*, LXI (1960), 34; see also *De Bow's Review*, XXIV (1858), 383.

43. Susan F. H. Tarrant, ed., *Hon. Daniel Pratt: A Biography with Eulogies on His Life and Character* (Richmond, Va., 1904), 13–16, 106–8; Merrill E. Pratt, *Daniel Pratt: Alabama's First Industrialist* (Newcomen Society of England, American Branch, 1949); Merrill E. Pratt, "Daniel Pratt: Alabama's First Industrialist," *Cotton History Review*, II (1961), 18–29; "Daniel Pratt," DAB; Miller, *Cotton Mill Movement*, 38–39.

44. Griffin, "Poor White Laborers," 27; Griffin, "Industrial Revolution in Georgia," 356–58; Lander, *Textile Industry*, 13–28; Mitchell, *William Gregg*, 1–14, 66–72; Mitchell, *Rise of Cotton Mills*, 17–19; Broadus Mitchell and George S. Mitchell, *The Industrial Revolution in the South* (1930; rpt., New York, 1968), 71–73; George W. Smith, "Ante-bellum Attempts of Northern Business Interests to 'Redeem' the Upper South," *Journal of Southern History*, XI (1945), 177–213; on C. T. James, see Freeman Hunt's *Merchants' Magazine and Commercial Review*, XXII (1850), 107–9.

45. Josephson, *Golden Threads*, 101–3; Vera Shlakman, *Economic History of a Factory Town: A Study of Chicopee, Massachusetts* (Smith College Studies in History, vol. XX, nos. 1–4) (Northampton, Mass., 1935), 30–45; E. Digby Baltzell, *Puritan Boston and Quaker Philadelphia: Two Protestant Ethics and the Spirit of Class Authority and Leadership* (New York, 1979), 207–45, contrasts the close ties within the Boston elite with the looser associations of the Philadelphia upper class.

46. The literature on the early New England textile industry is substantial. In particular, see Robert B. Zevin, "The Growth of Cotton Textile Production after 1815," in *The Reinterpretation of American Economic History*, ed. Robert W. Fogel and Stanley L. Engerman (New York, 1971), 122–47; Lance E. Davis and H. Louis Stettler III, "The New England Textile Industry, 1825–60: Trends and Fluctuations," Conference on Resarch in Income and Wealth, *Output, Employment, and Productivity in the United States after 1800* (Studies in Income and Wealth, vol. XXX) (New York, 1966), 213–42; Ware, *Cotton Manufacture*, 110–

18; Paul F. McGouldrick, *New England Textiles in the Nineteenth Century: Profits and Investment* (Cambridge, Mass., 1968), 73–120; Dalzell, *Enterprising Elite*, 27–28, 49–55, 162–63, 225; Josephson, *Golden Threads*, 56, 206–7, 299–307; Thomas Dublin, *Women at Work: The Transformation of Work and Community in Lowell, Massachusetts, 1826–1860* (New York, 1979), 134–36.

47. Oscar Handlin and Mary F. Handlin, *Commonwealth: A Study in the Role of Government in the American Economy: Massachusetts, 1774–1861* (New York, 1947), 168–69; Dalzell, *Enterprising Elite*, 94–95; Josephson, *Golden Threads*, 128, 142–43.

48. Gerald T. White, *A History of the Massachusetts Hospital Life Insurance Company* (Cambridge, Mass., 1955), 60–97, 119–20; Gregory, *Nathan Appleton*, 287–90; Lance E. Davis, "The New England Textile Mills and the Capital Markets: A Study of Industrial Borrowing, 1840–1860," JEH, XX (1960), 1–30; Davis, "Sources of Industrial Finance: The American Textile Industry: A Case Study," *Explorations in Entrepreneurial History*, IX (1957), 189–203; Dalzell, *Enterprising Elite*, 96–106; Pease and Pease, *Web of Progress*, 20–21. The textile magnates enthusiastically supported the Provident Institution for Savings, a bank designed to promote thrift among the common folk. Founded in 1816, the Provident Institution paid interest only on sums of $500 or less. The Associates and other members of the elite donated their counsel and services. By 1829 the Provident had almost one million dollars in savings accounts. See Walter Muir Whitehill, *The Provident Institution for Savings in the Town of Boston, 1816–1966* (Boston, 1966).

49. Edward C. Kirkland, *Men, Cities, and Transportation: A Study of New England History, 1820–1900* (Cambridge, Mass., 1948), I, 92–122; Stephen Salsbury, *The State, the Investor, and the Railroad: The Boston & Albany, 1825–1867* (Cambridge, Mass., 1967), 65–112, 138–81; Pease and Pease, *Web of Progress*, 16–17, 64–69; Dalzell, *Enterprising Elite*, 82–89; Josephson, *Golden Threads*, 104–6; Appleton, *Power Loom*, 36.

50. Josephson, *Golden Threads*, 107, quotes Parker; Appleton, *Power Loom*, 13.

51. Ibid., 160.

52. Thomas H. O'Connor, *Lords of the Loom: The Cotton Whigs and the Coming of the Civil War* (New York, 1968), 67, 78, 94; Kinley J. Brauer, *Cotton versus Conscience: Massachusetts Whig Politics and Southwestern Expansion, 1843–1848* (Lexington, Ky., 1967), 8–12; Ronald P. Formisano, *The Transformation of Political Culture: Massachusetts Parties, 1790s–1840s* (New York, 1983), 283–86; Josephson, *Golden Threads*, 106–7, 160–74, 300–302; Dalzell, *Enterprising Elite*, 163–65, 194–99, 207–18.

53. William Gregg to Amos A. Lawrence, Sept. 2, 1850, "Advent of William Gregg," 422; Mitchell, *William Gregg*, 91; Dublin, *Women at Work*, 133; "Daniel Pratt," DAB, VIII, 170–71; Miller, *Cotton Mill Movement*, 40–58.

54. Mitchell, *William Gregg*, quotes on 113, 191; Pease and Pease, *Web of Progress*, 43–48; Ford, *Origins of Southern Radicalism*, 324–35.

55. Pease and Pease, *Web of Progress*, 21–22.

56. Gregg, *Essays*, 52; Pease and Pease, *Web of Progress*, 16–17, 56–62; Samuel M. Derrick, *Centennial History of the South Carolina Railroad* (1930; rpt., Spartanburg, S.C., 1975), 76–105; Ulrich B. Phillips, *A History of Transportation*

in the Eastern Cotton Belt to 1860 (1908; rpt., New York, 1968); Mitchell, *William Gregg,* 132, 167–79.

57. Genovese, *Political Economy,* 180–220; Mitchell, *William Gregg,* 164–201; Tarrant, ed., *Daniel Pratt,* 111–12.

58. Another area where the two cultures diverged was in their approach to charity. Northern industrialists gave only to the "deserving poor"— those who displayed the proper work ethic, while southerners were less restrictive in their definition of who should receive aid. See Pease and Pease, *Web of Progress,* 138–52; Dalzell, *Enterprising Elite,* 113–63.

59. Dublin, *Women at Work,* 14–57, quotes on 37–38; Dublin, *Transforming Women's Work: New England Lives in the Industrial Revolution* (Ithaca, N. Y., 1994), 77–114. Also see Loriman S. Brigham, "An Independent Voice: A Mill Girl from Vermont Speaks Her Mind," *Vermont History,* XLI (1973), 142–46; Nell Kull, ed., " 'I Can Never Be So Happy There Among All Those Mountains': The Letters of Sally Rice," ibid., XXXVIII (1970), 49–57; Allis R. Wolfe, ed., "Letters of a Lowell Mill Girl and Friends, 1843–1846," *Labor History,* XVII (1976), 96–102; Sandra Addickes, "Mind among the Spindles: An Examination of Some of the Journals, Newspapers, and Memoirs of the Lowell Female Operatives," *Women's Studies,* I (1973), 279–87. Consult also the valuable documents collected in Thomas Dublin, ed., *Farm to Factory: Women's Letters, 1830–1860* (New York, 1981). Dublin's introduction (pp. 1–36) notes that a minority of Yankee women helped support their families.

60. "Two Essays from *The Lowell Offering,* 1840," in *Major Problems in American Women's History: Documents and Essays,* ed. Mary Beth Norton (Lexington, Mass., 1989), 172–75, quote on 173; Josephson, *Golden Threads,* 193.

61. Susan E. Kennedy, *If All We Did Was to Weep at Home: A History of White Working-Class Women in America* (Bloomington, Ind., 1979), 42–43, 46, 50–51; Herbert J. Lahne, *The Cotton Mill Worker* (New York, 1944), 71–72; Norman Ware, *The Industrial Worker, 1840–1860: The Reaction of American Industrial Society to the Advance of the Industrial Revolution* (1924; rpt., Gloucester, Mass., 1959), 70–74, 133, 135, 201; Philip S. Foner, *The Factory Girls: A Collection of Writings on Life and Struggle in the New England Factories of the 1840s* (Urbana, Ill., 1977), 74–94, 215–70; Josephson, *Golden Threads,* 204–308; Dublin, *Women at Work,* 86–164; Dalzell, *Enterprising Elite,* 68–69.

62. Anthony F. C. Wallace, *Rockdale: The Growth of an American Village in the Early Industrial Revolution* (New York, 1972, 1978), esp. 355–94; Jonathan Prude, *The Coming of Industrial Order: Town and Factory Life in Rural Massachusetts, 1810–1860* (New York, 1983), 133–80; Josephson, *Golden Threads,* 72–74, 250–308; Dublin, *Women at Work,* 132–207.

63. Mitchell, *William Gregg,* 51–56, quote on 56; Collins, "Southern Industrial Gospel," 400; Lacy K. Ford, Jr. "The Tale of Two Entrepreneurs in the Old South: John Springs III and Hiram Hutchinson of the South Carolina Upcountry," *South Carolina Historical Magazine,* VC (1994), 213.

64. Ford, *Origins of Southern Radicalism,* 273; E. P. Thompson, "Time, Work-Discipline and Industrial Capitalism," *Past and Present,* XXXVIII (1967), 56–97.

65. William Gregg to Amos A. Lawrence, Sept. 2, 1850, "Advent of William Gregg," 421–22; Terrill, "Eager Hands," 86–97, quote on 96; Griffin and

Standard, "Cotton Textile Industry," 145–55; Mitchell, *William Gregg*, 51–90, 107–9; Griffin, "Poor White Laborers," 31–33; Griffin, "Industrial Revolution in Georgia," 363.

Chapter 7. Entrepreneurial Spirit in French Canada

1. "Louis-Joseph Papineau," DCB, X, 564–77, and particularly 568 on his views of the seigneury; Cole Harris, "Of Poverty and Helplessness in Petite-Nation," *Canadian Historical Review*, LII (1971), 23–50, reprinted in *Canadian History before Confederation: Essays and Interpretations*, 2d ed., ed. J. M. Bumsted (Georgetown, Ont., 1979), 329–54, quotes from 334, 344. Note that before 1826 the Patriote party was the Parti Canadien.

2. During the 1940s, 1950s, and 1960s Maurice Séguin, Guy Frégault, and Michel Brunet were the most outspoken advocates of this neo-nationalist position. Maurice Séguin, "The Conquest and French-Canadian Economic Life," in *Society and Conquest: The Debate on the Bourgeoisie and Social Change in French Canada, 1700–1850*, ed. Dale Miquelon (Toronto, 1977), 68–70, quote on 68; Guy Frégault, "The Colonization of Canada in the Eighteenth Century," ibid., 85–104; Michel Brunet, "The British Conquest and the Decline of the French-Canadian Bourgeoisie," in ibid., 143–71. Today many French-Canadian intellectuals accept this point of view; see Ramsay Cook, *Canada, Quebec, and the Uses of Nationalism* (Toronto, 1986), 90–91. For a critique of this outlook, see Fernand Ouellet, *Economic and Social History of Quebec, 1750–1850: Structures* and *Conjonctures* (Ottawa, 1980); Jean Hamelin, *Economie et société en Nouvelle-France* (Quebec, 1960), 135; Marcel Trudel, *Introduction to New France* (Toronto, 1968), 142, 182, 209. Cameron Nish, *The French Canadians, 1759–1766: Conquered? Half-Conquered? Liberated?* (Toronto, 1966), surveys this issue.

3. "Charles Aubert de La Chesnaye," DCB, II, 26–34; Yves Zoltvany, "The Business Career of Charles Aubert de la Chesnaye," *Communications historiques/Historical Papers* (Canadian Historical Association Annual Meeting) (1968), 12–23; much of La Chesnaye's career can be followed in the documents and notes in *Documents Relating to Canadian Currency, Exchange and Finance during the French Period*, ed. Adam Shortt, 2 vols. (Ottawa, 1925), I, 19–155; Guy Frégault, "The Colonization of Canada in the Eighteenth Century," in *Society and Conquest*, 85–105.

4. "François Martel de Brouague," "Pierre Trottier Desauniers," DCB, III, 433–34, 631–32. Desauniers's contract to fortify Quebec was canceled before the work was completed — and he had difficulty collecting from the government. Those problems illustrate the risks in relying too heavily on royal favors. See also Cameron Nish, *François-Etienne Cugnet: entrepreneurs et entreprise en Nouvelle-France* (Montreal, 1975).

5. The comparison with the merchants in the Thirteen Colonies (and particularly the northern ports of Boston, New York, and Philadelphia) is striking. Only during wartime did government contracts become an important source of revenue for the American merchants. And even then these funds usually made only a minor contribution to the net worth of traders. Marc Egnal, "The Pennsylvania Economy, 1748–1762: An Analysis of Short-Run Fluctuations in the Context of Long-Run Changes in the Atlantic Trading Community" (Ph.D. diss., Univ. of Wisconsin, 1974), 175–88; W. T. Baxter, *The House of*

Hancock: Business in Boston, 1724–1775 (Cambridge, Mass., 1945), 79–112, 136–40; Virginia D. Harrington, *The New York Merchant on the Eve of the Revolution* (New York, 1935), 291–304.

6. On the merchant community in Canada, Louise Dechêne, *Habitants et marchands de Montréal au XVIIe siècle* (Montreal, 1974), 171–231; James Pritchard, "Commerce in New France," in *Canadian Business History: Selected Studies, 1497–1971,* ed. David S. Macmillan (Toronto, 1972), 27–43; Alice Jean Lunn, "Economic Development in New France, 1713–1760" (Ph.D. diss., McGill Univ., 1942), 342–85; Dale Miquelon, *Dugard of Rouen: French Trade to Canada and the West Indies, 1729–1770* (Montreal, 1978); José E. Iguarta, "The Merchants of Montreal at the Conquest: Socio-Economic Profile," *Histoire sociale/ Social History,* VIII (1975), 275–293.

7. Lunn, "Economic Development," 244–341, provides a detailed account of the fate of shipbuilding and ironmaking in New France; Donald James Horton, "Gilles Hocquart, Intendant of New France, 1729–1748" (Ph.D. thesis, McGill Univ., 1974), 86–95, 331–33, discusses the frustration Hocquart experienced in trying to strengthen the Canadian bourgeoisie. And see Louise Trottier, *Les Forges: historiographie des Forges du Saint-Maurice, 1729–1883. 150 ans d'occupation et d'exploitation* (Montreal, 1980), 44, 72–73.

8. George M. Wrong, *The Rise and Fall of New France,* 2 vols. (Toronto, 1928), II, 719, 789, 826–33, 881–82, quote on 827; John Bosher and J.-C. Dubé provide an insightful essay on Bigot in DCB, IV, 59–71; Guy Frégault, *François Bigot: administrateur français,* 2 vols. (Montreal, 1948); Lunn, "Economic Development," 376–77, 439.

9. "François Bigot," DCB, IV, 59–71; John Bosher, *The Canada Merchants, 1713–1763* (Oxford, Eng., 1987), 80–82, 208–11; Pritchard, "Commerce in New France," 41–42.

10. Francis Maseres quoted in Donald Creighton, *The Empire of the St. Lawrence* (Toronto, 1937), 34.

11. For example, see biographies of Maurice-Régis Blondeau, Jean-Baptiste Cadot, Charles-Jean-Baptiste Chaboillez, and Pierre Guy in DCB, V, 89–90, 128–30, 178–79, 395–99.

12. "Jacques Baby," "François Baby," DCB, IV, 38–39, V, 41–45.

13. A. L. Burt, *The Old Province of Quebec* (New York, 1933), 63–64, 200–201, 258, 323–24, 446–48.

14. Report from Charles Grant to General Haldimand on the Fur Trade, April 24, 1780, *Documents Relating to the North West Company,* ed. W. Stewart Wallace (Toronto, 1934), 63.

15. David S. Macmillan, "The 'New Men' in Action: Scottish Mercantile and Shipping Operations in the North American Colonies, 1760–1825," in *Canadian Business History: Selected Studies, 1497–1971,* ed. David S. Macmillan (Toronto, 1972), 58–68; biographies of Robert Ellice, George Allsopp, William Grant, DCB, IV, 261–62, V, 19–23, 367–76.

16. R. Cole Harris, ed., *Historical Atlas of Canada,* vol. I: *From the Beginning to 1800* (Toronto, 1987), plates 61–63; Fernand Ouellet, "Economic Dualism and Technological Change in Quebec, 1760–1790," in Fernand Ouellet, *Colony, Class & Nation in Quebec: Interpretative Essays,* ed. and trans. Jacques Barbier (Toronto, 1991), 161–209, provides a valuable comparison of English- and French-Canadian fur traders.

17. The various reorganizations can be traced in the documents in Wallace, ed., *North West Company*. Majorie Wilkins Campbell, *North West Company* (Toronto, 1957), presents a solid, popular history of the company.

18. Simon McTavish to William Edgar, Dec. 24, 1774, March 9, 1778, *North West Company*, ed. Wallace, 48, 60; Campbell, *North West Company*, 19; "Simon McTavish," DCB, V, 560–66.

19. Wallace, ed., *North West Company*, 26–36; Campbell, *North West Company*, 219–80.

20. Ouellet, "Economic Dualism," 161–209, quote on 185; Ouellet, *Lower Canada, 1791–1840: Social Change and Nationalism* (Toronto, 1980), 329; Campbell, *North West Company*, 61–69; "Peter Pond," "Henry Hamilton," DCB, V, 681–85, IV, 321–25.

21. "Simon McTavish," "William Grant," DCB, V, 560–66, 367–76; Ouellet, *Lower Canada*, 343; John McCallum, *Unequal Beginnings: Agricultural and Economic Development in Quebec and Ontario* (Toronto, 1980), 28; Fernand Ouellet, "Colonial Economy and International Economy: The Trade of the St. Lawrence River Valley with Spain, Portugal and Their Atlantic Possessions, 1760–1850," in *The North American Role in the Spanish Imperial Economy, 1760–1819*, ed. J. Barbier and A. J. Kuethe (Manchester, Eng., 1984), table VII.

22. Arthur R. M. Lower, *Great Britain's Woodyard: British America and the Timber Trade, 1763–1867* (Montreal, 1973), esp. 31–33, 50–58, 97–110, 127–28, 144–47; "James McGill," DCB, V, 527–44.

23. Biographies of Pierre-Joseph Gamelin, François Baby, Pierre Guy, DCB, IV, 285–87, V, 41–46, 395–99.

24. "Petition for British Intervention to Secure Payment of the Canada Papers," Feb. 1763, in *Society and Conquest*, 199.

25. José Iguarta, "A Change in Climate: The Conquest and the *Marchands* of Montreal," *Canadian Historical Association Historical Papers* (1974), 122–23.

26. "Horatio Gates," DCB, VI, 277–80; Lorraine Gadoury and Jean-François Leclerc, "Profil de quelques bourgeois de Montréal, 1820–1825," *Les cahiers d'histoire*, V (1985), 7–24.

27. Gerald J. J. Tulchinsky, *The River Barons: Montreal Businessmen and the Growth of Industry and Transportation, 1837–53* (Toronto, 1977), 14–19, 221–29; George Bevin, *Québec au xix-e siècle: l'activité économique des grands marchands* (Quebec, 1991), shows that, as in Montreal, the wealthiest merchants in Quebec City were anglophones; M. Dennison, *The Barley and the Stream: The Molson Story* (Toronto, 1955); Jean-Claude Robert, "Les notables de Montréal au XIXe siècle," *Histoire sociale/Social History*, VIII (1975), 54–76; Brian J. Young, *Promoters and Politicians: The North-Shore Railways in the History of Quebec, 1854–1885* (Toronto, 1978), 25, 38–39, 45.

28. "Joseph Masson," DCB, VII, 592–96; Tulchinsky, *River Barons*, 16–18, 74–78.

29. Ramsay Cook, ed., *French-Canadian Nationalism: An Anthology* (Toronto, 1969), 85; Cook, *Canada, Quebec, and the Uses of Nationalism*, 99–100.

30. Tulchinsky, *River Barons*, 14–15, 25–26, 53–58, 178–80; Ouellet, *Economic and Social History*, 375–80; Yves Bélanger and Pierre Fournier, *L'entreprise québécoise: développement historique et dynamique contemporaine* (Quebec,

1987), 13–20; Ronald Rudin, *Banking en français: The French Banks of Quebec, 1835–1925* (Toronto, 1985).

Chapter 8. Intellectual Life

1. Elizabeth C. Stanton et al., eds., *History of Woman Suffrage,* 6 vols. (1881–1922; rpt., New York, 1969), I, 67–75, 802–10, quote on 72; Eleanor Flexner, *Century of Struggle: The Woman's Rights Movement in the United States* (Cambridge, Mass., 1959), 71–77; Blanche G. Hersh, *The Slavery of Sex: Feminist-Abolitionists in America* (Champaign, Ill., 1978).

2. For a more theoretical discussion of the impact of ideology, see George Lichtheim, "The Concept of Ideology," *History and Theory,* IV (1965), 164–95; Clifford Geertz, *The Interpretation of Cultures: Selected Essays* (New York, 1973), 191–233; Joyce Appleby, "Value and Society," in *Colonial British America: Essays in the New History of the Early Modern Era,* ed. Jack P. Greene and J. R. Pole (Baltimore, 1984), 290–316.

3. Brook Hindle, *The Pursuit of Science in Revolutionary America, 1735–1789* (Chapel Hill, N.C., 1956), passim.

4. Benjamin Franklin, *The Autobiography and Other Writings,* ed. L. Jesse Lemisch (New York, 1961), 95–101; Paul W. Conner, *Poor Richard's Politicks: Benjamin Franklin and His New American Order* (New York, 1965); A. Whitney Griswold, "Three Puritans on Prosperity," *New England Quarterly,* VII (1934), 475–93; Charles L. Sanford, "An American's *Pilgrim's Progress,*" *American Quarterly,* VI (1954), 297–310; see the essays in two valuable collections, Esmond Wright, ed., *Benjamin Franklin: A Profile* (New York, 1970), and Charles L. Sanford, *Benjamin Franklin and the American Character* (Boston, 1955); on the relationship between Franklin's thought and the capitalist order, see Appendix A.

5. Gordon S. Wood, *The Creation of the American Republic, 1776–1787* (Chapel Hill, N.C., 1969), 568.

6. L. H. Butterfield, ed., *Diary and Autobiography of John Adams,* 4 vols. (1961; rpt., New York, 1964), quotes on I, 8, 31, and see III, 261–64; Peter Shaw, *The Character of John Adams* (Chapel Hill, N.C., 1976), 3–40.

7. "Thoughts on Government" reprinted in *The Political Writings of John Adams: Representative Selections,* ed. George A. Peek, Jr. (Indianapolis, 1954), 83–92, quote on 89; "A Defense of the Constitutions" is reprinted in *The Works of John Adams,* ed. Charles Francis Adams, 10 vols. (Boston, 1850–56), IV, V, and VI. The quote is from VI, 115. Henry F. May, *The Enlightenment in America* (New York, 1976), argues Adams abandoned the doctrine of original sin. However, quotes such as the one in the text suggest that this belief continued to play a role in Adams's outlook. May concedes that Adams's views "never carried him . . . into optimism about human nature or certainty about the nature of a liberal God" (279–86, quote on 280). See also H. O. Fielding, "John Adams: Puritan, Deist, Humanist," *Journal of Religion,* XX (1940), 33–46; Edmund Morgan, "John Adams and the Puritan Tradition," *New England Quarterly,* XXIV (1961), 418–529; John R. Howe, Jr., *The Changing Political Thought of John Adams* (Princeton, N.J., 1966).

8. For a discussion of the impact of commercial capitalism on the intellec-

tual life of the young republic, see Joyce Appleby, *Capitalism and a New Social Order: The Republican Vision of the 1790s* (New York, 1984); Joseph J. Ellis, *After the Revolution: Profiles of Early American Culture* (New York, 1979), 23–38; Steven Watts, *The Republic Reborn* (Baltimore, 1987).

9. Washington Irving, *The Sketch Book* (1820; rpt., New York, 1961), 47, 49, with "Afterword" by Perry Miller, 371–78; Ralph M. Aderman, ed., *Critical Essays on Washington Irving* (Boston, 1990).

10. Conrad Wright, *The Beginnings of Unitarianism in America* (Boston, 1955); Nathan O. Hatch, *The Democratization of American Christianity* (New Haven, Conn., 1989), 40–42, 170–75.

11. Gilbert H. Barnes, *The Antislavery Impulse, 1830–1844* (New York, 1933), 3–16; John L. Thomas, "Romantic Reform in America, 1815–1865," *American Quarterly*, XVII (1965), 656–81, quote on 658; Bertram Wyatt-Brown, *Lewis Tappan and the Evangelical War Against Slavery* (Cleveland, 1969), quote on 287; Wyatt-Brown, *Yankee Saints and Southern Sinners* (Baton Rouge, La., 1985), 13–41; John R. McKivigan, *The War Against Proslavery Religion: Abolitionism and the Northern Churches, 1830–1865* (Ithaca, N.Y., 1984), 20–29, 37–38, 74–92; Nancy A. Hewitt, *Women's Activism and Social Change: Rochester, New York, 1822–1872* (Ithaca, N.Y., 1984), 28–33, 45, 73–76, 123, 177, discusses the impact of Finney's revival on women's rights; Whitney R. Cross, *The Burned-Over District: The Social and Intellectual History of Enthusiastic Religion in Western New York, 1800–1850* (New York, 1965); Michael Barkun, *Crucible of the Millennium: The Burned-Over District of New York in the 1840s* (Syracuse, N.Y., 1986); Randolph A. Roth, *The Democratic Dilemma: Religion, Reform, and the Social Order in the Connecticut River Valley of Vermont, 1791–1850* (New York, 1987), 104–15, 142–86; Hugh Davis, *Joshua Leavitt: Evangelical Abolitionist* (Baton Rouge, La., 1990); Victor B. Howard, *Conscience and Slavery: The Evangelistic Calvinist Domestic Missions, 1837–1861* (Kent, Ohio, 1990); Howard, *Religion and the Radical Republican Movement, 1860–1870* (Lexington, Ky., 1990); Alice F. Tyler, *Freedom's Ferment: Phases of American Social History from the Colonial Period to the Outbreak of the Civil War* (Minneapolis, 1944); Ronald G. Walters, *American Reformers, 1815–1860* (New York, 1978), 21–37, 145–72; Lewis Perry, *Childhood, Marriage, and Reform: Henry Clarke Wright, 1797–1870* (Chicago, 1980), discusses the impact of the breakdown of Calvinism on one reformer; Robert L. Hampel, *Temperance and Prohibition in Massachusetts, 1813–52* (Ann Arbor, Mich., 1982); Daniel J. McInerney, " 'A Faith for Freedom': The Political Gospel of Abolition," *Journal of the Early Republic*, XI (1991), 371–97.

12. Russel Blaine Nye, *Society and Culture in America, 1830–1860* (New York, 1974), 1–31, quote on 27; Arthur E. Bestor, Jr., "Patent-Office Models of the Good Society: Some Relationships between Social Reform and Westward Expansion," *American Historical Review*, LVIII (1953), 505–26, emphasizes the "sense of rapid growth and vast potentiality" that marked this era (p. 514).

13. David J. Rothman, *The Discovery of the Asylum: Social Order and Disorder in the New Republic* (Boston, 1971), 79–130, quote on xviii; Paul E. Johnson, *A Shopkeeper's Millennium: Society and Revivals in Rochester, New York, 1815–1837* (New York, 1978), quote on 138; Clifford S. Griffin, *Their Brothers' Keepers: Moral Stewardship in the United States, 1800–1855* (New Brunswick,

N.J., 1960), x–xiii, 23–43, 135–51, 242–64; Fred Somkin, *Unquiet Eagle: Memory and Desire in the Idea of American Freedom, 1815–1860* (Ithaca, N.Y., 1967); Lois W. Banner, "Religious Benevolence as Social Control: A Critique of an Interpretation," *Journal of American History,* LV (1973), 23–41.

14. David Donald, *Lincoln Reconsidered: Essays on the Civil War Era* (New York, 1956), 19–36, quote on 33; James B. Stewart, *Holy Warriors: The Abolitionists and American Slavery* (New York, 1976), quote on 38; Joseph R. Gusfield, *Symbolic Crusade: Status Politics and the American Temperance Movement* (Urbana, Ill., 1963); Stanley M. Elkins, *Slavery: A Problem in American Institutional and Intellectual Life* (Chicago, 1959), 140–222; Paul Goodman, *Towards a Christian Republic: Antimasonry and the Great Transition in New England, 1826–1836* (New York, 1988), 29–33, 37–79; Lawrence J. Friedman, *Gregarious Saints: Self and Community in American Abolitionism, 1830–1870* (New York, 1982); Richard O. Curry and Lawrence B. Goodheart, " 'Knives in Their Heads' ": Passionate Self-Analysis and the Search for Identity in Recent Abolitionist Historiography," *Canadian Review of American Studies,* XIV (1983), 401–14; Lawrence B. Goodheart, *Abolitionist, Actuary, Atheist: Elizur Wright and the Reform Impulse* (Kent, Ohio, 1990); Donald M. Scott, "Abolition as a Sacred Vocation," in *Antislavery Reconsidered: New Perspectives on the Abolitionists,* ed. Lewis Perry and Michael Fellman (Baton Rouge, La., 1979), 51–74; Bertram Wyatt-Brown, "Conscience and Career: Young Abolitionists and Missionaries," in *Anti-slavery, Religion, and Reform: Essays in Memory of Roger Anstey,* ed. Christine Bolt and Seymour Drescher (Folkestone, Eng., 1980), 183–203. For critiques of this approach, see Robert A. Skotheim, "A Note on Historical Method: David Donald's 'Toward a Reconsideration of Abolitionists,' " *Journal of Southern History,* XXV (1959), 356–65; and Ian R. Tyrell, *Sobering Up: From Temperance to Prohibition in Antebellum America, 1800–1860* (Westport, Conn., 1979).

15. Michael B. Katz, "Origins of the Institutional State," *Marxist Perspectives,* I (1978), 6–22, quotes on 20; Katz, *The Irony of Early School Reform: Educational Innovation in Mid-Nineteenth Century Massachusetts* (Cambridge, Mass., 1968); Jonathan A. Glickstein, " 'Poverty is not Slavery': American Abolitionists and the Competitive Labor Market," in *Antislavery Reconsidered,* 195–218.

16. Channing, "The Moral Argument Against Calvinism," 1820, in *William Ellery Channing: Selected Writings,* ed. David Robinson (New York, 1985), 119.

17. Channing, "Likeness to God," 1828, in ibid., 146, 148.

18. Garth M. Rosel and Richard A. G. Dupuis, eds., *The Memoirs of Charles G. Finney: The Complete Restored Text* (Grand Rapids., Mich., 1989), 27, 48; "Charles Grandison Finney," DAB, III, part 2, pp. 394–96. Historians refer to the many sporadic and widespread revivals in the period from 1800 to 1840 as the "Second Great Awakening."

19. Hatch, *Democratization of American Christianity,* 162–93; John Lee Eighmy, *Churches in Cultural Captivity: A History of the Social Attitudes of Southern Baptists* (Knoxville, Tenn., 1972), 3–92; Frederick A. Norwood, *The Story of American Methodism: A History of the United Methodists and Their Relations* (Nashville, Tenn., 1974), 119–239, 292–330; Donald G. Mathews, *Religion in the Old South* (Chicago, 1977), 75–80.

20. *Channing: Selected Writings*, 4, quotes Emerson; Ralph L. Rusk, *The Life of Ralph Waldo Emerson* (New York, 1949), 101–4; Stanley Cavell, *In Quest of the Ordinary: Lines of Romanticism and Skepticism* (Chicago, 1988), 27–40, 106–20.

21. Quote from "Ralph Waldo Emerson," DAB, III, 134; Anne C. Rose, *Transcendentalism as a Social Movement, 1830–1850* (New Haven, Conn., 1981), 38–44, 70–93, makes clear that the Unitarians did not want the Transcendentalists to remain within their church. See also George Kateb, "Thinking About Extinction (II): Emerson and Whitman," *Raritan*, VI (1987), 1–22; Mary K. Cayton, *Emerson's Emergence: Self and Society in the Transformation of New England, 1800–1845* (Chapel Hill, N.C., 1989), 73, 107–11, 128–31, 174; Cayton, "The Making of an American Prophet: Emerson, His Audiences, and the Rise of the Culture Industry in Nineteenth-Century America," *American Historical Review*, XCII (1987), 597–620.

22. Robert E. Spiller, ed., *Selected Essays, Lectures, and Poems of Ralph Waldo Emerson* (New York, 1965), 211.

23. The quote about 'no history; only biography' is drawn from Emerson's essay on "History." The other quotes are from "Self-Reliance."

24. Tyler, *Freedom's Ferment*; Cross, *Burned-Over District*; Lori D. Ginzberg, *Women and the Work of Benevolence: Morality, Politics, and Class in the 19th-Century United States* (New Haven, Conn., 1990). On utopian communities, see Carl J. Guarneri, *The Utopian Alternative: Fourierism in Nineteenth-Century America* (Ithaca, N.Y., 1991); Robert Fogerty, *Dictionary of American Communal and Utopian History* (Westport, Conn., 1980); Edward Spann, *Brotherly Tomorrows: Movements for a Cooperative Society, 1820–1920* (New York, 1988).

25. Henry David Thoreau, *Walden* (1854), in *Thoreau: Walden and Other Writings*, ed. Joseph Wood Krutch (New York, 1962), 109; Lewis O. Saum, *The Popular Mood of Pre-Civil War America* (Westport, Conn., 1980), argues that Americans were less optimistic during these years than most historians have suggested. See also T. Scott Miyakawa, *Protestants and Pioneers: Individualism and Conformity on the American Frontier* (Chicago, 1964); Robert Gross, "Culture and Cultivation: Agriculture and Society in Thoreau's Concord," *Journal of American History*, LXIX (1982), 42–61; Gross, "Transcendentalism and Urbanism: Concord, Boston, and the Wider World," *Journal of American Studies*, XVIII (1984), 361–81.

26. Thomas Jefferson, "Autobiography," in *The Writings of Thomas Jefferson*, ed., Andrew A. Lipscomb, 18 vols. (Washington, D.C., 1903), I, 3; Garry Wills, *Inventing America: Jefferson's Declaration of Independence* (New York, 1978), 176–80; Joyce Appleby, "What Is Still American in the Political Philosophy of Thomas Jefferson?" WMQ, 3d Ser., XXXIX (1982), 287–309; Appleby, "Jefferson and His Complex Legacy," in *Jeffersonian Legacies*, ed. Peter S. Onuf (Charlottesville, Va., 1993), 1–16; Douglas L. Wilson, "Jefferson and the Republic of Letters," in ibid., 50–76; Daniel Boorstin, *The Lost World of Thomas Jefferson* (New York, 1948); Drew R. McCoy, *The Elusive Republic: Political Economy in Jeffersonian America* (Chapel Hill, N.C., 1980), 13–16; Richard Ellis, "The Political Economy of Thomas Jefferson," in *Thomas Jefferson: The Man, His World, His Influence*, ed. Lally Weymouth (London, 1973), 81–95. Peter S. Onuf, "The Scholars' Jefferson," WMQ, 3d Ser., L (1993), 671–99, surveys recent writing on Jefferson. More broadly, Joyce E. Chaplin, *An Anx-*

ious Pursuit: Agricultural Innovation and Modernity in the Lower South, 1730–1815 (Chapel Hill, N.C., 1993) 23–65, discusses ideas of progress in the Lower South. May, *Enlightenment in America*, 133–49, 244–50, examines the climate of opinion in the southern colonies.

27. Wills, *Inventing America*, quotation on 374; Michael P. Zuckert, "Self-Evident Truth and the Declaration of Independence," *Review of Politics*, XLIX (1987), 319–39.

28. James Madison, *The Federalist*, no. 14; Gaillard Hunt, *Life of James Madison* (New York, 1902), 4–5; Harold Schultz, *James Madison* (New York, 1970), 16–19; Esmond Wright, "Great Little Madison: Father of Constitution," *Proceedings of the British Academy*, LXVII (1981), 229–30.

29. Thomas Jefferson, *Notes on the State of Virginia* (1787; rpt., Chapel Hill, N.C., 1954), quotes from query 8, and also see queries 14 and 18; Records of the Constitutional Convention, June 6, 1787, in *The Mind of the Founder: Sources of the Political Thought of James Madison*, ed. Marvin Meyers (Indianapolis, Ind., 1973), 102; Drew R. McCoy, *The Last of the Fathers: James Madison and the Republican Legacy* (New York, 1989), 260, 283–84, 305; Clement Eaton, *A History of the Old South: The Emergence of a Reluctant Nation*, 3d ed. (New York, 1975), 369; William W. Freehling, "The Founding Fathers and Slavery," *American Historical Review*, LXXVII (1972), 81–93; Robert E. Shallope, "Thomas Jefferson's Republicanism and Antebellum Southern Thought," *Journal of Southern History*, XLII (1976), 537–45.

30. Jefferson and Lafayette quoted in McCoy, *Last of the Fathers*, 269–70; Ira Berlin, "Time, Space, and the Evolution of Afro-American Society in British Mainland North America," *American Historical Review*, LXXXV (1989), 44–78. Several writers have been highly critical of Jefferson's position on slavery. See Robert McColley, *Slavery and Jeffersonian Virginia* (Urbana, Ill., 1964, 2d ed, 1973); Paul Finkleman, "Jefferson and Slavery: 'Treason Against the Hopes of the World,' " in *Jeffersonian Legacies*, 181–221; William Cohen, "Thomas Jefferson and the Problem of Slavery," *Journal of American History*, LVI (1969), 503–26; David Grimstead, "Anglo-American Racism and Phillis Wheatley's 'Sable Veil,' 'Length'ned Chain,' and 'Knitted Hearth,' " in *Women in the Age of the American Revolution*, ed. Ronald Hoffman and Peter J. Albert (Charlottesville, Va., 1989), 338–444. For a recent defense of Jefferson on the slavery issue, see Douglas L. Wilson, "Thomas Jefferson and the Character Issue," *The Atlantic*, CCLXX (Nov. 1992), 57–74.

31. John Lynch, *The Spanish-American Revolutions, 1808–1826* (New York, 1973), 83–86, 154–56, 189–93, 288–89, 340. In many instances slavery in Latin America was replaced by a form of peonage. More broadly, on the changing outlook of the South, David M. Potter, *The Impending Crisis, 1848–1861* (New York , 1976); Charles Sydnor, *The Development of Southern Sectionalism, 1819–1848* (Baton Rouge, La, 1948); Don. E. Fehrenbacher, *The South and Three Sectional Crises* (Baton Rouge, La., 1980); William J. Cooper, Jr., *The South and the Politics of Slavery, 1828–1856* (Baton Rouge, La., 1978).

32. Among the many works taking this point of view, see W. J. Cash, *The Mind of the South* (New York, 1941), 59–99; William R. Taylor, *Cavalier and Yankee: The Old South and American National Character* (New York, 1957), 46–55, 177–201; Allen Tate, *Essays of Four Decades* (New York, 1970), 535–92; Louis D. Rubin, Jr., *The Writer in the South: Studies in a Literary Community*

(Athens, Ga., 1972); Rubin, *William Elliott Shoots a Bear: Essays on the Southern Literary Imagination* (Baton Rouge, La., 1975); C. Hugh Holman, *The Roots of Southern Writing: Essays on the Literature of the American South* (Athens, Ga., 1972), 87–95; Lewis P. Simpson, *The Man of Letters in New England and the South: Essays on the Literary Vocation in America* (Baton Rouge, La., 1973), 201–28.

33. Eugene D. Genovese, *The Slaveholders' Dilemma: Freedom and Progress in Southern Conservative Thought, 1820–1860* (Columbia, S.C., 1992), 2.

34. Michael O'Brien, *Rethinking the South: Essays in Intellectual History* (Baltimore, 1988), 37; James Oakes, *The Ruling Race: A History of American Slaveholders* (New York, 1982), argues that between the colonial era and the Civil War the outlook of the slaveholders shifted from paternalism to liberal capitalism.

35. While a complete list of recent works on southern intellectuals would run many pages, among the more important books are James O. Farmer, Jr., *The Metaphysical Confederacy: James Henley Thornwell and the Synthesis of Southern Values* (Macon, Ga., 1986); Elisabeth Muhlennfeld, *Mary Boykin Chesnut: A Biography* (Baton Rouge, La., 1981); John McCardell, *The Idea of a Southern Nation: Southern Nationalists and Southern Nationalism, 1830–1860* (New York, 1979); William B. McCash, *Thomas R. R. Cobb (1823–1862): The Making of a Southern Nationalist* (Macon, Ga., 1983); Drew Gilpin Faust, *A Sacred Circle: The Dilemma of the Intellectual in the Old South, 1840–1860* (Baltimore, 1977); Faust, *James Henry Hammond and the Old South: A Design for Mastery* (Baton Rouge, La., 1982); E. Brooks Holifield, *The Gentlemen Theologians: American Theology in Southern Culture, 1795–1860* (Durham, N.C., 1978); Robert M. Calhoon, *Evangelicals and Conservatives in the Early South, 1740–1861* (Columbia, S.C., 1988).

36. Genovese acknowledges "the slaveholders displayed a conflicted attitude toward historical progress," in *Slaveholders Dilemma*, 5; and see Allen Kaufman, *Capitalism, Slavery, and Republican Values: Antebellum Political Economists, 1819–1848* (Austin, Tex., 1982), 37–81, 82–103; more broadly, consult David Brion Davis, *Slavery and Human Progress* (New York, 1984).

37. O'Brien, *Rethinking the South*, 57–83, quotes on 66, 67.

38. "Thomas R. Dew," DAB; Thomas R. Dew, "Review of the Debate in the Virginia Legislature, 1831–32" [1832], in *The Pro-slavery Argument* (1852; rpt., New York, 1968), 287–490, quotes from 342 and 354–55. Also on Dew see Eugene D. Genovese, *Western Civilization Through Slaveholding Eyes: The Social and Historical Thought of Thomas Roderick Dew* (New Orleans, 1986); Kaufman, *Capitalism, Slavery, and Republican Values*, 82–103; Alison Goodyear Freehling, *Drift Toward Dissolution: The Virginia Slavery Debate of 1831–1832* (Baton Rouge, La., 1982), 196–263. Some historians have noted that proslavery arguments were present in the South before the 1830s. See McColley, *Slavery and Jeffersonian Virginia;* Drew Gilpin Faust, "The Proslavery Argument in History," in *The Ideology of Slavery: Proslavery Thought in the Antebellum South, 1830–1860,* ed. Drew Gilpin Faust (Baton Rouge, La., 1981), 1–20. Lary E. Tise, "The Interregional Appeal of Proslavery Thought: An Ideological Profile of the Antebellum American Clergy," *Plantation Society in the Americas,* I (1979), 58–72, and Tise, *Proslavery: A History of the Defense of Slavery in America, 1701–1840* (Athens, Ga., 1987), finds exponents of proslavery views in both the North and South.

39. Dew, "Review of the Debate," quotes on 459 and 359.

40. Ibid., 478–79.

41. Eugene D. Genovese, "The Southern Slaveholders' View of the Middle Ages," in *Medievalism in American Culture*, ed. Bernard Rosenthal and Paul E. Szarmach (Binghamton, N.Y., 1989), 31–52, quote on 41; Genovese, *Slaveholders' Dilemma*, 4–6, 13–18, 96–98.

42. George Fitzhugh, *Sociology for the South, or the Failure of Free Society* (1854; rpt., New York, 1965), quote on 179; more generally on Fitzhugh, see Eugene D. Genovese, *The World the Slaveholders Made: Two Essays in Interpretation* (New York, 1969), 114–244; and Harvey Wish, *George Fitzhugh: Propagandist of the Old South* (Baton Rouge, La., 1943).

43. Quotes from Fitzhugh, *Sociology for the South*, 35; George Fitzhugh, *Cannibals All!; or, Slaves Without Masters*, ed. C. Vann Woodward (1857; rpt., Cambridge, Mass., 1960), 18.

44. Quotes from Fitzhugh, *Cannibals All!*, 103; Fitzhugh, *Sociology for the South*, 206.

45. Quote from Fitzhugh, *Sociology for the South*, 157.

46. Thomas, "Romantic Reform in America," 656–81; Anne C. Loveland, *Southern Evangelicals and the Social Order, 1800–1860* (Baton Rouge, La., 1980), 159–85; Mitchell Snay, *Gospel of Disunion: Religion and Separatism in the Antebellum South* (New York, 1993); Mathews, *Religion in the Old South*, 66–80; John B. Boles, *The Great Revival, 1787–1805* (Lexington, Ky., 1972), 193–95; Holifield, *Gentlemen Theologians*; Stanley K. Schultz, "Temperance Reform in the Antebellum South: Social Control and Urban Order," *South Atlantic Quarterly*, LXXXIII (1984), 323–39; John C. Dann, "Humanitarian Reform and Organized Benevolence in the Southern United States, 1780–1830" (Ph.D. diss., College of William and Mary, 1975); Joanne V. Hawks, "Social Reform in the Cotton Kingdom, 1830–60" (Ph.D. diss., Univ. of Mississippi, 1970); Ian R. Tyrell, "Drink and Temperance in the Antebellum South: An Overview and Interpretation," *Journal of Southern History*, XLVIII (1982), 485–510. For a discussion of the literature of reform in the South, see Drew Gilpin Faust, "The Peculiar South Revisited: White Society, Culture, and Politics in the Antebellum Period, 1800–1860," in *Interpreting Southern History: Historiographical Essays in Honor of Sanford W. Higginbotham*, ed. John B. Boles and Evelyn T. Nolen (Baton Rouge, La., 1987), 92–96.

47. "Roland-Michel Barrin, comte de La Galissonière," DCB, III, 26–32; Adolph B. Benson, ed., *Peter Kalm's Travels in North America: The English Version of 1770*, 2 vols. (1937; rpt., New York, 1966), II, 504 (Sept. 11, 1749), 374 (July 2, 1749). Carl Linnaeus, who taught Kalm botany, was renowned for his work classifying plants and animals.

48. [Antoine-Denis Raudot], *Letters from North America*, trans. Ivy Alice Dickson (Belleville, Ont., 1980); Jean-Claude Dubé, "Les intendants de la Nouvelle-France et la république des lettres," *Revue d'histoire de l'Amérique française*, XXIX (1975–76), 31–48, quote from *Gazette of Holland* on 31; "Claude-Thomas Dupuy," DCB, II, 207–13; Jean-Claude Dubé, *Claude Thomas Dupuy: intendant de la Nouvelle-France* (Montreal, 1969), 317–54; John A. Dickinson, "Un aperçu de la vie culturelle en Nouvelle-France: l'examen de trois bibliothèques privées," *Revue de l'Université d'Ottawa*, XLIV (1974), 453–66.

49. Allan Greer, *Peasant, Lord, and Merchant: Rural Society in Three Quebec Parishes, 1740–1840* (Toronto, 1985), 18, 115–18; Greer, "L'habitant, la paroisse rurale et la politique locale au xviii-e siècle: quelques cas dans la vallée du Richelieu," Société canadienne d'histoire de l'église catholique, *Sessions d'études,* XLVII (1980), 19–33; Pontbriand is quoted in "Dubreil de Pontbriand, Henri-Marie," DCB, III, 197; Cornelius Jaenen, *The Role of the Church in New France* (Toronto, 1976); Amédée Gosselin, *L'Eglise du Canada: depuis Monseigneur de Laval jusqu'à la Conquête,* 3 vols. (Quebec City, 1911–14), 24–36, 237–58, 431–34, 522–52; Marcel Trudel, "La servitude de l'Eglise catholique du Canada Français sous le régime anglais," *Communications historiques/Historical Papers* (1963), 42–64; John S. Moir, *The Church in the British Era* (Toronto, 1972); for a different viewpoint on the relationship between state and church, Hilda Neatby, "Servitude de l'Eglise catholique: A Reconsideration," *Canadian Catholic Historical Association, Study Sessions* (1969), 9–25.

50. Micheline Dumont et al., *Quebec Women: A History,* trans. Roger Gannon and Rosalind Gill (Toronto, 1987), 103–7.

51. Greer, *Peasant, Lord and Merchant,* 118–19; Allan Greer, *The Patriots and the People: The Rebellion of 1837 in Rural Lower Canada* (Toronto, 1993), 56–68; Richard Chabot, *Le curé de campagne et la contestation locale au Québec de 1791 aux troubles de 1837–1838* (Montreal, 1975).

52. Jean-Paul Bernard, *Les Rouges: libéralisme, nationalisme et anticléricalisme au milieu du xix-e siècle* (Montreal, 1971), 321; Mason Wade, *The French Canadians, 1760–1967,* rev. ed., 2 vols. (Toronto, 1968); see also the essays in *France et Canada française du xvi-e au xx-e siècle,* ed. Claude Galarneau and Elzéar Lavoie (Quebec, 1966); Philippe Sylvain, "Libéralisme et ultramontanisme au Canada française: affrontement idéologique et doctrinal (1840–1965)," in *The Shield of Achilles/Le bouclier d'Achille,* ed. W. L. Morton (Toronto, 1968), 111–38, 220–55.

53. Before 1950 this view dominated French-Canadian historiography. See, for example, Lionel Groulx, *La Confédération canadienne* (Montreal, 1918); Théophile Hudon, *L'Institut canadien de Montréal et l'affaire Guibord* (Montreal, 1938). Some writers have continued these themes; see Gilles Chaussé, *Jean-Jacques Lartigue: premier évêque de Montréal* (Montreal, 1980).

54. Wade, *French Canadians,* 127–35; Fernand Ouellet, *Lower Canada, 1791–1840: Social Change and Nationalism* (Toronto, 1980), 173–76, 190–97, 214–24, quote on 224; Greer, *Patriots and the People,* 120–36, 190, 203–10; Fernand Ouellet, *Papineau* (Quebec, 1959), 100–1, quotes Papineau on the Declaration of Independence; this quote is repeated and translated in Denis Monière, *Ideologies in Quebec: The Historical Development,* trans. Richard Howard (Toronto, 1981), 100.

55. Gilles Chaussé, "Lartigue et Lamennais," *University of Ottawa Quarterly,* LVII (1987), 81–86; Fernand Ouellet, "La vallée du Saint-Laurent au temps des paroles d'un croyant," ibid., LVII, 87–99. The French philosopher's full name was Hugues Félicité Robert de Lamennais; some writers use Félicité as a first name.

56. "Jean-Jacques Lartigue," DCB, VII, 485–90; Fernand Ouellet, "Le mandement de Mgr. Lartigue et la réaction libérale," *Bulletin de recherches historiques* (1952); J.-P. Langlois, "L'Eglise face aux patriotes en 1837–1838,"

Société canadienne d'histoire de l'Eglise catholique, session d'études (1984); Chaussé, *Jean-Jacques Lartigue,* 137–45, 167–226; Nadia Fahmy-Eid, "Ultramontanisme, idéologie et classes sociales," *Revue d'histoire de l'Amérique française,* XXIX (1975), 49–68.

57. Biographies of Jean-Jacques Lartigue and Ignace Bourget, DCB, VII, 485–90, IX, 94–105. The number of Catholics per priest in Lower Canada/Quebec declined from 1,375 in 1810 to 1,080 in 1851 and 652 in 1911. The number of Catholics per member of religious order over the same timespan fell from 912 to 722 to 96. Fernand Ouellet, "The Quiet Revolution: A Turning Point," in *Towards a Just Society: The Trudeau Years,* ed. Tom Axworthy and Pierre Elliot Trudeau (Markham, Ont., 1990), 326; W. J. Eccles, "The Role of the Church in New France," in *Essays on New France,* ed. W. J. Eccles (Toronto, 1987), 26–37; Wade, *French Canadians,* I, 341–42; Léon Pouliot, *Monseigneur Bourget et son temps,* 5 vols. (Montreal, 1955–77).

58. Jacques Monet, S.J., "French-Canadian Nationalism and the Challenge of Ultramontanism" (orig. pub. in *Canadian Historical Association Historical Papers* [1966]), in *Canadian History before Confederation: Essays and Interpretations,* 2d ed., ed. J. M. Bumstead (Georgetown, Ont., 1979), 416–24; "Ignace Bourget" DCB, XI, 101, quotes the bishop; Wade, *French Canadians,* I, 341–46; Fernand Ouellet, *Economic and Social History of Quebec: 1760–1850:* Structures *and* Conjonctures (Ottawa, 1980), 382, 387, 602–3; Ouellet, *Lower Canada,* 168–71; Philippe Sylvain, "Liberalisme et ultramontanisme," 111–38; Bernard, *Les Rouges;* and see the documents in *Histoire des idées au Québec: des troubles de 1837 au référendum de 1980,* ed. Georges Vincenthier (Montreal, 1983), 43–59.

59. Ouellet, *Lower Canada,* 122–26; Catherine L. Cleverdon, *The Woman Suffrage Movement in Canada* (Toronto, 1950, 1974), 214–16; Allan Greer, "La république des hommes: les patriotes de 1837 face aux femmes," *Revue d'histoire de l'Amérique française,* XLIV (1991), 507–28; Greer, *Patriots and the People,* 197–218. An 1834 law barring women from voting was vetoed by the Crown. This measure—even though disallowed—seems to have sharply reduced the participation of women in politics. Constance Backhouse, "Married Women's Property Law in Nineteenth-Century Canada," *Law and History Review,* VI (1988), 211–57; Backhouse, *Petticoats and Prejudice: Woman and Law in Nineteenth-Century Canada* (Toronto, 1980), 176–80.

60. "François-Xavier Garneau," DCB, IX, 297–99; Wade, *French Canadians,* I, 285, quotes Garneau.

61. "Garneau," DCB, IX, 299–301; quotes in Wade, *French Canadians,* I, 287; Serge Gagnon, *Quebec and Its Historians, 1840 to 1920,* trans. Yves Brunelle (Montreal, 1982), 9–43.

62. "Garneau," DCB, IX, 301–5; Wade, *French Canadians,* I, 287–89. Garneau's contemporaries and historians have debated whether Garneau truly changed his views or simply was forced by Church pressure to take a pro-clerical stance. Gagnon, *Quebec and Its Historians,* 38–43.

63. Quoted in Taylor, *Cavalier and Yankee,* 267.

64. In particular, see Andrew Carnegie, *Triumphant Democracy* (New York, 1886); Carnegie, *The Gospel of Wealth and other Timely Essays,* ed. Edward C. Kirkland (1900; rpt., Cambridge, Mass., 1962).

Chapter 9. The Gap Widens: 1860s to 1940

1. Boucher's account is taken from Jacques Rouillard, *Ah les Etats: les travailleurs canadiens-français dans l'industrie textile de la Nouvelle-Angleterre d'après le témoignage des derniers migrants* (Montreal, 1985), 87–91. I have translated Boucher's remarks from the French.

2. Andrew Carnegie, *The Gospel of Wealth and Other Timely Essays*, ed. Edward C. Kirkland (1900; rpt., Cambridge, Mass., 1962), 23; Carnegie, *Triumphant Democracy* (New York, 1886); Carnegie, *The Empire of Business* (Garden City, N.Y., 1902), 3–18, 125–50. John G. Cawelti, *Apostles of the Self-Made Man* (Chicago, 1965), 167–99, discusses Carnegie and the "Philosophers of Success."

3. Irvin G. Wyllie, *The Self-Made Man in America: The Myth of Rags to Riches* (New York, 1954), 126, quote on 42–43; Gary Scharnhorst with Jack Bales, *The Lost Life of Horatio Alger, Jr.* (Bloomington, Ind., 1985), 150–51; Edwin P. Hoyt, *Horatio's Boys: The Life and Works of Horatio Alger, Jr.* (Radnor, Pa., 1974), 1–48; more broadly, for a discussion of children's stories and the entrepreneurial spirit, David C. McClelland, *The Achieving Society* (Princeton, N.J., 1961), 70–79.

4. Conwell quoted in Agnes Rush, *Russell H. Conwell and His Work* (Philadelphia, 1923), 327; along with Conwell's "Acres of Diamonds," two didactic works that enjoyed widespread popularity around the turn of the century were Elbert Hubbard, *A Message to Garcia* (East Aurora, N.Y., 1901), and George H. Lorimer, *Letters from a Self-Made Merchant to His Son* (Boston, 1902). See John Tebbell, *George Horace Lorimer and the Saturday Evening Post* (Garden City, N.Y., 1948).

5. See, for example, Henry James, *The American* (1877), and William Dean Howells, *The Rise of Silas Lapham* (1885); neither author, however, was unreserved in his praise of self-made men. Wyllie, *Self-Made Man*, 122–23. A separate question is, How realistic was the success myth? Studies of the business elites of the 1870s and 1901–10 indicate that most leaders came from middle-class or upper-class families. For the 1870s elite only 33 percent had fathers who were farmers or workers, while 64 percent of the fathers were businessmen or professionals. For the elite of 1901–10 a mere 16 percent came from farmer or worker homes, while 77 percent came from the homes of businessmen and professionals. Affluence to riches was far more likely than rags to riches. Frances W. Gregory and Irene D. Neu, "The American Industrial Elite in the 1870s: Their Social Origins," in *Men in Business: Essays on the Historical Role of the Entrepreneur*, ed. William Miller (New York, 1952, 1962), 193–94; William Miller, "The Business Elite in Business Bureaucracies: Careers of Top Executives in the Early Twentieth Century," in ibid., 286–305; William Miller, "The Recruitment of the American Business Elite," in ibid., 329–37.

6. Wyllie, *Self-Made Man*, 168–72; Richard M. Huber, *The American Idea of Success* (New York, 1971), 165–76, 186–209; Cawelti, *Apostles of the Self-Made Man*, 201–36; and see Bruce Barton, *The Man Nobody Knows* (Indianapolis, Ind., 1925), 103–57, in which he portrays Jesus as "The Founder of Modern Business."

7. This account of the rise of big business follows the broad outlines of the magisterial work by Alfred D. Chandler, Jr., *The Visible Hand: The Managerial Revolution in American Business* (Cambridge, Mass., 1977).

8. Ida M. Tarbell, *The History of the Standard Oil Company*, 2 vols. (New York, 1904), II, 31–62, 437; Allan Nevins, *Study in Power: John D. Rockefeller, Industrialist and Philanthropist*, 2 vols. (New York, 1953), I, 56–76, 132–267; and see the essays in Otto Mayr and Robert C. Post, eds., *Yankee Enterprise* (Washington, D.C., 1981).

9. David F. Noble, *America by Design: Science, Technology, and the Rise of Corporate Capitalism* (New York, 1977), 20–32; Chandler, *Visible Hand*, 345–76; Olivier Zunz, *Making America Corporate, 1870–1920* (Chicago, 1990), 37–66.

10. Chandler, *Visible Hand*, 331–44, 361–69, 426–33, 460–63; Thomas K. McCraw and Forest Reinhardt, "Losing to Win: U.S. Steel's Pricing, Investment Decisions, and Market Share, 1901–1938," JEH, XLIX (1989), 593–619; Alfred P. Sloan, *Adventures of a White-Collar Man*, with Boyden Sparkes (Garden City, N.Y., 1941), 91–166; Sloan, *My Years with General Motors* (Garden City, N.Y., 1963), 42–57, 149–68; Harold C. Livesay, "Entrepreneurial Persistence Through the Bureaucratic Age," in *Managing Big Business: Essays from the Business History Review*, ed. Richard S. Tedlow and Richard R. John, Jr. (Boston, 1986), 107–35.

11. Nathan Rosenberg, "Technological Change in the Machine Tool Industry, 1840–1910," in *Perspectives on Technology*, ed. Nathan Rosenberg (New York, 1976), 9–31; Chandler, *Visible Hand*, 269–82, 365–66; Robert Averitt, *The Dual Economy: The Dynamics of American Industry Structure* (New York, 1968), 9–21; Jeremy Atack, "Industrial Structure and the Emergence of the Modern Industrial Corporation," *Explorations in Economic History*, XXII (1985), 29–52; Donald R. Hoke, *Ingenious Yankees: The Rise of the American System of Manufactures in the Private Sector* (New York, 1990), 258–66; Edwin A. Battison, *Muskets to Mass Production: The Men & the Times That Shaped American Manufacturing* (Windsor, Vt., 1976), 6–19, 27–31.

12. C. Vann Woodward, *Reunion and Reaction* (Boston, 1951), 54–61. Arguing that the Civil War accelerated industrialization are Charles A. Beard and Mary R. Beard, *The Rise of American Civilization* (New York, 1930), 166–210; and Louis M. Hacker, *The Triumph of American Capitalism* (New York, 1940), 339–45, 361–73. Among those questioning these assertions are Thomas C. Cochran, "Did the Civil War Retard Industrialization?" *Mississippi Valley Historical Review*, XLVIII (1961), 191–201; Stanley Coben, "Northeastern Business and Radical Reconstruction: A Re-examination," ibid., XLVI (1959), 67–90; and Stanley L. Engerman, "The Economic Impact of the Civil War," in *The Reinterpretation of American Economic History*, ed. Robert W. Fogel and Stanley L. Engerman (New York, 1971), 369–79. Stephen Salsbury, "The Effects of the Civil War on American Industrial Development," in *The Economic Impact of American Civil War*, ed. Ralph Andreano (Cambridge, Mass., 1962), 161–68, comes to a balanced conclusion. Several key essays on this topic are reprinted in the Andreano collection.

13. Gilbert C. Fite, *The Farmers' Frontier, 1865–1900* (New York, 1966), 75–94; Earl W. Hayter, *The Troubled Farmer, 1850–1900: Rural Adjustment to Industrialism* (Dekalb, Ill., 1968), 3–14, 145–211; J. Sanford Rikoon, *Threshing in the Midwest, 1820–1940: A Study of Traditional Culture and Technological Change* (Bloomington, Ind., 1988), 20, 58; U.S. Bureau of the Census, *Statistical Abstract of the United States, 1936* (Washington, D.C., 1936), 580, 597; Paul-

André Linteau, René Durocher, and Jean-Claude Robert, *Quebec: A History, 1867–1929*, trans. Robert Chodos (Toronto, 1983), 384; and see the sources in note 64 below.

14. Key works on corporate liberalism include James Weinstein, *The Corporate Ideal in the Liberal State: 1900–1918* (Boston, 1968); Noble, *America by Design*; Martin J. Sklar, *The Corporate Reconstruction of American Capitalism, 1890–1916: The Market, the Law, and Politics* (New York, 1988); Gabriel Kolko, *The Triumph of Conservatism: A Reinterpretation of American History, 1900–1916* (New York, 1963). Also see Ellis W. Hawley, "The Discovery and Study of a 'Corporate Liberalism,' " *Business History Review*, LII (1978), 309–20; Kim McQuaid, "Corporate Liberalism in the American Business Community, 1920–1940," ibid., LII (1978), 342–68.

15. Weinstein, *Corporate Ideal*, 3–39, and passim.

16. John A. Garraty, *Right-Hand Man: The Life of George W. Perkins* (New York, 1960), 15–235; Robert Ozanne, *A Century of Labor-Management Relations at McCormick and International Harvester* (Madison, Wis., 1967), 71–95, quote on 73.

17. Ronald W. Schatz, *The Electrical Workers: A History of Labor at General Electric and Westinghouse, 1923–60* (Urbana, Ill., 1983), 10–14, quote on 14; David Loth, *Swope of G.E.: The Story of Gerard Swope and General Electric in American Business* (New York, 1958), 17–38, 80–92; Noble, *America by Design*, 279–80; Richard Edwards, *Contested Terrain: The Transformation of the Workplace in the Twentieth Century* (New York, 1979), 105–7; June C. Nash, *From Tank Town to High Tech: The Clash of Community and Industrial Cycles* (Albany, N.Y., 1989), 65–66, 115–16.

18. Schatz, *Electrical Workers*, 53–59, quotes on 56; William E. Leuchtenburg, *Franklin Roosevelt and the New Deal, 1932–1940* (New York, 1963), 56–57.

19. Schatz, *Electrical Workers*, 12–13; Thomas Ferguson, "Industrial Conflict and the Coming of the New Deal: The Triumph of Multinational Liberalism in America," in *The Rise and Fall of the New Deal Order, 1930–1980*, ed. Steve Fraser and Gary Gerstle (Princeton, N.J., 1989), 3–31.

20. Kolko, *Triumph of Conservatism*, 305; Sidney Kaplan, "Social Engineers as Saviours: Effects of World War I on Some American Liberals," *Journal of the History of Ideas*, XVII (1956), 347–69; Samuel Hays, "The Politics of Reform in Municipal Government in the Progressive Era," *Pacific Northwest Quarterly*, LV (1964), 157–69; Hays, *Conservatism and the Gospel of Efficiency: The Progressive Conservation Movement, 1890–1920* (Cambridge, Mass., 1959), 2–3; Robert H. Wiebe, *Businessmen and Reform: A Study of the Progressive Movement* (Cambridge, Mass., 1962), 6–15.

21. Weinstein, *Corporate Ideal*, quotes on 47, 54, 152–53. Response to pressure often meant half-hearted support for reform. Few liberal executives allowed their factories to be organized. Most, including Perkins and Swope, felt that *their* workers had no need of a militant union. Ozanne, *A Century of Labor-Management Relations*, 110–13; Nash, *From Tank Town to High Tech*, 115–16; Schatz, *Electrical Workers*, 170. More broadly, on the evolving relationship between government, business, and labor, see Steve Fraser, "The 'Labor Question,' " in *Rise and Fall of the New Deal Order*, 55–84; David Montgomery, *The Fall of the House of Labor: The Workplace, the State, and American Labor Activism, 1865–1925* (New York, 1987).

22. Theda Skocpol, *Protecting Soldiers and Mothers: The Political Origins of Social Policy in the United States* (Cambridge, Mass., 1992), 526; Molly Ladd-Taylor, *Mother-Work: Women, Child Welfare, and the State, 1890–1930* (Champaign, Ill., 1993), 3–7; Lori Ginzberg, *Women and the Work of Benevolence* (New Haven, Conn., 1990), 174–213; see the valuable essays in *Gender, Class, Race and Reform in the Progressive Era*, ed. Noralee Frankel and Nancy S. Dye (Lexington, Ky., 1991); Robyn Muncy, *Creating a Female Dominion for Reform* (New York, 1991), esp. xi-xii; Kathleen D. McCarthy, *Women's Culture* (Chicago, 1991), esp. xii-xvi; Kathleen D. McCarthy, "Parallel Power Structures: Women and the Voluntary Sphere," in *Lady Bountiful Revisited: Women, Philanthropy, and Power*, ed. Kathleen D. McCarthy (New Brunswick, N.J., 1990), 1–31.

23. Daniel Nelson, *Frederick W. Taylor and the Rise of Scientific Management* (Madison, Wis., 1980), 21–34, 68–100; Chandler, *Visible Hand*, 275–78, quote on 276. Daniel Nelson, "Scientific Management and the Workplace, 1920–1935," in *Masters to Managers: Historical and Comparative Perspectives on American Employers*, ed. Sanford M. Jacoby (New York, 1991), 74–89, makes clear that while many corporations were influenced by "scientific management," few adhered strictly to the principles of Taylorism.

24. Zunz, *Making America Corporate*, quotes on 78; Alfred D. Chandler, Jr., and Stephen Salsbury, *Pierre S. DuPont and the Making of the Modern Corporation* (New York, 1971), 104–20, 428; Gerald Colby, *DuPont Dynasty* (Secaucus, N.J., 1974, 1984), 151–202; Robert Cuff, "Private Success, Public Problems: The DuPont Corporation and World War I," *Canadian Review of American Studies*, XX (1989), 173–189; Robert F. Burk, *The Corporate State and the Broker State: The DuPonts and American National Politics, 1925–1940* (Cambridge, Mass., 1990), 143–69.

25. For overviews of the debate between "Continuitarians" and "Discontinuitarians" see Jack Temple Kirby, "Passion and Discontinuities: A Semicycle of *Mind, 1941–1991*," in *W. J. Cash and the Minds of the South*, ed. Paul D. Escott (Baton Rouge, La., 1992), 207–25; and Harold D. Woodman, "Economic Reconstruction and the Rise of the New South, 1865–1900," in *Interpreting Southern History: Historiographical Essays in Honor of Sanford W. Higginbotham*, ed. John B. Boles and Evelyn Thomas Nolen (Baton Rouge, La., 1987), 254–307. Also consult Jonathan M. Wiener, "Class Structure and Economic Development in the American South, 1865–1955," *American Historical Review*, LXXXIV (1979), 970–92; "Comments" by Robert Higgs, ibid., 993–97, and Harold D. Woodman, ibid., 997–1001; and Wiener's "Reply," 1002–6.

26. Various historians (who do not always agree with each other) emphasize market forces and the role of a new middle class in shaping the South. Among those focusing on market forces are Stephen J. DeCanio, *Agriculture in the Postbellum South: The Economics of Production and Supply* (Cambridge, Mass., 1975); Joseph D. Reid, Jr., "Sharecropping as an Understandable Market Response: The Post-bellum South," JEH, XXXIII (1973), 106–30; and Robert Higgs, *Competition and Coercion: Blacks in the American Economy, 1865–1914* (New York, 1977). David L. Carlton, *Mill and Town in South Carolina, 1880–1920* (Baton Rouge, La., 1982), 8–9, 82–128, 271, discusses the role of the new, commercially minded, "town classes"; Lacy K. Ford, "Rednecks and Merchants: Economic Development and Social Tensions in the South Carolina Upcountry, 1865–1900," *Journal of American History*, LXXI (1984), 294–318,

also sees a "new economic elite" (p. 318); as does Justin Fuller, "Alabama Business Leaders: 1865–1900," *Alabama Review*, XVI (1963), 279–86. C. Vann Woodward, *Origins of the New South* (Baton Rouge, La., 1951), esp. 291–320, argues for the role of a new middle class. He also faults northerners for treating the South as a colonial economy. Pete Daniel, *Standing at the Crossroads: Southern Life in the Twentieth Century* (New York, 1986), emphasizes the colonial economy argument. Two important works generally accept the importance of market forces, but argue that distorting features kept the southern economy from operating efficiently. Gavin Wright, *Old South, New South: Revolutions in the Southern Economy since the Civil War* (New York, 1986), points to the impact of a closed labor market; Roger L. Ransom and Richard Sutch, *One Kind of Freedom: The Economic Consequences of Emancipation* (New York, 1977), notes the effects of racism on transactions in the South. For a fuller discussion of this historiography, see Woodman, "Economic Reconstruction," 273–78.

27. Among those arguing the case for continuity are Dwight B. Billings, Jr., *Planters and the Making of a "New South": Class, Politics, and Development in North Carolina, 1865–1900* (Chapel Hill, N.C., 1979); Jonathan M. Wiener, *Social Origins of the New South: Alabama, 1860–1885* (Baton Rouge, La., 1978); Jay R. Mandle, *Roots of Black Poverty: The Southern Plantation Economy after the Civil War* (Durham, N.C., 1978); Carl N. Degler, *Place over Time: The Continuity of Southern Distinctiveness* (Baton Rouge, La., 1977); and Michael Wayne, *The Reshaping of Plantation Society: The Natchez District, 1860–1880* (Baton Rouge, La., 1983).

28. Steven Hahn, "Class and State in Postemancipation Societies: Southern Planters in Comparative Perspective," *American Historical Review*, XCV (1990), 85.

29. W. J. Cash, *The Mind of the South* (New York, 1941), esp. 105–89, is a seminal work that examines these beliefs and values.

30. On the maincurrents (and crosscurrents) of southern literature between 1870 and 1910, Edward L. Ayers, *The Promise of the New South: Life after Reconstruction* (New York, 1992), 339–72; for changes in southern thought in later years, see Daniel J. Singal, *The War Within: From Victorian to Modernist Thought in the South, 1919–1945* (Chapel Hill, N.C., 1982).

31. These quotes are taken from Theodore L. Gross, *Thomas Nelson Page* (New York, 1967), 24, 27, 43–44.

32. Walter Hines Page, "The Rebuilding of Old Commonwealths," *Atlantic Monthly*, LXXXIX (1902), 651–61, quote on 654; John Milton Cooper, Jr., *Walter Hines Page: The Southerner as American, 1855–1918* (Chapel Hill, N.C., 1977), 35–37, 53–59, 87–89.

33. During this era African-American writers presented a very different view of the races and the South. In particular, see the works of Charles W. Chesnutt, who was born in the North but grew up in the South; as well as two northern blacks, Paul Laurence Dunbar and Frances W. Harper. See William L. Andrews, *The Literary Career of Charles W. Chesnutt* (Baton Rouge, La., 1980), 175–208; Hugh M. Gloster, *Negro Voices in American Fiction* (Chapel Hill, N.C., 1948), vii, 252–53; Ayers, *Promise of the New South*, 365–71.

34. *The New South: Writings and Speeches of Henry Grady* (Savannah, Ga., 1971), 18–29, 64–86, quote on 20; Harold E. Davis, *Henry Grady's New South: Atlanta, a Brave and Beautiful City* (Tuscaloosa, Ala., 1990), 111–82. Michael

O'Brien, *The Idea of the American South, 1920–1941* (Baltimore, 1979), 107–10, discusses "New South" writers who criticized Grady for adhering to the myths of an Old South.

35. Ransom and Sutch, *One Kind of Freedom*, 68–94, 120–48; Mandle, *The Roots of Black Poverty*, 44–46; Eric Foner, *Reconstruction: America's Unfinished Revolution, 1863–1877* (New York, 1988), 173–75; Wiener, "Class Structure and Economic Development," 973–76; Gerald David Jaynes, *Branches Without Roots: Genesis of the Black Working Class in the American South* (New York, 1986), 156–57; Gavin Wright, "The Economics and Politics of Slavery and Freedom in the U.S. South," in *The Meaning of Freedom: Economics, Politics, and Culture after Slavery*, ed. Frank McGlynn and Seymour Drescher (Pittsburgh, Pa., 1992), 90–99; William Cohen, *At Freedom's Edge: Black Mobility and the Southern White Quest for Racial Control, 1861–1915* (Baton Rouge, La., 1991), 3–43; Alan Conway, *The Reconstruction of Georgia* (Minneapolis, Minn., 1966), 109–30; Lewis Nicholas Wynne, *The Continuity of Cotton* (Macon, Ga., 1986), 90–92.

36. Mandle, *Roots of Black Poverty*, 44–51; C. O. Brannen, *Relation of Land Tenure to Plantation Organization*, U.S. Department of Agriculture, Department Bulletin No. 1269 (Oct. 1924), 42; Alfred H. Stone, "A Plantation Experiment," *Quarterly Journal of Economics*, XIX (1905), 270–87; Woodman, "Comment," 1000; Ray Stannard Baker, *Following the Color Line: American Negro Citizenship in the Progressive Era* (1908; rpt., New York, 1964), 76–78; Barbara Jeanne Fields, "The Nineteenth-Century American South: History and Theory," *Plantation Society*, II (1983), 24–25; Jay R. Mandle, "Black Economic Entrapment after Emancipation in the United States," in *The Meaning of Freedom*, 69–78. Harold D. Woodman, "Post-Civil War Southern Agriculture and the Law," *Agricultural History*, LIII (1979), 319–37, argues that the status of sharecroppers worsened during the last decades of the nineteenth century.

37. Theodore Rosengarten, *All God's Dangers: The Life of Nate Shaw* (New York, 1974), 102, 222; Charles Denby, *Indignant Heart: A Black Worker's Journal* (Montreal, 1979), 6–7.

38. Wright, *Old South, New South*, 52–54; Ransom and Sutch, *One Kind of Freedom*, 40–55, 98–99, 186–89, 283, quote on 161; U.S. Bureau of the Census, *Historical Statistics of the United States, Colonial Times to 1970*, 2 vols. (Washington, D.C., 1975), I, 517–18.

39. Rosengarten, *All God's Dangers*, 86, 194–96; Wright, *Old South, New South*, 159–64, 179.

40. See Chapter 6.

41. Wright, *Old South, New South*, 138–46; Jacquelyn Dowd Hall et al., *Like a Family: The Making of a Southern Cotton Mill World* (Chapel Hill, N.C., 1987), 37, 52, 114, 122–24, 183–236; Billings, *Planters and the Making of a "New South"*, 42–69; Cathy L. McHugh, *Mill Family: The Labor System in the Southern Cotton Textile Industry, 1880–1915* (New York, 1988), 6–10; I. A. Newby, *Plain Folk in the New South: Social Change and Cultural Persistence, 1880–1915* (Baton Rouge, La., 1989), 25–26, 117–229; Ronald D. Eller, *Miners, Millhands, and Mountaineers: Industrialization in the Appalachian South, 1880–1930* (Knoxville, Tenn., 1982), 86–127; Ayers, *Promise of the New South*, 104–31; J. Carlyle Sitterson, "Business Leaders in Post-Civil War North Carolina, 1865–1900," in *Studies in Southern History*, ed. J. Carlyle Sitterson (Chapel Hill, N.C.,

1957), 111–21. For a contrasting viewpoint, one that emphasizes market forces rather than class persistence as the key to understanding southern industrialization, David L. Carlton, "The Revolution from Above: The National Market and the Beginnings of Industrialization in North Carolina," *Journal of American History*, LXXVII (1990), 445–75. For recent trends in the study of southern textile mills (and challenges to notion of a docile labor force), see Robert H. Zieger, "Introduction," in *Race, Class, and Community in Southern Labor History*, ed. Gary M. Fink and Merl E. Reed (Tuscaloosa, Ala., 1994), 1–8; Bess Beatty, "Gender Relations in Southern Textiles: A Historiographical Overview," ibid., 9–16; David L. Carlton, "Paternalism and Southern Textile Labor: A Historiographical Review," ibid., 17–26; Gary R. Freeze, "Patriarchy Lost: The Preconditions for Paternalism in the Odell Cotton Mills of North Carolina, 1882–1900," ibid., 27–40.

42. John K. Winkler, *Tobacco Tycoon: The Story of James Buchanan Duke* (New York, 1942), 17–78, quotes on 38, 60; John Wilber Jenkins, *James B. Duke: Master Builder* (New York, 1927), 1–123; Chandler, *Visible Hand*, 290–91, 382–91. Ernest Woodruff was another successful entrepreneur and atypical southerner. A Georgia banker and industrialist who headed the consortium that bought the Coca-Cola Company in 1919 for $25 million, Woodruff was the son of a New Englander who came south to seek his fortune. Asa Candler, however, who between 1892 and 1916 built Coca-Cola into a national company, was the scion of a slaveholding family. Candler was a prosperous Atlanta pharmacist whose bent for business was evident as a child. Few other southerners headed nationwide businesses during this era. J. C. Louis and Harvey Z. Yazijian, *The Cola Wars* (New York, 1980), 13–48.

43. Pitirim Sorokin, "American Millionaires and Multi-Millionaires: A Comparative Statistical Study," *Journal of Social Forces*, II (1924–25), 627–40. Maryland with seven millionaires and Missouri with one are not included here in the "South."

44. Wright, *Old South, New South*, 80, quote on 177; Ransom and Sutch, *One Kind of Freedom*, 180; in 1916 the average per capita expenditure for education in the southern states was $10.32 for whites and $2.89 for blacks. See Carole Marks, *Farewell—We're Good and Gone: The Great Black Migration* (Bloomington and Indianapolis, Ind., 1989), 76; Robert A. Margo, *Disenfranchisement, School Finance, and the Economics of Segregated Schools in the United States South, 1890–1910* (New York, 1985), 20–26; William A. Link, *A Hard Country and a Lonely Place: Schooling, Society, and Reform in Rural Virginia, 1870–1920* (Chapel Hill, N.C., 1986), 7, 40–41.

45. These stirrings of change were also reflected in the intellectual sphere. See three thoughtful works on this era: O'Brien, *Idea of the American South*; Singal, *War Within*; Richard King, *A Southern Renaissance: The Cultural Awakening of the American South, 1930–1955* (New York, 1980). Several important pieces are collected in Michael O'Brien, *Rethinking the South: Essays in Intellectual History* (Baltimore, 1988).

46. Jack T. Kirby, "The Southern Exodus, 1910–1960: A Primer for Historians," *Journal of Southern History*, XLIX (1983), 585–600; Neil Fligstein, *Going North: Migration of Blacks and Whites from the South, 1900–1950* (New York, 1981), 75–85; *U.S. Historical Statistics*, I, 89–95; Marks, *Farewell—We're Good and Gone*, 19–34, 173; Wright, *Old South, New South*, 144–55, 176–77, 202–

6; Joe W. Trotter, ed., *The Great Migration in Historical Perspective: New Dimensions of Race, Class and Gender* (Bloomington, Ind., 1991), contains several excellent essays. And see Florette Henri, *Black Migration: Movement North, 1900–1920* (Garden City, N.Y., 1975); Arna Bontemps and Jack Conroy, *Anyplace but Here* (New York, 1966). Why few blacks went North before 1914 has been the cause of debate. Both the "pull" factor of an expanding labor market in the North and the "push" of poverty in the South were present. Nor does it appear that sharecropping forced blacks to remain in the South, although some historians such as Jonathan Wiener have made that case. African Americans regularly moved from farm to farm and into southern cities. Most likely, the racism of northern employers meant there was little call for black laborers (except as strikebreakers) before World War I ended the influx of Europeans. Stanley Lieberson, *A Piece of the Pie: Black and White Immigrants since 1880* (Berkeley, Calif., 1980), 31–35, 348–69, discusses the attitudes of businessmen in the North; Mandle, "Black Economic Entrapment," 78–82; Cohen, *At Freedom's Edge*, 201–98, examines both the efforts of southern states to limit black mobility and the movement of African Americans.

47. Pete Daniel, "The New Deal, Southern Agriculture, and Economic Change," in *The New Deal and the South*, ed. James C. Cobb and Michael V. Namorato (Jackson, Miss., 1984), 37–61; J. Wayne Flynt, "The New Deal and Southern Labor," in ibid., 65–73; *U.S. Historical Statistics*, I, 517–18; Wright, *Old South, New South*, 216–18; James A. Hodges, *New Deal Labor Policy and the Southern Cotton Textile Industry, 1933–1941* (Knoxville, Tenn., 1986), 59–70. Also see Pete Daniel, *Breaking the Land: The Transformation of Cotton, Tobacco, and Rice Cultures since 1880* (Urbana, Ill., 1984), 72–150; Jack Temple Kirby, *Rural Worlds Lost: The American South, 1920–1960* (Baton Rouge, La., 1987), 51–79; Frank Freidel, *F.D.R. and the South* (Baton Rouge, La., 1965), 57–66; Raymond Wolters, *Negroes and the Great Depression: The Problem of Economic Recovery* (Westport, Conn., 1970), 5–6, 83–90, 124–25.

48. Quoted in Frank Freidel, "The South and the New Deal," in *The New Deal and the South*, 33; Gilbert C. Fite, *Cotton Fields No More: Southern Agriculture, 1865–1980* (Lexington, Ky., 1984), 125–60.

49. Among those emphasizing the outlook of French Canadians as the reason for slow economic growth are Norman W. Taylor, "French Canadians as Industrial Entrepreneurs," *Journal of Political Economy*, LXVIII (1960), 37–52; Taylor, "The Effects of Industrialization—Its Opportunities and Consequences upon French-Canadian Society," JEH, XX (1960), 638–47; Maurice Tremblay, "Orientations de la pensée sociale," in *Essais sur le Québec contemporain*, ed. Jean-Charles Falardeau (Quebec, 1953), 193–208; Ronald Rudin, "Revisionism and the Search for a Normal Society: A Critique of Recent Quebec Historical Writing," *Canadian Historical Review*, LXXIII (1992), 30–61; Jean-Charles Falardeau, "Des élites traditionnelles aux élites nouvelles," *Recherches sociographiques*, VII (1966), 131–45; Fernand Ouellet, "The Quiet Revolution: A Turning Point," in *Towards a Just Society: The Trudeau Years*, ed. Thomas S. Axworthy and Pierre Elliott Trudeau (Toronto, 1990, 1992), 357–85. These works typically see the Quiet Revolution of the 1960s as a turning point, a time when an older society finally gave way to a new more entrepreneurial one. Several key essays on this topic are brought together in René Durocher and Paul-André Linteau, eds., *Le "retard" du Québec et l'infériorité*

économique des Canadiens français (Montreal, 1971). During the 1930s, 1940s, and 1950s many sociologists and anthropologists asserted that rural Quebec was a "folk society" marked by traditional values and behavior. See Horace Miner, *St. Denis: A French-Canadian Parish* (Chicago, 1939); Everett C. Hughes, *French Canada in Transition* (Chicago, 1943); Marcel Rioux, *Description de la culture de l'Ile Verte* (Ottawa, 1954); and the articles in *Essais sur le Québec contemporain*.

50. Kenneth McRoberts, "The Sources of Neo-Nationalism in Quebec," in *Quebec since 1945,* ed. Michael D. Behiels (Toronto, 1987), 80–107, quote on 91; McRoberts and Dale Posgate, *Quebec: Social Change and Political Crisis,* rev. ed. (Toronto, 1988), 20. Albert Faucher and Maurice Lamontagne, "History of Industrial Development," in *Essais sur le Québec contemporain,* 23–37, are the best known advocates of a geographical explanation of Quebec backwardness. Faucher develops the same theme in *Histoire économique et unité canadienne* (Montreal, 1970) and *Québec en Amérique au XIXe siècle* (Montreal, 1973).

51. Linteau, *Quebec: A History,* quote on 128, and on race and class structure, see 140–55; André Raynauld, *Croissances et structures économiques de la province de Québec* (Quebec, 1961); Brian Young and John Dickinson, *A Short History of Quebec: A Social and Economic Perspective* (Toronto, 1988).

52. John H. Dales, "A Comparison of Manufacturing Industry in Quebec and Ontario, 1952," in *Canadian Dualism/La dualité canadienne,* ed. Mason Wade (Quebec, 1960), 203–21, offers a critique of Faucher and Lamontagne; John McCallum, *Unequal Beginnings: Agriculture and Economic Development in Quebec and Ontario until 1870* (Toronto, 1980), 6–7.

53. Hughes, *French Canada,* 151. Hughes calls this town "Cantonville." For its identification as Drummondville, see Herbert Guindon, *Quebec Society: Tradition, Modernity, and Nationhood* (Toronto, 1988), xiv; for a discussion of other sermons, consult Serge Gagnon and René Hardy, *L'Eglise et le village au Québec, 1850–1930: l'enseignement des cahiers de prônes* (Montreal, 1979), 92–104, and esp. 143–60, which provides excerpts from the *cahier* of Sainte-Eulalie, 1885–99; René Hardy and Jean Roy, "Mutation de la culture religieuse en Mauricie, 1850–1900," in *Evolution et éclatement du monde rural,* ed. J. Goy and J.-P. Wallot (Montreal, 1986), 406–7, discusses another curé warning parishioners about the danger of "luxuries" and American influences; René Hardy, "Le greffier de paix et le curé: à propos l'influence du clergé paroissial en Mauricie," *Annales de Bretagne* (1988), 447–63.

54. William F. Ryan, *The Clergy and Economic Growth in Quebec (1896–1914)* (Quebec City, 1966), 210–400.

55. Ouellet, "Quiet Revolution," 369–70.

56. Ibid., 370–71, 376; Linteau, *Quebec: A History,* 205–14; U.S. Census Office, *Census Reports,* vol. II: *Population, 12th Census of the United States, Taken in the Year 1900* (Washington, D.C., 1902), tables 4 and 57.

57. Mordecai Richler, *Oh Canada! Oh Quebec! Requiem for a Divided Country* (Toronto, 1992), 95, quotes Ryan. Richler emphasizes Groulx's anti-Semitism. So does Esther Delisle, *The Traitor and the Jew: Anti-Semitism and Extremist Right-Wing Nationalism in Quebec from 1929 to 1939* (Montreal, 1993).

58. Georges-Emile Giguère, *Lionel Groulx: Biographie* (Montreal, 1978), 11–121; Susan Mann Trofimenkoff, *The Dream of a Nation: A Social and Intellec-*

tual History of Quebec (Toronto, 1982), 219–21; J.-P. Gaboury, *Le nationalisme de Lionel Groulx: aspects idéologiques* (Ottawa, 1970), 94–95.

59. Quotes from Susan Mann Trofimenkoff, *Action Française: French Canadian Nationalism in the Twenties* (Toronto, 1975), 68, 83, 135, 139; Trofimenkoff, *Dream of a Nation*, 221–30; Guy Frégault, *Lionel Groulx tel qu'en lui-meme* (Ottawa, 1978); Ramsay Cook, *The Maple Leaf Forever: Essays on Nationalism and Politics in Canada* (Toronto, 1971), 107–9, 123–27; Serge Gagnon, *Quebec and Its Historians, 1840–1920*, trans. Yves Brunelle (Montreal, 1982), 111–21.

60. Ronald Rudin, *In Whose Interest: Quebec's Caisses Populaires, 1900–45* (Montreal, 1990), 17–51, 77–104.

61. Micheline Dumont et al., *Quebec Women: A History* (Toronto, 1987), 185–269; Linteau, *Quebec: A History*, 186–94, 441–50.

62. Fernande Roy, *Progrès, harmonie, liberté: le libéralisme des milieux d'affaires francophones de Montréal au tournant du siècle* (Montreal, 1988), examines the francophone business press in Montreal; Claude Couture, *Le Mythe de la modernisation du Québec: des années 1930 à la révolution tranquille* (Montreal, 1991), 13–31.

63. Ryan, *Clergy*, 80–84, 109–11, 200–7; Trofimenkoff, *Action Française*, 67. For a dissenting view, see two works by Jacques Rouillard: *Les Syndicats nationaux au Québec de 1900 à 1930* (Quebec, 1979) and "Le militantisme des travailleurs au Québec et en Ontario," *Revue d'histoire de l'Amérique française*, XXXVII (1983), 201–25. But note the critique of Rouillard in Rudin, "Revisionism and the Search for a Normal Society," 49–50.

64. Quebec farmers: (1) *Were far less productive.* The average cash receipts for a Quebec farm were $670 (in U.S. dollars), compared to $1,875 for the northern states. Earnings in the South were $660. (2) *Used much less machinery.* See figures for tractors presented earlier in the chapter. (3) *Stood apart from the labor market.* Only 28 percent of Quebec farms hired laborers, and few of these individuals were employed for long. Family members remained the mainstay of the labor force. Northern farms were far more likely to employ outside workers. (4) *Rarely borrowed money for capital improvements.* Just over one-fifth of Quebec farms had a mortgage debt, compared to 48 percent in the North and 34 percent for independent farms in the South. F. H. Leacy, ed., *Historical Statistics of Canada*, 2d ed. (Ottawa, 1983), series M93, M67–77; U.S. Bureau of the Census, *Statistical Abstract of the United States for 1934* (Washington, D.C., 1934), 566–67; U.S. Department of Commerce, *Statistical Abstract of the United States, 1936* (Washington, D.C., 1936), 578, 588, 591, 597; George V. Haythorne and Leonard C. Marsh, *Land and Labour: A Social Survey of Agriculture and the Farm Labour Market in Central Canada* (Toronto, 1941), 198–203, 213–29, 532, 543. More broadly, on the cultural factors slowing change in Quebec agriculture, see John Isbister, "Agriculture, Balanced Growth, and Social Change in Central Canada since 1850: An Interpretation," *Economic Development and Cultural Change*, LIV (1977), 673–97.

65. Quote from Rouillard, *Ah les Etats*, 107–8; Linteau, *Quebec: A History*, 374–75; Charles Lemelin, "Social Impact of Industrialization on Agriculture in the Province of Quebec," *Culture*, XIV (1953), 35–39.

66. On colonization, see Jean Hamelin and Yves Roby, *Histoire économique du Québec, 1851–1896* (Montreal, 1971), 169–72; Normand Seguin, "L'histoire de l'agriculture et de la colonisation au Québec depuis 1850," in *Agriculture et*

colonisation au Québec: aspects historiques, ed. Normand Seguin (Montreal, 1980), 27–37; On the inheritance patterns of French-Canadian farmers, see Léon Gérin, *Aux sources de notre histoire* (Montreal, 1946); Philippe Garigue, *Etudes sur le Canada français* (Montreal, 1958), 8–15; Miner, *St. Denis;* Hughes, *French Canada,* 4–21; Guindon, *Quebec Society,* 8–14; Gérard Bouchard, "La dynamique communautaire et l'évolution des sociétés rurales québécoise aux 19e et 20e siècles," *Revue d'histoire de l'Amérique française,* XL (1986), 51–71; J. I. Little, *Nationalism, Capitalism and Colonization in Nineteenth-Century Quebec: The Upper St. Francis District* (Montreal, 1989), xi, 3–35. On urbanization, consult Fernand Ouellet, "General Works: Urbanization and Industrialization," in Ouellet, *Economy, Class, & Nation in Quebec: Interpretative Essays,* ed. and trans. Jacques A. Barbier (Toronto, 1991), 234–50.

67. Hughes, *French Canada,* 4–22; Ryan, *Clergy,* 31; Linteau, *Quebec: A History,* 28–34, 155; Yves Roby, *Les franco-américains de la Nouvelle-Angleterre, 1776–1930* (Quebec, 1990), 33–99; Ralph D. Vicero, "Immigration of French Canadians to New England, 1840–1900: A Geographical Analysis" (Ph.D. diss., Univ. of Wisconsin, 1968), 191–203; Albert Faucher, "L'émigration des Canadiens français au xix-e siècle: position du problème et perspectives," *Recherches sociographiques,* V (1961), 277–317. Some French Canadians did go to western Canada and the U.S. Midwest. See André Lalonde, "The French Canadians of the West: Hope, Tragedy, and Uncertainty," in *French America: Mobility, Identity, and Minority Experience Across the Continent,* ed. Dean R. Louder and Eric Waddell (Baton Rouge, La., 1993), 100–16; D. Aidan McQuillan, "French-Canadian Communities in the Upper Midwest during the Nineteenth Century," ibid., 117–42. But the much larger emigration was to New England; Pierre Anctil, "The Franco-Americans of New England," ibid., 33–52. For maps illustrating the patterns of migration from French and English Canada, see R. Louis Gentilcore et al., eds., *Historical Atlas of Canada,* Vol. II: *The Land Transformed, 1800–1891* (Toronto, 1993), plate 31.

68. Linteau, *Quebec: A History,* 145, 314, 334, 402–3, 412; Ryan, *Clergy,* 69, 91, 131–77, 202–3, 282, and esp. 286–88, which discusses the reluctance of English speakers to promote francophones; Hughes, *French Canada,* 46–64, 202–6; Yves Bélanger and Pierre Fournier, *L'entreprise québécoise: développement historique et dynamique contemporaine* (Quebec, 1987), 20–58. Also see Ronald Rudin, *Banking en français: The French Banks of Quebec, 1835–1925* (Toronto, 1985), 22–25, 146–48; Paul André Linteau, "Quelques réflexions autour de la bourgeoisie québécoise, 1850–1914," *Revue d'histoire de l'Amérique française,* XXX (1976), 55–66; Gilles Pièdalue, "Les groupes financiers au Canada, 1900–1930," ibid., XXX (1976), 3–34; Margaret W. Wesley, *Grandeur et déclin: l'élite anglo-protestante de Montréal, 1900–1950* (Montreal, 1990), 7–8, 15–41; Yves Roby, *Les Québécois et les investissements américains (1918–1929)* (Quebec, 1976), 11–30.

69. Ryan, *Clergy,* 80.

70. Ouellet, "Quiet Revolution," 373–74; Hughes, *French Canada,* 212–17; Ryan, *Clergy,* 109–10, 201–6. Compare the behavior of Catholic unionists in the United States. Neil Betten, *Catholic Activism and the Industrial Worker* (Gainesville, Fla., 1976), 12–15, 77–81, 150, argues Catholics played a conservative role in U.S. unions.

71. Ouellet, *Economy, Class, & Nation,* 242; *U.S. Historical Statistics,* I, 22.

72. Hughes, *French Canada*, 22–28; Linteau, *Quebec: A History*, 19, 128, 234, 357, 429–36; *Statistical Abstract, 1936*, 761–63; John H. Dales, *Hydroelectricity and Industrial Development: Quebec, 1898–1940* (Cambridge, Mass., 1957), 156–94; Bernard L. Vigod, *Quebec before Duplessis: The Political Career of Louis-Alexandre Taschereau* (Kingston and Montreal, 1986), 15–17, 31–32, 43, 250–51; U.S. Bureau of the Census, *Historical Statistics of the United States, Colonial Times to 1970*, 2 vols. (Washington, D.C., 1975), I, 24–36. Church efforts to control the work force were less successful in Montreal (which had a sizable English-speaking minority) than in the smaller centers; Ryan, *Clergy*, 204–8; Ouellet, "Quiet Revolution," 372–74. For maps of Montreal, see *Historical Atlas of Canada*, II, plate 49.

73. Richard Jones, "Duplessis and the Union Nationale Administration," in *Quebec since 1945*, 11–12; Andrée Lévesque, *Virage à gauche interdit: les communistes, les socialistes et leurs ennemis au Québec, 1929–1939* (Montreal, 1984).

Chapter 10. The Paths Converge: 1940 to 1975

1. Robert B. Reich, *The Work of Nations: Preparing Ourselves for 21st-Century Capitalism* (New York, 1991), 43–46; on the location of head offices, see the information (organized by state and year) in *Fortune*, April 20, 1992, p. 290. Maryland was now a member of the "Greater Northeast" and one of the wealthiest ten states among the Lower Forty-eight.

2. Bennett Harrison and Jean Kluver, "Deindustrialization and regional restructuring in Massachusetts," in *Deindustrialization and Regional Economic Transformation: The Experience of the United States*, ed. Lloyd Rodwin and Hidehiko Sazanami (Boston, 1989), 104–10; Bennett Harrison, "Regional Restructuring and 'Good Business Climates': The Economic Transformation of New England since World War II," in *Sunbelt/Snowbelt: Urban Development and Regional Restructuring*, ed. Larry Sawers and William K. Tabb (New York, 1984), 48–78; Robert J. S. Ross and Kent C. Trachte, *Global Capitalism: The New Leviathan* (Albany, 1990), 176–83; James M. Howell, "Alternatives for the Northeast: Choices and Costs," in *The Massachusetts Miracle: High Technology and Economic Revitalization*, ed. David Lampe (Cambridge, Mass., 1988), 89–114; U.S. Bureau of the Census, *Historical Statistics of the United States, Colonial Times to 1970* (Washington, D.C., 1975), 89–92; see also the essays in Benjamin Chinitz, ed., *The Declining Northeast: Demographic and Economic Analysis* (New York, 1978).

3. Robert R. Reich, *The Next American Frontier* (New York, 1983), 121, 174–75; Ross and Trachte, *Global Capitalism*, 115–19; John Case, *From the Ground Up: The Resurgence of American Entrepreneurship* (New York, 1992), 44.

4. John B. Rae, *The American Automobile Industry* (Boston, 1984), 107, quotes Wilson.

5. Henry W. Broude, *Steel Decisions and the National Economy* (New Haven, Conn., 1963), 235–36, quotes Blough.

6. Works praising the large corporation include John Kenneth Galbraith, *New Industrial State* (Boston, 1967); David Lilienthal, *Big Business: A New Era* (New York, 1953); Richard Hofstadter, "What Happened to the Antitrust Movement?" in his *The Paranoid Style in American Politics and Other Essays* (Chicago, 1952). After 1975 many works examining this era sharply criticized

businesspeople. See Reich, *Work of Nations*; Case, *From the Ground Up*, 17–19; Ira C. Magaziner and Robert B. Reich, *Minding America's Business: The Decline and Rise of the American Economy* (New York, 1982), 143–54, 191–202; John P. Hoerr, *And the Wolf Finally Came: The Decline of the American Steel Industry* (Pittsburgh, Pa., 1988), 2–23; Maryann Keller, *Rude Awakening: The Rise, Fall, and Struggle for Recovery of General Motors* (New York, 1989), 19–54; David Halberstam, *The Reckoning* (New York, 1986), 460–81.

7. J. Patrick Wright, *On a Clear Day You Can See General Motors: John Z. DeLorean's Look Inside the Automotive Giant* (New York, 1979), 10. Among the most prominent works on the "organization man" are Sloan Wilson, *The Man in the Gray Flannel Suit* (New York, 1955); David Riesman, *The Lonely Crowd* (New Haven, 1950); William H. Whyte, *The Organization Man* (New York, 1956); C. Wright Mills, *White Collar* (New York, 1951); Alan Harrington, *Life in the Crystal Palace* (New York, 1959).

8. "How Reynolds Foiled Big Steel," *Globe and Mail*, July 4, 1992.

9. Hoerr, *The Wolf Finally Came*, 14–16.

10. Glenn Rifkin and George Harrar, *The Ultimate Entrepreneur: The Story of Ken Olsen and Digital Equipment Corporation* (Rocklin, Calif., 1990), 57.

11. Reich, *Work of Nations*, 48, 197.

12. Halberstam, *The Reckoning*, 23, italics added; Keller, *Rude Awakening*, 19–54.

13. Magaziner and Reich, *Minding America's Business*, 155–68, quotes on 163.

14. Halberstam, *The Reckoning*, quotes on 385, 510–11; Lee Iacocca, *Iacocca: An Autobiography* (New York, 1984), 34–66, 90–95, 309–16.

15. Reich, *Next American Frontier*, 117–18, 140–72; Ann R. Markusen and Virginia Carlson, "Deindustrialization the American Midwest: Causes and Responses," in *Deindustrialization*, 47; Neil Fligstein, *The Transformation of Corporate Control* (Cambridge, Mass., 1990), 191–312.

16. In 1964 the U.S. produced a million color television sets, and Japan only a few thousand—and none for export. Gains in Japanese productivity, however, far outpaced those in the U.S. By the early 1970s, when the Japanese began selling sets in the U.S., their televisions had far fewer defects and were produced more efficiently and cheaply. See Magaziner and Reich, *Minding America's Business*, 169–80. On the impact of defense spending, see the tables in Markusen and Carlson, "Deindustrialization in the American Midwest," 41–47; David L. Warsh, "War Stories: Defense Spending and the Growth of the Massachusetts Economy," in *Massachusetts Miracle*, 314–30; John C. Hoy, "Higher Skills and the New England Economy," in ibid., 331–47.

17. Carl Abbott, "The American Sunbelt: Idea and Region," *Journal of the West*, XVIII (1979), 5–18; "The South as the New America, Special Report," *Saturday Review*, Sept. 2, 1976, pp. 8–41; "The South Today," *Time*, Sept. 27, 1976, pp. 22–99. Charles P. Roland, "Sun Belt Prosperity and Urban Growth," in *Interpreting Southern History: Historiographical Essays in Honor of Sanford W. Higginbotham*, ed. John B. Boles and Evelyn Thomas Nolen (Baton Rouge, La., 1987), 434–53, surveys the literature on the sunbelt.

18. Bernard L. Weinstein and Robert E. Firestine, *Regional Growth and Decline in the United States: The Rise of the Sunbelt and Decline of the Northeast* (New York, 1978), contends that southern efforts to attract industries had little

impact on growth. For a different point of view, see James C. Cobb, *The Selling of the South: The Southern Crusade for Industrial Development, 1936–1980* (Baton Rouge, La., 1982); Daryl A. Hellman, Gregory H. Wassall, and Laurence H. Falk, *State Financial Incentives to Industry* (Lexington, Mass., 1976). Also consult the essays in *The Economics of Southern Growth,* ed. E. Blaine Liner and Lawrence K. Lynch (Durham, N.C., 1973).

19. Kevin P. Phillips, *The Emerging Republican Majority* (New Rochelle, N.Y., 1969), coined the term "Sun Belt" (p. 437) and was critical of the region; so was Kirkpatrick Sale, *Power Shift: The Rise of the Southern Rim and Its Challenge to the Eastern Establishment* (New York, 1975). More positive are the essays in *You Can't Eat Magnolias,* ed. H. Brandt Ayers and Thomas H. Naylor (New York, 1972).

20. Three valuable works that complement each other examine this change: Gilbert Fite, *Cotton Fields No More: Southern Agriculture 1865–1980* (Lexington, Ky., 1984), 150–57, 168; Pete Daniel, *Breaking the Land: The Transformation of Cotton, Tobacco, and Rice Cultures since 1880* (Urbana, Ill., 1985), 168–83, 225–40, 260–70; and Jack T. Kirby, *Rural Worlds Lost: The American South, 1920–1960* (Baton Rouge, La., 1987), 13–16, 25–80, 334–60. Kirby provides the fullest account of how these changes affected the lives of ordinary people.

21. Quote from Richard A. Couto, *Ain't Gonna Let Nobody Turn Me Round: The Pursuit of Racial Justice in the Rural South* (Philadelphia, 1991), 126; Jonathan M. Wiener, "Class Structure and Economic Development in the American South, 1865–1955," *American Historical Review,* LXXXIV (1979), 990–91; Jay R. Mandle, *The Roots of Black Poverty: The Southern Plantation Economy after the Civil War* (Durham, N.C., 1978), 85–89; *Statistical Abstract of the United States* for 1941, 1947, and 1955 provides information on number of tractors; Pete Daniel, "Going among Strangers: Southern Reactions to World War II," *Journal of American History,* LXXVII (1990), 886–911; James C. Cobb, " 'Somebody Done Nailed Us on the Cross': Federal Farm and Welfare Policy and the Civil Rights Movement in the Mississippi Delta," ibid., LXXVII (1990), 916–17.

22. Nicholas Lemann, *The Promised Land: The Great Black Migration and How It Changed America* (New York, 1991), 3–58, quote on 49–50; Hopson wanted to "equalize the white and negro population" because blacks were a majority in the Mississippi Delta. Gavin Wright, *Old South, New South: Revolutions in the Southern Economy Since the Civil War* (New York, 1986), 241–48; Pete Daniel, "The Crossroads of Change: Cotton, Tobacco and Rice Cultures in the Twentieth-Century South," *Journal of Southern History,* L (1984), 429–56; Fite, *Cotton Fields No More,* 180–206.

23. George W. Groh, *The Black Migration: The Journey to Urban America* (New York, 1972), 48, 63–68; Lemann, *Promised Land,* 6; Wright, *Old South, New South,* 254–57.

24. Robert C. McMath, Jr., "Variations on a Theme by Henry Grady: Technology, Modernization, and Social Change," in *The Future South: A Historical Perspective for the Twenty-first Century,* ed. Joe P. Dunn and Howard L. Preston (Urbana, Ill., 1991), 83, quotes Carter. The visitor to the White House was the Chinese leader Deng Xiaoping. Income data from U.S Bureau of the Census, *Statistical Abstract of the United States,* various years. On shifts in southern agricultural production, see the maps in National Geographic Society, *Historical*

Atlas of the United States (Washington, D.C., 1988), 133. See also Harry D. Fornari, "The Big Change: Cotton to Soybeans," *Agricultural History*, LIII (1979), 245–53; Zena Beers, "The New Face of Southern Agriculture: The Delta," *Farm Chemicals*, CXXX (March 1967), 30–37; Daniel, "Crossroads of Change," 429–56.

25. Wright, *Old South, New South*, 258–59; James C. Cobb, *Industrialization and Southern Society, 1877–1984* (Lexington, Ky., 1984), 58–66; Cobb, *Selling of the South*, 70–121; Hellman, Wassall, and Falk, *State Financial Incentives*, 1, 5–7, 16; Gurney Breckenfield, "Business Loves the Sunbelt (and Vice Versa)," *Fortune* (June 1977), 132–46; "Recruiting Industry Abroad," *South*, V (Apr. 1, 1978), 31–32.

26. Wright, *Old South, New South*, 250–63; Cobb, *Industrialization*, 51–52; Groh, *Black Migration*, 69–87; Bruce J. Schulman, *From Cotton Belt to Sunbelt: Federal Policy, Economic Development and the Transformation of the South, 1938–1980* (New York, 1991), 135–73; "The Second War between the States: Special Report," *Business Week*, May 17, 1979, pp. 92–114; "Federal Spending: The North's Loss Is the Sunbelt's Gain," *National Journal*, VIII (June 26, 1976).

27. Charles R. Wilson et al., eds., *Encyclopedia of Southern Culture* (Chapel Hill, N.C., 1989), 321–23, quote on 322; Raymond Arsenault, "The End of the Long Hot Summer: The Air Conditioner and Southern Culture," in *Searching for the Sunbelt: Historical Perspectives on a Region*, ed. Raymond A. Mohl (Knoxville, Tenn., 1990), 176–211; Margaret Ingels, *Willis Haviland Carrier: Father of Air Conditioning* (Garden City, N.Y., 1952).

28. John Hoffman, *Racial Discrimination and Economic Development* (Lexington, Mass., 1975); Howell Raines, *My Soul Is Rested: Movement Days in the Deep South Remembered* (New York, 1977), 425–31; James Gaskins, *Andrew Young: Man with a Mission* (New York, 1979); Eddie Stone, *Andrew Young: Biography of a Realist* (Los Angeles, 1980).

29. Cobb, *Industrialization*, 49–50, 69–96, quotes on 49; Groh, *Black Migration*, 48; Benson Soffer and Michael Korenich, " 'Right to Work' Laws as a Location Factor: The Industrialization Experience of Agricultural States," *Journal of Regional Science*, III (1961), 41–56; F. Ray Marshall, *Labor in the South* (Cambridge, Mass., 1967), 319–20; F. Ray Marshall, "Impediments to Labor Union Organization in the South," *South Atlantic Quarterly*, LVII (1958), 409–18; Robert E. Botsch, *We Shall Not Overcome: Populism and Southern Blue-Collar Workers* (Chapel Hill, N.C., 1980); Joe Persky, "The South: A Colony at Home," *Southern Exposure*, I (1973), 14–22; Cliff Sloan and Bob Hall, "It's Good to Be Home in Greenville. . . . But It's Better If You Hate Unions," ibid., VII (1979), 82–93.

30. Luther H. Hodges, *Businessman in the Statehouse: Six Years as Governor of North Carolina* (Chapel Hill, N.C., 1962), quotes on 57, 177; Cobb, *Selling of the South*, 151–78.

31. Hodges, *Businessman*, quotes on 94, 118, 230; Cobb, *Industrialization*, 111–15; also see the case studies in *Southern Businessmen and Desegregation*, ed. Elizabeth Jacoway and David R. Colburn (Baton Rouge, La., 1982). This work suggests that Hodges's outlook was similar to that of most businesspeople in the South. See also James A. Hodges, "J. P. Stevens and the Union: Struggle for the South," in *Race, Class, and Community in Southern Labor History*, ed. Gary M. Fink and Merl E. Reed (Tuscaloosa, Ala., 1994), 53–64.

32. Guy Rocher, "A Half-Century of Cultural Evolution in Quebec," *Quebec since 1945: Selected Readings,* ed. Michael D. Behiels (Toronto, 1987), 289.

33. Mason Wade, *The French Canadians, 1760–1967,* rev. ed., 2 vols. (Toronto, 1968), II, 982–1015; Paul-André Linteau, René Durocher, and Jean-Claude Robert, *Quebec: A History, 1867–1929,* trans. Robert Chodos (Toronto, 1983), 464; Fernand Ouellet, "The Quiet Revolution: A Turning Point," *Towards a Just Society: The Trudeau Years,* ed. Tom Axworthy and Pierre Elliot Trudeau (Toronto, 1990, 1992), 378–82.

34. Richard Jones, "Duplessis and the Union Nationale Administration," in *Quebec since 1945,* 15–20; Michael D. Behiels, "Quebec: Social Transformation and Ideological Renewal, 1940–1976," in ibid., 20–33; Rocher, "Half-Century of Cultural Evolution," 303; Kenneth McRoberts and Dale Posgate, *Quebec: Social Change and Political Crisis,* rev. ed. (Toronto, 1980), 60–93; Conrad Black, *Duplessis* (Toronto, 1977), 660–82.

35. Pierre Elliott Trudeau, "Quebec on the Eve of the Asbestos Strike" (1956), in *French-Canadian Nationalism: An Anthology,* ed. Ramsay Cook (Toronto, 1969), 33; Wade, *French Canadians,* II, 1108–9; Behiels, "Quebec: Social Transformation," 25–27; Michael Behiels, *Prelude to Quebec's Quiet Revolution: Liberalism vs. Neo-Nationalism, 1945–1960* (Montreal, 1985), 124–29; Jacques Rouillard, "Mutations de la Confédération des travailleurs catholiques du Canada," *Revue d'histoire de l'Amérique française,* XXXIV (1980), 377–405; Ramsay Cook, *Canada, Quebec, and the Uses of Nationalism* (Toronto, 1986), 60–86, discusses the evolution of Quebec nationalism in the years before the Quiet Revolution.

36. Dale C. Thomson, *Jean Lesage & the Quiet Revolution* (Toronto, 1984), 88–161.

37. Fernand Ouellet, "The Quiet Revolution," in *Economy, Class, & Nation in Quebec: Interpretative Essays,* trans. Jacques A. Barbier (Toronto, 1991), 291–97; also see two valuable collections of essays: J. F. Léonard, ed., *George-Emile Lapalme* (Montreal, 1988), and R. Comeau, ed., *Jean Lesage et l'éveil d'une nation* (Montreal, 1989).

38. On this debate, see Herbert Guindon, "The Modernization of Quebec and the Legitimacy of the Canadian State," in *Modernization and the Canadian State,* ed. Daniel Glenday et al. (Toronto, 1978), 212–46; Pierre Fournier, "Les nouveaux paramètres de la bourgeoisie québecoise," in *Le capitalisme au Québec,* ed. Pierre Fournier (Montreal, 1978), 137–80; Dorval Brunelle, "Le capital, la bourgeoisie et l'état du Québec, 1959–1976," in ibid., 81–108; Louis Maheu, "La conjoncture des luttes nationales au Québec," *Sociologie et société,* XI (1979), 125–44; Gilles Bourque and Anne Legaré, *Le Québec: la question nationale* (Paris, 1979); Jorge Niosi, "La nouvelle bourgeoisie canadienne-française," *Les cahiers du socialisme,* I (1978), 5–50; Jean-Jacques Simard, *La longue marche des technocrates* (Montreal, 1979); Jacques Grand'Maison, *La nouvelle classe et l'avenir du Québec* (Montreal, 1979).

39. Thomson, *Jean Lesage,* 290–321; Matthew Fraser, *Quebec Inc.: French-Canadian Entrepreneurs and the New Business Elite* (Toronto, 1987), 69–97; Jean-Marie Toulouse, *L'entrepreneurship au Québec* (Montreal, 1979), 104–11.

40. Ouellet, "Quiet Revolution," 379–80; Fraser, *Quebec Inc.,* 2–15, 88–89; by contrast the birth rate in the United States fell between 1948 and 1972 from 25 to 16 per 1000; *Historical Statistics of the United States,* I, 49; *Statistical*

Abstract of the United States, 1980, 62; McRoberts and Posgate, *Quebec,* 57–58. Several works explore the impact of declericalization on Quebec society. In particular, see Colette Moreux, *Fin d'une religion? Monographie d'une paroisse canadienne-française* (Montreal, 1969); Moreux, *Douceville en Québec: la modernisation d'une tradition* (Montreal, 1982); Paul André Turcotte, *Saint-Viateur et la révolution tranquille* (Montreal, 1981); Micheline D'Allaire, *Vingt ans de crise chez les religieuses du Québec* (Montreal, 1983).

41. Fraser, *Quebec Inc.,* 70–71.

42. Thomson, *Jean Lesage,* 233–89; McRoberts and Posgate, *Quebec,* 61, 106, 125; Jorge Niosi, *La bourgeoisie canadienne: la formation et le développement d'une classe dominante* (Montreal, 1980), 129–34.

43. McRoberts and Posgate, *Quebec,* 106–11, 125–26; Fraser, *Quebec Inc.,* 77–97; Niosi, *La bourgeoisie canadienne,* 134–49.

44. Fraser, *Quebec Inc.,* 151–201; Yves Bélanger and Pierre Fournier, *L'entreprise québécoise: développement historique et dynamique contemporaine* (Quebec, 1987), 93–145.

45. Alain-G. Gagnon and Mary Beth Montcalm, *Quebec: Beyond the Quiet Revolution* (Toronto, 1990), 113–16; J. M. Toulouse, *L'entrepreneurship au Québec* (Montreal, 1979), 20–45; F. Vaillancourt and Y. Carpentier, *Le contrôle de l'économie du Québec: la place des francophones en 1987 et son évolution depuis 1961* (Quebec, 1989); Pierre Fournier, "Les nouveaux paramètres de la bourgeoisie québécoise," in *Le capitalisme au Québec,* ed. Pierre Fournier (Montreal, 1978), 137–80; Dorval Brunelle, "Le capital, la bourgeoisie et l'état du Québec," in ibid., 79–108.

46. Gagnon and Montcalm, *Quebec,* 18–34.

47. Statistics Canada, *Labour Force Annual Averages: 1975–1983* (Ottawa, 1984), 91.

48. See, for example, the various statements in *Histoire des idées au Québec: des troubles de 1837 au référendum de 1980,* ed. Georges Vincenthier (Montreal, 1983), 332–92.

Chapter 11. The Post-Industrial Economy, 1975 to the 1990s

1. "America's Fastest-Growing Companies," *Fortune,* Oct. 5, 1992, pp. 58–82, quote on 62.

2. Daniel Bell, *The Coming of Post-Industrial Society* (New York, 1974). Other writers, however, emphasize the continuing importance of manufacturing and question the existence of a "New Economy." See Stephen S. Cohen and John Zysman, "The Myth of a Post-Industrial Economy," *New York Times,* May 17, 1987, p. F2; Cohen and Zysman, *Manufacturing Matters* (New York, 1987); Barry Bluestone, "Is Deindustrialization a Myth? Capital Mobility versus Absorptive Capacity in the U.S. Economy," *Annals of the American Academy of Political and Social Science* (Sept. 1984), 39–51.

3. Along with the maps in this chapter, see the information for 1989–91 displayed in Rodger Doyle, *Atlas of Contemporary America: Portrait of a Nation* (Hong Kong, 1994), 26–27, 120–21, 124.

4. Robert B. Reich, *The Work of Nations: Preparing Ourselves for 21st-Century Capitalism* (New York, 1991), 72; Ann R. Markusen and Virginia Carlson, "Deindustrialization in the American Midwest: Causes and Responses," in *Deindus-*

trialization and Regional Economic Transformation: The Experience of the United States, ed. Lloyd Rodwin and Hidehiko Sazanami (Boston, 1989), 29–59; Robert J. S. Ross and Kent C. Trachte, *Global Capitalism: The New Leviathan* (Albany, N.Y. 1990), 119–35; Lucy Gorham, *No Longer Leading: A Comparative Study of the U.S., Germany, Sweden, and Japan* (Washington, D.C., 1986); Clyde V. Prestowitz, Jr., *Trading Places: How We Allowed Japan to Take the Lead* (New York, 1988).

5. Reich, *Work of Nations,* 120–22; Bennett Harrison and Barry Bluestone, *The Great U-Turn: Corporate Restructuring and the Polarizing of America* (New York, N.Y., 1988), 25–38; Ross and Trachte, *Global Capitalism,* 82–114; "U.S. Businesses Loosen Link to Mother Country," *New York Times,* May 21, 1989; Joseph Grunwald and Kenneth Flamm, *The Global Factory: Foreign Assembly in International Trade* (Washington, D.C., 1985); Folker Froebel et al., *The New International Division of Labor* (New York, 1980).

6. Michael J. Piore and Charles F. Sabel, *The Second Industrial Divide* (New York, 1984), 19–48, 165–220, 281–308.

7. John P. Hoerr, *And the Wolf Finally Came: The Decline of the American Steel Industry* (Pittsburgh, Pa., 1988), 158–61, 427–39, quote on 435; Paul A. Tiffany, *The Decline of American Steel* (New York, 1988), 5–41; Dick Blin, "Steelworkers Give Up Jobs, Work Rules, Money, Benefits, Holidays to USX," *Labor Notes* (Feb. 1987); Gregory L. Miles and Matt Rothman, "The Steel Deal That Everybody's Watching," *Business Week,* April 21, 1986.

8. "Deindustrialization in the American Midwest," 32–33; John Case, *From the Ground Up: The Resurgence of American Entrepreneurship* (New York, 1992), 32–35; Candee S. Harris, "The Magnitude of Job Loss from Plant Closings and the Generation of Replacement Jobs: Some Recent Evidence," *Annals of the American Academy of Political and Social Science,* CCCCLXXV (Sept. 1984), 15–27.

9. "The Job Drought," *Fortune,* Aug. 24, 1992, pp. 62–74; Harrison and Bluestone, *The Great U-Turn,* 21–52; Peter H. Lindert and Jeffrey G. Williamson, "Growth, Equality, and History," *Explorations in Economic History,* XXII (1985), 345, suggests that for the U.S. as a whole the reversal of the long-term trend toward equality of income was evident as early as the mid-1960s; Lester Thurow, "A Surge in Inequality," *Scientific American* (May 1987), 30–37; Thierry Noyelle, *Beyond Industrial Dualism* (Boulder, Colo., 1987), discusses the restructuring of labor markets; Eileen Appelbaum, "Restructuring Work: Temporary, Part-Time, and At-Home Employment," in *Computer Chips and Paper Clips: Technology and Women's Employment,* ed. Heidi Hartmann (Washington, D.C., 1987), 268–310.

10. Reich, *Work of Nations,* 174–80; with the emergence of a new entrepreneurial ethos the advice to an aspiring businessperson changed. Gone were the books that praised conformity and the "organization man." In their place were works that told men and women to be hard-driving and more self-centered. Among these new self-help books were Robert J. Ringer, *Looking Out for #1* (New York, 1977); Michael Korda, *Success!* (New York, 1977); Betty Lehan Harragan, *Games Mother Never Taught You* (New York, 1977). See the discussion of these works in Peter Baida, *Poor Richard's Legacy: American Business Values from Benjamin Franklin to Donald Trump* (New York, 1990), 336–41.

11. Bennett Harrison, "Regional Restructuring and 'Good Business Cli-

mates': The Economic Transformation of New England since World War II,"
in *Sunbelt/Snowbelt: Urban Development and Regional Restructuring,* ed. Larry
Sawers and William K. Tabb (New York, 1984), 48–96; and see the articles
reprinted in *The Massachusetts Miracle: High Technology and Economic Revitalization,* ed. David Lampe (Cambridge, Mass., 1988), 19–168; Benjamin Chinitz,
"Manufacturing Employment in New York State: The Anatomy of Decline," in
The Declining Northeast: Demographic and Economic Analyses, ed. Benjamin Chinitz (New York, 1978), 45–65; Peter D. McClelland and Alan L. Magdovitz,
Crisis in the Making: The Political Economy of New York State since 1945 (Cambridge, Eng., 1981), 15–142, 294–342.

12. "After Gains of 80s, Northeast Is Lagging in the Growth of Jobs," *New
York Times,* April 25, 1990; "New England's Siren Call of 80s Becomes Echo of
the Depression," ibid., Dec. 15, 1991; *Massachusetts Miracle,* 169–357; Bennett
Harrison and Jean Kluver, "Deindustrialization and Regional Restructuring in
Massachusetts," in *Deindustrialization,* 104–31; Saskia Sassen, "Finance and
Business Services in New York City: International Linkages and Domestic Ef-
fects," in ibid., 132–54; Ross and Trachte, *Global Capitalism,* 180–91; Michael
S. Dukakis and Rosabeth Moss Kanter, *Creating the Future: The Massachusetts
Comeback and Its Promise for America* (New York, 1988), 107–79.

13. National Geographic Society, *Historical Atlas of the United States* (Washington, D.C., 1988), 75.

14. Lester C. Thurow, "Regional Transformation and the Service Activities," in *Deindustrialization,* 179–98.

15. Patricia Aburdene and John Naisbitt, *Megatrends for Women* (New
York, 1992), 61–81; U.S. Bureau of the Census, *Statistical Abstract of the United
States: 1991* (Washington, D.C., 1991), 533–34.

16. Case, *From the Ground Up,* 32–35; "The Job Drought," *Fortune,* Aug.
24, 1992, pp. 62–65, presents a slightly different set of figures that make the
same point; "Small Manufacturers Lead Revival," *New York Times,* Feb. 11,
1988.

17. "GE Keeps Those Ideas Coming," *Fortune,* Aug. 12, 1991, pp. 40–49,
quotes on 41; Ira C. Magaziner and Robert B. Reich, *Minding America's Business: The Decline and Rise of the American Economy* (New York, 1982), 176; *Fortune,* April 20, 1992, p. 250; *New York Times,* May 3, 1992. On the turnaround
in some large firms, see "Competitiveness: How U.S. Companies Stack Up
Now," *Fortune,* April 18, 1994, pp. 52–64; Rosabeth Moss Kanter, *When Giants
Learn to Dance* (New York, 1990).

18. *New York Times,* April 25, 1990; "The Job Drought," *Fortune,* Aug. 24,
1992, p. 70; on interstate migration, see U.S. Bureau of the Census, Current
Population Reports, Series P23, No. 175, *Population Trends in the 1980s* (Washington, D.C., 1992), 26–40.

19. For other discussions of the idea of two "Souths," see Joe P. Dunn,
"The Quest for the South's Future: An Overview," in *The Future South: A His-
torical Perspective for the Twenty-first Century,* ed. Joe P. Dunn and Howard L.
Preston (Urbana, Ill., 1991), 1–9.

20. For these migration statistics the "South" consists of the eleven states
of the Confederacy; Earl Black and Merle Black, *Politics and Society in the South*
(Cambridge, Mass., 1987), 16–19.

21. Alexander P. Lamis, "The Future of Southern Politics: New Directions

for Dixie," in *Future South*, 51–53; Black and Black, *Politics and Society in the South*, 16–19. On p. 18 the Blacks present a county map of the South showing the concentration of northern settlement. Areas of high Yankee population include a retirement community in northern Arkansas.

22. Howard N. Rabinowitz, "The Weight of the Past versus the Promise of the Future: Southern Race Relations in Historical Perspective," in *Future South*, 111, quotes Wilder; Lynn E. Brown, "High Technology and Business Services," July 1983, in *Massachusetts Miracle*, 215–18; "First Black Governor, If Recount Upholds Vote," *New York Times*, Nov. 8, 1989. Along with the impact of northerners, the emergence of a large population of foreign-born, Spanish-speaking individuals in the southern periphery has sharpened the entrepreneurial ethos of that area. See Elliott Barkan, "New Origins, New Homeland, New Region: American Immigration and the Emergence of the Sunbelt, 1955–1985," in *Searching for the Sunbelt: Historical Perspectives on a Region*, ed. Raymond A. Mohl (Knoxville, Tenn., 1990), 124–48; Raymond A. Mohl, "Miami: New Immigrant City," in ibid., 149–75; General Dynamics moved to Virginia in 1992.

23. V. O. Key, *Southern Politics in State and Nation* (New York, 1949), 254; this passage is also quoted in Black and Black, *Politics and Society in the South*, 30.

24. Joe R. Feagin, "Sunbelt Metropolis and Development Capital: Houston in the Era of Late Capitalism," in *Sunbelt/Snowbelt*, 99–127; Feagin, *Free Enterprise City: Houston in Political and Economic Perspective* (New Brunswick, N.J., 1988); on the growth of small companies, see "America's Fastest Risers," *Fortune*, Oct. 7, 1991, pp. 46–68; "America's Fastest-Growing Companies," ibid., Oct. 5, 1992, pp. 58–82; "The 1991 *Inc.* 500," *Inc.*, Dec. 1991, pp. 34–123; "The *Inc.* 500: America's Fastest-Growing Private Companies," ibid., Oct. 1992, pp. 71–143. In all these lists California has the largest number of these fast-growing firms. Texas stands second, followed by Florida (or in one instance, by Virginia with Florida fourth). On a per capita basis, however, the New England states rank above Texas and Florida.

25. "America's Fastest Risers," *Fortune*, Oct. 7, 1991; "Holy PCs! This Kid's Turbo Charged," *Entrepreneur*, Nov. 1990.

26. Norman J. Glickman and Amy K. Glasmeier, "The International Economy and the American South," in *Deindustrialization*, 72–73.

27. *Statistical Abstract: 1991*, 29–31. By 1990 metropolitan Atlanta had surpassed Baltimore in population; David R. Goldfield, "The City as Southern History: The Past and Promise of Tomorrow," in *Future South*, 11–48.

28. Thomas A. Lyson, *Two Sides to the Sunbelt: The Growing Divergence between the Rural and Urban South* (New York, 1989).

29. Bradley R. Rice, "Searching for the Sunbelt," in *Searching for the Sunbelt*, 220, quotes the chairman of Equitable Real Estate Group; Ronald H. Bayor, "Models of Ethnic and Racial Politics in the Urban Sunbelt South," in ibid., 108–11; "The Best Cities for Business," *Fortune*, Nov. 4, 1991, pp. 52–84; *Wall Street Journal*, Feb. 29, 1988; Goldfield, "The City as Southern History," 16–42; Alton Hornby, Jr., "A City That Was Too Busy to Hate: Atlanta Businessmen and Desegregation," in *Southern Businessmen and Desegregation*, ed. Elizabeth Jacoway and David R. Colburn (Baton Rouge, La., 1982), 120–36; Dana White and Timothy Crimmins, "How Atlanta Grew: Cool Heads, Hot

Air, and Hard Work," *Atlanta Economic Review*, XXVIII (Jan.-Feb. 1978), 7–15; Truman Hartshorn, *Metropolis in Georgia: Atlanta's Rise as a Transaction Center* (Cambridge, Mass., 1976); Harold H. Martin, *William Berry Hartsfield: Mayor of Atlanta* (Athens, Ga., 1978); Carl Abbott, *The New Urban America: Growth and Politics in Sunbelt Cities* (Chapel Hill, N.C., 1981), 94–102, 226–28.

30. "Military and Economy" in *Encyclopedia of Southern Culture*, ed. Charles Reagan Wilson et al. (Chapel Hill, N.C., 1989), 731–32; Glickman and Glasmeier, "International Economy", 70–72; *Statistical Abstract: 1991*, 338.

31. *Historical Atlas*, 210; *Statistical Abstract: 1991*, 149.

32. "White-Black Disparity in Income Narrowed in 80's, Census Shows," *New York Times*, July 24, 1992; Rabinowitz, "Weight of the Past," 112–17; Richard A. Couto, *Ain't Gonna Let Nobody Turn Me Round: The Pursuit of Racial Justice in the Rural South* (Philadelphia, 1991), 58–156.

33. James Allan Davis and Tom W. Smith, *General Social Surveys, 1972–1991* (machine-readable file), NORC ed. (Chicago: National Opinion Research Center, producer, 1991; Storrs, Conn: Roper Center for Public Opinion Research, Univ. of Conn, distributor), 1 data file (27,782 logical records) and 1 codebook (989 pp). I am grateful for the assistance provided by Mirka Ondrack of the Institute for Social Research at York University in helping to analyze these data. Also see Norval D. Glenn and Charles N. Weaver, "Regional Differences in Attitudes Toward Work," *Texas Business Review*, LVI (1982), 263–66.

34. "Goldfield," City as Southern History," 37–39; Glickman and Glasmeier, "International Economy," 74–76; "The Boom Belt," *BusinessWeek*, Sept. 27, 1993, pp. 98–104, focuses on growth along I-85, particularly the stretch from Durham, N.C., to Atlanta, Ga.

35. James C. Cobb, "The Sunbelt South: Industrialization in Regional, National, and International Perspective," in *Searching for the Sunbelt*, 25–46, quotes on 35, 36; "Why Japan Keeps on Winning," *Fortune*, July 15, 1991, pp. 76–85; Glickman and Glasmeier, "International Economy," 62–80.

36. Couto, *Ain't Gonna Let Nobody Turn Me Round*, 82–157, quotes Mants on 117; "Reminders of Its Old Poverty Hit South in Recession's Grip," *New York Times*, Sept. 10, 1991, quotes White; Robert C. McMath, Jr., "Variations on a Theme by Henry Grady: Technology, Modernization, and Social Change," in *Future South*, 90–94; John D. Kasarda, Holly L. Hughes, and Michael D. Irwin, "Demographic and Economic Restructuring in the South," in *The South Moves into Its Future: Studies in the Analysis and Prediction of Social Change*, ed. Joseph S. Himes (Tuscaloosa, Ala., 1991), 32–68.

37. Statistics Canada, *System of National Accounts* (Ottawa, 1976), 90–93; F. H. Leacy, ed., *Historical Statistics of Canada*, 2d ed. (Ottawa, 1983), series A7, F95–F96; U.S. unemployment and per capita income figures from U.S. Bureau of the Census, *Statistical Abstract of the United States*, various years; for Quebec unemployment, see Bureau de la Statistique du Québec, *Le Québec statistique*, 59th edition (Quebec, 1989), tables 5–9; Statistics Canada, *Canada Year Book*, various years.

38. "The Decline and Fall of Montreal," *Financial Times of Canada*, Dec. 23, 1991; *Globe and Mail*, Dec. 18, 1991, p. B3; typically, the successful firms are located in the suburbs while Montreal itself has languished. Economists refer to the Montreal region as a "doughnut" with the city as the hole in the

center. "In the hole . . . and there's no easy way out," ibid., Jan. 8, 1993; "Quebec's Vital Signs Strong," ibid., Nov. 10, 1992.

39. Matthew Fraser, *Quebec Inc.: French-Canadian Entrepreneurs and the New Business Elite* (Toronto, 1987), 2–6, passim; Jorge Niosi, *La bourgeoisie canadienne: la formation et le développement d'une classe dominante* (Montreal, 1979), 49–95. Another sign of the changing mind-set in Quebec was seen in the awarding of engineering degrees. Between 1936 and 1955 anglophone universities awarded nearly 68 percent of engineering degrees. By 1980 francophone universities awarded 66 percent of these degrees. William D. Coleman, "From Bill 22 to Bill 101: The Politics of Language under the Parti Québécois," *Canadian Journal of Political Science/Revue canadienne de science politique,* XIV (1981), 459–86; "The Sound of Two Solitudes, Applauding," *Canadian Business,* July 1993, pp. 79–81, documents Laurent Beaudoin's popularity. In fall 1995 Beaudoin's outspoken opposition to Quebec sovereignty made him a more controversial figure. See also Dave Greber, *Rising to Power: An Unauthorized History of Paul Desmarais and Power Corporation* (Toronto, 1987); Colette Chabot, *Péladeau* (Montreal, 1986); Ramsay Cook, *Canada, Quebec, and the Uses of Nationalism* (Toronto, 1986), 87–104, profiles the training of young businesspeople at the Ecole des Hautes Etudes Commerciales.

40. Fraser, *Quebec Inc.,* 188–207, quote on 191; "Lortie Quits as Chairman of Provigo Inc.," *Montreal Gazette,* Oct. 25, 1989; "PM Picks a Quick Study for a Slow Job," *Toronto Star,* March 15, 1990.

41. Alain-G. Gagnon and Mary Beth Montcalm, *Quebec beyond the Quiet Revolution* (Toronto, 1990), 64–66; "Bombardier Profit Edges up in First Half," *Globe and Mail,* Aug. 22, 1991; Fraser, *Quebec Inc.,* 94–97; Yves Bélanger and Pierre Fournier, *L'entreprise québécoise: développement historique et dynamique contemporaine* (Quebec, 1987), 150–87.

42. "Quebec Plans to Jump Start Montreal," *Globe and Mail,* Dec. 18, 1991.

43. "Socanav-Caisse Claims Victory for Steinberg," ibid., Aug. 22, 1989; "SNC Buys Lavalin's Prized Engineering Firm," ibid., Aug. 13, 1991; "Caisse Taking a Chance as It Tries to Prop up Steinberg," *Montreal Gazette,* Nov 16, 1990; "Quebec Reported Backing Merger of Lavalin, SNC to Form a Giant Firm," *Toronto Star,* Aug. 6, 1991. Despite the growing importance of the state, both the Parti Québécois and the Liberals have made ringing statements declaring their dedication to free enterprise. See Gagnon and Montcalm, *Quebec,* 61–68, 90–92. Such rhetoric professing a new emphasis on the marketplace is undercut by the rapid expansion of provincial government spending (and the provincial deficit) after 1975. See the figures presented in the *Public Accounts of the Province of Quebec* for the years 1961 through 1990. A similar but not identical series is presented in Paul-André Linteau et al., *Le Québec depuis 1930* (Montreal, 1986, 1991), 514. Pierre Arbour, *Quebec Inc. and the Temptation of State Capitalism* (Montreal, 1993), argues that billions of dollars of taxpayer money were wasted in efforts to promote francophone control of the economy.

44. Fraser, *Quebec Inc.,* quote on 1.

45. "The Decline of Quebec Inc.," *Globe and Mail,* Oct. 18, 1991; ibid., Dec. 18, 1991, Sept. 17, 1992; "Montreal Mounts Comeback," ibid., Jan. 9, 1995, discusses the restructuring of employment in the Montreal area; "The

Enduring Charm of Montreal," *Macleans*, Oct. 19, 1992, pp. 46–50, provides an overview of these changes.

46. "Survival at Heart of Concerns," *Toronto Star*, Oct. 18, 1992. Several works reflected (and heightened) the concerns of French Canadians about the declining rate of natural increase. Province du Québec, Secretariat au développement social, *L'évolution de la population du Québec et ses conséquences* (Quebec, 1984); Jacques Henripin, *Naître ou ne pas être* (Quebec, 1989); Jacques Henripin and Yves Martin, *La population du Québec d'hier à demain* (Montreal, 1991).

47. Robert Chodos and Eric Hamovitch, *Quebec and the American Dream* (Toronto, 1991), 227, quotes Levesque; Fraser, *Quebec Inc.*, 88–92; Mordecai Richler, *Oh Canada! Oh Quebec!: Requiem for a Divided Country* (Toronto, 1992), 36, 48–50, 180.

48. Gagnon and Montcalm, *Quebec*, 175–85; Richler, *Oh Canada!*, 12; Fraser, *Quebec Inc.*, 88.

49. Fraser, *Quebec Inc.*, 88–93, quote on 88; "Quebec Plans to Jump Start Montreal," *Globe and Mail*, Dec. 18, 1991; Bureau de la statistique du Québec, *Le Québec statistique 1989* (Quebec, 1989), 139, 141; Graham Fraser, *René Levesque and the Parti Québécois in Power* (Toronto, 1984), 111, 133–35, 212, 353–54; Pierre Fortin, *Unemployment, Inflation, and Economic Stabilization in Quebec* (Montreal, 1980), 10–17.

50. Gagnon and Montcalm, *Quebec*, 189–91; Richler, *Oh Canada!*, 1–32, 51–57, 261–62, provides a critical look at the impact of Bill 178.

51. The broader use of French in Quebec is clear. According to *L'Actualité* (Jan. 1991), 23, in 1961 only 47 percent of jobs were in French hands or were in companies where the language of work tended to be French. By 1987 the figure was 60 percent. In 1982 only 20 percent of businesses had their certificate of francization. By 1990 fully 63 percent of big businesses and 76 percent of small and medium-sized enterprises complied with provincial language regulations. The other firms were moving steadily toward this goal. See also François Vaillancourt and Y. Carpentier, *Le contrôle de l'économie du Québec: la place des francophones en 1987 et son évolution depuis 1961* (Quebec, 1989); Vaillancourt and A. Raynaud, *L'appartenance des entreprises: le cas du Québec en 1978* (Quebec, 1984). The movement toward francophone control accelerated after 1978. Between 1961 and 1978 the proportion of jobs in francophone-controlled companies increased less than half a percentage point a year. Between 1978 and 1987 the rate was 0.74 percent; and 1987 to 1991 nearly one percentage point a year. See "Power Shifts at Quebec Inc," *Globe and Mail*, Nov. 3, 1993, p. B4. The gap between francophone and anglophone incomes in Quebec virtually disappeared. In 1977 anglophone families earned 8.2 percent more than francophones. By 1992 the difference was only 1.9 percent. Ibid., March 23, 1994, p. A7.

52. On regional disparity in Quebec, "Quebec Blamed for Collapse of Poor Areas," *Globe and Mail*, March 10, 1992, p. A8; Quebec Council on Social Affairs, *Deux Québecs dans un: rapport sur le développement social et démographique* (Quebec, 1989), 61–77. Marc Lesage and Francine Tardif, eds., *Trente ans de révolution tranquille: entre le je et le nous itinéraires et mouvements* (Quebec, 1989), presents several commentaries on the changing outlook of Quebeckers since the Quiet Revolution.

53. Statistics Canada, *Adult Literacy: Results of a National Study* (Ottawa,

1991), 9–27; Hélène Blais et Marcel Lavallée, *Du crayon à l'imprimante: alpha-bétisation, micro-informatique et sémiotique* (Quebec, 1988), 77–85.

54. "Qui nous sommes: anatomie d'une société distincte," *L'Actualité*, Jan. 1992, pp. 19–23. Only 61 percent of Quebeckers approved of busi-nesspeople, a rating that puts this group in sixth place behind professors, po-lice, environmentalists, judges, and generals. Outside of Quebec, 77 percent of Canadians gave businesswomen and men a vote of confidence, and placed them third behind professors and police. But see Cook, *Canada, Quebec, and the Uses of Nationalism*, 92. Cook discusses Pierre Laurin's views of a Gallup poll that showed Quebeckers feared big business *less* than other Canadians did.

55. Another poll presented Americans and French-speaking Quebeckers with a list of qualities and asked which ones children should be encouraged to learn at home. Americans chose "hard work" more often than did Quebeckers. These surveys are discussed in Seymour Martin Lipset, *Continental Divide: The Values and Institutions of the United States and Canada* (Toronto, 1989), 127–28, 157–58.

56. Marshall Frady, "Gone with the Wind," *Newsweek*, July 28, 1975, quote on 11; Howard L. Preston, "Will Dixie Disappear? Cultural Contours of a Region in Transition," in *Future South*, 188–216; James C. Cobb, "Tomorrow Seems like Yesterday: The South's Future in the Nation and the World," in ibid., 217–37; John Shelton Reed, "New South or No South? Regional Culture in 2036," in *The South Moves into Its Future*, 225–35; John Egerton, *The Ameri-canization of Dixie: The Southernization of America* (New York, 1974); William Reynolds, "The South: Global Dumping Ground," *Southern Exposure*, VII (1979), 49–56. On Quebec see Alain-G. Gagnon and Daniel Latouche, *Allaire, Bélanger, Campeau et les autres: les Québécois s'interrrogent sur leur avenir* (Mon-treal, 1991), 187–206, 231–64, 391–409; Gabriel Dussault, ed., *Questions de culture 10: l'état et la culture* (Quebec, 1986).

A Concluding Note

1. The Twain quote concludes: "persons attempting to find a plot in it will be shot." *The Adventures of Huckleberry Finn* (1884; rpt., New York, 1962), 10.

2. Thomas M. Doerflinger, *A Vigorous Spirit of Enterprise: Merchants and Economic Development in Revolutionary Philadelphia* (Chapel Hill, N.C., 1986), 2, 335–64. Doerflinger draws his title from statements made by Philadelphia merchants. Also see Edwin J. Perkins, "The Entrepreneurial Spirit in Colonial America: The Foundations of Modern Business History," *Business History Re-view*, LXIII (1989), 160–86.

Appendix A

1. Fernand Braudel, *The Wheels of Commerce* (New York, 1982), 231–39; Rodney Hilton, "Introduction" and "Capitalism: What's in a Name?" in *The Transition from Feudalism to Capitalism*, ed. Paul Sweezy et al. (London, 1976); Maurice Dobb, *Studies in the Development of Capitalism* (New York, 1947); Fred-erick C. Lane, "Meanings of Capitalism," JEH, XXIV (1969), 5–13.

2. On the urban sources of funding for New England settlements, John

Frederick Martin, *Profits in the Wilderness: Entrepreneurship and the Founding of New England Towns in the Seventeenth Century* (Chapel Hill, N.C., 1991), 46–110.

3. Eugene D. Genovese and Elizabeth Fox-Genovese, *Fruits of Merchant Capital: Slavery and Bourgeois Property in the Rise and Expansion of Capitalism* (New York, 1983), 3–25, 59, 188–91, 272–73. Genovese and Fox-Genovese remark: "The Old South emerged as a bastard child of merchant capital and developed as a noncapitalist society increasingly antagonistic to, but inseparable from, the bourgeois world that sired it" (p. 5). Also see Gregory Nobles, "Capitalism in the Countryside: The Transformation of Rural Society in the United States," *Radical History Review*, no. 41 (1988), 163–77; Luis Llambi, "Small Modern Farmers: Neither Peasants nor Fully-Fledged Capitalists?" *Journal of Peasant Studies*, XV (1988), 350-72; Robert E. Mutch, "Colonial America and the Debate about the Transition to Capitalism," *Theory and Society*, IX (1980), 847–63; Mutch, "Yeoman and Merchant in Pre-industrial America: Eighteenth-Century Massachusetts as a Test Case," *Societas*, VII (1977), 279–302; Elizabeth Fox-Genovese, *Within the Plantation Household: Black and White Women of the Old South* (Chapel Hill, N.C., 1988).

4. Braudel, *Wheels of Commerce*, 401–3, 567–76, quote on 576.

5. Ibid., quote on 578; Max Weber, *The Protestant Ethic and the Spirit of Capitalism* (1920; New York, 1958).

6. Louis B. Wright, "Franklin's Legacy to the Gilded Age," *Virginia Quarterly Review*, XXII (1946), 268–79; Thomas Mellon, *Thomas Mellon and His Times* . . . (1885; rpt., New York, 1969).

Index